Enigma Books

Also published by Enigma Books

Hitler's Table Talk: 1941–1944
In Stalin's Secret Service
Hitler and Mussolini: The Secret Meetings
The Jews in Fascist Italy: A History
The Man Behind the Rosenbergs
Roosevelt and Hopkins: An Intimate History
Diary 1937–1943 (Galeazzo Ciano)
Secret Affairs: FDR, Cordell Hull, and Sumner Welles
Hitler and His Generals: Military Conferences 1942–1945
Stalin and the Jews: The Red Book
The Secret Front: Nazi Political Espionage
Fighting the Nazis: French Intelligence and Counterintelligence
A Death in Washington: Walter G. Krivitsky and the Stalin Terror
The Battle of the Casbah: Terrorism and Counterterrorism in Algeria 1955–1957
Hitler's Second Book: The Unpublished Sequel to *Mein Kampf*
At Napoleon's Side in Russia: The Classic Eyewitness Account
The Atlantic Wall: Hitler's Defenses for D-Day
Double Lives: Stalin, Willi Münzenberg and the Seduction of the Intellectuals
France and the Nazi Threat: The Collapse of French Diplomacy 1932–1939
Mussolini: The Secrets of His Death
Mortal Crimes: Soviet Penetration of the Manhattan Project
Top Nazi: Karl Wolff—The Man Between Hitler and Himmler
Empire on the Adriatic: Mussolini's Conquest of Yugoslavia
The Origins of the War of 1914 (3-volume set)
Hitler's Foreign Policy, 1933–1939—The Road to World War II
The Origins of Fascist Ideology 1918–1925
Max Corvo: OSS Italy 1942–1945
Hitler's Contract: The Secret History of the Italian Edition of *Mein Kampf*
Secret Intelligence and the Holocaust
Israel at High Noon
Balkan Inferno: Betrayal, War, and Intervention, 1990–2005
Calculated Risk: World War II Memoirs of General Mark Clark
The Murder of Maxim Gorky
The Kravchenko Case: One Man's War On Stalin
Operation Neptune
Paris Weekend
Shattered Sky
Hitler's Gift to France
The Mafia and the Allies
The Nazi Party, 1919-1945: A Complete History
Encyclopedia of Cold War Espionage, Spies, and Secret Operations
The Cicero Spy Affair
A Crate of Vodka
NOC
The First Iraq War: Britain's Mesopotamian Campaign, 1914-1918
Becoming Winston Churchill

Hitler's Intelligence Chief: Walter Schellenberg
Salazar: A Political Biography
The Italian Brothers
Nazi Palestine
Code Name: Kalistrat
Pax Romana
The De Valera Deception
Lenin and His Comrades
Working with Napoleon
The Decision to Drop the Atomic Bomb
Target Hitler
Truman, MacArthur and the Korean War
Working with Napoleon
The Eichmann Trial Diary
Stalin's Man in Canada
The Parsifal Pursuit

Hunting Down the Jews

Vichy, the Nazis, and Mafia Collaborators
in Provence, 1942–1944

Isaac Levendel and Bernard Weisz

Enigma Books

Copyright © 2011 by Isaac Levendel

First Edition

Printed in the United States of America

ISBN: 978-1-936274-31-4
e-ISBN: 978-1-936274-32-1

Publisher's Cataloging-In-Publication Data

Lewendel, Isaac, 1936-
   Hunting down the Jews : Vichy, the Nazis, and Mafia collaborators in Provence,
1942-1944 / Isaac Levendel and Bernard Weisz ; [preface by Serge Klarsfeld]. -- 1st
ed.

   p. : ill., maps ; cm.

   Issued also as an ebook.
   Includes bibliographical references and index.
   ISBN: 978-1-936274-31-4

   1. Holocaust, Jewish (1939-1945)--France--Vaucluse (Dept.) 2. Jews--Persecutions-
-France--Vaucluse (Dept.) 3. Vaucluse (France : Dept.)--History--German
occupation, 1940-1945. 4. Antisemitism--France--Vaucluse (Dept.) I. Weisz,
Bernard. II. Klarsfeld, Serge, 1935- III. Title.

DS135.F83 L28 2011
940.531/81/094492

Contents

Southeastern France

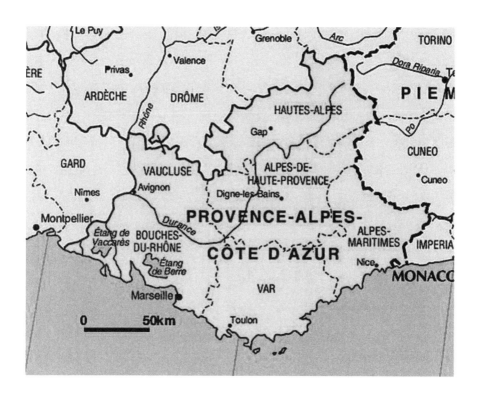

The Départment of the Vaucluse and Avignon

The locations

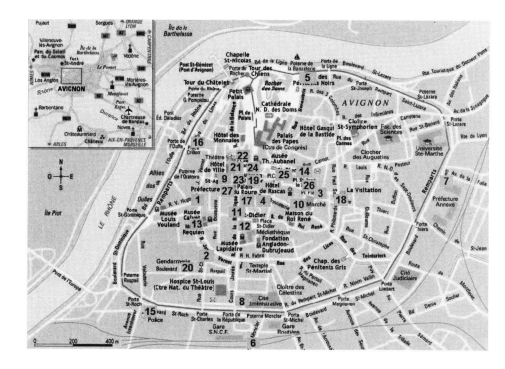

1	Kommandantur	Hôtel de Brancas, 35, rue Joseph Vernet
2	Military command	Hôtel Dominion, bd Raspail
3	Feldgendarmerie	Hôtel St Yves, rue Thiers at place Pie
4	Geheime Feld Polizei	Hôtel de la Cigale, 11, rue Bancasse
5	GFP French auxiliaries	Naquet Villa, 2, rue Rempart de la Ligne
6	SiPo-SD	Dr. Pons Villa 32, Bd Monclar
7	Wehrmacht	Chabran barracks, avenue de la Folie
8	Wehrmacht	7ième Génie barracks, rue de la République
9	German Propaganda	21, rue St Agricol
10	OPA former location	rue Grivolas
11	OPA new location	8, rue de la République
12	German Bookstore	18, rue de la République
13	Milice of Vaucluse	71, rue Joseph Vernet

14	Centre de Propagande pour la Révolution Nationale	6, rue Carnot
15	STO	de Salles barracks, bd St Roch
16	PPF former location	place Crillon
17	PPF new location	7, rue de la République
18	LVF former location	rue Thiers
19	LVF new location	rue des Marchands at place de l'Horloge
20	Légion	3, bis rue Violette
21	Bar le Crillon	place de l'Horloge
22	Central Bar	place de l'Horloge
23	Brasserie de l'Horloge	place de l'Horloge
24	Café Glacier	place de l'Horloge
25	Bar Carnot	near Eglise St Pierre
26	Bar de l'Olivier	place Pie
27	Prefecture of Vaucluse	4, rue Viala

Chronology

June 22, 1940	Germany and France sign an armistice. Two major zones are created : 1- The Northern Zone (3/5 of the metropolitan territory) is occupied by Germany, 2- The Southern – so called free - Zone is entirely controled by France; the colonies and overseas territories remain under French control A few northern sections are annexed by Germany and a "forbidden" zone is created along the Atlantic Ocean. After signature of a second armistice with Italy on June 25, 1940 a small Italian zone is created in the free zone along the Italian border. France remains sovereign on the entire territory, but Germany exercises "the right of the occupying power" on the north. The occupied zone includes several special zones: 1- The forbidden zone along the Atlantic coast 2- The part covering the northern *départements** is a military zone attached to the German military command in Belgium 3- Alsace-Lorraine is practically annexed by Germany 4- On the western side of Alsace-Lorraine, a territorial strip forms a zone "reserved " for German settling France commits, amongst others, to pay occupying fees which will amount to close to 400 million of francs per day.
September 25, 1940	Louis Valin is named prefect, replacing Louis Martin
October 3, 1940	First Statute of the Jews
March 29, 1941	Creation of the CGQJ – Xavier Vallat is its first Commissioner
	The PQJ is created and attached to the national police
	Henri de Camaret is named delegate of the CGQJ for the Vaucluse; Antoine d'Ornano serves as inspector of the PQJ for the Gard and the Vaucluse
November 29, 1941	French law creating the UGIF by orders of the Germans
December 1, 1941	Prefect Henri Piton replaces Louis Valin

---

* A *département* is an administrative geographic division of France, not to be confused with the departments as organizational divisions

May 6, 1942	Louis Darquier de Pellepoix becomes the next CGQJ Commissioner
August 26, 1942	Arrest and deportation of foreign Jews to the camp of les Milles, then to the camp of Drancy
	The PQJ is replaced by the SEC which is attached to the CGQJ
November 8, 1942	Allied landing in North Africa

November 11, 1942	**Invasion of the "free" zone. The Germans seize a narrow strip along the left bank of the Rhône, and the remainder of the *département* passes under Italian control.**

December 1, 1942	Jean Lebon is named inspector of the SEC for the Vaucluse and the Gard *départements*
March 16, 1943	Prefect Georges Darbou replaces Henri Piton
March 31, 1943	The role of Henri de Camaret is eliminated; he remains a simple AP (Administrateur Provisoire – Provisional Adminsitrator)
April 12, 1943	Arrest of several French Jewish notables in the Vaucluse
September 8, 1943	**Italy capitulates, and the Italian occupation zone is eliminated. The Germans take control of the former Italian zone and now occupy metropolitan France.**
December 1st, 1943	The gang leader Georges Parietas arrives in Avignon; he takes control of the local gang of Alfred André already in place.
December 16, 1943	Prefect Jean Benedetti replaces Georges Darbou who is designated representative of the southern zone prefects before Vichy
February 1944	Charles du Paty de Clam becomes the third Commissioner of the CGQJ
March 1, 1944	Charles Palmieri officially arrives in Avignon; he takes control of the local gang of Lucien Blanc, who had been already active and brings in reinforcements from Marseille when needed
March 28 and 29, 1944	Large roundup in Avignon
May 11, 1944	Prefect Jean Benedetti is arrested by the Germans; a vacancy is created
June 5 and 6, 1944	Large roundup in Avignon and surroundings
June 6, 1944	Allied landing in Normandy and declaration of insurrection in the various maquis
June 1944	Joseph Antignac replaces du Paty de Clam as General secretary of the CGQJ
August 26, 1944	**Liberation of Avignon**

August 29, 1944	**Liberation of Marseille**
August 31, 1944	Last payday of Jean Lebon, inspector of the SEC

September 1944 – July 1949	After a few weeks of "savage" justice, the trials of collaborators from the Vaucluse are carried out by the Courts of Justice of the Vaucluse, of the Gard, of the Bouches du Rhône, and of the military Justice in Marseille. On September 20, 1944, prefect Jean Charvet fills the vacancy.

Abbreviations

AE	Aryanisation économique – Economic Aryanization
AO	Autorités d'Occupation – Occupation Authorities
AP	Administrateur Provisoire – Provisonal Administrator (of Jewish Assets)
CDJC	Centre de Documentation Juive Contemporaine – Centre for Contemporary Jewish Documentation
CDL	Comité Départemental de Liberation – *Département* Liberation Committee
CGQJ	Commissariat général aux questions juives – General commission for Jewish affairs
FFI	Forces Francaises de l'Interieur – French Forces of the Interior
Gestapo	Geheime Stat Polizei – Secret State Police
GFP	Geheime Feld Polizei – Secret Field Police
GMR	Groupes Mobiles de Réserve – State Police charged with political repression
KdS	Kommando der SiPo/Gestapo und des Sicherheitsdienstes – Command of the unified German polices
LFC	Légion Française des Combattants – French Legion of Combattants
LVF	Légion des Volontaires Français – French Units of the Wehrmacht
OPA	Office de Placement Allemand – German office of employment
OSE	Œuvre du Secours aux Enfants – Taskforce for Children Aid
PPF	Parti Populaire Français – Popular French Party
PQJ	Police aux questions juives – Police for Jewish affairs
RG	Renseignement Généraux – Intelligence section of the police
RSHA	Reichssicherheitshauptamt - Central Office of Reich Security
SD	Sicherheitdienst – Security Service
SEC	Section d'Enquête et de Contrôle – Section for Investigation and Control
SiPO-SD	Sicherheit Polizei - Sicherheit Dienst
SOL	Service d'Ordre Légionnaire – Legion Police
SS	Schutzstaffel – Protection Squad
STO	Service du Travail Obligation – Service of Compulsory Labor
UGIF	Union Générale des Israélites de France – Union of the Jews of France

Preface

Isaac Levendel offers us an unconventional and even atypical book that is fascinating to read from beginning to end. This work belongs to the set of noteworthy regional, departmental and municipal studies that I was always hoping to see grow and that increasingly illuminate the more comprehensive historical works. However rather than proceed as the mainstream historians that set out to describe arrest operations, the itineraries of Jewish families or the biographies of the victims, this author has focused on the agents who were carrying out the persecution of the Jews, their court files, modus operandi, and psychological makeup. I have known what a dogged and methodical researcher Isaac Levendel is; I have known him for some thirty years since he came to France from the United States to retrieve the keys to his own fate. His motivations were rather straightforward: as a very young boy he had survived his mother's arrest. He never could accept the disappearance of the mother he loved so much; he continued his dialog with her and set himself the task of finding out the truth and telling the truth about the barbaric treatment that turned him into a victim as well. The Vaucluse was and remains the geographical framework of this investigation. His previous book, *Not the Germans Alone,* told his story from a very personal viewpoint and enjoyed considerable literary and historical critical acclaim as it found an appreciative readership.[1] He is a pioneer of an often fascinating category of books: reporting on a personal tragedy that involves the author. As Isaac Levendel returns to these same facts he comes to them with the greater detachment of the historian motivated by the passion to discover those responsible for the crimes against the Jews and their motivations.

The reconstruction that he offers is clear and unambiguous: in August 1942 the Vichy government had promised to hand over 10,000 stateless Jews living in the free zone to the Germans. Based on that commitment, the French national police did the arithmetic and limited the categories to be arrested to those Jews having entered France after January 1, 1936: the former Germans, Austrians, Poles, Czechs and Russians or Soviets. The quota for the Vaucluse was set; the gendarmes rounded up the agreed numbers of Jews on the basis of the census. They could have picked up ten or fifteen times more had they been ordered to round up all the Jews present in the *département*. Such an order was not issued. While Vichy wanted to reduce the Jews to the condition of pariahs it didn't seek to kill them but knowing that the Germans wanted to exterminate them, it became an accomplice to the genocide. The xenophobic anti-Semitism of Vichy placed the foreign Jews on the front line in the occupied zone. Had the population and the churches not protested, Vichy could well have continued those arrests throughout the entire country with the same intensity as during the summer of 1942. There came a reprieve that lasted until September 1943 in the Vaucluse thanks to the Italian military occupation authorities. Following the German invasion of the Italian zone of occupation the condition of the Jews in the Vaucluse worsened very quickly. Levendel describes very effectively how small numbers of German policemen led to the surfacing of gangsters and thugs who became the long arm of the Gestapo. Just as the author was able to show how Vichy's state sponsored anti-Semitism had given rise to anti-Semitic attitudes often motivated by lucre in the confiscations and aryanizations among France's bourgeois class and those among them who had lost their status. As to the careerism of the top civil servants Levendel's description fits in perfectly with the example of Maurice Papon, known to the French public since 1997.

Given the advantages it had in 1942 because of the empire, the fleet and the fact that France was quietly working in support of the Nazi war economy, Vichy had made its contribution to the final solution by a decision it took freely in the territory under its control where there were no Germans. Following the German invasion of the southern zone Vichy stopped handing down orders to the administrators of the prefectures for massive arrests of the Jews, with two exceptions, leaving the initiative to the Germans whose approach it was in each and every *Kommando* in each *département* to attract those individuals ready to do anything out of hatred for the Jews or for money. Levendel clearly shows how the Jews, registered on the census or just known as such, became easy prey to the Gestapo that managed to grab three times more in 1943–44 than the Vichy police had in 1942 because it only considered the Jews as having one nationality that of being Jewish and because there wasn't a preset number as in august 1942. In all about one quarter of the Jews in the Vaucluse died while the rest survived. The same scale of numbers appears for the whole country: 80,000 were lost; 240,000 were saved. Levendel can't quite tell who saved them; yes; the population didn't denounce them as the legend goes, yes there were acts of solidarity and yes, the allied victory helped the survival rate. What he does know and describes to perfection is the involvement of French gangsters being handled by the SS to undertake the dirty work that Vichy refused to continue ordering its police to do and that the Germans couldn't carry out since they were giving priority to the fight against the resistance and the security of the German army.

Isaac Levendel also established the minor role played by the Milice in the hunt for the Jews. By using the archives of the Courts of justice he describes fifteen cases of members of the Milice who helped some Jews in dangerous circumstances. This is not indeed as giving them an award as Righteous among nations but to understand the complicated reactions of some and show how the resistance fighters were often somewhat indifferent to the plight of the Jews.

The course of justice in the immediate postwar period indicates how far behind the punishment of crimes the persecution endured by Jewish families had been relegated. What was true for the Vaucluse also applied to the rest of France. It took the sons and daughters of Jews of France who were deported to take charge of the issue, change the memory of Vichy and inform the public conscience of this country what truly did take place and in what kind of crimes Vichy had been an accomplice. I read "*The Hunt for the Jews*" in just one sitting. You shall also read as I did because it is useful, hard, and true.

Serge Klarsfeld

Foreword

My *Libération*

... How do we react to unadulterated crime, when the foundations of human behavior are at stake? Can we then attempt to isolate the crime from its category, history from morality, and science from conscience?

François Bedarida[1]

On June 7 or 8, 1944, during the final hours before *Libération*, I was sitting on the rack of Monsieur Steltzer's bike. We left Carpentras early in the morning and wound our way through the country roads to the village of Sarrians. Monsieur Steltzer turned right and onto a cart lane. Once in a while, a tire kicked up a pebble with a pop. On both sides of the lane, were fields of tomato plants, and plum trees; at the end of the lane, an old farm with a huge door in the middle—it looked huge to me; this was the shed, and the small door to the living quarters on the right side, behind the well. All around the farm house, hedges of tall fir trees served as windbreaks for the cultivated plots.

I arrived at the Brès family farm, a few days after the arrest of my mother. I was not yet 8 years old, and I escaped arrest by sheer luck. During the years that followed, outwardly, I behaved as if none of this had ever happened; until January 1992.

Shortly after my arrival, Michel Brès, who was two years older than me, led me to one row of fir trees that hid the lifeless remains of a British fighter plane: a cockpit without the wings. Burnt patches of silk and loose ropes—what was once a parachute—were scattered all around, attesting to the tragic end of the pilot. Although the farm was isolated from the road to the town of Orange and from the village of Sarrians, it was located exactly on the path of waves of bomber and fighter planes on their way north. On June 15, they were targeting the two Luftwaffe air fields—Caritat and Plan de Dieu. On July 18 and 25 it would be the turn of the railroad tracks and the strategically positioned Orange train station that was used by the Germans as a communication hub for supply to the wide southeast area and the eventual retreat to the north, along the narrow Rhône valley. On August 13 a steady flow of bombers converged on the bridges and major roads. It looked like the allies were cutting the essential communication arteries.

From the roof top of the Brès family farm, we could see the devastation. Flames in the distance flared up long into the silence of the night. Libération was now at hand. Everyone was rejoicing, since it would all finally be over. Life would soon be back to normal for everybody. Well, for most people.

On August 26, 1944, the word was out: the Germans have left; they ran away as fast as they could. They took with them their most valuable collaborators; the others would have to fend for themselves. The entire Brès family rushed to the village; I follow.

The square is packed in front of the village hall where a self-proclaimed council is in session. The agenda does not include the reestablishment of essential services. First things first: the popular court of justice of Sarrians was in session. Outside, on the square, there is talk of revenge against a doctor and his wife who performed abortions for the benefit of some Sarrians "women of easy virtue," the grocer who profited from black market and a manufacturer who denounced Resistance fighters. Suddenly, a shot is fired. Everyone looks at the village hall door. A man staggers out and collapses at the bottom of a few steps. He is bleeding at his temple. "Serves him right!" breaks the tense silence, and the people on the square burst into applause. This is what Libération is supposed to be.

For the collaborators who were lucky to escape summary execution, there would be trials and sentencing. For their families and children, shame was to last forever.

My own Libération took a lifetime of waiting. At first, waiting desperately for my mother's return, and when that hope dwindled and vanished, waiting for the courage to face reality and seek the truth.

On a warm summer evening in 1994, at the darker corner of a Marseille outdoor café, a kind Marseille archive employee was holding a single sheet of paper, the report of the confrontation* that took place before Judge Jean Fabre, at the Marseille Court of justice on July 20, 1945, between Moise Benyacar, an Auschwitz survivor from Le Pontet, my village near Avignon, and Charles Palmieri, a notorious Marseille gangster:

Moise Benyacar:

I was arrested in Le Pontet on June 6, 1944, at half past noon, by 5 men, among whom Charles Palmièri being now present. I was arrested together with my wife and a baby, three and a half months old, we were brought to the village hall of Le Pontet; there several people were brought, first my sister in law Mme. Kremer, presently deported and without any news, Mme. Levander [*sic*] from Le Pontet, presently deported and without any news, as well as Mme. Bitran who was liberated and is now in Avignon... We were taken by the same people to the barracks of the Engineering Regiment, and then to the Sainte-Anne prison, then to Drancy, Auswich [*sic*], Bukenwal [*sic*] and Dachau, where I was liberated. My wife and my child were deported at the same time as me, and I have no news from them.

Charles Palmieri:

I do not contest having made the arrest in company of Billartz who was the boss; he belonged to the Gestapo of Marseille under the orders of Bauer; also were present Bergeron and Blanc; Bride was with us that day, I do not know whether he stayed at the village hall or went to the house of Benyacar. I want to make it known that one member of our team told to the wife of Benyacar not to come, this happened after the departure of the German Billartz, but the woman said that she did not want to separate from her husband and she came with her child...

This was the first time I became truly aware of the fate of my mother; fifty years later. More than a year has passed since Gaston Vernet, our long lost next door neighbor, had told me over the phone that the men who had arrested my mother were not Germans, since I had accepted Madame Steltzer's statement *"C'est les Allemands qui l'ont fait!"* (The Germans did it!) *"They spoke French with the accent of Marseille,"* said Gaston. He tersely explained: *"Mme. Levandel had run away from the Marseille men through her back door and taken*

---

* In the French judicial system, the confrontation is a procedure which takes place under the supervision of an investigating judge and during which a witness testifies in the presence of the defendant who is asked to react.

refuge in my home across the street. They were on her heels. In our kitchen, she seized a knife and tried to cut her veins. Then, they dragged her bleeding to their vehicle waiting outside…"

"They spoke French with the accent of Marseille." It was this testimony of Gaston that had brought me to the Marseille archives and to the sympathetic employee seated across the table from me, at the Marseille coffee shop, on this 1994 summer evening. He was holding tight on the document and did not want to let go of it. I would have to send in the usual official request for release… The writing of *Un Hiver en Provence*[2] and its American translation[3] put some order in my childhood memories.

I tried to imagine Charles Palmieri. What kind of person would want to do such a job, and why? How did he get from Marseille to Le Pontet and how did he become aware of us? And all the men who are mentioned in the confrontation report: Billartz, Bauer, Bergeron, Blanc, and Bride?

Maybe they were the four or five "Gestapo" men whom I remember from a hot day in May 1944. I was taking a hot bath outside, on the sidewalk in the back of our store; as usual, my mother had set up the water tub to heat in the sun, a few hours earlier. Suddenly, the men burst out of a grey Citroën "*traction-avant familiale,*"* stopped next to the sidewalk, and rushed into the "Sporting Bar" two doors away. They were all in dark tailored suits, wearing the distinctive "*chapeau mou*"† and carrying brown leather brief cases. All the neighbors stopped in their tracks and everyone hurried inside. My mother quickly picked me up, and wrapped me in a towel. In a few seconds the street was empty, although nothing happened that day. The men were just going to a "routine" meeting in a back room of Monsieur Gros's Sporting Bar; maybe they were meeting with their informers?

I saw those men again a few days later, at the end of May 1944, when, "in spite of the events," we went to the yearly horse races at the Roberty race track in Le Pontet. They were engaged in a friendly conversation with German officers in uniforms, next to the paddock. As soon as my mother saw them, she turned on her heels, and pulled me away. "We'll watch the horses later!"

No wonder I "took the bait" when Bernard Weisz presented me in 2005 with a list of more than 200 deportees from the Vaucluse. The list was obviously incomplete as some names were missing, and I could not resist the drive to find all the victims. When we reached together the 400 deportee

---

* A Citroen family-size front wheel drive car, that was popular with the police and the mob, among others.
† Fedora

mark, I asked him a question that each new name would bring up all along in my mind: "Would you want to know who arrested them, how did they do it and why?" He did not hesitate a minute.

Bernard was born in Marseille shortly after the war, and did not experience the Holocaust. But he lived it deeply. He lived it as a young child, holding the hand of his mother, née Mossé, on her way to errands in their native neighborhood. "This store owner was a collaborator and that one too!" as the boy was learning the local geography of the Holocaust.

Like many Jews, the Weiszes and the Mossés had lost a significant number of their family members, uncles, aunts, and cousins.

Without Bernard, this book would never have seen the light of day. Tireless in the archives, relentless in clarifying the obscure, persistent in exploring "other angles," always ready to reconsider when a new fact emerges, he has the mindset of a researcher. I could not have dreamt of a stronger partner.

Neither of us is a detached observer of the Holocaust. We are both irresistibly engaged.

Isaac Levendel

Introduction

From State Anti-Semitism to Mob Rule

Throughout the period from June 1940 to November 1942, the prefecture, the municipalities, the police and gendarmerie units followed Vichy policies regarding the persecution of the Jews *à la française*. Their goal was essentially to eliminate them from the national economy and strip them of all basic rights. If the destruction of the Jews down to the last individual was the cornerstone of the German "solution" of the Jewish problem,[1] this didn't apply to the French strategy. According to the terminology of the period, the "collection" and the "expulsion" of foreign Jews during the summer of 1942 was "nothing more" than returning to Germany those Jews that had come from the countries the Reich was occupying. Every European country would therefore settle its Jewish problem in its own specific way. To the deep disappointment of the ultra-collaborationists, Vichy resisted the German demands to deport the French Jews or those who had been living in France for a long time.

Things changed with the invasion of the free zone on November 11, 1942. Most of the Vaucluse was under Italian occupation, while the Germans kept the control over Avignon and the main communication passageways along the Rhône valley. From that date, the prefecture appears to have considerably reduced its anti-Jewish activity, even against the foreign Jews, limiting itself to specific individual requests that often originated from higher up. In some cases, Jews were interned in camps for foreign workers or "moved away" out of the larger cities, but always in response to a request from the CGQJ (*Commissariat Général aux Questions Juives*) or Vichy itself. The gendarmerie labeled the documents of the Jews with the stamp "JUIF" at the beginning of 1943, and the prefecture continued to maintain its Jewish files through the census of September 1943 and that of May 1944 as well as eventual updates. The orders came from Vichy responding to German pressure. However, there are no traces of roundups initiated by the prefecture and the gendarmerie during that period. The municipality and the prefecture were seldom forced to participate in actions against the Jews; they even have at times passively resisted German requests.

Once, on September 16, 1943, the Germans arrested, with the help of the *Groupements mobile de réserve* and the *Milice*, scores of "Gaullist" insubordinates to force the Vaucluse establishment to toe the line, but that measure was not aimed at the Jews. Although the operation was relatively limited, it bears resemblance to the major clean up of the Vieux Port of Marseille on January 22 to 24, 1943, by the French police, the Gardes mobiles de reserve and the gendarmes, following an agreement between René Bousquet, General Secretary of the Vichy French police, and Karl Oberg, Supreme Commander of the SS and German police in France. This operation did not specifically target the Jews either, and was aimed at cleaning the area, that the Germans regarded to be a warren of gangsters. This kind of action was rather rare in France in 1943-1944.

The arrival of the Germans in the Southern zone dampened the zeal of the bureaucrats who were in charge of implementing the French solution of the Jewish question at the Vaucluse prefecture. They were in fact overtaken by the agents of the CGQJ. Towards the end, understandably, the "settlement of the Jewish question" became an embarrassing smoking gun for the prefecture, as we learn from the regional director of the SEC (*Section d' enquête et de controle*) of Marseille in his monthly report of July 31, 1944:

> ...on 7/1/44, the prefect of the Vaucluse was asking me to inform him whether it would be possible, with respect to his département, to transfer his service in charge of "Jewish affairs" to my inspector on assignment in Avignon.
>
> I replied in the negative, because the prefectural attributions are different from mine in the Jewish domain.
>
> In addition, his service, already overloaded because of these attributions, would hence not be able to focus the attention necessary for the analysis of the Jewish affairs which are incumbent to prefectural competence.[2]

Actually, contrary to what the report appears to say, it was not the prefect of the Vaucluse, Jean-Baptiste Benedetti, who wrote to the director of the SEC, simply because he had been arrested by the Germans on May 11, 1944, and had not been replaced. It was in fact the General Secretary of the Prefecture, Jean Reiller, who had been empowered to sign the acts of the prefecture, starting May 12, 1944, and at least until August 5, 1944. It is therefore likely that Reiller would not have taken the initiative of discussing a partial reorganization of the Prefecture without Vichy's approval.

The distancing of the Prefecture immediately poses a fundamental question: who was arresting the Jews in 1943–1944?[3] The responsibility went directly to the Germans, the "sole masters of the ship" together with the "miliciens," as mentioned by a great number of witnesses.

The Actors and the Sources

Strictly speaking, a *milicien* was a card carrying member of the *Milice* (Militia), a paramilitary organization created in February 1943 out of the membership of the *Légion Francaise des Combattants*. A *milicien* was expected to wear the *Milice* uniform. However, for most people, a *"milicien"* was a French individual, usually dressed in civilian clothes or in uniform, vested with a certain amount of power and actively collaborating with the Germans. In that sense, a member or an adjunct of the Gestapo, for instance, was considered to be a *milicien*. Similarly, the term "collaborator" designated a broad range of sympathizers, not all of whom were actually inclined to take action. Collaborators included all those who favored or helped the occupiers to one degree or another. This covered the despised "horizontal collaboration" of prostitutes as well as the black market, denunciations, and the direct actions of the *miliciens*. The uniform tended to complicate things because a member of the *Milice*, a true *milicien*, could take part in an action in civilian clothes, thus making him a *"milicien"* or a "collabo," depending upon the extent of his involvement.

How does one account for the parish priest of Gadagne,* who was a true member of the *Milice* while still wearing his cassock?

The linguistic confusion between these different forms of collaboration has made it difficult to evaluate claims made by witnesses. A similar confusion affected the German police, often called the "Gestapo" by witnesses, in spite of the diversity of the units to which its members belonged. Contemporary intelligence reports, provided by members of the Resistance on the

---

* We will come back to this person in Part Two, Chapter 9

ground and found in the London Files (*Dossiers de Londres*), suffer at times from the same ambiguity.

A previous book by this author entitled *Not the Germans Alone* has sparked particular interest in the "francs-tireurs" (free agents) of Jewish persecution in the Vaucluse.[4] The author had traced through the Marseille archives two "members of the Gestapo" who had arrested his mother in Le Pontet and "spoke French with a Marseille accent."[5] Charles Palmieri, a boss from Marseille working for the Germans, was identified, together with a few of his acolytes, as the perpetrator of the arrest of seven Le Pontet Jews, amongst them Sarah Levendel, on June 6, 1944. How many more Jews had Palmieri and his gang arrested? How many more "francs-tireurs" had been involved in the hunt for the Jews? Who were they and what was their relationship to the Germans? These questions are the crux of this book.

To conduct the investigation, the procedural files of the Courts of Justice in the region (Vaucluse, Gard, and Bouches du Rhône) remained privileged sources of information. In some cases, the military Courts of Justice provided additional important data. The archives of the CGQJ (AJ38 series), in particular those of the Police for Jewish Questions and of the Section of Investigation and Control (SEC), as well as the archives of the Vaucluse were of critical importance. Each file yielded new discoveries, and often provided vital cross-references.

The Legal Basis for the Post War Purges

In 1944, before the end of the war, de Gaulle insisted on putting in place a military structure, the FFI (French Forces of the Interior), based on the unification of the various Resistance groups, and an administrative system based on the CDLs (*Comité départemental de Libération*). Through the description of his own role, as a *Commissaire de la République** for the region of Marseille, in the reconstruction of an administrative structure, Raymond Aubrac explains de Gaulle's rationale:

> The invention of the commissaires de la République results exclusively from the invention by the allies of an administration for the occupied territories. The goal is to prevent the Americans from applying the tool thaye had prepared to administer the territory during the combats for Liberation. They had prepared en entire administration, including instruction booklets. They applied it in Italy and they are ready to apply it in France. This administration of French territory by

---

* The role of *Commissaire de la République* for the Marseille region is that of regional prefect.

the allies is not acceptable. The refusal is natural with de Gaulle, but it the same with the Resistance. To avoid this situation, two mecanisms were also invented: first the CDLs, to prepare the liberating combats and to manage them according to the circumstances that will prevail. And also the commissaires de la République, whose very simple mission is to restore the République. When de Gaulle visits the provinces, the key word he uses everywhere is "the State," namely the tool of unification…[6]

In this context of restoring control over the country, de Gaulle's provisional government also "invented" a provisional legal system which consisted of the High Court of Justice (*Haute Cour de Justice*) in Paris, and the regional Courts of Justice (*Cours de Justice*) and Civic Chambers (*Chambres Civiques*). The ordinance of June 26, 1944, establishing the system envisioned a Court of Justice "*in the capital of each area under the jurisdiction of a Court of Appeal.*" After sentencing, the accused could request that the highest court, in this case the court of cassation, overturn the verdict, or he could also ask for a pardon, but the intermediate stage, the court of appeals, was not involved. This resembled the accelerated judicial process that existed during the previous Vichy regime. To curb unbridled popular purges (*l'épuration sauvage*[7]) and foil a burgeoning rebellion by some segments of the Résistance, Raymond Aubrac, Regional Commissioner of the Republic (*Commissaire Régional de la République*) for Marseille, named an early member of the Resistance, Maxime Fischer, second in command of the Maquis Ventoux, as sub-prefect in charge of the purges, a function he held for a few months after Liberation before returning to his home in Paris. Aubrac also set up the Court of Justice of the Vaucluse by the decree of September 5, 1944, long before most other regions and without a transition period, when "*the military or criminal courts are normally competent,*" as recommended by Article 5 of the ordinance of June 26, 1944. Early on in the Vaucluse, a race had pitted the delegates of the provisional Government against the local *Comité de Libération,* (CDL) that was demanding the establishment of a court martial that would be more severe and summary. The decree issued by Aubrac thus short-circuited the CDL and, in an indication of hasty justice, did not give the defendant the right to appeal in front of the court of cassation, contrary to the decree of June 26, 1944.[8] Max Fischer had confirmed this state of affairs in a personal letter. However, the exception did not last long, because Aubrac rapidly reaffirmed the right to appeal to the court of cassation in spite of the contrary opinion of the prefect and his entourage, as expressed in his reports to Aubrac of November 10 and 23, 1944:

... in my judgment, the reinstatement of the right of appeal to the court of cassation is a mistake. It is a measure that could become acceptable only in a few months.[9]

The court of the Vaucluse was officially created by Aubrac on September 20, 1944, and rendered its first verdict on September 28, 1944, a death sentence for Waffen-SS Jean-Daniel Michon and *milicien* André Rouyalroux, two minor collaborators; a verdict meant to serve as an example and to satisfy popular wrath.

In spite of the speedy establishment of the Court of Justice, the Vaucluse would remain the stage of a protracted conflict between the return to a more equable justice and the pursuit of "justice of the people"—summary executions, acts of personal vengeance, disproportionate sentences. Numerous bodies were found on the road sides and floating in the rivers.

This summary justice did of course not leave many documentary sources. Prefect Jean Charvet even noted that gangs of hoodlums in search of plunder crisscrossed the liberated Vaucluse, under the cover of the wild purges. Max Fischer became a sort of mediator between the *"francs-tireurs"* of justice and the prefectural authorities: *"I have been de facto the true boss of the Vaucluse during five months, and specifically in charge of the purges. Prefect Charvet was not doing much, and he and the military authorities accepted all my proposals without argument..."*[10] Max Fischer's job was to manage a strong symbolic element of justice, against the backdrop of generalized tension between the CDL and a prefect who didn't enjoy unanimous support from the various factions of the Resistance since his selection in April 1944. In order to take justice back in hand without alienating the Resistance and public opinion, Aubrac, Fischer and the Court returned exemplary verdicts, and the first defendants had to pay the ultimate price of the pacification of liberated Vaucluse.

The Courts of Justice were eliminated by the law of July 29, 1949, and military justice took over after 1951.

Article 1 of the law of June 26, 1944, defined crimes as *"acts, committed between June 16, 1940, and the date of Liberation, which constitute infractions to the penal laws in force on June 16, 1940, when they demonstrate the intentions of their authors to favor any of the enterprises of the enemy, and this regardless of any legislation in force."* This article put "the laws in force on June 16, 1940" at the center of the procedures to avoid retroactivity and all the disputes that might have caused. In addition, the intentions of the defendant had to be demonstrated in the application of this article. Because of the difficulty in establishing these intentions, the courts required proof of a contact to that effect between the defendant and the Germans.

Article 3 placed a limit on the defendant's responsibility: *"There is neither a crime nor a misdemeanor, when the facts consisted on the part of their author of the strict execution—exclusive of any personal initiative—of orders or instructions received, without any excess, or of the sole performance of professional obligations without the voluntary participation in an antinational act."* This article made up for it a little later by stating that an order received can provide no justification *"when the defendant, who had a managerial or a commanding positions, had the opportunity of getting out of it on his personal initiative. Similarly, the measure indicated in the first paragraph of the present article is applicable neither to acts of denunciation or delivery of people, nor to acts of violence…"* Although not directly mentioned, the deportation of Jews was implicitly covered by this ordinance in articles 1 and 3. According to the strict application of the law, a gendarme who arrested and delivered a person was not able to invoke as a defense the receipt of orders from higher up, as long as it was clear that he was aware that his action has served the enemy. Of course, this became more complicated when the chain of delivery includes several intermediaries.

A separate ordinance, issued on August 26, 1944, and amended on December 26, 1944, establishd Civic Courts to judge crimes of "national indignity." These were minor crimes broadly defined on the basis of a generic description as well as of a non exhaustive list introduced by the term "amongst others":

1. To have belonged, under whatever denomination, to governments or pseudo-governments which have exercised their authority in France between June 16, 1940 and the installation, on the metropolitan territory, of the Provisional Government of the French Republic, or
2. To have served in the management of the central, regional or département services of said governments, or
3. To have served in the management of the central, regional or département services of the Commission for Jewish Affairs, or
4. To have become or remained a member, after January 1, 1941, … of any collaboration organization, and particularly, of one of the following organizations: the SOL, the Milice, the Collaboration group, the LVF, the PPF, … [partial list], or
5. To have participated in the organization of demonstrations… in favor of the enemy, or
6. To have published articles, brochures or books, or given speeches in favor of the enemy, of collaboration with the enemy, of racism or of totalitarian doctrines

The anti-Jewish activity of the CGQJ came clearly under the jurisdiction of the Civic Court, and did not expose the defendant to sentences beyond national degradation.

In reality, these ordinances were not always enacted consistently. The rapid decrease of the severity of the courts became acutely visible as time passed.

Local History and History at the Top

Contrary to our earlier investigations, this time there was no need to resort to political support for the special permissions necessary to consult documents which will be open to the public in 2035 and 2045. They were granted without undue difficulty, with the exception of a few temporary absurdities linked to the Archives of the Gard *département* but fortunately corrected after an appeal to the *Commission d'Accès aux Documents Administratifs* (CADA).

We have undertaken this voyage inside the archives convinced that micro-history will contribute to the understanding of the larger History. Let the eventual skeptics be reminded that everything did not happen inside the offices of Vichy, Paris, or Berlin. Quite the opposite! It is the translation of the intentions from higher up by individuals in the streets, the cafés and the houses of Avignon, Carpentras, Pertuis, Sorgues, Bollène, Apt, which has often brought the Vaucluse to the edge of the abyss, and in some cases, ennobled it. It is through the strength or the weakness of the chain of command that slowdowns or initiatives beyond the call of duty emerge in the persecution of the Jews. Finally, the courage or baseness of individuals at the bottom of this chain of command often determined the fate of the victims one way or the other.

As for the broad historical framework, so essential to understand the "energy" gains and losses all along the chain of command, we have drawn our knowledge from works that preceded ours. In particular, our discoveries lie within the global work of Serge Klarsfeld about the Shoah in France, and provide a local perspective to the Vaucluse and Provence.

In this local study of the destruction of the Jews, we have contributed to the reconstruction of an "impressionist" history where the full picture will unfold out of a multitude of small brush strokes. For instance, claiming that the relatively lower percentage of Jewish victims in France testifies to the sympathy of the French population is too hasty a conclusion, because the survival of potential victims depended on multiple factors whose diversity on the ground must be recognized in the proper context.

Throughout our efforts testimony was critical, because many things did occur outside government spheres. Limiting ourselves to administrative archives would have yielded a truncated view of those events. However, this will open several fundamental questions. Must a testimony be rejected if it is too subjective, if a detail does not fit or if the witness might have benefitted from lying? We are of course aware of the weaknesses of memory and of the human tendency to be selective, voluntarily or not. But, is the document immune from this kind of problem, since it has in a certain way been written by a "witness"? Without rejecting any source off hand, we used whatever material was available, but cautiously. In the course of our analysis, we have noted those deficiencies which will leave some questions unresolved. Apparently, the "Memory of the State," to use an eloquent title of Lucie Favier, will not be sufficient.[11]

The Economy of Evil

Contrary to an agreed upon tradition in historical research, we have chosen to conduct our analysis through the individuals who marked that period. On one hand, the official titles of these individuals and their functions in the traditional organisms of the occupation and collaboration did not necessarily determine their actions. On the other hand, it was their ability to associate with one another to create the "networks of evil" and to infiltrate the official organizations which was at the core of their effectiveness. With their partners and associates, they formed the network fabric of collaboration dedicated both to hunting the Jews and pursuing the other "enemies of the Reich." Both these activities were often inextricably connected.

Some took an active part, weapons in hand, in the hunt for the Jews, while others used their leadership positions to foster anti-Semitic hostility in the Vaucluse, thereby helping the designs of the activists. The "blue collars" and the "white collars" of anti-Semitism would be a fitting name. There was something in it for everybody. Our decision to give priority to personal relations over chronology will at times make it difficult to memorize all the names flashing by. Fortunately, this memorization is not necessary to grasp the extent of this spiderweb network.

The state of political insignificance that the Vichy regime had progressively slipped into in 1943 and 1944 allowed gangs of violent criminal types to comb the Vaucluse in search of Jews under the supervision of the German police. This amid the indifference of a large part of the population that had subscribed to the slogans of Vichy and the Maréchal not long before. Of course, the hoodlums were not strangers to anti-Semitism, but the free exercise of their criminal activities was what they sought. Latent anti-Semitism was just helping them in their designs. The German police needed reinforcements, since they counted only a little more than one hundred individuals for all the *départements* of the region of Marseille.[12] The German police, itself bristling with hoodlums and shady characters, found natural allies in the French gangsters, with whom they could communicate in the common language of manipulation and violence.

Without underestimating the importance of traditional anti-Semitism in the persecution of the Jews, this formed an ideal base for an "economy of evil*" between an array of shady characters, the institutions of Vichy, and the German police. Those who felt like it and had no scruples did participate; everyone got his share. Often with the help of a corrupt establishment possessed by an irrational reactionary hope, this economy took root in a paralyzed and crippled society—in bistros, in private homes, in requisitioned and despoiled buildings, at the headquarters of the German police. This "economy of evil," also carved in the stones of the Vaucluse, paradoxically, did not yield the return the Germans in Berlin had hoped for. A significant number of Jews were released for a ransom, that was shared at times with the Germans. Other times, they were robbed behind the back of the occupying forces. Some owed their life to luck; others were protected by good people. A certain number, whose addresses were known to the authorities, seem to have been "forgotten" or perhaps their time had not yet come. The result was a cruel, but fortunately unaccomplished, persecution.

The German "masters," under such constraints, had the time to deport "only" a little more than 300 Jews of a total of more than 1500 of those registered, and probably 300–400 more unregistered individuals. These came in addition to the hundred or so deported by Vichy during the summer of 1942, before the German invasion of the Southern zone.

But suppose their reign had lasted longer…

In the final analysis, the numbers testify to a significant disparity between Berlin's genocidal intentions and the actual results attained "on the ground" in the Vaucluse. This poses the central question of this work: how did each actor contribute to this disparity, and in particular, did Vichy truly shield the Jews against Nazi plans?

---

* To better appreciate this "economy of evil," a table in Appendix A provides the value of the French franc between 1940 and 1945 in 2010 US dollars. This table will serve as a reference all along this book.

Part One

The "French Solution" to the Jewish Question in the Vaucluse

The French Solution to the Jewish Question was not a single set of rules and decisions. Vichy government policy often fluctuated, and even then, it was not enforced uniformly across all the *départements* and municipalities.

Changes came under the pressure of tactical realities. Contradictions became apparent. For example, the deportation of foreign Jews to Germany in 1942 was not in the spirit of the laws that made up the Statute of the Jews[*] promulgated between October 1940 and June 1941. France was sacrificing these undesirables in the hope of preventing the delivery of French Jews in the short term. This "compromise" didn't come as a demonstration of sympathy for French Jews, but was instead, a device meant to protect a remnant of sovereignty by Vichy in the face of the Nazi victor. In addition, the verbal protests by a part of the population confirm that for some people these deportations were beyond the scope of the "French solution" to the Jewish question they had come to accept. They saw it as a far reaching decision that was difficult to swallow, even if the deportations were the logical extension of the anti-Semitic decrees. Indeed, physical abuse against an already weakened group is never surprising.

How should one qualify the more or less overt collaboration by some functionaries with the German designs? For instance, the activity of the collaborationist Prefect of the Gard (from 1940 to the beginning of 1944), Angelo Chiappe, who was executed during the Liberation, is as much part of the "French Solution" as the ambiguous attitude of a Vichy functionary who would have applied measures against the Jews according to the dispositions of the Statute of the Jews while at the same time helping other Jews.

The CGQJ, another branch of the Vichy government, seemed to harbor a more radical anti-Semitism than the Prefecture and the Ministry of Internal Affairs.

The implementation of the measures against the Jews along the Statut des Juifs did not follow a strict pattern and resulted in a significant diversity of action across French territory and in particular in the Vaucluse. The

---

[*] The Statute of the Jews falls within the context of a global European anti-Jewish hostility, but it must be noted that each country had its own legislation, modified by German decrees.

guiding line of these measures did not include by and large the active and systematic deportation of Jews, except for the notorious roundups of the summer of 1942. All these measures converged however to a core issue: turning the Jews into outcasts in French society.

With all its specificity, the "Vaucluse solution to the Jewish question" falls within the framework of this complex body of actions that we shall call the "French solution" within these pages.

Chapter 1

The Forgotten Jews of 1942

The history of the persecution of Jews in the Vaucluse has remained hidden for decades in the confines the synagogue and the Jewish cemetery of St. Roch in Avignon; places that are almost exclusively visited by Jews. The Jews feared that a simple public reference to past abuse would be construed by the "others" as an accusation and an indictment. It is what many young Jews growing up in Vaucluse experienced immediately after the war. That issue had to be forgotten once and for all.

In fact, this was the general consensus, and certainly that of Michel Hayez, the director of the archives of the *département* of Vaucluse, when he essentially told the author, at the beginning of 1992: *"There is no need to look at the archives. The history of Vaucluse during Second World War has already been written. Why don't you read the book by Aimé Autrand instead? He provided the lists of all the deportees."*

Aimé Autrand, the Vaucluse representative in the Committee for the History of Second World War, presided over by Henri Michel, had been designated to provide the official view of those events. In his 1965 book, Autrand published the "authorized list" of victims, amongst them "82 racial arrestees."[1] This Vaucluse list, which is unbelievably short, will in turn be sanctioned by Henri Michel's Committee as an official component of the national synthesis. The significant errors and omissions in the list of the Vaucluse originate mostly from methodological flaws. The basic documents are incomplete, and in particular, the lists of arrests made directly under German control, as acknowledged by Autrand himself.

> … However, in the absence of any police report on this topic (and for a good reason) we could unfortunately not indicate (even approximately) the number of people arrested and directly taken to the German prison after these operations…[2]

To establish his "authorized list" of those arrested and deported, Autrand did not use sources external to the Vaucluse, which could have filled the gaps and provided additional names. To be fair, it must be said that some of these sources were not readily available in the sixties as they are today, such as the data bases of Yad Vashem[3] and of the *Centre de documentation juive contemporaine* (CDJC).[4] However, most of the archives of the Vaucluse municipalities, rich in detail, as shown by Michèle Bitton and Jean Priol for the deportees of Pertuis[5] and Villelaure,[6] and by Bruno Tognarelli[7] for the children of the Vaucluse, were ignored by Autrand.

Since Aimé Autrand did reconstruct his lists in part by using testimonies and statements from survivors, some errors are directly linked to new arrivals from other *départements*, and to the absence of testimony about some deportees. This explains the presence in his book of people who had resided in other *départements* during the war, as well as the absence of the names of some victims of the Vaucluse, because no witness came forward on their behalf.

These factors alone resulted in the omission of more than 220 victims. But there is a far more serious historical shortcoming, which attests to multiple breaks of professional ethics: the hundred or so foreign Jews deported during the summer of 1942 are not documented anywhere. Yet, it was Autrand himself who had organized their deportation in August 1942.[8] He was at the time the Head of Division in charge of Police Affairs, Weapons, Foreigners and Jews, a position he held at the Prefecture of the Vaucluse from July 1940 to September 1943.

These arrests were made following orders of Pierre Laval and took place all across the free zone with the support of the Gendarmerie. On August 24, 1942, the prefect of the Vaucluse wrote:

> As a follow up to the conversation you had this morning with the competent division Head in my prefecture and with the General Secretary, I am honored to request that you order the arrest on <u>Wednesday 26 of the current month starting at dawn,</u>* of all the foreign Jews on the list attached.

---

* The sender had underlined two important elements

These individuals will have to be assembled in the nearest barracks and taken to the "camp of les Milles" near Aix-en Provence with two buses which I will make available to that effect and that will arrive <u>at 7 a.m. that day in front of the Avignon city hall</u>.

The list in question is that of the Jews of the Vaucluse who had entered France after New Year's Day 1936; it includes 110 people.[9]

The "competent division Head" is no other that Aimé Autrand himself, and in fact, he is the author of this letter in the name of the prefect, as attested by the letterhead label D1 B2.* Several months later, the *Rapides du Sud Est* bus company will remind Autrand that he still owes them some 2,866.50 francs for this "transport of August 26 to the camp of *les Milles.*"

It is, to say the least, a strange omission for a man who had himself been at the center of these arrests. His services had even prepared the list. One could begin to see a few "explanations." *"Oh, come on, Monsieur Levendel, these people were not his Jews,"* an archive employee had suggested in 1992. One can "understand"—the people deported in August 1942 were not "the Jews of Aimé Autrand." Many of them were indeed refugees in the Vaucluse. To be "a Jew of Autrand," one had to be a French Jew or to have arrived in the Vaucluse before January 1, 1936, according to Vichy's criteria. So be it!

This explanation is however not very convincing, when one sees that Aimé Autrand had published the name of Simon Ebstein who was on the victims' list provided to the Gendarmerie on August 24, 1942. Simon Ebstein, who was to be arrested two days later, escaped and was picked up a few weeks later near the Swiss border; yet he was not "a Jew of Autrand." In fact, the most probable explanation for the omission is that Autrand had not wanted to give to the Committee of History of the Second World War the list of his own victims. Remorse? Embarrassment? Fear of the consequences? It is also possible that the committee of Henri Michel was not that interested in the list of the Jewish victims of 1942.

Robert Bailly, the other historical icon of Avignon, provides an answer for both himself and his illustrious predecessor, Aimé Autrand. First, the deportation of Jews rates only a few words in his book about Avignon. In addition, on the page he dedicated to the Gestapo, Bailly sympathizes with Autrand.

> It is not appropriate for us to mention here its activities [the Gestapo], the time has not yet come! In addition, as written so well by Aimé Autrand: **"It is**

---

* The prefecture is composed of divisions supervised by the prefect and his secretary. Each division includes several bureau (departments). Autrand was the head of Division D1, *Bureau* (department) B2.

better not to mention these things, so as not to run the risk of awakening resentments which have not been completely forgotten…"* It should be added that many of the actors of some dramas are still around amongst us.[10]

So, now we know. These "historians" have no business in the actual history of the Vaucluse. Their main aim is to boost the prestige of the *département* without making too many waves. If one was not aware of the exceptional work of some historians, this could cast a shadow on the entire profession.

Vichy had been planning the measures against the foreign Jews long before August 1942. On March 25, the regional director of the CGQJ had forwarded to the regional chief of Police for Jewish Affairs the following report provided a few days earlier by Henri de Camaret, delegate of the CGQJ for the Vaucluse.

SUBJECT: Census of the Jews who had entered France since January 1, 1936
In the Vaucluse: 177 were counted as follows:
- Men younger than 18   – 30
- Men from 18 to 55   – 58
- Men older than 55   – 15
- Women   – 74

As a matter of course, the commission for the enlistment of foreign workers in Avignon has already enlisted 24 of those who currently hold a job in a profession useful to the National Economy—particularly in agriculture…

The delegate for the Département of the Vaucluse
H. de Camaret[11]

The date of entry in France, mentioned in this letter of March 25, 1942, strangely coincides with the cutoff date for the deportees of August 26, 1942, which implies that this deportation had been planned for a long time. But this also reveals a discrepancy. Why did Henri de Camaret gather the names of 177 people in this category, while Autrand only uses 110 of them—a difference of 67 individuals? This difference can be explained—but only in part—by the 24 foreign Jews enlisted "as a matter of course" by the commission for the enlistment of foreign workers. (Incidentally, this commission was presided by no other than Aimé Autrand himself.) In the end, at least 43 Jews—some of them arrested after August 26 and not accounted for—seem to have slipped through the cooperation between Autrand and de Camaret. Could it then be that Autrand had dragged his feet?

---

* Bold in the original text.

There is an irony in the description of his own role during the war by Autrand, the delegate of the Vaucluse in Henri Michel's committee.

> Autrand Aimé, born on April 11, 1892, in Camaret (Vaucluse). Head of a division in the cabinet of the Prefect of the Vaucluse in November 1940, when the purges were decided by the Vichy government. With three or four of his colleagues at the Prefecture, he was to become the targeted victim, under the pretext "that he had served the republican regime too loyally" (this was, at least literally, the reason invoked in the report which Special police superintendant Nouvet had addressed to the Prefect of the Vaucluse on November 10, 1940). If he was not fired (as the new leaders of the Légion des Combattants demanded), it is because the new Prefect, air force general Louis Valin, a high government officer of exceptional probity, deemed that under these circumstances, it would be sufficient for the head of the division to be "moved away" from the cabinet of the Prefect. In exchange, he entrusted him with the management of police affairs, including: control of foreigners, Jews and weapons. This was indeed a particularly thankless administrative attribution…[12]

Aimé Autrand almost succeeds in making us lose sight of who the victims were.

This text however still holds a residual ambiguity: Autrand does not state his own title. The answer is provided by a fanatic of the new regime, Jacques Petit, the president, for the Vaucluse, of l'Amicale de France:

> M. Autrand had been named head of division. But the Prefecture, being of the third class, was supposed to have only two divisions instead of the four that had been created to "find a spot" for friends. M. Autrand had to be demoted to the rank of department head. However, it seems that, in spite of it, he has kept his salary level and his mail signature delegation.
>
> This sectarian officer and staunch supporter of the Front Populaire was chosen by Prefect Valin to establish the political files of the officer of the département [of the Vaucluse].
>
> This nomination, extraordinary to say the least, was made with full knowledge of the facts by M. Valin, who had made a point to please senator [Ulysse] Fabre, a friend of [Edouard] Daladier, and M. Gonnet, who states everywhere that, although a strong supporter of the Front Populaire, he is strongly backed, in Vichy, by a high ranking officer of the Ministry of the Interior.[13]

This makes Autrand's position look like a pro forma demotion since he kept his salary and several functions were still under his authority. In fact, he used the label D1 B2* while dealing with Jewish affairs.

---

* 1st Division, 2nd Department (Bureau).

This note confirms what has been known from other sources. Before the war, Autrand had been a *radical socialiste* close to Edouard Daladier, who was mayor of Avignon before moving up to the national scene and becoming prime minister. He was an "enlightened" member of the Vaucluse establishment and showed no sympathy for fascism. His political circle included people on the left. Some, like Jean Garcin, later chose to resist. After the 1940 defeat, Joseph Cucumel, a resistance member from the beginning, in charge of infiltrating public administration in the Vaucluse, had criticized Autrand for staying on within the administration of Vichy.[14]

This raises a fundamental ethical question. Were Autrand and the prefecture aware, between 1940 and 1942, of the seriousness of their actions against the Jews? This can be placed on two levels: that of systematic discrimination—census, spoliation, house arrests, professional destitution—and that of pure and simple deportation, as in August 1942. On the first level, how could Autrand accept the blacklisting of human beings protected by the fundamental principles at the heart of the Republic? How could he justify it? Were the moral standards of that period so different from ours? And if that had been the case, why did others make very different choices?

On the second level, did Autrand and his peers know—even vaguely—the consequences of the deportations they had carried out in August 1942? On September 12, 1942, the department of foreigners and police affairs of Autrand had intercepted a letter of Léon Rosenthal, the shoemaker of rue Joseph Vernet. This document, addressed to the office of *l'Œuvre du secours aux enfants* in Montpellier, speaks volumes on the question.

> To the Union O.S.E.
> It is in the name of a desperate mother whose husband has just died that I appeal to you. It is about saving the lives of two children, one five and a half years old and the other seven; as well as their mother, Mrs. Régine Bobryker, all interned in the Camp of Les Milles. I beg you to intervene urgently; because we are talking about human beings and <u>above all children</u>.* I am sending you my last cry of desperation. Be merciful. This cry is of a dying woman. Save the two children and react urgently... Save them immediately. Take pity on these children lives.[15]

What this letter does not mention is that the father, Joseph Bobryker, was in fact alive. He was not arrested, because he was not sleeping at home, like many others at the time. So far, only men had been targeted for deportation. But, aware of the danger after the arrest of his wife and children, he

---

* Underlined in the police report and possibly in the original letter of Rosenthal.

behaved discreetly. Léon Rosenthal, the intermediary and a communist, was a reliable source of information circulating amongst the members of the communist party.[16] The two children, Norbert and Rachel, will be saved by the OSE; they now live in Australia. It appears that at least a few Jews were keeping their eyes and ears open. One can understand the blindness of some. But how is it possible that the police services of Autrand and the *Renseignements généraux* had no knowledge of this information?

The "Non Crime" of August 1942

Autrand was not indicted at the Liberation for what he had done during the war, in spite of the fact that he had presided over anti-Jewish measures as early as November 1940. Actually he would return to the prefecture as a head of division, a position that he had de facto occupied during the war. "*Apparently, no charges were filed against him,*" said Joseph Cucumel, secretary of the Prefecture after Liberation, who was aware of Autrand's collaboration with Vichy, as we noted earlier.[17] This is confirmed by Maxime Fischer, a refugee from Paris who became a resistant, co-founder of Maquis-Ventoux and sub-prefect in charge of the purges for a few months after Liberation. He explained: "*How was I supposed to know, if nobody complained about it?*"[18]

An important event contributed to covering up Autrand's responsibility in the deportation of Jews in 1942. His arrest for supporting de Gaulle on September 16, 1943, along with 123 others from the Vaucluse, in the vast political crackdown organized by the Germans with the participation of the *Milice* and the *Groupes mobiles de Réserve*. That roundup was meant in part at shaking the inertia and the passive resistance of the administration toward the designs of the German occupying forces. Six days later, on September 22, 1943, Autrand forwarded to prefect Georges Darbou a letter written in pencil on a few pages torn out of a notebook.

> You have surely been informed, Mr. Prefect, that I was arrested last Thursday by units of the German police.
>
> I have not worried until now, because I thought that this was a general security measure taken against some categories of French people, or that I had been the victim of an error and that I would soon be freed.
>
> If I am taking the liberty of writing to you today, it is to protest vehemently to you regarding my complete innocence.
>
> I give my word as a family man that I have never done nor attempted nor conceived anything against the operational authorities [the Germans].
>
> Also, I am awaiting with confidence, but also with the impatience that you can imagine, the moment of my interrogation so that I may justify myself.

I assure you, Mr. Prefect, of my respectful devotion and my loyal commitment to my duties.[19]

These few lines did not have the desired effect, and despite everything, he was sent to a labor camp in Linz, Austria. He was released for health reasons before the end of the war and repatriated to Avignon. Obviously, the arrest reflected a change of mind on his part, but it also came as convenient protection when he returned from captivity.

Aimé Autrand later was co-opted as a representative of the Vaucluse in the *Comité pour l'histoire de la seconde guerre mondiale* despite his antecedents, that Henri Michel knew about thanks to Robert O. Paxton.[20] There was a document concerning Autrand available to the public at the CDJC concerning his role at the Prefecture of Vaucluse. "*One can expect from M. Autrand a good collaboration*," a visitor from Vichy had reported in 1941 regarding the census of the Jews delivered by Autrand.[21]

Paradoxically, the fox was set to mind the geese, and in his capacity as an official historian of the Vaucluse, he was granted free access to the archives documenting his own misdeeds, while the law hampered the steps of most other "innocent" researchers.

How many people in the know have remained silent, or kept their voices too low to be heard, or saw nothing wrong with the deportations, all along? Would it have been the same if Aimé Autrand had organized the deportation of resistance fighters? The answer can be found in the trial of the prefect of the neighboring Gard *département*, Angelo Chiappe, sentenced to death on December 21, 1944, for collaboration and intelligence with the enemy, and executed one month later. The charges against Chiappe included belonging to the Group Collaboration, his active support for the milice, and his zeal in increasing the enrollment for the STO (Compulsory Labor Service). But the heaviest element of all—the one that cost him his life—was a list of 50 hostages* he had provided to the Germans, following a bombing, where five Germans soldiers and two French women lost their lives at the "Maison Caro," a brothel reserved for the German army. Although Chiappe had also organized the roundup of Jews in 1942 in step with the other prefects of the free zone, that charge was not brought against him.[22] Just as in the trials of Marshal Philippe Pétain[23] and Pierre Laval,[24] the persecution of the Jews was seldom explicitly taken into account in the indictments of individuals who operated in the Vaucluse. This was a recurring pattern in the trial files at the base of our work, even when the testimonies spoke to the contrary. Masking the impact of the Holocaust was not an accident, and seemed to result from a

---

* The 50 hostages were released after the discovery of the authors of the bombing.

convergence of several interests, a kind of implicit consensus between various segments of society.

Let us now turn to the way Autrand describes the role he played during the war in his own words:

> Thanks to the kindness of the population, and the "complicity" of the competent service of the Prefecture, numerous Jews worthy of interest were able to elude, for a few months, the zealous inspectors of the CGQJ of Vichy, but this was to change starting in 1943, when many miliciens or members of the PPF were able to obtain their addresses.[25]

First, Autrand informs us that the "competent service of the Prefecture"—a bureaucratic euphemism to designate the service that he managed—had snatched "numerous Jews worthy of interest" from the clutches of "the zealous inspectors of the CGQJ of Vichy." Of course, we know the fate of the other Jews—those who had not been "worthy of interest"—arrested during the operations which Autrand himself had organized in August 1942. All were deported in convoys 29 to 33 and murdered, with the single exception of Icek Agjengold from Villelaure, who survived Auschwitz and returned without his wife and two children.

Autrand also gave the impression that the arrests of Jews in 1942 were the doings of the "zealous inspectors of the CGQJ of Vichy," while he concentrated on saving a few victims of choice. The truth is sadly different.

Two questions still remain. The first relates to historical fact: what was the true nature of the relations between Autrand and those "zealous inspectors of the CGQJ of Vichy"? The second has to do with the addresses of the Jews which "numerous miliciens or members of the PPF were able to obtain." How did these addresses find their way into the "wrong hands"?

The Accomplices

The deportations of 1942 were exclusively organized by the Vichy government in the free zone, and Autrand was not the sole "contributor" to this operation for the Vaucluse. It began with the measures against the Jews promulgated by Vichy including the census managed by Autrand with the assistance of the municipalities. The conspiracy continued with house arrests or internment in the GTE by the head of the division, Aimé Autrand. This made it easier to find the foreign Jews when the time came.

Of course, all those actions were covered by the prefects succeeding one another in Avignon: Louis Valin from September 1940 to November 30, 1941, Henri Piton from December 1, 1941, to March 15, 1943, Georges

Darbou from March 16, 1943, to December 15, 1943—later as the representative of the prefects of the free zone to Pierre Laval—and Jean Benedetti from December 16, 1943, until his arrest on May 11, 1944. Every one of them countersigned the measures against the Jews. Even though Benedetti was considered a friend by the CDL (Committee of Liberation), this does not change the fact that the last census of the Jews of May 1944 was prepared under his authority. Apparently, in those days, one could at the same time make a list of Jews and remain a friend of the Resistance.

Torpedoing the hunt for the Jews was not in the radar screen of the Resistance of the Vaucluse. In 1994, Maxime Fischer was asked why his network did not attack a German deportation train that was forced by the allied bombardments to stop for more than 24 hours in Sorgues (Vaucluse) on August 18, 1944. His answer was simple: "*I had only about 80 men at my disposal in the entire département; nobody had informed me about the deportation train, and even if I had known, the allies had not provided us with any heavy weaponry for fear of a communist takeover; our limited individual weapons were no match for the heavily armed German detachment on the train.*"[26] Also in 1994, while explaining his role in fighting the Germans, Jean Garcin, the former head of the *Groupes Francs** for the R2 région (Vaucluse, Bouches-du-Rhône, Gard, Var, Basses-Alpes and Alpes-Maritimes), mentions several daring operations to free "comrades" from the hands of Germans in Marseille. "*M. Garcin, did you organize any action to free Jews?*" He gives a simple and eloquent answer: "*We were fighting the common enemy.*"[27]

On the allied side, all the way to the top, the "Jewish issue" did not weigh much. Even the word "Jew" is strangely absent from a 39 page study of the BBC and the propaganda war in occupied France.[28] "Anti-Semitism" appears only once. In a cooperative publication, Sébastien Laurent poses a simple quandary "The French Military Secret Services and the Holocaust, 1940–1945: Omission, Blindness, or Failure?"[29] The answer may lie in a conversation between two men specialized in the French sector: on January 2, 1943, Peter Storrs (Special Operations Executive) spoke with Lewis Gielgud (Political Warfare Executive). In the eyes of Storrs, emphasizing the persecution of the Jews was counterproductive:

> In conversation with two young Frenchmen who have just arrived in this country after doing good work for us in France, I learn that the continued reference in BBC broadcasts to the persecution of the Jews tends to be resented by the French, who themselves have so many relatives imprisoned in German prison camps or concentration camps.[30]

---

* The *Groupes Francs* (Free Groups) were a segment of the Resistance movement.

Silence during the war and silence after the war.

The deportations of August 1942 were prepared and executed at the direction of Prefect Henri Piton, a long-time official at the ministry of Interior. In 1943, Piton moved on under Max Bonnafous, Secretary of State for agriculture and food supply, and after the Liberation, he resurfaced as Prefect of the *département* of Maine et Loire, a position he held from May 11, 1945, until his retirement the following year. The change of heart of the prefecture after the German invasion served as a screen for others besides Autrand.

One must not forget the denouncers of all sides, and in particular, the representative of the CGQJ, Henri de Camaret, who made it his duty and was often too pleased to reveal how the Jews avoided the census.

A close accomplice of Autrand, Tainturier, the commander of the Gendarmerie of the Vaucluse, put together the detailed logistics of the arrests carried out on August 26, 1942. He was also responsible for the transfers before that date of the Jews assigned to the GTE under his control. On August 26, 1942, Tainturier dispatched his gendarmes to the towns and villages of the Vaucluse to "collect" the foreign Jews. A multitude of reports written on the same day bear witness to the systematic effort invested in the operation. Captain Ferrier, commander of the Gendarmerie Section of Orange gave an account of his action in Orange, Sablet, Bollène, Valréas et Vaison.

> The collection operations of the foreign Jews in the list attached to note Nr. 1704 from the Prefect dated August 24, 1942, began on August 26, 1942, at daybreak and went off without any major incident.

His team did not let go of its victims easily.

> After arriving at 4:15 a.m. at the home of the family of Osias Tieder in Sablet, the gendarmes could not get any answer to their calls. At 5:15 a.m., they had to seek the mayor who had to call a locksmith to open the door. The bedrooms and attic were searched to no avail. They discovered the husband hidden behind the door of the basement, the wife Brucha Tieder was lying in a corner, entirely hidden under a pile of garbage.

Brucha and Osias perished in Auschwitz. Absent from home, their three children, Ida, Martin and Sarah, were saved. The gendarmes probably could have listened to their conscience and discreetly sabotaged the orders of Tainturier. They are not the only ones who did not do so. For instance, two gendarmes of Bollène had visited the Sapirs, their friends, on the evening of August 25, 1942, to have an aperitif, as usual. They could have warned them, allowing them to flee, but they did not and they returned the next day at dawn to arrest the family.[31] The Sapirs (the mother, Szayne, and her children, Estelle and Yehuda) and the sisters Margolis (Estéra and Rose) who lived with them owed their lives to the presence of mind of Szayne and to the help of two doctors, Basch and Descalopoulos. Indeed, Estéra Margolis was declared unfit to travel by the two doctors following an appendectomy that was completely healed. As to Szayne Sapir, Captain Ferrier wrote:

> The woman named Szayne Sapir had a strong fit of hysterics upon the arrival of the gendarmes, and it became necessary to call a doctor who stated that her transport was impossible.

Marianne Basch, the doctor in question, had helped Mrs. Sapir by finding that she suffered from several fictitious "ailments." During her fit, Szayne was muttering unintelligible words, but in fact, she was warning her family in Yiddish, thus allowing them to flee through a back window. Ferrier concluded:

> Out of 14 people targeted in this residence [Bollène], only 9 could be arrested.

Apparently, there were not enough merciful acts as remarkable as those of the two doctors, since the gendarmerie of the Vaucluse could claim approximately one hundred arrests of Jews who were unable to find help.

To our knowledge, no one was ever brought to trial for the action of August 1942 against the foreign Jews of the Vaucluse (or any other *département* of the free zone for that matter). It was a crime that did not exist in the eyes of Justice.

As to Marianne Basch, harassed by Jean Lebon, the SEC delegate for the Vaucluse, and targeted by the German police, she was finally forced to flee for her life in early December 1943; since her husband, lieutenant Georges Basch,* dead in June 1940, was Jewish, so were her two children, André and Françoise.

Full Circle

In the CDL meeting of October 11, 1944, the President, Paul Faraud, informs the committee: "*I have received a request from M. Autrand, head of Division and President of the purge committee of the Prefecture, a request expressing his desire to obtain access to M. Pleindoux' file…*"[32] The CDL which had already examined the

---

* Georges Basch was the son of Victor Basch, the president of the Ligue of Human Rights, and his wife Hélène. Both his parents were assassinated on January 10, 1944, by members of the Milice under direct supervision of Paul Touvier.

Pleindoux case does not deem it necessary to transfer the file. In the session of January 12, 1945, André Genin, a former member of the Resistance who takes over the coordination of the purges, pays tribute to the work of his predecessor, Maxime Fischer, *"in particular in the management of the purges, the relations with the FFI,* and the advocacy for the Resistance before the Prefecture."* He underscores that Fischer has worked under appalling conditions, and he adds: *"From now on, it is M. the Prefect who will rule on the files I will bring before him. M. Autrand has accepted to assist me on a voluntary basis."*

Aimé Autrand has come full circle to respectability. First, he is appointed to supervise the purges in the Prefecture staff. Then, he volunteers to help M. Genin in ridding all Vaucluse of collaborators.

To complete the circle, Michel Hayez, the retired director of the *archives départementales de Vaucluse*, informs us that a street has been named in honor of Aimé Autrand.

> Since December 21, 1990, a stone's throw from St. Joseph church, Aimé Autrand (1892–1980) and Robert Bailly (1922–1988) each has his own place. Aimé Autrand, an officer of the Prefecture, cultivated the taste of archives to the point that, after his retirement, he took on the job of classifying and filing those of the city [Avignon]; in addition to various studies related to the département, his work, le Département de Vaucluse de la Défaite à la Libération† (1965), stands out in the field...[33]

Of course, Michel Hayez keeps from mentioning Autrand's burdensome past which he knew well and had "laundered" for the occasion.[34] It would be more fitting to remove the street plate with the name of the man in charge of the "collection" of the 1942 deportees, and find, instead, a street name commemorating the victims.

---

* French Forces of the Interior, name used by de Gaulle toward the end of the war to designate the diverse body of Resistance fighters. The FFI would be incorporated in the regular army as early as October 1944.
† The *département* of Vaucluse from Defeat to Liberation

Chapter 2

The CGQJ: Legalized Looting

The statute of individuals and economic "Aryanization" were the two main strategic functions of the CGQJ, which was created on March 29, 1941, under German pressure. On one hand, it was necessary to ensure that every Jew be registered in the census, forced to be located at a fixed residence, and reduced to a second class citizen, and on the other hand, the Jews were also to be eliminated from the economy and dispossessed of all means. Their assets were to be transferred to non-Jews, the "aryans" according to the CGQJ terminology.

Of course, there is some irony in this choice of words, especially in Provence, where large segments of the non Jewish population hardly fit the "Aryan" profile.

The CGQJ started as a bureaucracy to implement the measures taken against the Jews, and in response to German pressure, it was progressively radicalized. The Germans at first pressed for a more aggressive leader. Then they tried to take control of the local and regional operations of the agency. In the end, they brought its most relentless agents into their sphere of influence. This trend became the norm in the Vaucluse as well.

Xavier Vallat, the first CGQJ commissioner, was given the mission of consolidating the anti-Jewish legislation and setting up the administrative framework required for its application. Even if some aspects of the Vichy legislation (for instance, the definition of who is a Jew)* were more severe than in the equivalent German legislation,† its objective remained confined to social and economic exclusion. If it contributed in any way to the extermination that was brewing, it was mainly by enhancing the status of the Jews as pariahs.

Shortly after the creation of the CGQJ, Henri de Camaret, a pillar of the Avignon establishment, became its delegate for the Vaucluse, a position he held until the elimination of the position on March 31, 1943.

During most of this period, he worked hand-in-hand with Antoine d'Ornano from Nîmes. D'Ornano served, for both the Gard and the Vaucluse, as inspector of the "Police" for Jewish Affairs (PQJ), which, in spite of its name and its incorporation in the national police, was not operating as a true "police force," because it did not have any executive power; therefore, it had no power to apply the Statute and no right to carry firearms. Should the need arise, d'Ornano had to rely on the regular police.

D'Ornano was in charge of investigations on behalf of Henri de Camaret, with whom he eventually exchanged information. His role as anti-Jewish policeman seemed to have gone to his head. Like a novice who has just been propelled into a position of responsibility well beyond his capabilities, he showed off his power wherever he went, to the point that he poached on other people's territory, even when vacationing in his native Corsica. Following the creation of the SEC, which replaced the PQJ, its regional director in Nice, responsible for Corsica amongst others, wrote to his colleague, the regional director of the SEC of Marseille on September 25, 1942.

> I was very surprised to learn through a letter I received from Corsica that, after having alerted the Jewish population by spreading the rumor that he was charged with the immediate application of the law of June 2, 1941, an investigator of your service, passing in Ajaccio, had requested an office to be put at his disposal in the building of the Prefecture of Corsica, where he had summoned the Jews for the purpose of questioning.
>
> … I think that we have here a strictly personal initiative, coming form an investigator whose zeal has gone beyond the framework of his attributions.

---

* Article 1 of the Vichy law defines a Jew as "a descendant of three grandparents of Jewish race, or two grandsparents of the same [Jewish] race, if the spouse is also Jewish."

† The German ordinance of September 27, 1940, states: "Are recognized as Jews the people who belong or belonged to the Jewish religion, or have more than two Jewish grandparents (grandfathers and grandmothers). Are considered as Jews the grandparents who belong or belonged to the Jewish religion."

… the Jews, whose apprehensions we have tried very hard to calm until now… will now have all the time they need to prepare self-defense measures by liquidating or camouflaging their merchandise.[1]

D'Ornano did make a mess of things. His zeal in economic Aryanization drew a remark from the director of food supply in the Gard: *"He is showing intense pleasure in the activity in which he excels… He is having a wonderful time."*[2]

In May 1942, Henri de Camaret witnessed a change of management at the top of his hierarchy; Xavier Vallat was replaced by Louis Darquier de Pellepoix.[3] Although executed by Laval, the designation of Darquier had been instigated by Theodor Dannecker, at the time the Paris head of the Juden-referat* (Jewish Unit) of the SD, Sicherheit Dienst or Security Services, and sometimes referred to by the French as *Police de Sûreté*, who saw in Darquier someone who could free the CGQJ from the shackles of Vichy, personified by Vallat, and put it at the service of the final solution. Darquier did not disappoint his German supporters, at least with fine words. At the meeting of July 4, 1942, with Bousquet, general secretary of the Police since April, Dannecker picked up on the suggestions made by Darquier and asked Bousquet to prove that the national police were capable of pursuing the Jews, given their recent shortcomings and lack of zeal.

Under German pressure and with Bousquet's report regarding the meeting of the day before, the Vichy government provided Dannecker with a decisive victory. By a decree of July 5, 1942, Laval separated the PQJ from the national Police, making it an autonomous organization. But above all, the "stateless" foreign Jews were to be "evacuated" while other repressive measures were also in the making. A radiant Darquier even declared *"I can hope that the turn of the French [Jews] will come!"* Fearing that such a task would be unappetizing, Bousquet tried to eliminate it and proposed the creation of an executive committee under the leadership of the CGQJ. Faced with the large scale of the mission, Darquier hesitated, prompting Dannecker to state that he did not have the makings of a policeman.

After long negotiations, Laval finally decided on August 13, 1942, to do away with the PQJ, and replace it with the SEC, directly under the CGQJ, in spite—and maybe because—of Dannecker's reservations. Moreover, Laval subsequently put spokes in the wheel of the anti-Jewish legislative zeal of Darquier, who struggled to no avail against the craftiness of his boss. Disappointed and frustrated by the "centrist" line of Xavier Vallat, the Germans

---

* Dannecker will serve in this capacity until July 1942, before he was transferred to Bulgaria as the top man in charge of the Jewish Question.

didn't appear to obtain a better deal from his successor, whom they had imposed on their "counterparts."

Following the deployment of the SEC, Jean Lebon replaced d'Ornano. Recently arrived in Marseille from Calavados, Lebon settled in Avignon, where he served as inspector of the SEC for the *départements* of Gard and Vaucluse, and occasionally for a few municipalities from the *département* of the Bouches du Rhône that was neighboring Avignon. It would indeed be more convenient to ask Lebon to conduct an investigation in Châteaurenard or Arles rather than sending in an inspector from Marseille.

As to d'Ornano, he joined the regional offices of the CGQJ in Marseille after attempting to organize an "Aryan" group in Nîmes,[4] the "Union Française pour la Défense de la Race."[*] Later, he was wise enough to switch to a different administration. He returned to Nîmes as assistant to the director of manpower, and in the STO, he moved skillfully by trying to prevent departures to Germany in spite of the pressures of the OPA.[†] He even put himself at the service of the Resistance in August 1944, thus trading the wrath of the Court of Justice for the more measured severity of the Civic Chamber, which in such cases often limited its sentences to the loss of national degradation (less or more loss of civil rights).

Lebon's bosses followed one another as regional delegates of the SEC in Marseille. Starting in November 1942, Edmond Favier became the master of the SEC until the appointment of Emile Madelin, his new boss and the regional delegate of the CGQJ, with whom significant tensions came to light. In August 1943, Madelin finally succeeded in getting rid of Favier, following complaints against him about apartment and paintings theft. Briefly, Armand Malye replaced Favier, and when he resigned, Raymond Guilledoux, the last regional head of the SEC, who took on the "disorder left behind by his predecessors." He introduced stronger and more bureaucratic discipline in launching and conducting investigations, and in the administration of the files.[5] This change of management style affected Lebon, without toning down his anti-Semitic enthusiasm.

The creation of the SEC, set up for the application of the Statute of the Jews, a process which made it possible to diminish the role of Henri de Camaret on April 1, 1943. He became a simple provisional administrator of Jewish assets after having been the head of provisional administrators. It would appear that financial difficulties led the leaders of the CGQJ towards this solution which, at least on the surface, provided savings while increasing

---

[*] The French Union for the Defense of the Race.
[†] The OPA was in charge of securing a French work force for German endeavors.

the number of assets moved into non Jewish hands. However, the lack of buyers of Jewish assets foiled this plan once the return of those dispossessed was anticipated. This flaw however did not reduce the destructive effect of the CGQJ on the Jews, since they were hunted down, despoiled and eliminated from the professions forbidden by the statute.

While de Camaret had administered the Statute of individuals as well as the economic Aryanization until April 1943, Jean Lebon served as a catalyst for the executive responsibility to move from Avignon to Marseille. Lebon flushed out the Jews from the Vaucluse and the Gard, and pinpointed their assets on behalf of the Marseille CGQJ. With the help of Lebon, Marseille then completely took over the designation and the management of the provisional administrators to accelerate the sale of Jewish assets. However, a significant number of obstacles stood in the way, and it wasn't easy for Marseille to ensure the success of the process from a distance. Jean Lebon was not satisfied with investigating the Jews and their assets. Eventually, he evaluated the loyalty of the provisional administrators, because he suspected that some of them were unreliable and at times of playing a double game.

Henri de Camaret and Jean Lebon, were two visceral anti-Semites with fundamentally different personalities as we shall discover. It is probably no accident that Lebon, a relentless and violent go-getter, replaced, after the German occupation, de Camaret, a bureaucrat of the reactionary Vichy establishment. Was this to change the activity of the CGQJ from a bureaucratic anti-Jewish persecution to criminal fury, as it took place in other regions of France?

The attributions of the CGQJ overlapped in large parts on those of Division 1 *Bureau* 2 of the Prefecture. It will then be essential to determine how the encounter between two Vichy institutions in charge of the resolution of the "Jewish problem" took place.

The answers to these questions can be found in the procedural files of the Court of Justice of Vaucluse. The archives of the CGQJ often bring in an additional point of view which had surprisingly been absent during the conduct of the purge trials in Vaucluse. This gives a unique view of the relations between the CGQJ and the prefectural authorities.

The progressive hardening of some elements in the CGQJ shall also become apparent.

Finally, it must be noted that during the period when the largest part of Vaucluse was controlled by the Italian troops, there was no mention of the Italian presence. Although based in the German zone, de Camaret and Lebon operated as if the Italians did not exist.

Chapter 3

Henri de Camaret and His Network: The CGQJ Delegate for the Vaucluse

A "White Collar" Agent of Anti-Semitism: 1941–March 1943

On December 16, 1941, Henri de Camaret wrote to his regional manager in Marseille:

> I made contact with the service chief who has taken care of the census [of the Jews] for the Vaucluse. There are approximately 1600 Jews registered including their name, address, origin, situation, etc. For the benefit of my control and searches, it would be extremely useful to put this list on index cards. But it is a significant task which I estimate would require one week of work (done at the prefecture itself, because the list cannot leave the office). The cost of the index cards (only, and not the file cabinet which I already own) and of the person, who will fill them, should be between 350 and 400 francs. May I go ahead with this expense?[1]

The service chief mentioned in the letter was none other than Aimé Autrand, head of the division of Police affairs, foreigners and Jews (2nd department), with whom de Camaret would have continuous dealings in the application of the Statute of the Jews. But how can one not detect that, by pointing out his own zeal to his boss, by the same token he emphasizes Autrand's shortcomings?

Nine months later, in a note dated September 24, 1942, Henri de Camaret trumpeted to his boss the great benefits of his own far-sighted investment:

> The number of Jews currently domiciled in the Vaucluse who have not been registered in this département in July 1941 appears extremely large. This is explained by the numerous moves the Jews have made during the preceding year and during the first months of this year. As a result, their number that was officially 1457 in July 1941 must, in my opinion, currently reach 1800 and perhaps exceed this number. As an example, I want to bring to your attention the case of Vaison which is typical. The mayor of this town informs me that there are currently 34 Jews. Out of this number, 15 only have come forward. The others escape any control.
>
> The general file of all the Jews of the département, which I have established and strive to keep current, does not concern economic Aryanization directly which I am in charge of. It permits to follow families, their employment, their movement, and because of this, it has come in handy by allowing me to detect Jewish businesses or [Jewish] interests in Aryan businesses...[2]

Henri de Camaret could never have imagined that his zealous initiative would become one of the counts in his sentence to hard labor for life on June 21, 1945. Before that, came a glorious period when the amateur bureaucrat created a file that was more complete than anything at the prefecture and police headquarters. How was this possible?

In fact, de Camaret was able to mobilize his relations and associates without any strike force—he had no subordinates at the prefecture, no personnel of any significance. He was a simple cog in the machine; a relay between the provisional administrators and the CGQJ.

To create a network of voluntary informers covering 71 municipalities, his closeness to Régis d'Oléon, the President of the *Légion des Combattants* of Vaucluse, who shared his political views, was of great help. Beyond the diversity of the members of the Légion, there are their sheer numbers; no village was without its section. Being able to draw on them alone provided the grassroots support he needed.

The list of his correspondents—he wrote their names himself on loose sheets with annotations as for their title, their profession or the level of trust they inspired in him—would delight researchers. It is a jewel of micro-sociological history. Amongst 120 people, one can find 10 priests. The most cited professions are: career officers, doctors, dentists, *notaries,** pharmacists, insurance agents, industrialists, merchants, craftsmen, even a wine grower. It is worth noting a few mayors and deputy mayors, and three women, probably deserving widows with aristocratic names that were over-represented in the list. In short, it was the top of the heap of the establishment of provincial towns and villages.

This list that is so revealing, would almost sound comical, except for the consequences. De Camaret, would invariably send a written request: "*I would be grateful if you would tell me, to the best of your knowledge, whether there are Jews, Jewish business or businesses under Jewish influence in which there are Jewish interests.*"[3] Although all the members of de Camaret's network were sympathizers, they did not show an equal zeal, and ranged from the smooth talker to the visceral anti-Semite. Over time, some were even to switch to the other side.

The rate of responses and the personal involvement of the correspondents are not known. However, the impact of de Camaret's network was considerable since he succeeded in establishing a file whose size exceeds by two to three hundred the official list of Jews of Vaucluse during the war, and it has been possible to verify independently of de Camaret that the list of the prefecture underestimated the number of Jews of Vaucluse by at least the same number.

So far, we have been unable to find the Jewish index cards created by de Camaret in the archives of the Court of Justice of Vaucluse. The only available lists concern Jews from Carpentras, Cavaillon, Vaison, and others provided by his informers, which indicate a continuous flow of names of Vaucluse Jews. It is likely that the census files went to the man who succeeded him in April 1943, Jean Lebon, secretary of the census at the CGQJ in Marseille before he was named as SEC representative in Avignon. Having shared the office of de Camaret after his arrival in Avignon, Lebon had free access to those lists. The establishment of an independent Jewish census is a significant element of de Camaret's operation aggravated by the fact that this information will be made available to the German police after the invasion of the free zone in November 1942.

Within his informers' network including several members of the PPF, the LVF and the Milice, some will become ardent collaborators with the Nazis in 1943–1944. Let us cite for instance Célestin Sandevoir from l'Isle sur la

---

* A *notaire* (civil law notary) is a sworn in law specialist who oversees several domains: estate law, real estate law and real property title certification. The *notaire* offices are limited in numbers in proportion to local population size. Their function is a hybrid between private practice and government office. A young aspiting *notaire* must work for an existing *notaire* until an existing office is put up for sale at an affordable price.

Sorgue, sentenced to death at the Liberation; a publicist, Henri Guillerault from Séguret and Doctor Victor Gaillard from Vaison, both sentenced to 20 years of hard labor. One may wonder today why participation in de Camaret's network had not been considered a crime, but it is likely that the Court of Justice took a position in keeping with the climate of the times.

Was de Camaret credible when he claimed, during his questioning of April 14, 1945, that he had maintained a link with only a dozen of his informers? He adds "*I had noted the names of eventual correspondents of known respectability.*" As for his information requests, they were modestly aimed at completing his census. He assures us: "*When some Jews were not in order, I would give them the necessary instructions. Lastly, out of 1700 Jews of Vaucluse, I took interest in no more than 200 of them.*" This assertion definitely underestimated de Camaret's role and impact.

His case file provides an interesting exchange about this issue.[4] On August 18, 1941, the director of the CGQJ informed the prefecture that his "*services have directly warned*" a certain number of Jews (Bigard, Kahn, Kauffmann, and Benichou) who had not come forward for the census, and demands a list of non compliant Jews which the prefecture, specifically Aimé Autrand, provides on August 27, 1941. De Camaret had informed the Jews in question of this failure, and particularly his bosses in Vichy to underscore Autrand's sloppiness. On September 12, 1941, the CGQJ in Vichy demanded explanations about the list of noncompliant Jews of August 27. Autrand answered quickly and in two installments. On September 30, 1941, the case of each Jew was detailed in a first answer.

> The results of these investigations show
> 1- That the individuals named Jacques Brom, Yvette Jung, Henri and Victor Goldblum, Simone Roche and Stern have given a sworn statement claiming that they are not Jewish.
> 2- That the individuals named Pinchos Estryn, Berthe Haas, Aucher Kauffmann, Levendel and his wife, Hoffning née Kurover, Miss Maitre, Léo Ruttembach, Joseph and Szayna Sapir, and Hélène Schwartz had indeed come forward to register in a municipality other than that of their residence.
> ...
> 5- That the individual named Albrecht Marienfeld was interned last August 15 [1941] in the camp of Gurs, in execution of an order of the Minister Secretary of State for the Interior dated on July 18.

Therefore, amongst the individuals presumed Jewish that I had reported to you in my letter of last August 27, only the man named Maurice Geismar, born on February 7, 1869, in Grüssenheim, currently residing in Monteux, had in fact filled, on September 17 current, the attached declaration attesting that he is Jewish. He did so 47 days past the prescribed deadline and only after having been ordered.

I think that I need to leave it to you to decide whether he should be punished according to Article 2 of the law of June 2, 1941, instituting the census of the Jews.

The penalties in question are indeed detailed in Article 2: "*Every infraction… is punished with a prison sentence of one month to one year and a fine of 100 to 10,000 francs… without prejudice to the right of the prefect to mandate internment in a special camp, even if the interested party is French.*"

On October 8, the CGQJ responded that "*the sworn declaration*" of the 5 Jews in question "*attesting that they do not belong to the Jewish race is not sufficient to exempt them from registering as mandated by the law of June 2, 1942.*"

The answer, on October 13, of division D1-B2 in the name of the prefect, testified to the growing irritation of Aimé Autrand against the accusations of the CGQJ in Vichy masterminded by de Camaret. Autrand complained about the excessively short deadline given to the prefecture of Vaucluse, and he added:

> Anyway, you will understand that I cannot overlook, without rising up against this assertion, the terms of the handwritten note in the margin of the copy of the letter which is attached to your communication of October 4 and which is formulated as follows: "No response, attract the attention of M. Gazagne[*] to the <u>lack of goodwill</u>[†] of the P. of V."[‡]

But beyond the irritation, the ratting of de Camaret had already created at least one victim. Pressed to act against the Jews who had eluded the census, Autrand had already seen to it to send Albrecht Marienfeld to Gurs from where he had been deported to Drancy, then to Auschwitz with convoy 19 on August 14, 1942. His presence at Gurs ahead of the deportations of August 1942 had already singled him out as a warning to other non-compliers. Was Albrecht Marienfeld, who had been severely punished by Autrand and the prefecture for eluding the census, the only person from Vaucluse deported early? Because this kind of deportation took place far from Vaucluse, it would be more difficult to establish than the roundups of August 26, 1942.

The network of de Camaret and his census were for Autrand a constant source of irritation. De Camaret delighted in sending zealous complaints

---

[*] René Gazagne is the directorr of the CGQJ section of the Statute of the Jews.
[†] Underlined by Aimé Autrand.
[‡] P. of V. stands for "Prefecture of Vaucluse."

against the excessively conciliatory attitude of the prefecture to his Marseille boss, and particularly to the leaders of the Vichy CGQJ, who then spurred the prefecture on. In the same way, the CGQJ brought up the "problem" of the presence of Jews on the board of the association of reserve officers, denounced Jews involved in illegal activities, became the spokesperson of anti-Semites who saw in him a means to get rid of troublesome competitors, and continually tried to demonstrate the feebleness of the prefecture's measures.

Always on the look-out, de Camaret did not limit himself to Vaucluse. After getting wind of the presence of Charles Mossé as a bookkeeper at the Marseille office of the Main d'œuvre Indigène, a branch of the Ministry of Labor, de Camaret informed the CGQJ of that town on February 23, 1942. He added that the son of Charles Mossé worked for a brokerage enterprise. However, de Camaret was not aware that on September 22, 1941, Charles Mossé had been one of the few beneficiaries of an exemption for military distinctions from the anti-Jewish measures enacted by Xavier Vallat.

This frantic correspondence prompted Jean Lebon to write in his first report of December 3, 1942, shortly after his arrival in Avignon:

> As for my collaboration with M. de Camaret, I think that it will be possible for the purpose of "information"* only, because he deals with business exclusively in writing. Nevertheless, his numerous connections will be invaluable to me.[5]

The Entente "Cordiale"

In fact, de Camaret had no major problems in taking advantage of the data accumulated against the Jews by the prefecture during those years when Vichy was triumphant. Most of the notorious documents, written for the most part by Aimé Autrand under the label D1 B2[6] can also be found in the files confiscated in de Camaret's home during his pretrial investigation:

- census data arranged by nationality, town, profession
- statistics on Jewish businesses by profession and nationality
- communication from the prefecture for the first division, second department concerning the ban on Jews to acquire businesses without authorization
- minutes of the commission in charge of the "grouping" of foreign workers, presided over by Autrand (reports sent to Vichy by telegram)
- minutes of the screening commission, presided over by Autrand. The commission was in charge of examining the cases of French and

---

* Underlined by Jean Lebon.

foreign Jewish refugees who came to Avignon after the German invasion, and who could be subjected to removal and scattering, as mandated by the decrees of the interior minister on November 3, 1941, and January 2, 1942 (reports sent to Vichy by telegrams)

- reports sent to Vichy by Autrand about the late registration of a group of Jews
- documentation of the deportations of the summer of 1942, prepared and sent to Vichy by Autrand:
  o list of foreign Jews who entered France after January 1, 1936, who were subjected to the measures mandated by the instructions of the interior minister of August 5 and 15, 1942
  o list of foreign Jews from the above category who had already been sent to the camp of Les Milles (near Aix en Provence) between August 23 and 26, 1942, by the head of the Vaucluse group of foreign workers [M. Deluc])
  o list of the foreign Jews sent on August 26, 1942, to the camp of Les Milles by the gendarmerie
  o list of foreign Jews who eluded the grouping measures imposed on them

Although most of the documents were annotated "copy for de Camaret" by Autrand, he was careful not to mention this active collaboration and will pretend later to have been under *"close surveillance... on the part of both the administrator* [de Camaret] *and the controller* [Lebon] *of the Jewish affairs of the département, and of the zealous collaborators of the Vichy government..."*[7] As we will see subsequently, this is a half truth. One can only imagine what it would have been if Autrand had "really" collaborated with de Camaret!

Obviously, the recovery of duplicate documents from the department of foreigners and police affairs was working very well. One can find in the Vaucluse archives a mail exchange which proves it. On July 3, 1942, de Camaret wrote to the prefect:

> I am honored to acknowledge receipt of your letter of the 24th in which you are asking me to indicate the nature of the information which I would find necessary in order to undertake my mission. In principle, I am interested in all the information about the Jews in the département, because it enables me to track their activity. It is therefore useful for you to keep me informed of all internments or house arrests enacted against them. I would find it also invaluable to know whether the aforementioned individuals are in possession of safe-conducts. I am indeed aware that some abuse the facilities which are granted to them. I would also value being immediately informed of eventual sale of buildings belonging to Jews. Finally, I would want that those considered to be suspects are pointed out to me.[8]

In the margin of this letter, Autrand wrote in his own hand: "*Agreed for the first two points*" and for the third, he adds "*Copy provided to M. Lacoue, head of the department of real estate transactions, for his information.*"

The requests were immediately fulfilled.

The Chain of Accomplices

De Camaret took advantage of his connection to his cousin Régis Dubout, director of the "General Insurance Companies" at Avignon, to obtain information concerning the Jews in that profession, if we believe Dubout's account.[9] But this was not the opinion of Pierre Bernard-Laroche, an insurance agent in Carpentras. He accused Dubout of having provided a file of all insurance agents of Vaucluse to an anti-Semitic Vichy organization. He stated: "*Some Vaucluse insurers, notably from Carpentras, and myself have been particularly targeted because of our family links or relations with Jewish families.*" On that subject, there is a far more compromising letter from de Camaret to his cousin. On April 8, 1942, he wrote: "*My dear Régis, you have informed Mr. Verny* [the head of de Camaret's service in Marseille] *that the Jew Bernard worked as an insurer in Carpentras. I immediately started an investigation, and I will be grateful if you can send me, as soon as possible, all the information you have collected on this subject…*"[10]

De Camaret admitted writing that letter. But he claimed in his defense that he had decided not to send it at the last minute, because "*he had mistaken a conversation with Verny about the investigation of the Aryan origins of M. Bernard with a previous conversation with Dubout about the general organization of the insurance profession.*" In addition, the Court of Justice confused things further by dismissing the charges against Dubout. A simple question could have cleared up the matter: if de Camaret did not send the letter, did Dubout receive it? And even if this letter was never sent, does it not illustrate de Camaret's attitude towards the Jews?

With Maurice Rambaud, things are even murkier.[11] A manufacturer of candied fruit in Apt, he was a notorious royalist, who coerced his employees into joining the Légion des Combattants and subscribing to the newspaper of the *Action Française.*[*] The marquis Helen des Isnards, owner of the collaborationist newspaper *Le Ventoux* in Carpentras, aligned with the *Action Française*, kept him regularly abreast of the instructions of the movement. Rambaud, in charge of reporting left-wing individuals to the subprefect of Apt, was also a member of de Camaret's network.

---

* *L'Action Française,* founded in 1898, was a French monarchist movement. Charles Maurras was its founder and main ideologue.

During de Camaret's trial, the Court of Justice had pondered his association with Rambaud and his possible role in the slaughter that took place in Saignon, five miles from Apt, on February 17, 1944. On that day, Gaston Dreyfus and his brother Felix, two very rich Jews who had taken refuge in the village, were shot on the spot when they refused to obey the "miliciens" and Germans who had come to arrest them. Gaston's wife, who was at her husband's side during this bloody operation and survived severe wounds, demanded an investigation by the court to prove de Camaret's responsibility.

Did Rambaud inform de Camaret of the presence of the Dreyfus family? The court had doubts about Rambaud so his case was closed. However, a deeper look into de Camaret's file reveals several clues. Amongst the files of his informers were two answers to his requests for information about Jewish enterprises.

The first dated March 6, 1942, was signed by Maurice Rambaud who wrote: "*Dear Sir, In response to your letter of March 4, I am honored to inform you that I do not see here much in terms of Jewish enterprises. To the best of my knowledge, there is only a flower shop founded by a woman named Franck…*"

The second more significant one, was sent by Antonin Gay,[*] the mayor designate of Apt, five weeks later, on April 10, 1942:

> Monsieur
>
> Allow me to express my sincere condolences for the cruel bereavement which has stricken you in the person of your father.
>
> I had not yet responded to your request because I wanted to know as exactly as I possibly could the situation and the number of Jews in town.
>
> Before 1939, there was in Apt a Jewish family of three—very harmless French photographers, and a Polish Jew, the spouse of doctor Appy, as well as her sister.
>
> Since the defeat, the Jewish colony has grown and today comprises 41 people (expelled individuals, refugees, Poles, Germans, etc.).
>
> One family settled here as flower merchants—Franck—the business is registered in his wife's name, a catholic French woman. The husband is a Jew (a small camouflaged propagandist, anti-government).
>
> A well-off family—Dreyfus—four people, big cattle tradesman from the forbidden zone,[†] an independent refugee, just took up residence in Apt.
>
> Finally, the Meyers, three people landed up in Apt, a fabric and garments manufacturer from Mulhouse. Pretends to be short of cash but still lives very comfortably.

---

[*] It should be noted here that the title of "Righteous Among the Nations" was posthumously granted by Yad Vashem to Antonin Gay in 1989. Testimonies for this title were provided by A. Grumbach and F. Thau.

[†] The Lorraine was declared "forbidden zone" by the Germans.

To the best of my knowledge, there is no industry financed by Jews.

It is as the mayor of the city of Apt that I can provide you with these various reports for you to use at your discretion.

Please accept the assurance of my respectful consideration.

De Camaret transferred this information to his regional director in Marseille on July 13, 1942:

M. Desayes, subprefect of Apt, had replaced in that function, M. Kahn, a Jew who is underlined* in Vaucluse, and said to be now counselor in the prefecture of Clermont Ferrand.

M. Desayes is said to be the son of a Jewish mother. Married for the first time and divorced, he is known to have remarried, while he worked at the prefecture of Clermont Ferrand, to the daughter of a mistress of Peyrouton† who is said to be Jewish and of easy virtue.

In Apt, he is the great protector of the Jews, receives them at the subprefecture, sits with them at the café, and in particular with a very rich Jewish refugee, formerly a cattle trader, named [Gaston] Dreyfus, who has not registered in Vaucluse and whom I am about to interrogate on this matter.

M. Dautry, the former Minister of Armament, visits him once in a while.

Two months ago, M. Desayes was named department head at the Ministry of Interior in Vichy, but he is still in Apt, awaiting the designation of his successor.

Could we find out in Clermont Ferrand whether it is true that his mother and his wife are Jewish?

The answer of the regional director to de Camaret left no doubts whatsoever:

Further to your report of July 13, I am honored to inform you that I have informed the head of the CGQJ on the matter of M. Desayes .

An investigation was requested by our central service of the PQJ, and the problem has been referred to The head of the government, and minister secretary of state for the interior [Laval].

It is imperative to order Mr. Dreyfus to register without delay, and in case of refusal, to apply the disciplinary measures as mandated by the law.

You are requested to keep me informed of this individual's compliance with your order.

---

* The three words in the letter were underlined by de Camaret.
† Marcel Peyrouton, Secretary of State for the Interior who signed the law of October 3, 1940, on the Statute of the Jews. Later, he turned against Vichy.

When confronted with this document during the pre-trial investigation, de Camaret revealed his attitude towards certain Jews. He was questioned by Louis Béral, the investigating judge from Avignon:

> Louis Béral:
> Please, indicate the circumstances in which you intervened in the case of M. Gaston Dreyfus (d'Apt) whom you brought to the attention of your bosses by the report July 13, 1942, for not having registered as a Jew in the département of Vaucluse.
>
> De Camaret:
> From different sources, people alerted me that rich Jews were often buying choice properties by using front men. I was made aware of M. Dreyfus' enterprise through a letter from the mayor in response to a request I had made to give me the number of Jewish refugees in that town. M. Dreyfus was known to be very rich, and since his name did not appear on the census lists at the prefecture of Vaucluse, I had written to him to inquire where he had registered. He told me that he had done it at the prefecture of Soissons. I intended to meet him some day in Apt, but I did not go to Apt and I did not pursue my investigation.

De Camaret turned the spotlight on the Dreyfus brothers. He transferred the information about their presence in Apt to the CGQJ regional manager, who was more radical towards the Jews than the minister of the interior, when he agreed to deliver the foreign Jews while trying to prevent the deportation of French Jews.

De Camaret shared the responsibility for their murder. On the date of the execution, he was no longer the CGQJ delegate for Vaucluse: he had been replaced by Jean Lebon. The information and the network set up by de Camaret were now operated by the SEC, and they were working shoulder-to-shoulder with the Nazis.

Facing Justice

The life of de Camaret can be traced through the procedural files. At the time of his verdict, he was 58 years old. Born in Avignon on August 21, 1886, the son of Louis de Camaret and Isabelle de Labastide, Henri studied at St. Joseph Catholic high school (in his days, a Mecca for learning and education of the conservative-thinking Avignon elite) before being awarded a high school diploma in science. He then started a two year preparation at *l'Ecole des Beaux Arts* (architecture section), followed by military service in Nîmes. After that he was hired by the *Crédit Lyonnais* in Lyon. In January 1914, he married Christine d'Adhémar; everything seemed to fit well with this marriage within the same social class. He volunteered in the Great War as a non-commissioned officer, and later held various positions in two companies, first at *La Société des Pierres Ouvrées* de la vallée du Rhône, then at *Bâton Provence*.

This is when he made the mistake of his life by creating his own company; it failed and he emerged completely destitute; this total failure led him, in his own words, to accept a CGQJ position, which Marseille proposed but he had not sought. He claimed: "*I was also looking for a job, because an unsuccessful business launch, La Société Provençale des Lampes Electriques, had swallowed up my personal fortune as well as an important contribution made by my wife.*" For a meager monthly income of 2,000 francs, de Camaret took a "position" which was to become a demanding burden.

He did not elaborate about his other "position," as the correspondent of the newspaper *L'Eclair*, where he had worked since 1936. His monthly income at the newspaper increased from 600 francs to 750 francs, starting May 1, 1943.[12] *L'Eclair* was an important daily paper, based in Montpellier, with circulation covering all of southern France and several local editions. No sooner had he become the correspondent for the Vaucluse that de Camaret wrote on April 3, 1936, to inform the manager of *l'Action Française* in Marseille that "*You will always be able to rely on me to pursue the just struggle for the triumph of our ideas of national salvation for the King.*" The next day, commandant Louis Dromard, who was heading the federated sections of Provence, Corsica and the Alps region of *l'Action Française* "*congratulate[s] him for such a fortunate choice of* l'Eclair *in taking him as correspondent at Avignon.*"

At the same time, de Camaret also informed Régis d'Oléon, whom we will meet again later:

> You know that *l'Eclair* does its best to defend all the political and religious ideas that we cherish. It is far from having in our region of Vaucluse the place it deserves; I am asking you to push it amongst our friends whom you see in such large numbers in all the meetings you attend, and as far as I am concerned, never refrain from giving me advice or even criticism that you deem beneficial. I thank you in advance for both. I assure you, my dear Régis, of my warmest feelings.

There was no answer from "dear Régis," but de Camaret could undoubtedly count on his support. The two provincial aristocrats, old school friends from St. Joseph high school, were on the same wavelength: a Maurrassien kind of nationalism, maybe even more clerical with de Camaret.

In 1936, de Camaret viewed himself as an elite member of a fan club of scribblers in awe of the future immortal of the Académie Française

---

* Pierres ouvrées: finely carved stones.

[Maurras]—who had probably given him some encouragement; throughout the years, de Camaret had carefully kept an autographed picture of Maurras, that was discovered in his house after Liberation. Here, de Camaret, a Catholic monarchist, was lifting his sword against France, a land won to republican secularism. The year 1936 was also a key moment in the re-awakening of anti-Semitism. When the right wing representative, Xavier Vallat, the future founder and first head of the CGQJ, spitefully proclaimed, on the day of Léon Blum's investiture by the Assembly, *"For the first time, this old Gallo-Roman country will be governed by a Jew."* But the Front Populaire of 1936 did not last long, and with the advent of Vichy, more than one notable of Vaucluse saw his ideas at the center of the governing power. Despite the defeat, even among the numerous germanophobes of *l'Action Française*, the time for revenge had struck. Anti-Jewish legislation seemed natural, and keeping the Jews out of the French community was self-evident. It was all simple common sense and did not offend too many people.

By choosing the CGQJ, Henri de Camaret entered an organization that will not be condemned, and was quite the opposite had he joined one of the organizations labeled as an "anti-national group," as they were called at the Liberation. During his trial, de Camaret denied harboring any anti-Semitic sentiments. If we follow his reasoning, he almost protected Jews, as he testi-fied:

> Since I had never handled Jewish questions and I was aware that the popes had always been the defenders of the Jews, that the bishops had interceded in their favor so that the statute would be interpreted with kindness, I asked for the position of the Church towards the Jews to be confirmed by consulting with Reverend Father d'Anselme who, to my knowledge, had carefully studied the issue. I have always conformed to those rules of strict justice and charity.

The testimony of d'Anselme at the trial confirmed this declaration of de Camaret:

> December 1944
> Early in 1942, I had the visit of M. de Camaret who had just been desig-nated for the Commissariat aux Questions Juives. M. de Camaret asked me very kindly to share with him the thinking of the Catholic Church regarding the Jewish question.
> I responded that the thinking of the Church was firm and kind toward the Jews, that it wanted them to be treated with strict justice and charity, without any consideration of race and that the best proof of this Christian and humane doctrine was the way, in practical and always equitable terms, the Jews had been administered throughout the residence of the Supreme Pontiffs in this town and

the Jews have continuously thanked the Popes for their equitable kindness towards them.

L. d'Anselme

Collège St. Joseph – Avignon

So, de Camaret claimed he had no anti-Semitic ideas. But the documents seized at his home contained many newspaper clippings meticulously kept, and it will suffice to quote a few of the titles to appreciate the "kindness" of de Camaret towards the Jews.

- The Statute of the Jews in the Papal States
- The Israelites and French Business
- For a French anti-Semitism: The Statute of Jewish Assets
- For a French anti-Semitism: The Statute of Jewish Individuals
- Who is a Jew?
- For a French anti-Semitism: Police Measures
- For a French anti-Semitism: The Commissariat General aux Questions Juives
- In order for the Jew to Restitute Ill-gotten Gains
- For a French anti-Semitism: The Jew must be Forced to Work
- For a French anti-Semitism: Anti-Semitic Propaganda
- For a French anti-Semitism: The Certificates of Non-belonging to the Jewish Race
- The Application of the "Numerus Clausus" to the Jewish Dentists in Algeria
- Romanian Jews will not be Allowed Anymore to have Aryan Servants
- 80,000 Jews of Paris are wearing the Yellow Star
- The Jews and their False Names
- No more Jews in Limited Liability Companies
- Occult Forces in the Modern World: Masonic, Jewish and Communist Influences
- Jewish Demography
- How France became Anti-Semitic
- The Idleness of the Jews
- For a French Anti-Semitism: Let the Jew work for us
- The Patronymic Names of the Jews
- Excesses and Shamelessness of the Jews
- Jewish Duper, the Duped French
- The Jews and Black Market
- The Jews and France: Let the Others Run to War
- The Jewish Problem in the non Occupied Zone: 2,700,000 Jews in France—An Anti-Jewish Police has become Necessary

This last clipping is particularly illustrative of the anti-Semitic bugaboo haunting de Camaret and his peers. In France, there were fewer than 300,000 Jews out of a total of 41,900,000 people, while anti-Semitic propaganda "counts" 2,700,000 of them. The census of de Camaret provided 1,800 names out of a total Vaucluse population of 245,508 in 1940,[13] about 0.73%, a percentage consistent with the national ratio. They saw Jews everywhere, even when there were far less than expected.

De Camaret was not just content with collecting gems of anti-Semitic journalism. He put them into action, and on June 26, 1942, he "denounced" the protestant Pastor Marc Boegner to his Vichy superiors (who were already well aware of him):

> I have been given the following information which I am forwarding to you for you to use as you please. Pastor Boegner, the head of the Protestant Church of France, left Paris in 1940, in spite of his duty to stay put, just as the Cardinal Archbishop of Paris did to protect his flock.
>
> He settled in Nîmes, which counts 35,000 Protestants, and established his headquarters in that town.
>
> Since then his action has never ceased to be:
> 1- In support of communism, through the inferences of his speeches, in particular about the Charter of Labor and social laws
> 2- In support of Gaullism, which conceals, under a mask of patriotism, the personal interests of the rich protestant bourgeois, whose assets are, for many of them, located in foreign countries...
> 3- Against the spirit of the Révolution Nationale by giving his subordinates specific orders to mix politics and religion, and that, if they were bothered, to cry "persecution," which carries particularly far in this region of the Cévennes which was the scene of extremely violent religious wars and whose memory still divides Catholics and Protestants in two opposed—and sometimes hostile—camps
> 4- In support of freemasonry, the protestant circles being in large parts subservient to freemasonry
> 5- Finally, in favor of the Jews. Attached a copy of the letter from Pastor Boegner to the Chief Rabbi[*] of France to protest against the law of October 1940 regarding the Jews. Later, he wrote to the Maréchal asking him to stop the anti-Semitic persecutions. A campaign, backed up by some pastors, is being launched in protestant circles to clear the Jews of any fault or excess

De Camaret then went on a crusade against the "enemies" of the Church—Protestants and Jews. Strangely, he raised the specter of religious

---

[*] Isaïe Schwartz was the Chief Rabbi of France during German occupation.

wars, apparently still alive in this *département* bordering with the Gard, a more Protestant *département* on the other side of the Rhône. However, amongst the seized documents, side by side with this "denunciation" of Pastor Boegner, de Camaret had kept a copy of the poignant messages delivered in September 1942 by two members of the Catholic hierarchy, Mgr. Pierre-Marie Gerlier, archbishop of Lyon, and Mgr. Pierre-Marie Théas, bishop of Montauban, who had been moved by the Jew hunting initiative of August 1942 by the Vichy government in the free zone. Of course, the operation led by the prefecture of Vaucluse and Aimé Autrand was part of this initiative. We will cite only Gerlier's message:

> The execution of the deportation measures which are currently taking place against the Jews gives rise on the entire territory to scenes so distressing that we have the imperative and painful duty to rise in protest in the name of our conscience. We are witnessing a cruel dispersion of families where nothing was spared, neither age, weakness, or illness. A pang of anguish seizes us at the thought of the treatment suffered by thousands of human beings, and more so, as we think about what may be foreseen.

> We do not forget that French authorities have a problem on their hands, and we are aware of the difficulties that lay ahead for the government.

> But who would blame the Church for strongly affirming, during this dark hour and in the face of all that is imposed upon us, the unalienable rights of the human being, the sacred character of family ties, the inviolability of the right of asylum and the pressing demands of this fraternal charity of which Christ had made the distinctive mark of his disciples. It is to the honor of Christian civilization, and it must be the honor of France never to abandon such principles.

> It is not on the basis of violence and hatred that we will be able to build the new order. One will build it, and have peace with it, only in the respect of Justice, in the kind union of spirit and heart, to which the great voice of the Maréchal is inviting us and where the century-old prestige of our motherland will bloom again.

> May our Lady of Fourvière help us in hasting its return!

If de Camaret was moved by the cry of alarm from these two leaders of the church, he showed it only during his trial. Moreover, was it "charity" which brought him to open a "discreet inquiry" about Jews who were frequenting the reception center of the boulevard Raspail in Avignon? This center, open to refugees of modest means, was an object of controversy. Jews were singled out for eating there. De Camaret raised the issue with the person in charge of the Secours National, who responded on October 15, 1942:

> In response to your letter of October 3, it is absolutely true that some Jews are eating at the reception center. This is quite normal and I do not see on what grounds this could be denied them. Moreover, most of them are refugees. How-

ever, all refugees without distinction of religion are taken care of by the service of refugees which does not report to the Secours National, but to the prefecture, and they are all authorized by the prefecture to eat at the reception center. If the CGQJ considers that this is going too far, it must write to the prefecture and not to the Secours National. Concerning the article from Gringoire*, it is absolutely false that the proportion of Jews eating at the center is that high, and it is even less true that the returning prisoners of war are treated less favorably than the Jews.

After noticing that five foreign Jews coming to this center were not on his lists, de Camaret became immediately worried, probably out of "compassion." Let us remind for the record that October 25, 1942, followed by a few weeks the massive deportations of August 1942, and that, amongst the Jews eating at the Raspail center, four will be deported later: Sally and Joseph Beinovitz, Nathan Majzels and Jacques Senator, in convoys 59, 59, 73, and 76, respectively.

During his trial, de Camaret did not hesitate to state that he was close to Gaullism in explaining his actions. Let us skip the feats of arms of his son, his brother and his nephews, true patriots who rejoined the army in Algiers; actions that he will later use for his own defense. However, in his capacity of administrator of Jewish assets, he sees no contradiction whatsoever. In discussing the persecution of the Jews at his trial,

> I was aware of these measures (internment, deportation) and I became indignant about their inhumanity. But I knew the anti-German sentiments of my hierarchy which made no secret of their feelings. As for myself, I have always considered Gaullism as movement favorable to French interests, since it allowed us to maintain contact with our allies and create a new army.

Was de Camaret hoping, like some of his Parisian CGQJ colleagues who returned to work after the arrival of the allies in Paris,[14] that his worries were temporary, and that once General de Gaulle had things back in hand, he—de Camaret—would be asked once again to handle the Jewish question? This would not be the last time that some elements of French society were to pin false hopes on the General.

This wishful thinking followed a very peculiar kind of logic. For a certain number of Catholics, the transition from "maréchalisme" to Gaullism was nothing like the attitude towards the Jews that de Camaret kept until Liberation. In "L'Etude de l'Esprit Public en Vaucluse: Mai/Juin 1940–Août 1944,"[15] Serge Issautier observed that a significant proportion of Catholics

---

* *Gringoire* was a right wing literary and political weekly. Founded in 1928, it emerged during the war as a leading anti-Semitic propaganda sheet.

switched to Gaullism after the round-up of the Jews in the Paris Vélodrome d'Hiver in 1942 and the protest of Mgr. Jules-Géraud Salièges, repeated by Les Cahiers de Témoignage Chrétien, which described the Jews as "*poor people whom one must take pity on.*" Issautier pointed out that in Avignon, "*in fact, college St. Joseph, the Convents of the Sacred Heart and of Immaculate Conception, the most important Vaucluse society of mutual assistance of catholic inspiration, are at the same time vital centers of Gaullist resistance and the safest refuges for Jews.*"

"Taking pity on the Jews" could lead, if not to saving them, at least to doing them no harm. But one searches in vain in Henri de Camaret's activity for any signs of the spirit of such a recommendation. Indeed, de Camaret was not indicted only for the establishment of his census of the Jews of Vaucluse and of a network of informers. The charges, the witnesses and the verdict indicate his continuing desire to finish the job. He had:

- sought information about the Jews
- suggested a special card to regulate the travel of Jews by train
- facilitated the roundup by Germans of typewriters belonging to Jewish enterprises
- established reports on the political opinions of various individuals, in particular the Valabregue and Dreyfus families, while causing or attempting to cause their arrest, by denouncing Mrs. Granoff and the individuals Laroth and Lazarus, residing in Ardèche
- denouncing non Jews hostile to Vichy (Pastor Boegner)
- organizing the sale of the assets of Mrs. Goetschel and her sons, in spite of the fact that the co-owners of the assets were prisoners of war
- providing information about doctors, Jewish or Aryan, regarding their political orientation (Gobeil, Lazard, Altman,[*] Descalopoulos) which led or could have led to their arrest, internment or expulsion from the order of doctors
- demonstrated excessive zeal or personal initiative going beyond orders or instructions received
- guilty either by his words or his actions of having collaborated with the Germans

Note that the republican court still uses the term "Aryan."

The Impunity of the CGQJ Delegate for the Vaucluse

Strangely, the indictment did not mention the role of de Camaret as a delegate of the CGQJ, which was meant to organize, from 1941 to 1943, the detection of Jewish assets, the dispossession of the victims, the assignment of

---

[*] A Jewish doctor residing in Gordes arrested by the Nazis, then liberated by the Resistance in August 1944.

provisional administrators, and their supervision, although these activities were occasionally mentioned in testimonies and file documents. The seizure of Jewish assets fell under the jurisdiction of the Civic or Commercial Courts and within the competence of the Civic Courts.[16] A few individual cases of provisional administrators' files were transferred to the Civic Court, as well as the case of d'Ornano, inspector of the PQJ for the Gard and the Vaucluse. The Court of Justice, would indict administrators—like de Camaret, when they were over-zealous or exceeded the functions prescribed by their roles.

The case of the provisional administrator Victor Dupeyre provides an insight into the legal perspective on this topic.[17] Samuel Mossé, a horse trader in Orange, lodged a complaint against Victor Dupeyre, administrator of his business, general agent of the Caisse d'Epargne* in Orange, and a member of the Groupe Collaboration. Mossé accused Dupeyre of having sold off his business to a man named Guigue, a horse trader in Beaucaire. In his report, the investigating judge wrote:

> The Courts of Justice are meant to judge acts that took place between June 16, 1940 and the date of Liberation, when they reveal the intention of the author to encourage all kinds of initiatives taken by the enemy. It does not appear that the sole fact of having been an administrator of Jewish assets constitutes a crime under the law, as long as this administration was not aimed at or has not resulted in encouraging these enterprises. It is apparent from the Dupeyre file that this man exercised his functions without becoming guilty of national division, denunciations, police or administrative assistance for the benefit of the enemy. The only charges against him by the sole plaintiff M. Mossé are uniquely related to the material management of the assets he was in charge of.
>
> It must be noted that the plaintiff, M. Mossé, requests protective measures, in particular the seizure of the his administrator's assets. He can possibly use the procedure of ordinary law, these protective measures being under the authority of the Commissioner of the government only when criminal responsibility appears to be established.

M. Mossé was sent to the Civic Court (*Chambre Civique*). The same reasoning can be used for de Camaret, who was the manager of the provisional administrators before he himself became an ordinary administrator in March 1943. This explains why his role as the Vaucluse delegate of the CGQJ, and later, as administrator of Jewish assets, did not by themselves end up in the list of charges against him.

---

* A savings institution.

However, although the seizure of Jewish assets was undertaken by the CGQJ and its subordinates in the field, it remained an essential German objective in their fight against the Jews. The Germans were the ones who made sure that Xavier Vallat was replaced as the head of the CGQJ by Darquier de Pellepoix, whom they regarded as their loyal collaborator. As a result, the spoliation organized by French organizations was indeed a central act of collaboration with the enemy. Moreover, it represented a serious violation of human rights, according to legislation in force before the war.

In the Avignon of 1944–1945, we are still far away from the spirit of the Nuremberg trials for crimes against humanity, an expression already used by the allies in 1915 to describe the Armenian genocide. Partially defined in their essence in the Manifest of the third Moscow Conference in October 1943, crimes against humanity were established for the first time in 1945 as a strictly legal notion by Article 6, *littera* (c), of the charter of the Nuremberg Tribunal.[18] Crimes against humanity were defined as *"assassination, extermination, enslavement, deportation, and any other inhuman act committed against any civilian population, before or during the war; or persecutions for political, racial or religious motives, committed as a result of any crime falling within the competence of the International Tribunal or associated with it, whether or not these persecutions had constituted a violation of the internal law of the country in which they have been perpetrated."*

The ban from professions, the dispossession, the liquidation of assets and other arbitrary measures, which the Jews had been the victims of and which de Camaret had made himself the promoter of, all fit well into the definition of crimes against humanity. Unfortunately, the Nuremberg Tribunal had no authority over the Avignon Court of Justice, and it was not until December 26, 1964, that the law for crimes against humanity without statute of limitations would enter French law.

The relationship between de Camaret and Antoine d'Ornano, which testified to a great concern for efficiency, also qualifies as crimes against humanity. They kept each other informed about the Jews. In response to a question by d'Ornano asking whether he had noticed any reaction in the Vaucluse during the celebration of Passover, de Camaret replied that he had not, but mentioned a search, carried out in Sorgues on August 28, 1942, at the house of the Rappoport family, which uncovered a certain quantity of unleavened bread for the ceremony. De Camaret and d'Ornano undertook jointly to "regularize" Jews who refused to toe the line. Dr. Paul Brunschwig from Avignon, who did not accept the ban to practice imposed upon him and refused to apply for an exemption, stated that de Camaret and d'Ornano went to the prefecture at the end of May 1942 and asked for him to be interned. This measure taken against Brunschwig could have cost him his life, as it tragically happened to Albrecht Marienfeld following his internment.

The Organization of Spoliation

De Camaret put in place the legal mechanism for the spoliation of the Jews. First, he designated provisional administrators. In March 1942, he received a visit from Roger Alphonse Villard who would end up as the agent of the "Gestapo of rue Bancasse" in Avignon. Here are the terms of his evaluation of Villard that were sent to the Marseille manager: "*Catholic, very active salesman, intelligent, in good health, very national. Prisoner escaped from Eastern Prussia, refugee in Carpentras, all his assets blocked in Germany, needs to work, would go anywhere.*" Marseille was altogether convinced, and on May 22, Villard was proposed as provisional administrator for two Jewish businesses in the Gard.[19] De Camaret also supported the candidacy of Jean Gaugler who would eventually become the president of the *Groupe Collaboration* for the Vaucluse.

In September 1942, there were about 30 provisional administrators for the Vaucluse, half of them in Avignon. These were people whose names de Camaret had in part received from d'Ornano, and from his dear friend d'Oléon, who answered him on February 1, 1943:

> You have asked me to suggest the names of administrators for seized Jewish businesses.[20] I want to remind you that I have already suggested Colonel Desprez in Orange as a candidate. I am adding:
> - Jean Lagrange, member of the board of directors of the Vaucluse Legion, formerly director of the BNCE (Banque Nationale pour le Commerce Exterieur).
> - Léon Marcellin, president of the Mormoiron section of the Legion
> - Amédée Pons, merchant for pharmaceutical products, district head of the Legion - Avignon
> - De Villemandy, formerly lawyer at the Paris court, Legion - Avignon
> - [Victor] Chanoux, packaging manufacturer - Cavaillon
> - Sigalas, director of the company l'Union - Cavaillon
> - Léopold Aubert, Legion - Vaison

Of course, these were persons of "known honorability," to use Camaret's own expression. Amongst these seven candidates, four were to be tried by the Court of Justice, and the man named Sigalas, the treasurer of the Groupe Collaboration, would be sentenced to 20 years of hard labor for having produced a list of Gaullists and communists for the Milice to use.

An estimation of the value and the condition of each property was effected by a pre-screened architect. As early as June 12, 1942, de Camaret received, upon his request, the complete list of the Vaucluse architects, from Jean Mognetti, member of the council of the order of architects. Amongst the 25 architects politically screened by Mognetti, de Camaret eliminated those "*who are not reliable from the national point of view*," including one suspected of being a freemason, and selected those whom "*appraisals can be entrusted to in complete confidence.*" These were of course Mognetti himself, Henri Mazet, Jean Gaugler, Charles Girard, Pierre Jacquet, Pastre (father and son), Ludovic Demeure, Hébrard, Valentin.[21]

Mognetti was not only an appraisal expert; he would also serve as provisional administrator of the Bernheim-Lyon apartment buildings. His beginnings were very promising since, during its session of August 17, 1945, the CDL of Vaucluse alluded to a document from Mognetti to de Camaret concerning the architects of the *département*. As we just saw, it was a list assessing their racial and ideological purity. De Camaret had definitely found in Mognetti an ally in the hunt for Jews, since at the same meeting, one of the members of the CDL declared that it was Mognetti who had denounced the architect Georges Amoyel as a Jew and a Gaullist.[22] One less competitor!

After the decision to sell was reached by the regional manager in Marseille, *notaires* were needed to transfer the assets to "Aryans," an easy task in Avignon. He obtained the paid collaboration of a dozen *notaires*, designated in turn by the president of the Chamber of *Notaires*.

The Zealous Provisional Administrator of Jewish Assets

At the beginning of 1943 the landscape changed: the Germans took control of the free zone. Starting in May 1943, de Camaret concentrated on his role as provisional administrator after the reorganization of the CGQJ. At his trial, he stated: "*My activity having been deemed insufficient, at the beginning of 1943, my position of delegate was cancelled, and I was only in charge of the provisional administration of different businesses and apartment buildings. Starting in March 1943, I did not have to provide any information about the Jews. This role had then passed on to the inspector of the section of investigations,* Lebon.*"

On July 1, 1943, de Camaret was named by decree provisional administrator of the personal assets "abandoned" by the Jews who had been deported by the prefecture of Vaucluse almost one year earlier, in August 1942. Their names: Berta Eiseman from Merindol, Emmanuel and Marie Freundlich from le Crestet, Anna Rochwerger from Apt and Léopold

---

* This is the SEC.

Schoenfeld from Carpentras. In fact, Emmanuel and Marie Freundlich had succeeded in fleeing and eluding arrest, but months passed since Berta Eiseman, Anna Rochwerger, and Léopold Schoenfeld, deported by convoy 29, had been exterminated.

Just before the 1943 summer holidays, de Camaret provided the list of his assignments. He was already administrator of the Troller company (after the resignation of Charles Bonnard at the beginning of 1943), and of the assets of Garson, Berrebi, Bernheim, and Goetschel. Starting in April 1943, Alice Goetschel, the widow of Max Goetschel, owner of this Haussmann style building at the corner of 8, avenue de la République and 1-3, avenue Viala in Avignon, had taken refuge in St. Christol, near Sault in Vaucluse. Her two sons, Jean and Raymond, were prisoners of war. The Goetschels were Alsatians who had settled in Avignon, because the parents had refused German citizenship after the defeat of 1870 to Prussia and the subsequent annexation of Alsace. Owners of a haberdashery business, the Goetschels acquired this important building and set up the Parisette store, known throughout Avignon.

The "Parisette" business rights were rented out by Alice Goetschel to an LLC since May 14, 1941, for 70,000 francs per year. On June 14, 1943, Mrs. Goetschel informed de Camaret that she would not be able to respond to his summons, because she was near Sault "for health reasons," and was sending him the documents he has asked for: the list of tenants, two pay stubs of her two sons who were prisoners, the document of inheritance of her husband, and the titles for the buildings. She also gave instructions to a *notaire*, Pierre Geoffroy, to provide the rental agreement of "Parisette," and she insisted "*on reminding that all the assets inherited from her husband are still owned jointly by her and her two sons who are prisoners.*" She stressed that the assets of the family should not be touched, since her two sons were prisoners of war, and relied on the arrangement wisely put in place by Geoffroy on May 14, 1941. Providentially, article 7 of the Statute of the Jews of June 2, 1941 (transfers of Jewish assets to Aryans), stipulated that "*the application of the dispositions of the present law to prisoners of war is deferred until their return from captivity.*" The subterfuge did not go unnoticed by Jean Lebon, the delegate of the SEC, who observed in his report of April 1, 1943: "*From the account above, we are dealing with a Jewish business, skillfully camouflaged behind a fictitious company created in anticipation of the law of June 2, 1941.*"[23]

De Camaret carried on regardless, and on December 18, 1943, he placed an ad in the "Nouvelliste" to put "Parisette" up for sale, after which he received threats by mail. Shaken, on January 17, 1944, he wrote a letter to his Marseille boss, in which he inquired "*whether in Algeria Jewish assets which had been put under provisional administration had to be returned or on the contrary the buyers had kept the assets and the Jews had received only the money"* and *"whether legal action had been taken against provisional administrators."*[24] Only a few weeks before the provisional government of de Gaulle in Algiers issued the decree of November 12, 1943, purely and simply cancelling the measures against the Jews. Despite the clear language of that decree, de Camaret, who could see the German defeat and the collapse of Vichy, did not grasp the incompatibility between the measures against the Jews and the new republican order about to be reinstated.

De Camaret hounded the Goetschels. First he fired the wife of Raymond Goetschel, under the pretext that she was absent, while she was actually traveling to refill the store, thereby depriving her and her two young children of their livelihood.[25] Then, he attempted to sell the apartment building after negotiations with the Germans who had requisitioned the "Parisette" store which occupied the ground floor and the basement of the Goetschel building in order to house the German Office of Employment. De Camaret succeeded in delaying the requisition by one month, enough time to facilitate the sale and move "Parisette" to the previous location of the German Office of Employment, 1, rue Grivolas. One must say that "Parisette" was a successful business giving de Camaret excellent profits.

Nevertheless, the auction of "Parisette" did take place on January 28, 1944, in the office of M. Henri de Beaulieu, *notaire*, with an opening bid of 500,000 francs.[26] There were two approved candidates: Hubert and Agnès Rosier, but they abstained from bidding. A new auction was set for May, this time with a lower starting bid of 400,000 francs. The Rosiers seemed to hesitate; they were mostly interested in the location but not in the merchandise. They finally did not buy it because they had just acquired the store "Lydie" belonging to René Zarade.

The "Goetschel apartment building" was put on the market on May 30, 1944, for the price of 2,500,000 francs through the services of Joseph Martin, *notaire*, with an office at 22, rue Carnot.[27] No buyers showed up, and a certificate of failure was issued. De Camaret persisted; the building was again put up for auction at a starting price of 1,250,000 francs. But the sale didn't take place, and de Camaret was angry at not being able to close a deal, and losing a large commission. On July 22, 1944, one month before the Liberation of Avignon, Joseph Martin, in a letter to de Camaret, cynically analyzed the failure:

> In all sincerity, I must confess that, because of the current events, fear of
> bombing or of landing, people are no more disposed to buy houses and prefer

to keep their cash positions. Moreover, concerning assets that belonged to Jews, the clientele has little confidence in such sales, if unfortunately, we were to return to the pre-war régime.

In her complaint dated December 14, 1944, Alice Goetschel reiterated that the building was jointly owned with her sons, and that de Camaret had no right to administer assets belonging to prisoners of war. As to de Camaret, he hid behind a decree which he had obtained on November 20, 1943, and which extended his powers to the assets of the two Goetschel sons, both co-owners and both POWs. However, the decree, obtained on the advice of Jean Lebon and his boss at the SEC, was contrary to Vichy law.[28]

Could it be that money and greed had been all along one of the main motivations of this anti-Semite? Money was never acknowledged because it had been made on the backs of the persecuted Jews. But was de Camaret a charitable man of faith when he executed the order coming from the Marseille office on June 6, 1944, concerning the apartment building of David Palombo, put up for auction with a starting bid of 200,000 francs?

> Since the Jew and his family who occupied the entire apartment building, 3, rue Paul Saïn in Avignon were arrested on March 30, 1944, by the German authorities, the central management is considering a sale of the property. The file of this case will be brought to the consultative committee. It is time to look for buyers and to inform me of all offers you may receive.

David Palombo was the sole survivor of his family, deported on convoy 71; his wife Rose, and their daughters Laurette and Suzanne did not survive. Their names are engraved in the synagogue on the memorial to the victims of the Holocaust. The archives do not indicate whether their apartment building had found a buyer that close to Liberation. On the other hand, they do specify that de Camaret's life sentence to hard labor was quickly reduced to 7 years in prison.

The Man and His Limitations

"My activity has been deemed insufficient." This was the way he had explained his replacement by Jean Lebon. Was it also a way to minimize his role to the Court of Justice or is there any basis to this statement? The documents speak eloquently for themselves.

Clearly at the outset some difficulties arose because of his working conditions. It was not easy to find buyers for several reasons. On one hand, the buyer had to declare the true value of the property, and that might have unfortunate consequences on the taxes owed. On the other hand, the thought of a possible return of the victims or their successors did not make things any easier.[29] The provisional administrators also did not always play into de Camaret's hands. For instance, Charles Bonnard was recruited to administer the business of Suide at 18, rue de la République; he was also in charge of the assets of 4 other Jewish businesses.* At his trial, Bonnard offered a letter from A. Suide dated September 3, 1944, in his own defense. ...

> Dear Sir,
> Back in Avignon after too long an absence, I am now living a naturally and mentally normal life with my family.
> I was pleased to learn that you and your family have been able to come out largely unscathed from these critical times our city has gone through, but I have been extremely surprised that you have had problems about your role as provisional administrator of Jewish assets. In my opinion, it is the opposite that should have happened, since everybody in Avignon must know the kind and unselfish devotion which you have shown in the business you managing and which we have discussed so often in the course of a long year working together.
> Personally, I will give you, if needed, the testimony of my gratitude as well as the same moral support as the one I found in you during difficult circumstances.
> Madame Suide joins me in sending you the assurance of her friendship and support.
> Hoping to see you soon, most sincerely yours.

Charles Bonnard received a similar letter from every Jew whose assets he had administered. He stated that he had done everything possible to hinder the spoliation process headed by de Camaret. A letter of October 1943 from the regional headquarters to de Camaret confirmed the failures of the provisional administrators and corroborated the claims of Bonnard after his resignation at the end of the summer of 1943.

Charles Bonnard was exonerated by the Court of Justice. However, in examining his file more closely, one discovers a reality that is somewhat different from that presented in his defense. Indeed, Jean Lebon, arriving in Avignon at the beginning of December 1942, had noted in his first report that same month, just after the arrival of the German troops: *"The following fact has been brought to my attention by M. Bonnard, delegate of the Maréchal for Propaganda. The man named Feldman (Jew) whose assets he is administering has received instructions from the prefecture ordering him to leave Avignon where there are occupying authorities and move to a municipality which is not occupied. Who gave this order? ..."* Before clearing

---

* Nahoum (1, rue St Jean-le-vieux), Endignoux (rue de la Masse), which belongs in parts to Dreyfus, Troller (Place Pignotte), and Feldman (rue Roquille); all in Avignon.

his own name, Bonnard has in any case joined the Vichy "Révolution Nationale." He had passed on the information that Feldman had entrusted him with. An anonymous resistant left this testimony:

> BONNARD:
> Provisional administrator of Jewish assets; has organized the center of propaganda and information of the révolution nationale. Wears the francisque. Very dangerous.[30]

As many officials, he seemed to have used a new line some time after the arrival of the Germans. He was not "very dangerous" compared to others.

De Camaret therefore did not have the support of all the members of his network whom he thought were well chosen. It resulted in dissatisfaction on the part of his boss. But this is not the first in the list of his reprimands.

At the beginning of his work as a delegate for the Vaucluse, de Camaret asked his boss from Marseille for a list of Jewish assets. His boss responded *"It is your job to obtain it."* Indeed, would a respectable employee ask his boss to do his job?

One senses in the responses de Camaret received from his supervisor a degree of contempt for his administrative abilities. On July 27, 1942, his boss wrote to him: *"I am honored to send you as an attachment a note of the head of the CGQJ about the information to be provided in the summaries. It is appropriate for you to take into account the instructions in this note when writing your reports."* And a few months later, on November 24, 1942, he was taught another lesson: *"You will please send me from now on, except for exceptional cases, only complete files whose documents have been carefully verified."*

On October 31, 1942, de Camaret asked his boss for the *"number and date of an article of the law that allows him to threaten a Jew with sanctions in case of an erroneous declaration on his part."* The response was not a long time coming, and on November 3, 1942, his boss reminded him that he ought to know the legislation relating to his job.

> I am honored to acknowledge receipt of your letter dated October 31, 1942, about the "threats" of sanctions mentioned by M. Verny during his last visit in Avignon.
> I am reminding you that the three principal laws bearing on the statute of the Jews are those of June 2, 1941, of July 22, 1941, and of November 17, 1941.
> It would be desirable for you to know them thoroughly.
> Concerning the article of the law "which permits to threaten with sanctions a Jew in case of erroneous declaration on his part," I am reminding you that it is article 24 of the law of November 17, 1941.

We find another sign of dissatisfaction by de Camaret's boss ten days later.

> In re: Grumbach Notaire
>
> I am honored to acknowledge receipt of your letter of November 10 about Grumbach, notaire in Lagnes, who is requesting the issue of a certificate of non belonging to the Jewish race.
>
> I am surprised that you still do not know the documents which are necessary to establish such a certificate. I am reminding you that the documents to be provided are the following: [follows a list of documents to be provided for a series of cases]

Another indication of his boss's displeasure was de Camaret's protesting tone. As the sound of allied guns grew louder, on June 30, 1944, de Camaret complained to his boss in his monthly report, while underlining that he expected reparation for the injustice he was the victim of:

> As I had the honor to write in my last report "as I could not hope to get a just remuneration for my work, because the apartment building could not be sold [he is writing about the Palombo building] because of a situation out of our control, <u>I demand that this remuneration be decided and paid</u>."*
>
> Let it also be known that I cannot continue indefinitely in the administration of this building and that, if on top of the payment past due, that of my work to come is no longer assured, I will not be able to see to this administration and I am asking to be relieved.[31]

The process of moving a large number of Jewish assets to Aryans in Vaucluse posed a significant number of problems. The Jewish owners, who knew the business, were expelled, and no one else could run the business efficiently. The revenues disappeared, and the balance sheet practically showed only expenses; charges accumulated. It was imperative to sell quickly, but buyers were hard to find, hence the boss' dissatisfaction. Even in the rare cases when a buyer was found, the process was extremely slow. At any rate, de Camaret must not have perceived the blunt refusals of his repeated demands for payment as indications of trust on the part of his supervisor.

What we know about de Camaret—his beliefs, the results of his work, the impatience of his boss, and the blocking of his salary—contributes to understanding his character. We are dealing with a hard-line doctrinaire ideologue, politically and socially involved as an assertive anti-Semite, a penniless aristocrat nostalgic for the Ancien Régime, perhaps hoping that a return to the past would spare him semi-destitution. His failures had thrown him into

---

* Underlined by de Camaret.

debt to the point that he could not afford a lifestyle commensurate with the social position he believed he deserved. He did not shine at the CGQJ, either as a delegate until April 1943 or as a simple provisional administrator until the end of the war, except through his anti-Semitic zeal. He was a man with limited abilities facing an extraordinary task.

However, this should not lead us to underestimate the damage he did. To the great chagrin of his bosses, de Camaret did not succeed in liquidating many Jewish assets and thus replenish the coffers of the CGQJ. Nevertheless, their owners lost the source of their revenues, and the fruit of their work was handed over to pillage by unscrupulous individuals. When looking at the arrests that were made, his responsibility was even greater because his census was turned into an instrument for Jew hunting. He had pointedly designated a certain number of richer Jews in his correspondence with his superiors. His letters on this topic show a definite hatred towards Jews who were richer than himself.

Let us imagine for a moment the damage that a delegate more efficient than de Camaret could have caused. This poses a fundamental question for history in general, and for that of the CGQJ in particular. The scope of the Statute is well known. We also know the intentions of the leaders of the CGQJ and those of their German masters. We have seen the many directives emanating from the CGQJ and their dissemination through its regional agencies. This was facilitated by the degree of efficiency of individuals all along the administrative chain as well as their paid or volunteer collaborators. In the case of de Camaret, he had set up a devastating mechanism for the physical and material persecution of the Jews. Fortunately for the designated victims, the approaching allied victory discouraged eventual buyers. This mechanism did not work to maximum efficiency, either because of the incompetence of its most zealous agents or because of the deliberate sabotage of others or their (even late) change of heart. Each region, each town, each individual created their own imprint on the impact of the CGQJ.

Chapter 4

The Trial of Jean Lebon

The Mad Drift of the SEC

Only one file at the Court of Justice of Vaucluse reveals that an indicted individual was judged almost exclusively for having either arrested or provoked the arrest of Jews. That was the case of Jean Lebon.

Inspector of the CGQJ SEC for the Vaucluse and the Gard[1] from November 1942 until his "dismissal" taking effect on August 31, 1944, Lebon could show an impressive list of successes. His file includes ten complaints, emanating from victims or victims' relatives testifying about the persecution of the Jews of Avignon.

A remarkable element also stands out: Lebon was almost exclusively judged on the base of testimonies, contrary to his predecessor, Henri de Camaret who was confronted with a combination of testimonies and file documents that were seized at his home. In the course of our research, we have naturally looked for and found abundant material concerning the activity of Lebon and de Camaret in the archives of the regional management of the CGQJ in Marseille, responsible for those two individuals.[2] Surprisingly this material was not presented at Lebon's trial by the prosecution even though its existence was mentioned and needs to be reviewed to reconstruct the course of his trial.

The decision to present here the essential elements of the procedure will undoubtedly result in some repetitions. This will however make it possible to clarify and question the conduct of the trial. This choice was made to give an idea about the atmosphere of the trial. Two dates frame the proceedings, January 18, 1945, the date of the first testimony written by the wife of a deportee, and June 29, 1945, the day of the public court session where Lebon was convicted.

The procedure file—with its hearings, confrontations and cross-examinations, with the statements of the court, the accused and the witnesses, and with the grounds for the verdict—must be compared to the archival documents not presented at the time. All of this will indicate if not our temptation to revise the trial, at least our desire to challenge the unacceptable "extenuating circumstances" of the verdict.

Witness Testimony and Cross Examination

The victims or the victims' relatives who lodged a complaint were heard before they were confronted with Lebon.

Court Testimony by Henri Kohn, February 28, 1945 (39 years old, 7, rue de la République, Avignon)

Henri Kohn was arrested in April 1943 and yet he survived. He was the owner of the "Marisse" hairdressing salon and perfume shop at 7, rue de la République à Avignon. It was to this store that the PPF moved its office from place Crillon in April 1944.

> I met Lebon for the first time at the beginning of 1943. He came to my store showing me his CGQJ credentials. He asked to see all my documents (ID card, official family record book, ration card). He verified whether all were indeed stamped "Jew."
>
> Then, he went on to examine the financial records of my store, and I had to provide him with the title of my business. After that date, he returned to my hairdressing salon as a customer, but he did not ask any questions. I was convinced that he was coming only to watch my business and to see what was going on.
>
> On April 19, 1943, at 7 in the morning, I was arrested at home by two individuals in plain clothes claiming to belong to the German police. They apprehended me, but before taking me away, they subjected me to questioning about all the information I had provided to Lebon.
>
> Moreover, during my interrogation, they kept referring to a paper that seemed to contain all the information they were asking me about. Then they

took me to the Hautpoul barracks. From there I was sent to Drancy, then to the Cherbourg area, and I was finally deported to the Anglo-Norman islands.

In May 1944, while being transferred to Germany, I managed to flee.

During our discussions, Lebon said, amongst others, "The Jews are not worth the price of the noose we would use to hang them."

The Lebon-Kohn Confrontation

Lebon: *I did not denounce Kohn, not to any French organization nor to the Gestapo. I simply provided information about his identity and his professional activity to the CGQJ that was asking for it. My report (to Marseille) would clearly indicate that I had not done anything that could harm the person and the assets of Mr. Kohn.*

Kohn: *I am convinced that Lebon was the cause of my arrest.*

Lebon: *I did what I could so that his store would not be requisitioned by the PPF. I had a conversation with Mrs. Kohn who told me "I thank you for what you have done for me, concerning the requisition of the store, but I do not forgive you for having been the cause of my husband's arrest." I assured Mrs. Kohn that I had absolutely nothing to do with his deportation and that, if I had actually been a member of the Gestapo, Mrs. Kohn would have also been arrested.*

Lebon was careful not to mention that the wife of Henri Kohn was a Catholic, a fact he knew very well, and that she should therefore not be targeted by the laws against the Jews.

Letter from Maria Weil Added to the File

Joseph Weil born on February 25, 1881, was the husband of Maria Weil. He was arrested in Le Thor on May 8, 1943, transferred to Drancy on May 16, 1943, and deported on convoy 55 on June 23, 1943. On January 18, 1945, Maria Weil sent a letter to a woman whose identity was not immediately clear.

I was very happy to receive your kind letter of January 7 and especially to read that your dear husband is safe and sound.

Alas, since your husband says that there are no more detainees on the Anglo-Norman islands, I have no further illusions about it. You may remember that I had the premonition that he was in Germany, even if the Gestapo of Paris maintained that he was near Cherbourg because I am a catholic and baptized…

I am not sure whether I had written to you that a charitable organization for the search for deportees, in rue d'Artois, in Paris, told me that, on the same day my husband was taken from Drancy, a convoy left for Birkenau, in Upper Silesia, and that it must be assumed that he was interned there, if he was not on the Anglo-Norman islands.

It was very cold there and he had no overcoat and only one pair of shoes.

As to this Jean Lebon, I am delighted that he is in prison. He caused us so much pain. I do not know whether I could recognize him. I was so distraught on the day he was in the car of the Gestapo and they came to take us from the Avignon prison to be transferred to the prison at the Avignon barracks. He was standing with his back towards us and turned briefly to me when the head of the Gestapo got out of his car. I took him for a prefecture employee and thought he was going to intervene with the Gestapo to get us freed.

Alas, I did not suspect his duplicity. He was so unctuous with me. He even betrayed himself and he introduced himself when he came to ask for information about us in Le Thor, when we were not at home. He said that he would come back, but he never did. If he had not said so himself in the car that he had come to our home, I would never have known it was him. He was telling me "I had come to Le Thor to see you. I had come to ask you about your income to know whether you needed help or not, because we have very humane laws for the Jews." My landlord from Le Thor could recognize him because he had spoken with her at length in the garden, having tried to worm information out of her (pardon the expression).

Coming back to this Jean Lebon, I prefer not to launch a complaint for the time being, because my husband is still in the hands of the Germans. If this Lebon creature were to be freed (we have already seen things like that recently), he would be able to get someone to seek revenge on my poor husband because I had launched a complaint. He may have kept connections with the Gestapo, if he has worked for them.

As long as my husband is not safe, I dare not do anything. I fear too much for him.

This letter was probably sent to Mrs. Kohn, whose husband had possibly been, in the mind of Mrs. Weil, companion in deportation of Joseph Weil, who never returned. The anguish of Maria Weil, like that of many others, had not disappeared with the Liberation. There was an additional fear that stirring up the past might irritate the non Jews. It was imperative above all to not make waves, as if the Liberation had not meant freedom for everybody.

Moreover, the representatives of the Avignon Jewish community, the officiating minister* accompanied by an official, expressed this malaise very well in the fall of 1944, during their visit to Max Fischer, then the sub-prefect in charge of the purges. A few weeks after the Liberation, Max Fischer had indeed been asked by Raymond Aubrac to establish and supervise the Court of Justice of Vaucluse. *"Monsieur Fischer,"* said the two representatives of the Jewish community, *"What you are doing now is not worthy of us* [the Jews]" Furious, Max Fischer showed them the door: *"Be sure to exit backwards, if you want to protect your behind..."*[3]

---

* An officiating minister is a non ordained member of the congregation who serves as rabbi.

This uneasiness of the Jewish population, destined to persist for decades to come with varying degrees of intensity, added to the general uneasiness of the rest of the population. The witnesses, who despite their hesitation, had decided to testify against Lebon in order for justice to be served, were to deserve that much more credit.

Henri Dreyfus' Audition of February 28, 1945
(69 years old, avenue Pasteur, Carpentras)

Henri Dreyfus, a nephew of Captain Alfred Dreyfus, was the mayor of Carpentras until his destitution in 1940. He was listed in the census, and was arrested in Pernes on April 12, 1943, by Gaston Mouillade, a collaborator, and Lieutenant Wilhelm Müller, chief of the German police. Interned in Drancy, he was not deported.

> I was arrested on April 12, 1943, and incarcerated at the St. Anne prison in Avignon.
> A few days later, while I had not been authorized to communicate with anybody, I received the visit of a few members of the Gestapo who had come to ask for the keys to my safes.
> I have positively identified a man named Lebon within that group, and it is my provisional administrator [Albert] Allard who informed me that he was an inspector at the CGQJ.
> This fact, that in itself is not of prime importance, does prove however that Lebon was in excellent terms with the Gestapo.

The Lebon-Dreyfus Confrontation

> Lebon admits to having accompanied Allard because the CGQJ had asked him to do so, and because Allard needed those keys. For those reasons, he did accompany Allard to Gestapo headquarters and to Dreyfus who surrendered the keys to Allard.

Dreyfus' testimony and Lebon's declaration underscore the level of collaboration between the SEC and the Gestapo, a collaboration reaching all the way up the chain of command.

Jacques Yenni's Testimony, March 12, 1945
(34 years old, 30, rue du Chapeau Rouge, Avignon)

Jacques Yenni was born on April 5, 1911. His name was registered in the census as an outdoor stall keeper.

Around the beginning of 1943, Lebon appeared at my domicile to check my identity documents. He was rather impertinent and verified whether the stamp "Jew" was indeed on all my documents. Since I had tried to scratch my identity card, he became violently angry and threatened to have me tried in court.

Shortly thereafter, I was summoned for the STO. I did not respond and went into hiding near Sault.

Sometime later, the STO papers arrived in Sault, but the gendarmes pretended not to find me. It is during my stay in Sault that Lebon seized my business license, and I think that it is on the basis of the reports he provided about me that I was summoned for the STO.

Lebon disputed the statements Yenni made about him. However, a report by Jean Lebon found in the archives of the CGQJ corroborates the essential parts of the statement by Yenni. On April 22, 1943, Jean Lebon proposed indeed to cancel his travel permit and business license, and to intern him in a GTE for mandatory labor.[4]

Victor Nahoum's Testimony on February 22, 1945
(25 years old, 24, rue Carnot, Avignon)

The entire Nahoum family was registered in the census and deported.
1- Sigma Blonstein, born Nahoum on September 18, 1907, deported on convoy 72
2- Maurice Nahoum, born on January 19, 1916, deported on convoy 74
3- Sarina Nahoum, born on October 8, 1898, deported on convoy 71
4- Isaac Nahoum, born on April 15, 1897, deported on convoy 71
5- Henri Nahoum, born on March 3, 1923, deceased before deportation at Tenon hospital in Paris

Victor Nahoum testifies:

At the beginning of 1943, I received the visit of a man named Jean Lebon who was an inspector of the SEC at the CGQJ. After checking my documents and those of my family, he stated that he was surprised to see me here, while there was so much work for young people.

I told him that I was working at the store run by my uncle in rue Carnot, but that did not seem to satisfy him.

Shortly thereafter, Victor Nahoum received an order to join the STO and decided to hide. His testimony continues.

On several occasions, Lebon came to the store to verify my uncle's financial records.

On March 29, 1944, my family, composed of my uncle, my aunt, my nephew, my brother and my sister, was arrested by the French members of the Gestapo.

I had no news of my family for many months.

After my uncle's arrest, the store has been administered by a man named Bonnet from Nîmes, but the warehouse was looted.

I cannot specify the exact role played by Lebon. Nevertheless, I can assure you that he is the only one we had any dealings with and that all the hardship we have had to go through since his first visit can only have originated from the reports he made about me and my family.

Lebon declared that he had *"nothing to do with the arrest of this family."* Victor Nahoum alludes to the looting of the store "The 200,000 stockings," which we will revisit in the case of Tiziano Feroldi.

Flore Asmanoff's Testimony of February 22, 1945
(39 years old, 14, rue d'Amphoux, Avignon)

Flore Asmanoff, née Cohen, was registered in the census. Her husband, Moïse Asmanoff, outdoor stall keeper, also in the census, was deported on convoy 73 after his arrest in Orange. He survived.

At the beginning of November 1943, I received a visit from a man who asked me where my husband was. He was actually working at his stall on Place Pie, but I answered that he was away. I feared that this individual belonged to the Gestapo, but he left me a card with his name and his position of inspector of the CGQJ.

He behaved brutally, and after he explained the goal of his visit which consisted of verifying my husband's identity, he began to speak about the situation at the time and said among other things that he had been born to harm the Jews. He continued on this subject for a long time while stressing that the Jewish race should not exist, and that all the wars would disappear if the Jews were also to disappear.

I presume that with such a frame of mind an individual of his kind could only harm people of the Jewish faith, and it is because I want to make sure that he is punished for his harmful actions that I have the duty to give evidence now.

Lebon *"denies the statements that were attributed to him."*

Moïse Yaffe's Testimony of February 22, 1945
(35 years old, 7 place des Carmes, Avignon)

Moïse Yaffe was a hosiery merchant also registered on the census. He was arrested, and then released in March 1944.

In February 1943 I received the visit of the man named Lebon who asked to see my identity documents. As I gave them to him, he put a stamp on them although there already was one.

Sometime later, I had to travel to Nîmes on business. I ran into Lebon who gestured me to come closer and asked what I was doing there. I told him that my papers were in order and that it was the Avignon police that had issued the safe-conduct necessary for my travel.

He said that I was not allowed to travel, and since I was convinced to the contrary, I understood that he intended to persecute us.

On another occasion, he told me that he wanted to rid Avignon of all the Jews. He also said that I was not authorized to conduct my business, and a short time later, I was given an administrator.

On numerous occasions, he came to see me as well as all my fellow merchants, and we were under his tight surveillance.

Lebon was also responsible for the deportation of my father, my brother and my nephew. He himself carried out their arrest under the pretext that they were of the Jewish faith.

The damage caused by Lebon to the Jews of Avignon is unimaginable, and it is certain that, if he had had full powers, we would have been all deported or killed.

Lebon denied the charge once again. *"I am surprised by the witness's statement, since I have met Mr. Yaffe often enough, and our relations were almost friendly. We always shook hands and I even had a cup of coffee with him in Nîmes."*

The presence of Lebon in Nîmes was linked to his dual role as inspector of the SEC for the Vaucluse and for the Gard. It is therefore surprising that he was not charged with any crime in the Gard and in some Bouches du Rhône cities bordering the Vaucluse (Chateaurenard, Arles, Tarascon).

Jean Marx' Testimony of February, 1945
(36 years old, 8, rue Ste. Garde, Avignon)

Jean Marx who was registered in the 1941 census was a refugee. He used to live in Ste. Marie aux Mines (Haut-Rhin).

During the summer of 1942 I received the visit of an individual named Lebon. He showed me documents on CGQJ stationary, and he told me that he had been appointed director for Jewish affairs for the département of Vaucluse, replacing a man named de Camaret.

This individual, after having checked my documents to verify that they were stamped with the word "Juif," not content to know that all the declarations about my assets had been given at the prefecture, he told me that he would take over all the investigations, and he checked whether I had stopped practicing medicine since February 11, 1942.

Having declared that I was employed as a concentrator of grape must at the fram of la Bathelasse, Lebon went there several times under the pretext of checking my presence and to extort some quantity of wine from the owner during each of his visits.

Lebon, during his visits to my home, claimed to be "proud of helping the purge of the country of this Jewish gangrene and that it was necessary to end the malfeasance of the Jews, the cause of all the misfortunes of France that fortunately thanks to the Maréchal and himself, this was about to be taken care of."

At my explanation that, after I was dispossessed of my assets and my parents had died (my father, French mayor of Willer on the Thur, Haut Rhin, during 12 years, my grandfather, military medal-holder in 1870), I needed a job to raise my children, he sniggered while promising more work than I wanted in a concentration camp. As he was leaving, he said "You will have a less luxurious apartment. I will see to it."

During my absence, I was a lieutenant doctor of the FFI in Haute Savoie, Lebon came to my home several times, wanting to know at all costs where I was hiding, and he threatened to deport to Poland the young catholic woman, a 1940 war widow, who was at my service, if she persisted and did not respond to his demands and continued working for Jews.

Jean Marx was probably mistaken about the date, because "during the summer of 1942" Lebon was still secretary of the census of the PQJ in Marseille.[5] He took up his post as inspector of the SEC only in November 1942.

Lebon was not as firmly righteous as one might think. He was using his position to get free wine from Marx's boss similar to mob practices. Did Lebon receive his share of the looting that took place during and after the arrests of Jews?

After the war, Dr. Marx became an influential member of the Jewish community. An ardent patriot, he was very anxious to see the Jews regain their place within the French nation.

Judith Cohen's Testimony of February 22, 1945
(49 years old, 109, rue des Infirmières, Avignon)

The entire Cohen family was registered during the census, the father Léon, the mother Judith, the children Raphael and Marguerite. Léon was a day worker at the silk manufacturing plant, Chemin de Bonaventure.

Raphael, born on June 24, 1920, was deported on convoy 81. In the Memorial of the Deportation, Serge Klarsfeld wrote that this convoy left the camp of Noé, passing through the camp of St. Sulpice, to reach Toulouse where Jewish internees were loaded at the Cafaretti barracks. The destination was Weimar-Buchenwald. Raphael Cohen was on "Autrand's list of deportees," with May 25, 1943, as the date of his arrest.[6] Autrand adds "Buchenwald—returned." Raphael was indeed a survivor. This was confirmed by his Yad Vashem testimony of October 8, 1992, regarding his father Léon Cohen, deported on convoy 75.

Judith Cohen states:

> Towards the end of 1943, I received the visit of a man who introduced himself as an inspector of the CGQJ.
>
> He asked me for details about my son who was then 22. At the time, he was working at Bouchara and was not at all involved in politics. Sometime later, my son became unemployed. Everywhere he applied, nobody wanted to hire him under the pretext he was Jewish.
>
> He also had to deal with Lebon who, later, wrote a report about my son. The latter was arrested at the beginning of June and sent to St. Sulpice La Pointe.
>
> I went to see him five months later and he smuggled out a copy of the report established against him by Lebon. In August, he was deported to Germany and I have had no more news from him.
>
> I categorically accuse the man named Lebon to be at the base of the arrest and the deportation of my son through the report he provided about him.

Lebon-Judith Cohen Confrontation

> Lebon: *I do not know Cohen's son. The information about the state of his baptism was give to me by the mother herself.*
>
> Judith Cohen: *Lebon knows my son. He has asked him the information mentioned in this report one day in front of the Regina* [café]. *I will even add that Lebon had told my daughter, whose identity card was not stamped "Juive," while she was protesting "Do you want me to send you to the Gestapo and be deported to Poland?"*
>
> Lebon: *I categorically contest this last statement.*

Elise Yaffe's Audition of February 22, 1945
(38 years old, 51, rue Carreterie, Avignon)

Elise Yaffe's husband, Elie, was born on March 1, 1898, her father-in-law, Jacob, in 1869, and his son, Jacques (Jackie), on June 8, 1930, in Avignon. The three of them were deported on convoy 72. The family was registered in the census of French or foreign Jews.

I have met a man named Lebon for the first time at the beginning of March 1943. When he arrived at my home, he introduced himself as inspector of the CGQJ of Avignon. As such, he required that we show all our identity and rationing cards in order to check whether they all had the mention "Juif." Afterwards, he asked for the size of our capital.

On March 29, 1944, at midnight, while my husband was returning from guarding the railroad, he was arrested by Lebon at the door of our home. Lebon was accompanied by seven men belonging to the Milice and the Gestapo. They locked my husband in one of the three cars which had brought them, and left him there under guard. Then, they conducted a roundup in the neighborhood and arrested approximately 40 Jews. It was Lebon who directed the operation. In general, they beat people up and operated with extreme violence. They gathered everybody and took them to the offices of the Milice, rue Joseph Vernet. At the end of the roundup, Lebon took my husband off the car and five of them came upstairs to my apartment. They all had their weapons in their hands.

Lebon then spoke to me, he asked for my identity and ration cards which, by the way, he never gave back to me, then seeing an empty bed, he asks me where the occupant was. I must tell you that it was my son Jackie, 14 years old, whom I had, as a precaution, hidden in the attic. Since I was refusing to tell him who it was, he threatened me and I had to resign myself and bring my son down.

Lebon then knocked on the door of my 75-year-old father-in-law. He ordered him to get dressed and follow them. My father-in-law resisted and on the orders of Lebon, he was pulled out of his bed and forcefully dressed. Near one in the morning, Lebon and his acolytes left with my husband, my son and my father-in-law. When it came time to leave, my daughter got closer to kiss her father good bye, but she was then brutally beaten by Lebon. I want to specify that all the men were speaking in perfect French. As they were leaving, they said they would be back the next morning.

The next day, one of the men who had come on the previous evening came to my home. He said that in return for a few one thousand francs in banknotes, my family would be released. I responded that I had no money, and he demanded that I surrender our car. As I was resisting him, he called a German who had been waiting downstairs and both of them asked me to take them to our store. They looted it, filled their car with merchandise and left, leaving my store open and ransacked. The following day, I left Avignon with my two children to take refuge in Carpentras.

I omitted to tell you that when Lebon and his accomplices were taking my family away, they also wanted me to follow them. I had a young baby of 14 months and I categorically refused. Lebon handcuffed me and hit me violently. After seeing the medical prescriptions, Lebon became aware that my son was sick, and agreed to leave me behind in order to take care of him.

I never got any news from my son, my husband, or my father-in-law and I think that they were deported to Upper Silesia.

Lebon-Elise Yaffe Confrontation

> Lebon: *I admit that I came in March 43 to the home of the witness... I indeed asked Mrs. Yaffe and her husband why they had not left for Turkey as they had been ordered to do... I deny having come to their home on March 29, 1944.*

The roundup of March 29, 1944, was conducted by the French auxiliaries of the German police. This emphasizes an occasional additional link between Lebon and the hoodlums engaged in the capture of Jews.

In 1943, for the Jews of Turkish origin, returning to Turkey was not an order, as Lebon claimed, but a noncompulsory proposal. According to the note of the prefecture of March 24, 1943, signed by Aimé Autrand and sent to the Central police superintendant of Avignon he states: "*I am asking you to contact urgently the heads of the families listed below, and inquire whether they would agree to return to their country of origin.*"[7]

Lebon provided an alibi for the night of March 28 to 29, 1944, which he spent in Marseille. His witness specified that Lebon was supposed to be in Avignon on the 29th to celebrate the birthday of his girlfriend. Contrary to his claim, it is clear that he was indeed in Avignon during the roundup in question, during the night from March 29 to 30.

Esther Revah's Audition of March 3, 1945
(26 years old, 2, rue Mijane, Avignon)

Esther Revah's husband, Victor, was deported by convoy 74. Her father, Moïse Mordoh, grocer, born on April 19, 1883, was deported by convoy 72. The family was registered in the census.

> On March 29, 1944, around one in the morning, eight individuals arrived at our home and after having introduced themselves as police, they told us they had come to arrest us because we were Jewish.
>
> The individual named Lebon was amongst them, as well as a man around 30 years old wearing a small moustache.
>
> During that night, we had to endure their threats, their insults and their beatings. They all behaved with unprecedented brutality. They were all armed with a handgun.
>
> Thanks to the commotion created by their arrival, I was able to escape alone, and I hid until Liberation.
>
> It is then that I learned that my father had been arrested and deported during the roundup of March 29, 1944. I must say that my husband had been deported since 1943.

It has been a long time I have had no news from them. I can also say that people who were living in the same building were arrested and deported. These are the Levy family, composed of two Levy brothers, three women and a 14 year old girl. I am bringing this family to your attention, since they will not be able to complain in person because it is the entire family.

There probably is an error in the transcription of the minutes concerning Esther's husband, Victor, born on January 10, 1908. He could not have been deported since 1943, because he was arrested on May 10, 1944, arrived in Drancy on May 19, 1944, coming from the Marseille region, and was on convoy 74, which left that camp the next day.

We have found the six members of the Levy family mentioned by Esther Revah. Arrested on March 29, 1944, and deported, they were all registered in the census at the address 2, rue Mijane. They were:

1- David (Dario) Levy, born on March 11, 1905, in Salonica, deported on convoy 71

2- Esterina Levy (née Almosnino), born on April 17, 1909, in Salonica, deported on convoy 71

3- Dora (Denise) Levy, born on March 18, 1931, in Avignon, deported on convoy 71

4- Mathilde Levy (née Matarasso), born on April 12, 1909, in Salonica, deported on convoy 72

5- Rachel Matarasso, born on January 25, 1917, in Salonica, deported on convoy 72

6- Ovadia Levy, born on January 21, 1906, in Salonica, deported on convoy 72, a survivor

The witness had to be unaware of the fact that Ovadia was the sole survivor of the Levy family. Esther Revah mentioned six members of the Levy family. The sixth one was Rachel Matarasso, the sister of Mathilde Levy, also née Matarasso.

The Cross-Examination of Jean Lebon

On March 12, 1945, the investigating magistrate, Louis Béral, interrogated Lebon for the first time, and with the assistance of Raoul Roux, he recorded the session in the minutes.

Jean Lebon
32 year old, ex-inspector at the CGQJ[8]
Avignon, avenue St. Paul Monclar

Born on March 17, 1913, in Ernée, département of the Mayenne, son of Eugène and of Clémentine Sinope.

Single

Charged with actions sanctioned by articles 75 and following of the penal code and by ordinance of November 28, 1944

At the beginning of the interrogation, Lebon said:

I agree to explain my actions while assisted by my council M. Ortial.

As an officer on armistice leave, I was hired in April 1941 as an accountant at the Secrétariat général à la Jeunesse. Since my salary was significantly insufficient, I accepted on February 5, 1942, a position as census secretary at the PQJ of the CGQJ*. On November 1, 1942, I was named an inspector at the CGQJ.

My functions consisted of investigating the professional and racial situation of the Israelites.

I was detached from the Marseille administration to operate in the Vaucluse, and this is how I ended up dealing with the situation of the Israelites of the region on the initiative of the CGQJ. I did nothing on my personal initiative. I am very surprised to have made myself a great many enemies in the region amongst the Israelites.

I have indeed fulfilled my function with the greatest possible moderation, and I am ready to face the confrontation with each witness who gave evidence against me.

Read, approved and signed.

During his defense, Lebon notably uses the more respectable term "Israelite," while during the war he had used the pejorative "Jew" in the official SEC documents. On April 17, 1945, the final interrogation took place under the direction of Judge Béral.

… You went to elementary school in Ernée, then to secondary school at the lycée of Laval and of Rennes. You obtained your high school diploma, and after high school, you worked for one year as a dental technician in Laval.

At the age of 18½, you enlisted in the 22nd BCA† in Nice. You were then assigned to the 1st RTA‡ in Blida. You were successively posted to Meknès, Tataouine, and later, you were demobilized in Blida after you asked to be put on leave because of the reduction of the officers due to the 1940 armistice.

---

* Note that the PQJ did not report to the CGQJ but to the national police.

† BCA: Bataillon de Chasseurs Alpins, Mountain Battalion.

‡ RTA: Régiment de Tirailleurs Algériens, Algerian Infantry Regiment.

You were promoted as an NCO in 1934 while serving in the 22nd BCA, staff sergeant and warrant officer at the No. 1 Infantry depot and second lieutenant while at the 33rd RTA.

In your quality of SEC inspector at the CGQJ, you are accused of having exhibited towards Israelites such an activity that some of them hold you clearly responsible for the trouble, the arrests, or the deportations they or their families have been the victims of.

1- M. Henri Kohn states that you are the cause of his arrest since he claims that no other person than you could have provided de precise details to the policemen who had arrested him. You are claiming that you had nothing to do with his arrest and you indicate that you did all what was in your power to prevent his store from being requisitioned by the PPF

2- Jacques Yenni declares that you came into his home in a rude manner at the beginning of 1943, and that after your visit, he was called for the STO. You deny having made the comments he attributes to you. You admit however having checked his documents, but you claim to have had nothing to do with the measures he was subjected to.

3- Esther Revah accuses you of having come to her home in the company of seven other individuals on March 29, 1944, at one in the morning. During that visit, she claims having been subjected to insults, threats and beatings. He father was arrested and later deported. On March 12, 1945, you were confronted with the witness. But on that day, Esther Revah declared that, after such on long time, she could not remember whether it was actually you, as she had asserted in front of police Inspector Leyris. You state, on the other hand, that you paid a visit to Mrs. Revah only once to make the customary verifications of her documents and those of her family.

4- Victor Nahoum reports that you visited him in the course of 1943. You checked his documents and those of his family, and you expressed surprise to still see him there, given his age. Shortly after your visit, he was taken by the Germans to build the fortifications of St. Nazaire. On March 29, his uncle, his aunt, his nephew, his brother and his sister were arrested by the Gestapo. The witness states that you certainly are at the origin of these measures, which you vehemently deny.

5- Judith Cohen categorically accuses you as responsible for the arrest and deportation of her son, which is attributable only to the report that you provided about him. You deny this accusation; you claim to not be at all the author of that report, a copy of which was given to the young man, Cohen, and was attached to the file. You also deny having asked Raphael Cohen for the information contained in this document, under the conditions reported by the mother during her deposition.

6- Flore Asmanoff assures us that during November 1943, she received your visit. You told her that you were born to harm Jews. You maintain that you have never said what is attributed to you.

7- Mr. Henri Dreyfus claims that on May 12, 1943, you arrived in the company of Mr. Allard at the Hautpoul barracks where he was detained to ask for the key to his safe. It has been established that it is at the request of Mr. Allard that you had come to the Haupoul barracks, because as an administrator of Jewish assets, Mr. Allard needed the keys of the safe which Mr. Dreyfus had with him at the time of his arrest, an arrest which you have nothing to do with.

8- On March 29, 1944, at midnight, in the company of seven men belonging to the Milice and the Gestapo,* you conducted the arrest of Mr. Yaffe. During the same evening and while directing the operations, you are said to have conducted a roundup and arrested around forty Jews. Madame Rachel Yaffe specifies also that on that evening you took away not only her husband, but her son and her father-in-law. You are even said to have hit the witness when she approached to kiss her father before you took him away†. You maintain that you never came on March 29, 1944, to the domicile of the Yaffe family together with miliciens and members of the Gestapo. You claimed to be absent from Avignon at the date reported by the witness. Indeed, a witness, Antonin Alesandrini, reports, through written deposition, that you spent the night from March 28 to March 29, 1944, at his home: 1, rue d'Hozier in Marseille.

9- René Mayer states that during May 1943 you subjected him to a two-hour interrogation to find out whether he belonged to the Jewish race. In the course of the interrogation, you told him "it is necessary to eliminate all the Jews." You deny having said the words he attributed to you.

10- Finally, Doctor Jean Marx declares that he received your visit during the summer of 1942. You verified whether he indeed had ceased to practice medicine. During your visits, you claimed that you were proud of helping this country to get rid of the Jewish gangrene and that it was necessary to put an end to the malfeasance of the Jews who were the cause of all the misfortunes of France

The judge asked: *"Do you wish to add anything to your previous statements?"* Lebon embarked on a long convoluted statement, aimed at exonerating himself and refuting every accusation. He even became the prosecutor.

… I therefore accuse the man named Villars,** a member of the Gestapo, of having arrested the people who accuse me now, or of having been the cause of their arrest.

---

* Here again, we see a confusion between various units of the German police, including collaborators. This issue will be clarified in a subsequent section.
† It is not the witness but her daughter who was hit by Lebon.
** This is probably Roger Alphonse Villard.

I accuse Debon, currently at the Beaumettes prison in Marseille, of having, perhaps thoughtlessly, given the information drawn from my reports, to Villars; this information was only of a conventional usefulness for the service of the CGQJ, but Villars used them for his personal financial profit through the usual route of the Gestapo…

Despite lies, half-truths and omissions, Lebon nevertheless admitted having been the author of the reports against the Jews.

The Presentation of the Facts

In his summing-up of June 8, 1945, the government commissioner first described the accused, and followed with all the charges brought up by the witnesses, including the arrests operated by Lebon during the roundup of March 29, 1944. He emphasizes his anti-Semitism.

…It is undeniable that Lebon is responsible for the arrest of numerous Jews. He could indeed not ignore the fate and the usefulness of the reports he was writing in manifestly anti-Semitic spirit.

The government commissioner concluded by requesting a verdict against the accused.

Considering that this information has resulted in sufficient charges against the man named Lebon, domiciled in Avignon (jailed), for having, in France, from 1942 to 1944, or in any case after June 16, 1940, undermined the external security of the state, a crime and offence, covered and punished by Article 75 and following articles of the penal code.

In view of the ordinances of June 26 and November 28, 1944, we have decided to refer the man named Jean Lebon to the Court of Justice of Vaucluse to be judged in accordance with the law.

A Verdict in Tune with the Times

At the public hearing of June 29, 1945, the president of the jury read the questions to the jury and the responses.

First Question:
Is the accused Jean Lebon guilty of having, in the Vaucluse, after June 16, 1940, undermined the external security of the state and had secret dealings with the enemy, while he was inspector at the SEC of the CGQJ, particularly by

provoking through his reports and investigations, the arrest, internment or deportation of numerous persons of Jewish race? Yes, by a majority
Second Question:
Is it constant that, in his actions, the accused has demonstrated an excessive zeal or personal initiative going beyond the orders or instructions he had received? Yes, by a majority.

The court pronounced a more nuanced verdict.

> The Court: in view of the responses to the questions posed,
> Considering that the existing facts as presented constitute the crime covered and punished by Article 75 paragraphs 2 and 5 of the penal code,
> Considering however that there are, by a majority of votes, extenuating circumstances in favor of the accused and that it is appropriate to apply article 463 of the penal code:
> Sentences, by a majority of votes, Jean Lebon to hard labor for life,
> Orders, by a majority of votes, the confiscation of all Jean Lebon's assets,
> Sentences him to bear the trial costs.

If one stops for an instant at the first question to the jury, one cannot help noticing that the notion of "Jewish race" had not disappeared with the Liberation. A period does not necessarily fade away with the even violent rejection of the previous institutions. This state of mind would definitely contribute one more element to the fears of the Jews after "Liberation," that single event that took many meanings. Contrary to the language in force for decades after the war, Jean-Pierre Azéma observed that there had been "several Libérations depending on who you were."[9] The people who had been on the side of the victors did not experience the "Liberation" in the same way as the collaborators and their families who were associated with the vanquished. On the surface, the "Liberation of the Jews" was supposed to be that of the victors, but the reality was far more complex, since Liberation had not erased their "defeat." After the war, the Jewish population was once again safe, but amputated of its victims, in a society it had not stopped fearing, despite the return of the Republic. And of course, the judges do not miss the opportunity of reminding this population that it is still a part of the Jewish race, namely the "vanquished." The Jews will not fully partake in the Liberation of the victors or in that of the vanquished; they will have their own Liberation, that of the "vanquished-victors."

It is remarkable that the only charges against Lebon retained by the jury are the reports he filed that provoked arrests and the excessive zeal in the exercise of his task. And yet, the commissioner of the government had mentioned in his opening statement Lebon's active participation in the arrests of

March 29, 1944, according to two independent witnesses. Was this accusation so extraordinary that two testimonies would not be sufficient to establish it?

As for the "extenuating circumstances... by a majority of votes," the procedure against Lebon gave no indication about them, with perhaps the exception of taking his denials into consideration. But who could take into account the denials of the accused in front of multiple testimony? This question raises another one which is much more disturbing: if Lebon had written about members of the resistance in his reports, thereby leading to their arrest or not, or if he had directly participated in the arrests of members of the resistance, would he have benefited from "extenuating circumstances with a majority of the votes"? The answer to this question would have raised no doubts: in the climate of that time, the life of a Jew is not worth that of a member of the resistance. It seems, indeed, that Liberation had not yet liquidated the "Jewish question."

This state of mind could be found almost everywhere in France. After Liberation, didn't some Paris employees of the CGQJ regularly come back to work, hoping that someone would finally take the seals off and open the doors?[10] In addition, didn't around 20 employees write a letter in December 1944 asking to be reinstated into the CGQJ so that they can "*lend their support to the necessary task of cleansing and rebuilding*"?

We can understand that employees and low level managers might have gone off their heads. But, how can one explain that, after the departure of the Germans and the arrival of the provisional government, Jean Armilhon, director of the legal services of the CGQJ, had designated himself as "Director of the CGQJ administration" after Joseph Antignac, its last acting director, had fled? From his office with the CGQJ sign on place des Petits Pères in Paris, Armilhon had written to the budget director in view of ensuring the remuneration of his agents: "*Moreover, the personnel is starting to come back with a keen desire to return to work.*"[11] For these people, the reconstruction of France was therefore hinging on the continuation of the CGQJ mission, and there was absolutely no doubt that the job needed to be finished.

In the court file, a last document emanating from the Resistance added to the disturbing aspect of the verdict. It is an undated letter number 2916.

> In July [1943], Mrs. Breillat, a short hand typist, infiltrated the regional office of the CGQJ, 49 cours Pierre Puget, in Marseille, in order to identify the police of the SEC of the said administration, and keep an eye over what the AP are up to.
>
> Having become in January 1944 the secretary to the regional director of the Commissariat, Mr. Ramaroni, our comrade (Mrs. Breillat) was able to obtain all

the information useful to prevent the arrest of some people by the German police and cause a delay in the sale of Jewish assets.

Some time before Liberation, we had in our possession the addresses of the administrators and functionaries of the CGQJ who belonged in large part to the Milice, and the PPF and whom we have arrested during the insurrection itself, starting on August 22, 1944.

Mrs. Breillat was able to overhear Lebon, inspector of the SEC at the CGQJ, who was in charge of tracking down Jews, Gaullists, etc.

This individual was a supporter of ultra-collaboration with the "boches" in his conversations, during his visits at the CGQJ in Marseille.

Edouard Padovani	Gabrielle Bordas
AS. Mle 211.31 bis	Member FFI in the Basses Alpes
Member of the group "Combat"	Region 42-44
No. 554 - Region R2	Charged with recruiting for the maquis
	Ex political internee, card 86
	Avignon

The Documents Speak

Jean Lebon was a disreputable person; the testimony by many witnesses confirms it. However, most of the proceedings would tend to cast doubt as for the severity of his actions. This comes of course from his own denials which one may or may not believe. But they cannot be rejected outright because there is always a possibility that he spoke the truth.

There are also questions which could affect the credibility of the testimony. Did the witnesses exaggerate Lebon's zeal in executing the measures which, even without any zeal, were already appalling? In addition, Esther Revah stated during the confrontation that "*she does not remember Lebon.*" This remark is essential because Lebon was accused of having participated in the arrest of her family that took place on the evening of March 29, 1944. Of course, Elise Yaffe, second witness, was much more categorical about the participation of Lebon in the round up of March 29; she had also faced his hostility during prior inquiries of Lebon at her domicile.

1. Omissions : Jean Lebon, Inspector of the PQJ et Inspector of the SEC for the Gard and some Municipalities of the Bouches du Rhône

Before we begin our examination of the charges against Lebon at the light of the documents of the AJ 38 series,* two omissions stand out in the

---

* AJ 38 Series, Archives of the CGQJ, Archives Nationales, Paris.

entire procedure, and in particular in the statement of the Commissioner of the government.

Nobody seemed to know that the accused was briefly an inspector at the PQJ after he resigned from his position of secretary of the census. A statement of February 24, 1942, confirms it:

> I undersigned Mr. [Jean] Pegeot, chief of the PQJ, certify that Mr. Jean Lebon, 24, rue des Beaux Arts, Marseille, serves as Police Inspector, section of the Jewish Questions and that as such he has to conduct investigations at night.
>
> The present certificate can be used as necessary and amongst others to obtain a ration card, category "T."*[12]

He became inspector of the SEC when the PQJ ceased to exist.

The second omission was much more important than the first: in addition to his role as inspector of the SEC for the Vaucluse, Lebon was not only inspector of the SEC for the Gard, but also executed targeted missions in municipalities of the Bouches du Rhône close to Avignon, depending on the needs of the director of the SEC of Marseille. No witnesses were called on this issue, and no documents were presented to the court. This is all the more regrettable since the Court of Justice was aware of Lebon's trips to Nîmes.

2. Using Half-Truths for his Defense

Let us revisit briefly the "Marisse" case. Lebon attributed to himself the merit of having helped the wife of Henri Kohn. Lebon stated "*I have done all that was in my power to prevent her store from being requisitioned by the PPF.*" In fact, this represents yet a new lie. First, we know that Mrs. Kohn was Catholic. On April 7, 1944, Lebon's boss sent him instructions concerning the "Marisse" business where he specifically wrote:

> … you should bring to the attention of Monsieur the Prefect that this business is half Aryan through the wife who, by her contribution, owns 16/28 of it, and in this case, it appears that he must intervene to safeguard the rights of an Aryan woman…[13]

It is clear that Lebon's boss urged him to be cautious in the preservation of the rights of an Aryan woman, even if she committed the crime of being the

---

* Ration category "T" is reserved for individuals who have a physically taxing job.

spouse of a Jew. Is it the late date of such an episode that induced the boss to cautiously avoid a blunder?

3. A Zealous and Enthusiastic Inspector

First, who was Lebon in the eyes of his boss in Marseille? In his self-evaluation of July 1943, one reads: "*Remains as serious and convinced an inspector as he has always been, perfectly sound, honest, skillful in his investigations, but really handicapped by his basic education.*" The handicap which Lebon alluded to is tied to the fact that he had only the first part of a high school diploma. Although a little more moderate, his chief of service was almost in agreement with Lebon's glorious view of himself: "*Inspector seriously convinced, full of enthusiasm, however keeps a young outlook. Discharges his mission as responsible for two départements conscientiously, in spite of the handicap of his basic education.*" In fact, overall, Lebon's colleagues did not have better credentials than he did; judging by the unrestrained behavior of most members of the SEC,[14] this organization was offering to young recruits easy prospects and power not found in "normal" positions.

Lebon's boss even proposed a promotion "one step above the current position." There were very good reasons for this. During this period, Lebon had indeed made almost one hundred inspections, of which we have sampled only 3 months. Out of 41 investigations, 27 were made on his own initiative while 14 had been requested by others, including his boss. The collection of his reports for 1943 and 1944 all showed the same zeal. At the beginning of 1944, one can feel a late change in his bosses which Lebon takes into account as indicated in this letter to his boss in Marseille:

> SUBJECT: Your note RG/SF No. 268 of March 2, 1944
> In response to your note cited above, I am honored to inform you that I am taking into account your observations that no mission or investigation can be performed if it does not originate from your services and if a signed order of mission is not addressed to me…
>
> In accordance with your instructions, I have informed this service [Service of foreigners of the prefecture, under Aimé Autrand] that they must send to your service any request of investigation for you to approve…

One senses a stronger hand in dealing with the inspectors of the SEC by Raymond Guilledoux, Lebon's boss at that time. As we already know, the boss had decided to restore order in the "*mess left behind by his predecessors.*" One can also see a manifestation of his desire to channel the zeal of his subordinate towards the "most serious issues." The instructions from Marseille covered investigation requests coming from outside the SEC and did not exclude the initiatives of Lebon himself, since he was part of the service. This limited and somewhat late moderation of Lebon in undertaking investigations was sufficient to repress his untidy zeal of the past 15 months, and had the advantage of better focusing his energy.

Lebon lied again in his statement and with good reason.

4. Authorized to Collaborate with the Milice

In 1943, Lebon had undertaken several investigations at the request of the Milice, without referring the matter to his boss. On March 22, 1944, he was contacted by Yves Thesmar, chief of the Milice of the Vaucluse. This time, Lebon informed his boss: "*The latter* [Thesmar] *did not hide his desire that I collaborate with him in order to make him aware of any obstruction by the Police, the Judges, the Prefecture and others.*" The response from Lebon's boss, on March 31, 1944, is a masterpiece of political obfuscation.

> In response to your letter No. 46 dated March 22, 1944, related to eventual relations with the Milice, inspired by the service note No. 62 from the Director of the SEC who specifies that our mission is to "investigate and control," these terms being understood in the largest possible sense, I am honored to inform you that your collaboration with the organization you had cited does not seem to me susceptible of having any drawbacks.
>
> Indeed, even if our respective attributions are different, they bear in common the political objective they are aimed at.
>
> It is for you to decide what can benefit to the Révolution Nationale and to give it your all.
>
> However, it matters to keep, as far as you are concerned, absolute independence, and avoid every unethical compromise by strictly remaining within the context of verbal relations.
>
> Finally, from the standpoint of pure intelligence, there is a rule for those who dedicate themselves to it: give little and wisely, to reap a lot, everywhere and always.

The roar of the allied guns seemed to encourage the boss of the SEC to more prudence, although he still maintained his fidelity to the impersonal Révolution Nationale; prudence towards his own bosses in Vichy and Paris, but also prudence in anticipation of the arrival of the future masters. Was Liberation already in line of sight? Perhaps, this explains why Lebon's boss was getting a better grip on his employee.

5. Monitors Public Opinion and the Notables

The Goetschel affair was not the only case raised to the credit of M. Geoffroy. Another case raised the suspicions of Jean Lebon.

In 1943, "Martine Couture" was an Aryan enterprise of womens' ready-to-wear, but Lebon noticed that it had been created on August 3, 1939, under the name of "Avignon Couture" by six Jews: Joseph Pilosoff, David Benveniste, Jacques Saportas, Maurice Benveniste, Joseph Benveniste, and Salvator Asseo.[15] On September 8, 1941, a bill of sale to two Aryans (Paulette Rampone and Alphonse Mailhos) was signed at the office of Maître Geoffroy; this caused Lebon to note in his August 3, 1943, investigation:

> After this sale, the LLC "Avignon Couture" becomes "Martine Couture." This sale does not include 100 shares of 1000 francs, and there is no mention of the intangible elements of the business—this is why I am inclined to believe that this operation was fictitious.

As a result, Lebon's boss decided to put "Martine Couture" under provisional administration *"in order to determine whether this business is under Jewish influence."*

In his second monthly report, of December 1942, Jean Lebon showed that he was aware that he could not rely on everybody.

> ACTIVITIES AND DIVERSE REACTIONS OF THE ARYANS
> In too many cases, the Aryans, in the spirit of <u>Christian charity</u> (?)[*] or out of pure self-interest, are passive or help the Jewish tribe in exchange for remuneration.
> In the first case, a wind of pessimism covers Avignon, where there are many Aryans who are <u>afraid that</u> <u>their present activity</u> might later disrupt their relations with the Jews, when these get the upper hand again. This situation is dangerous and deserves attention.[16]

Lebon underlined some terms and wondered about the motive linked to "Christian charity," a feeling he apparently did not share. Lebon's view was in sharp contrast with the analysis of public opinion in Vaucluse by prefect Piton following the arrests of August 1942. On October 5, 1942, the prefect wrote:

---

[*] The underlining and the question mark in this note were done by Lebon.

The measure taken against the foreign Jews have raised some emotion amongst the population which generally took pity of the fate of the regrouped people. The sentiment expressed by the Church on this issue was not without having an influence on public opinion.

However, the selfish preoccupations of everyone rapidly overtook the reaction mentioned which has now become a mere memory.[17]

One can probably assume that the judgment of the prefect was based on a more detached attitude that the obsessive militancy of Lebon, who brought everything back to his daily anti-Semitic mission.

6. Seeing the Jewish Conspiracy Everywhere

On March 20, 1943, Mr. Roger Bonpuis, chief of the Légion des Combattants in Le Thor, sent a complaint to the prefect:

> We have here a Jewish family, the father Stern, the mother and two daughters who maintain an anti-French propaganda to the utmost degree, and who did whatever was in their power to prevent my son from leaving [as a volunteer to Germany], the eldest Yvonne giving herself to my son as his fiancée, the second Maidy is in the process of causing the downfall of another honorable family of Le Thor…

In his investigation report of April 17, 1943, Lebon echoed the words of Roger Bonpuis and guarded the "purity of the race in Provence." Yvonne Stern, 21 years old, who was at the center of Lebon's concern, was baptized on January 15, 1943.

> On their arrival at Le Thor, this family again without a homeland, seeks a relation with the family of Mr. Bonpuis, a retired Captain, President of the Légion, residing in Le Thor; a family which includes <u>twelve children</u>* and whose last born is the godson of the Maréchal.
>
> It is thus on the romantic plane and through the agency of the daughter Yvonne Stern that this attempt of interference into this truly French family took place. The latter indeed is wooing one of the Bonpuis sons, <u>Fernand</u>, assiduously following an incident which has been referred to the public prosecutor's office (… it relates to a matter of abortion)…
>
> In the course of my investigation, after I asked young Yvonne Stern to provide her certificate of baptism, she brought me, five minutes later, the… entire Register of Baptism of the Parish!

---

* The two words were underlined by Jean Lebon.

I find it very odd that a priest would part with these documents, especially in the hands of a foreigner (the parish priest of Le Thor, is Abbot Jules Mazet).

I went to see the mayor [Dr. H Azais] who did not hide the interest he was taking in this family [Stern] and disavowed all the attempts by Mr. Bonpuis to break this union…

This doctor, Mayor of Le Thor, and vice-president of the Légion does not enjoy a good reputation in the Légion of Vaucluse and his replacement is requested.

The parish priest of Le Thor was not the only clergyman who had to be outwitted. Amongst the investigations requested of Lebon, there was a letter intercepted by the censors and marked "CONFIDENTIAL."[18] Abbot Bourdette, its author, was sending fake certificates of baptism to the mother of a Jewish family while exhorting her to use them *"… only to obtain the cards your children need, do not use them in a church, for instance for a church wedding, because they would be sent back."*

To track down the famous fake certificates of baptism and to enforce the *Statut des Personnes* (Statute of Individuals) Lebon repeatedly launched investigations aimed at proving the Judaism of suspects and then notified authorities. Another member of the clergy made his task easier. On June 22, 1943, Henri Audemard, priest at Our Lady of Les Blanches, wrote to the CGQJ.

From Lapalud (Vaucluse), where I went to visit friends, I am now returning nauseated by what they said when they told me that they are facing Jews living in opulence, insulting, by their great lifestyle and their excessive joy, to the misery of their neighbors, all true French people 100% for Pétain.

I imagine that it will be sufficient to notify you of the insulting and provoking attitude of these Jews in order for it to be put right soon. It goes without saying that, for the Jews I am mentioning to you, the black market is moving along briskly wherever they are. It is scandalous to see these foreigners starving the true French people.

Jews, freemasons, communists are swarming here. In a letter to Pétain of April 4, 1941, I took the liberty to expose a civil funeral where the barons and vassals of freemasonry had made an appointment.

One doesn't mind literally proclaiming this:

"Pétain believes he has killed us, we can see here, that we are more alive than ever, and happier than ever to have been able to surround Pétain with many of our own." I have since learned that amongst the people planted into Pétain's entourage, [Jean-François] Darlan has been amongst the winners and proved himself. I want to believe that your activity against the Jews does not allow this impertinence on their part…

It is a fact that the communists are raising their heads everywhere in the Vaucluse... Will there finally be an action against the freemasonry, the communists and the people in the pay of Moscow, as you are doing against the Jews? I have never been a pessimist, but what we are observing here frightens me.

The complaints of Lebon against the administration and the notables continued unabated. An incident dated June 29, 1943, provided another opportunity for Lebon to single out two Vichy officials. He wrote his boss:

On this day, 6/29/43 at 10 a.m., the superintendant, chief of the security police of Avignon called on me. After I arrived, I was shocked to hear his requests:

1- What do I have against Althuil*?
2- What is the basis for stating in my report that Althuil is Jewish?
3- What were the official documents leading me to say that Althuil had broken the law?
4- To surrender the certificates of baptism of Althuil which are in my possession

These questions emanated from Mr. Cord, investigating judge in charge of this matter.

I am taking the liberty to mention the particularly discourteous tone of this official, and this dialogue looked rather like the interrogation of someone accused and <u>seemed to ignore</u>† the functions you have entrusted me with...

Moreover, I just learned today that the <u>Security police</u> resorted to use a Jew (whose name I still ignore) to keep an eye on my work.

Given these facts, I am asking, Mr. Regional delegate, to inform me whether, in light of this fact, my mission in Vaucluse should be pursued.

Of course, Lebon added a small emotional blackmail to his boss at the end of his letter, but in the background, there is the case of René Altkuil. In a preceding letter of May 30, 1943, Lebon complained to his boss that Madame Altkuil had been allowed to read his report at the police station of the 1st district, by Mr. Roure, secretary to Superintendent Poggi. By showing Lebon's report to Madame Altkuil, this employee had *"divulged a professional secret."* What exactly was the "Altkuil affair"?

We have the report of an investigation initiated by Lebon, dated April 24, 1943, against René Altkuil, manager of the Sans Souci bar, 125, rue Carreterie in Avignon. Lebon states *"Althuil is a Jew according to the law of June 2, 1941. For*

---

* This is René Altkuil and not Althuil.
† The two expressions were underlined by Jean Lebon.

having failed to declare himself, he is therefore punishable by the sanctions enacted by the laws of 6/2/1941 and 12/11/1942." However, Altkuil had been baptized as a Catholic on June 11, 1924, at the age of 13. Lebon continues:

> The investigation permitted to establish that Althuil is indeed Jewish and that he has knowingly attempted to elude the laws against the Jews currently on the books.
>
> The bar he is managing is an agency for the black market and on the day of the investigation he was being prosecuted for the sale of forbidden apéritifs (pastis)…
>
> In conclusion, it is appropriate to:
> 1- Prosecute Althuil according to the laws of 6/2/1941 and 12/11/1942
> 2- Require his transfer to a group of foreign workers

This report of Lebon against Altkuil answered the questions of the investigating judge and of the chief of the security police, who do not seem to agree with the SEC. In fact, our verification shows that René Altkuil had been registered from 1941 to 1944, contrary to the claims of Lebon who refused to let go of his prey. Ironically, the Sans Souci, like other bars and cafés of Avignon, served as headquarters for the Avignon mob, some of whom participated in the hunt for the Jews. As to Altkuil, he survived thanks to this passive resistance that Lebon could not stand.

7. Demands Brutal Measures Against his Victims

Lebon had claimed *"When a request for investigation was communicated to me by Marseille, I would return it, after having filled the objective, with a hand written report and without any conclusion."* The initial report was indeed handwritten; it was then typed in Marseille. A section reserved for Lebon's boss contained his final decision. However, in all cases, without any exception, Lebon provided his own recommendation. In the quasi totality of his investigations against the Jews, he had asked for one or more of the following sanctions:

1- Put the business under provisional administration
2- Freeze the bank account
3- Prosecute the person for infractions to the Statut des Juifs
4- Cancel the permit of circulation
5- Cancel the stallholder's license
6- Assign the person to forced residence
7- Send the person to a camp

In a few rare cases, Lebon's boss sent the report back to be rewritten with even more severe recommendations. In all other cases, the boss countersigned Lebon's recommendations while specifying the branches of the administration that were to receive a copy of the report for further action.

Lebon lied again when he passed the ball back to his boss.

8. Author of Murderous Monthly Reports Against the Jews

In his own defense, Lebon tried to reassure the court about his attitude towards the Jews and his patriotism: *"I am not afraid to say that, very often, I took the side of the Israelites and that I never hesitated to notify my bosses as well as the prefectural and police authorities of the intrigues of some French individuals who were excessively slavish toward the German occupiers."* Let us shed light on this statement with the help of Lebon's fourth report of March 1943, which gives a good idea of his state of mind throughout his work.

> TECHNICAL INFORMATION
> From March 1 to 31, 1943, I have performed 22 investigations broken down as follows:
> 6 relating to economic Aryanization
> 10 relating to the statute of the persons
> 6 others
> The distribution of requests is as follows:

CGQJ Marseille	2
Milice Avignon	2
SEC Marseille	3
SEC Vaucluse	15

> These investigations resulted in requests from the competent authorities of various measures broken down as follows:

Nomination of APs	6
Administrative internment	5
GTE	1
Inculpation	5

> FUNCTIONING OF THE SERVICE
> Starting on March 1 when Mr. de Camaret, representative in Vaucluse left his job it is no longer possible for me
> 1- To use his office
> 2- To use his telephone
> I have to think about using an office and a telephone in an official administration in Avignon.

On the other hand, no AP possesses a place that can be used as an office. I am considering renting 2 or 3 furnished rooms so I can install a telephone.

This latter point remains conditional to the approval of the regional director.

THE DIFFICULTIES – THE NEEDS

I am taking the liberty to bring up once again the lack of means of transportation, a case I have submitted in detail in my previous report.

Since I know a person owning a moped, I am requesting whether the administrative services of our organization would cover the rental fees for this moped.

RELATIONS WITH THE AUTHORITIES

Upon the arrival of the new prefect of Vaucluse [Georges Darbou], I went to explain my duties. I found him an intelligent and understanding official with respect to Jewish affairs. He assured me of all his support.

OTHER EVENTS

During the month, other events have taken up my activity

1) The Rumanian Jew, Isaac Pascal, the object of my report of 12/8/1942, incorporated on 2/15/1943 in the camp of foreign workers has been detached starting on March 1 as a fur worker at Mme. Acton, rue des Fourbisseurs, Avignon. Contract signed between the latter and Mr. Montagu, chief of Group 148 in Le Pontet. The sanction imposed on this Jew is incompatible with this preferential measure taken in his favor. This removes the opportunity for a Frenchman, a father, to avoid being sent to Germany*.

2) A man named Schwarz, Swiss and Aryan subject, is president in Avignon of the Amicale des Volontaires Etrangers whose headquarters are in Limoges. This man is going to great lengths to favor Jewish members of this organization, under the pretext that, having served France during the war, they must be considered as citizens of our country. The blood shed by these foreigners for the defense of our Homeland does not justify in my opinion the favors that some services of the prefecture are inclined to grant them.

3) During my investigations this month, I was able to notice how much the stamp "Juif" on the identity and ration cards of the Jews is rapidly disappearing.
   i. Stamp barely readable
   ii. Scratching or smearing with a dirty thumb so that the sign of this inferior race will soon disappear from all cards

---

* A worker being sent to Germany would allow a French prisoner in Germany to come back; Lebon implies that Isaac Pascal should be sent to Germany.

On this topic, I am proposing that a control be done from time to time by the police and the gendarmerie during their investigations.

For my own use, I have asked and obtained at the prefecture a stamp "Juif," and since I have purchased an ink pad, I will put the stamp back on the cards of the Jews during my travels.

4)   During a visit in Apt, I have registered the agitation of the population concerning the measure (almost a favor) taken toward the Jew Dreyfus (report of 12/30/1942). Indeed, following an internment request by the regional director of the SEC, the prefecture of Vaucluse is leaving him in Apt in forced residence. This half measure is detrimental. On one hand, Dreyfus is the head of the gang of Jews who have swooped down on Apt, he gives the marching orders against the government, he initiates and directs the black market. After I brought it up to M. Autrand at the Prefecture, this measure was canceled and it was proposed that Dreyfus be assigned to a residence in Gordes. Always half measures.

5)   I have brought up in one of my recent reports the case of the young Jew, Raphael Cohen, who is not going to Germany because he is a Jew, and spends his time in cafés ranting against France and the Relève.* The case of this Yid† is not an isolated one. Too many individuals of this inferior race could not care less about the suffering imposed upon the French. And yet, while they accomplish the ordeal imposed on them by defeat, the Jews continue to lead the good life, buy and sell on the black market, work around our laws, and broadcast slogans of hatred against France.

REACTIONS OF THE ARYANS

At the moment, Avignon is inundated with lies, and overtly in cafés and public places, people publicly insult the Maréchal and his government. One cannot find one Frenchman, worthy of this name, to put an end to this campaign of false news whose goals—for the future—are filled with clouds when the worst events could take place.

CONCLUSIONS

From the aforementioned, it stands out that:

Too many officials, and not of the lowest ranking, consciously favor the Jews and too often thwart my action.

I am singling out for the prefecture:

M. Autrand F∴M∴ Head of Division, chief of the Service of Foreigners

M. Pleindoux, Head of the First Division

M. Gilles, Director of the Cabinet of the prefect

---

* The Relève, the relief, is the replacement of prisoners of war by able-bodied people who are sent to work in Germany.

† Lebon used the French term "youpin."

In the Police:

M. Bonnet, Superintendant of the south district [of Avignon]

M. Poggi, Superintendent of the north district

The activity of the secretary of the Chief of the Security named Hours has been brought to my attention; I will launch an investigation

In conclusion, almost all the officials in Vaucluse are vassals to the Jews.[19]

Next to the name of Autrand, the mention "F∴M∴" designates the freemasons, or the "Brothers Three Dots" in the parlance of the far right.[20] This notation can also be found in the writings of several collaborators dedicated to the far right ideology, and in particular Jean Mognetti in the list of architects he provided to Henri de Camaret.[21]

The original report by Lebon, written shortly after the beginning of the German occupation, reinforced the image of an ideologue, obsessed by his work against the Jews, who did not hesitate to contradict himself in his own defense: "*I am not afraid to say that, very often, I took the side of the Israelites.*" Whatever Lebon might say, he projected a fanatical anti-Semitism, which is obvious in all his investigative and monthly reports, and is confirmed by the testimony against him. He hounded individuals like Isaac Pascal, Henri Dreyfus and Raphael Cohen, who will be deported. Isaac Pascal would not survive.

On April 1, 1943, Lebon's boss saw it fit to send to the prefect a sweetened version of report No. 4. Interestingly, in this censored version, there are no further accusations against the Vichy official in Vaucluse, everything being centered on the "harmful activity" of the Jews.

On the first page of the expunged version of the report, there was a handwritten note by the boss: "*Copy of the monthly report of M. Lebon, whose original has likely been sent directly to the P. of Vaucluse. Perhaps, it would be better to do it through our channel.*"

The leader of the SEC of Marseille tried to look confident in the prefect and required his subordinate to follow suit. However, he forwarded everything to his own superiors, that brought down criticism upon the prefect. There is no doubt that the prefecture was not fooled by the friendly attitude of the SEC. The remarks by Autrand about the CGQJ in his 1965 book confirm this.[22]

9. Relentlessly Singled Out Officials Judged Not Aggressive Enough Against the Jews

Let us return to the attitude of Lebon towards the prefectural administration: "*I am not afraid to say that... I never hesitated to notify my bosses as well as the prefectural and police authorities of the intrigues of some French individual excessively servile toward the German occupiers.*" As we just saw, it was in fact the opposite that's true.

It was Lebon who had stated in his report No. 1 of December 1942 that "*...the man named Feldmann (Jew) has been instructed by the prefecture to leave Avignon where the occupying authorities are and to go to an unoccupied locality in the département. Who issued this order? ...*"

In the same report, Lebon had added "*Individuals named as dangerous in the Vaucluse administration: M. Autrand, head of the Service of Foreigners, who is the only one who can provide safe-conducts to Jews...*" It was not his first show of zeal. Immediately after he took office—which, by the way, coincided with the beginning of German occupation—Lebon's hostility towards Autrand and the prefecture was echoed up the line by his boss of Marseille to his own leadership in Vichy in a report dated December 10, 1942:

> While sending you report No. 1282,... I want to draw your attention to the schemes of the Public Prosecutor in Avignon.
>
> Our inspector, M. Lebon, discovers a Jew Holzmann, sought after by the Paris police as a dangerous individual who on top of it is not registered and has crossed the demarcation line clandestinely.
>
> The police superintendant of Avignon was tipped off and arrested this individual, sending him to the prosecutor's office. Twenty hours later, the Jew is acquitted on orders of the Prosecutor due to "Lack of evidence."
>
> This incident deserves a thorough investigation, but I already think that it is unacceptable under the present circumstances that the justice system be a hindrance to the national decontamination task which we are all committed to...
>
> Finally and most importantly, this example is contagious and disastrous.
>
> The information which I have already collected about the mentality of some officials in Avignon indicates that this mentality is clearly pro-Jewish. M. Lamorlette, general secretary of the prefecture, is married to a Deutch daughter who is presumed Jewish (investigation in progress). Mr. Autrand, in charge of Jewish affairs at the prefecture, is deemed favorable to the Jews. Today, we see that the public prosecutor of Avignon is taking a benevolent measure, to say the least, towards a Jew who satisfies all the conditions to remain incarcerated...
>
> I am therefore requesting that this incident be brought to the attention of Monsieur le Commissaire General aux Questions Juives, so that a good example be made to these who might be tempted to sabotage the actions of the government.[23]

Among others, Lebon also took on Autrand who, according to the reports of the SEC, had changed in the space of a few months; he was now hindering the efforts of Lebon and the CGQJ, and did not even pursue the foreign Jews who had escaped during the deportation of August 1942. He was not the only one amongst the high officials of Vaucluse who passively resisted the CGQJ in the execution of the anti-Jewish measures of Vichy.

The complaints of Lebon and his boss on top of those of other collaborators against these officials triggered the purges of September 16, 1943, when 127 people, including Autrand, were arrested for Gaullism by the occupying authorities and sent off to labor camps.[24] Exasperated by this passive resistance of the Vaucluse Vichy administration, the Germans tried to neutralize the prefecture and the establishment and leaned more and more on the "freelancers" of collaboration. One cannot help noticing a de facto alliance—if not of intention—between the SEC and the Germans. These changes will characterize the year 1944. Lebon's grievances were not limited to Autrand. He sent a note against the police superintendant of Chateaurenard to his superiors.

> Fate had it that I was at the central police station on 2/18/43 when the Jew Gutman came in.
>
> If the name of this individual intrigued me and induced me to ask for more details, two things caught my attention.
>
> 1- How come identity cards were delivered to these 2 Jews without a flag being raised by their names sounding so little like ours and mostly under the current circumstances where the Jewish question is on the agenda (census mandated by the law of 12/11/1942)
> 2- Without my intervention and the action that I immediately undertook, these two Jews who had been ignored by the police were about to leave Avignon. How many others have already left?
>
> I do not want to incriminate anybody, but I find it of essential importance that these kinds of things could happen at the moment.
>
> By note No. 36 of today, I am sending to the Superintendant a report concerning this affair where I am asking for legal proceedings according to the laws of 6/2/1941 and 12/2/1942.

Lebon's boss wrote a question mark in the margin, next to "2 Jews" since the letter seemed to refer to Gutman. A separate report, written by Lebon one day earlier and also sent to Vichy, provided the identity of the 2 Jews in question: Maurice Kaminer and Robert Herscovici who had also received help from the French authorities in Chateaurenard. "*It is common knowledge that the mayor and the police superintendant have been subverted by Jewish influence.*"* The boss transmitted the notes of his subordinate with his handwritten comments:

---

* Originally, "... *sont enjuivés.*"

Transmitted to M. le prefect of Vaucluse and to M. the Intendant of police*
while drawing their attention to the facts uncovered by the inspector of the SEC
for the Vaucluse. It is not the first time I observe that the Jewish question is not
given, by some elements in the police, the appropriate importance.

10. Obsessive Hunter of Jews

Let us go beyond Lebon's report No. 4, where we read his rantings against
Raphael Cohen, and for absolute certainty, we refer to Lebon's original report
(Investigation on the Activity of the Jew Raphael Cohen).

SUMMARY

Jew without a well defined job… he is a barfly; for whom the enlistment in
a grouping of workers is imperative…

EXPOSE OF THE INVESTIGATION

The Jew Raphael Cohen, 22 years old, catholic, baptized on 12/22/1942 at
the Church of Les Carmes in Avignon; his job consists of visiting cafés and bars,
where he is making antinational remarks and is poking fun at Aryans who leave
for the relief of war prisoners.

Signed Jean Lebon

CONCLUSIONS OF THE SEC DIRECTOR OF MARSEILLE

From the preceding report, it emerges that:

The Jew Cohen is an idle individual who is dangerous to moral order.

Consequently, I am asking Monsieur the prefect of Vaucluse to have him
urgently incorporated in a grouping of workers according to decree No. 3.593 of
November 25, 1942.[25]

Raphael Cohen's late baptism stood out, as the Germans had just arrived
in Avignon.

This report was sent to the prefect of Vaucluse, to the regional prefect of
Marseille, and to the SEC and CGQJ of Vichy. Obviously Lebon took the
initiative of the investigation and concluded that the internment of Raphael
Cohen was required. His boss informed the prefect and the higher-ups.
Raphael Cohen was interned, then deported.

Once again, Lebon had lied to save his neck. On April 28, 1943, Lebon
had also provided a report about Yuda Cohen, deported on convoy 75.

The entire family is not well-disposed towards our country, therefore it is
imperative to:

---

* This the Vichy government Superintendant of Police.

   1-   Enlist Yuda Cohen and his son Raphael in a G.T.E
   2-   Strip the children of their French citizenship.

In his report of April 28, 1943, about Victor Revah, the husband of Esther Revah, Lebon wrote:

> The Jew Revah is a dubious individual on whom the following sanctions must be imposed:
> 1-   Immediate enlistment in a GTE
> 2-   Repatriation to his country of origin.

For Victor Revah, who was of Serbian origin, "repatriation" meant deportation and death.

Lebon produced tens of reports in the same frame of mind and the same style. It would be sufficient to only change the name and description of the victims. Lebon traveled to Nîmes, Uzès, Pont-St. Esprit, Villeneuve, Arles, Chateaurenard, Tarascon, and to the municipalities of Vaucluse. He was everywhere and did not spare a soul: hundreds of victims, among them the eight brave witnesses for the prosecution, were caught in the web of this hateful and relentless inspector.

Report against Elie Yaffe: "*In the course of the investigation, Yaffe and his wife dared criticize overtly the laws against the Jews… It is imperative to rid the national economy of these little foreign swindlers whose exact activity is impossible to verify.*"

Report against Moïse Yaffe: "*… It is imperative to rid the economy of these undesirable swindlers.*" He was particularly hounding the stallholders, amongst them Elie Yaffe and Moïse Yaffe, so much so that, on May 17, 1943, he provided his boss with two lists he had obtained from the prefecture: the list of "Foreign stallholders and peddlers" and that of "French stallholders and peddlers" which included some 68 people.[26] Lebon harassed them by having their circulation permits and licenses cancelled and by putting their stocks under provisional administration prior to their liquidation. For him, they represent the dregs of the Jewish population. Is that because the large majority were foreigners living amongst their own tribe, speaking among themselves a strange language, and their French was terrible? He hounded them relentlessly. He proposed internment for many.

The same activity occurred in the Gard. Lebon, a relentless Jew hunter, was on the lookout for the slightest opportunity to harm the Jews. He chased them from their businesses. They tried to redeploy to survive, and some became sales representatives. On July 10, 1943, he had their licenses cancelled, and provided a list of 21 Jewish sales representatives to his boss for action.[27] "*The needs of their families do not justify this profession*" he wrote in his report. He also observed that these licenses had been "*delivered or renewed to*

Jews by the prefecture of the Gard since January 1, 1943." He was watching the prefecture of the Gard very closely.

The reports filed by Lebon had ugly consequences. The people whom he proposed to be eliminated from the economy lost their jobs; those whose assets he proposed to aryanize were dispossessed and found themselves without any resources; those whom he had proposed be interned were practically all deported.

Overall, Lebon was the representative of a fraudulent ideology. In his thirst for power over the weakened Jews, he was like the gangsters in the service of the Germans. His belonging to the CGQJ provided him with an ideological base.

11. Jean Lebon and the SEC of Marseille Collaborate with the Germans

On February 12, 1943, the SD Aussenkommando (external detachment) in Avignon had asked the prefecture for the list of Jews residing in the *département* of Vaucluse ("ein namenlistiches Verzeichnis sämtlicher im Departement Vaucluse wohnenden Juden").[28] On February 17, Aimé Autrand responded in the name of the prefect "*I must inform you that only the regional prefects have the authority to eventually provide information of this nature.*" We can't help noticing that, in Autrand's response, there was no polite closing greeting. In the meantime, Lebon was charged by his boss with obtaining the list from the prefecture, which ended in failure, except for the list of stall-holders. Autrand resisted. A few months later, on October 4, 1943, the regional delegate of the SEC in Marseille, Raymond Guilledoux, picked up the issue again and wrote directly to the Prefecture of Vaucluse, which had been brought in step by the arrests of September 16, 1943, and the re-shuffling that followed:

> OBJECT: List of foreign Jews of the Vaucluse
> For a reason of opportunity, and because of the present circumstances, it is absolutely necessary for me to have the list of foreign Jews in the départements placed under our control.
> Consequently, I have the honor to ask you to send me this list pertaining to your département as quickly as possible.[29]

This time, Georges Darbou's prefecture complied, and the successor of Autrand responded in the affirmative to the regional delegate of the SEC.

> In response to your letter cited in reference, I have the honor to include in this letter, the list of foreign Jews presently in residence in my département.

Probably with the tacit agreement of Vichy or even in line with its instructions, the prefecture of Vaucluse was now ready again to sacrifice the foreign Jews of Vaucluse in the name of the "opportunity" mentioned by the regional delegate of the SEC. All the more so since it would be difficult to tie the prefect to the arrests of foreign Jews by the German police, or how it obtained their names, as will be shown in the court procedural files of Charles Palmieri and his Avignon acolytes.

In his deposition of November 18, 1948, after Liberation, the prefect Darbou testified:

> I witnessed several times the efforts carried out with persistence and silent fortitude by Pierre Laval to unclench the stranglehold, every day more brutal; and personally, I could cite cases when his vehement interventions and his action in general helped me or my colleagues save Israelites or heads of Resistance, or also French people often blindly arrested for having expressed their feelings against the occupier.[30]

Once again, foreign Jews were not "worthy of interest."

In his monthly report No. 29 of April 30, 1944, the regional delegate of the SEC in Marseille unveiled the recipients of the list of Jews in his possession as well as the quid pro quo of his collaboration:

> We are flooded with requests for information by the German Jewish affairs, but with the most perfect courtesy, without any unpleasant indiscretions or the lightest pressure or constraint… In general, I am getting all satisfaction from the side of the German Jewish affairs. So much so that immediately after an arrest is operated… the keys are given to me with the full power to dispose of the buildings and the apartments…
>
> As well in agreement with them [German Jewish affairs], I visit them every Thursday morning, in their offices, where we settle verbally the questions whose character does not seem urgent.[31]

12. Jean Lebon, his Colleagues and the German Police

The case of Henri Dreyfus clearly showed that Lebon had easy access to the German police.[32] A letter sent on December 22, 1943, by the regional delegate of the SEC in Marseille, to the regional prefect of Marseille confirms this:

> I have the honor to forward to you the attached list of personnel of the SEC of Marseille authorized to possess and bear a defensive weapon, according

to Article 3 of the law of December 2, 1942, in order to obtain from the offices of the Police administration, the required authorizations to bear arms.

Concerning these authorizations which, as I am aware, need to be submitted for approval to the Occupation Authorities, I have the honor to report to you that it is at the instigation of those authorities—who are awaiting them—that I am sending you the attached request.[33]

A list of seven inspectors of the SEC of the Marseille region, among them Jean Lebon of Avignon, was attached to this letter. On March 9, 1944, the director of the SEC for both zones gave his agreement for the weapon permit. The authorization was received at Avignon on March 15, 1944, and as we have seen, Lebon, armed with a revolver, was among the hoodlums leading the great roundup of March 29.

Given the mounting disillusionment of the Germans, it is clear that the head of the German police of Avignon, in tune with his boss in Marseille, was anxious to arm his most loyal and aggressive collaborators, miliciens, hoodlums, "French Gestapo," and PPF. There is therefore no doubt that Lebon was working in close coordination with the German police. It would not be surprising if this were also the case with his boss and colleagues of the SEC in Marseille.

Lebon was in good company. His boss Guilledoux wrote in his report of May 31, 1944, what a great man the head of the Jewish Section of the German police was:

> I must recognize once again the magnificent conduct of Kommandeur Bauer in executing the measures the opportunity of which I cannot comment upon, since they come from the High German Authorities, his chiefs.

This admiration for Bauer is surprising because he had put in place a Jew hunting network of hooligans and outlaws, which spanned the entire prefectural region of Marseille and sometimes beyond.

Moreover, in a note dated April 27, 1944, to Director of the SEC for the free zone in Paris about "The bearing of arms by the personnel of the delegations," Lebon's boss wrote: "*...MM. Lebon and Regereau are already armed, the first by the prefecture of Vaucluse, the second by the P.P.F...*"[34]

Apparently, Regereau, a Marseille colleague of Lebon, was also a man trusted by the PPF with the approval of his boss at the SEC. As in other parts of France, the rogues of the SEC of Marseille went wild and worked hand in hand with the gangs of hoodlums.[35] The prefectures were marginalized for the benefit of the German police and the thugs at their service.

Lebon became more radical and played into the hands of the Nazis while many others who had been favorable to them had already moved away.

Ironically, on March 29, 1944, the same day of the roundup against the Jews, Lebon was required to provide the proof that he was an Aryan, while he had never stopped requiring the same proof from others. On April 14, he responded to his boss: "*In response to your letter mentioned in the margin, I have the honor to provide you with the documents which prove in an undeniable way my Aryan origin. For smooth running, I would ask you to confirm receipt by return.*"

13. Was Jean Lebon Present at the Arrest of the Jews on March 29, 1944?

Two key documents destroy Jean Lebon's alibi. His alibi situated him in Marseille during the day and night of March 28, 1944. The notice of information of the special superintendent of the Renseignements Généraux, dated March 30, 1944, specified that the arrests of Jews took place during the night of March 29 to March 30, 1944, and not one day earlier.

> The German authorities conducted a vast police operation in Avignon during the night of March 29 to 30, 1944. This operation, started with a roundup in a café named Palais de la Bière, and continued with arrests in the homes.
>
> During this roundup, a great number of people of the Jewish race were arrested. The exact number of people arrested is still unknown. According to public rumors, it would be approximately 90.[36]

This document points to an apparent contradiction, as the witnesses were unclear about the exact date; some place the roundup on March 28 and others on March 29. Lebon took advantage of this ambiguity to brandish his alibi stating that he was not present on March 28. However, in another document, the interrogation on September 18, 1944, of Jean Gibelin, a member of the Palmieri gang, clarified the situation once and for all refuting Jean Lebon's alibi.

> … Towards the end of March, the Avignon agent, Lucien Blanc, came to the office [of Palmieri in Marseille] with a list of approximately sixty Israelites to be arrested in the area. This decided Charles [Palmieri] to make the raid together with the SD of Avignon.
>
> Charles, Alfred [the brother of Charles Palmieri], Simon, Francois Heiter, and the Avignon [French] agents participated in this operation. The operation lasted two days and yielded the arrest of approximately 40 people from our lists; they were all turned over to the SD of Avignon.[37]

There were two days of roundups, on March 28 and on March 29. This practically lifted the veil of doubt about the dates cited by the witnesses as well as by Jean Lebon, and weakened his defense. Jean Lebon was indeed present at Avignon on the evening of March 29, and had no alibi. He was now face-to-face with the witnesses.

Had Lebon finally taken the "law" into his own hands in his anti-Jewish fervor? If so, the increasing half-heartedness of the prefecture would paradoxically have helped his pro-German drift.

The Imminent Return of "Republican Order"

Pretty late, Lebon took some—perhaps naïve—precautions, in his writing about his relations with the Gestapo. On June 13, 1944, seven days after the landing in Normandy, he wrote in his report to his boss the location of his office: "*As you ordered, I contacted the police of the AO,* which gave me a list of 50 names and addresses. Since no key had been provided and on the advice of the G— I went to the Quartieramt†…*" At this late date, it was ill advised to write Gestapo in full.

From then on events followed quickly, and on July 7, 1944, Lebon's boss informed him that the Secretary General instructed him to broadcast the following text: "*Agents of the CGQJ, stay at your post without taking care of anything! Should instructions be necessary, be assured that I will give them in due course.*" On August 17, 1944, 12 days ahead of the liberation of Marseille, the regional delegate send a letter to Lebon that began: "*I have the honor to inform you that you are relieved of your job as inspector starting August 31, 1944. In accordance with the law, you are entitled to accrued benefits and to one month's advance notice.*"

Lebon wasn't waiting at the door of the SEC in Marseille for the reopening of the offices after Liberation, like some of his Paris colleagues.[38] He was arrested in Chateaurenard on August 29, 1944, without the full benefit of his month of advance notice. On October 4, 1944, the police superintendant, Marcel Sancelme, described the last weeks of Lebon on the run, in his statement countersigned by the CDL and the Municipal Council of Chateaurenard.

> … We conducted a complete investigation of Jean Lebon … functionary of the CGQJ of Marseille, arrested in Chateaurenard on August 29, 1944, and transferred to Arles on September 13, 1944.

---

* Autorités d'Occupation (Occupation Authorities).
† The Intendant.

According to the new municipality and the CDL, the activity of the named was negative in Chateaurenard,* where he sought refuge at the end of the month of July or the beginning of the month of August, in an isolated farm. He was going out frequently at night on a motorcycle, but starting August 15, the date of the allied landing in the southern France, he stopped going out. According to public rumor, he was expecting to be arrested at any moment. He had not hidden his activity in the CGQJ, which provided him with some promotions...[39]

From Arles, Lebon was transferred to the Ste Anne prison and handed over to the Court of Justice in Avignon.

At the end of this examination, one question remains open: why did the Court of Justice not even try once to obtain the administrative documents produced during Lebon's tenure? It was peculiar because, during his confrontation with Henri Kohn, Lebon had mentioned the existence of these documents in Marseille. During the same period, other Courts of Justice, for instance in Paris, had examined thousands of documents during the investigation phase of the trials against members of the SEC and other branches of the CGQJ.

This omission was indicative of a minimalist form of justice which spared Jean Lebon the death penalty. The judicial apparatus of the Liberation was caught between two contradictory pressures. The new state realized that in order to govern, it must calm the people and restore a more serene justice, while the CDL demanded, in the name of public opprobrium, that actions be taken against the collaborators—big and small. In this conflict between the central power and the new local leaders, the needs for justice for the Jews was not a priority since they were not demanding it and French society was still steeped in anti-Semitic reflexes that had blossomed before and during the war. It is easy to imagine, on the other hand, Lebon's fate, if his victims had been Resistance fighters. For the Jews of 1944, Liberation was slow in coming.

To conclude, we return to Jean Lebon. In the darkness that surrounds his character, one case deserves to be mentioned. On June 17, 1943, his boss sent him a request for an investigation, triggered by the SEC of Vichy against Jane Mayrargues of Carpentras, following a denunciation by her tenant, Mme. Latard.[40] Lebon went to work, and on July 27, 1943, he wrote a report that is surprisingly conciliatory in its attitude towards Jane Mayrargues.

From the investigation, it appears that:

---

* This is obviously misinformed to the light of the complaint of Lebon against the police superintendant of Chateaurenard for helping Jews.

1- The revenue from her apartment buildings constitute the sole resource of the Jewess Mayrargues.

2- This person—who is handicapped—constantly needs a home nurse, Mme. Boyac, who lives in her home with her children and has little living space. This justifies the request from Mme. Latard to leave the apartment.

3- Moreover, the private life of Mme. Latard <u>who is said to receive night visits</u>* is the main reason for her eviction.

Now, Lebon's boss in Marseille took a tougher stand, depriving a Jewish handicapped woman of her revenues: *"Consequently, I am asking the director of the AE* [Aryanisation Economique] *to place the assets of the woman Mayrargues under the control of an AP."*

Could Lebon have been capable of some human feeling, at least once, after all?

---

* Underlined by Jean Lebon.

Chapter 5

A State-Sponsored Network
of Profiteers of Jewish Assets

The aryanization of an estate, the Domaine de la Gardine, through its
transfer to a provisional administrator and its sale to a buyer, and later
the return of the assets to the original owner, are at the same time typical and
exceptional. Such a "double success" was unusual. The reality of profiteering
will become clear, as we discuss additional examples. The need for a systematic in-depth study of the spoliations in Vaucluse, which has yet to be done,
remains.

The Domaine de la Gardine in Châteauneuf-du-Pape

> There was a master, who planted a vineyard.
> He put a wall around it, dug a winepress and built a watchtower…[1]

This is the beginning of the parable of the Wicked Vineyard Laborers which
Gaston Brunel cites in his 1980 book, *The Guide of Vine-growers and Cellars of the
Côtes du Rhône,** where he informs us that, after Liberation, he too constructed
a tower at La Gardine, thus creating its castle-like appearance, but he remains
silent about the history of the estate before Liberation.[2]

---

* Original French title: *Le Guide des Vignerons et Caves de Côtes du Rhône.*

The case of La Gardine, at the time an estate producing wine with the "appellation contrôlée" of Châteauneuf du Pape, spanned both the "reigns" of de Camaret and of Lebon. De Camaret had in Châteauneuf du Pape a reliable informer, himself a wine-grower wary of the purity of the land. According to the bill of sale, this property had belonged, since July 3, 1933, "*to Mme.* [Marie] *Esther Gommez-Pereire, the spouse of Alfred Isaac Rodrigues Pereire, man of letters, Knight of the Legion of Honor, with whom she lives in Paris, rue du Faubourg St. Honoré No. 35.*"[3] In 1941, Alfred Pereire had been denied a special dispensation from the measures against the Jews, which he had requested by invoking the services rendered to France by his famous family, since the time of Louis XV, and personally rendered by him to the Bibliothèque Nationale, as a volunteer librarian, curator, and patron.[4]

The Domaine de la Gardine, managed by a master farmhand for the benefit of Marie Pereire, was confiscated by de Camaret and taken under the provisional administration of Georges Bonjean in July 1942. The property was then unsuccessfully put up for sale on May 29, 1943, following an auction organized by M. Charles Rivollier, notaire in Châteauneuf du Pape and mayor of the village. Then, several candidates turned up amid intrigues and envy.

First, there was Joseph Casimir Charrasse, a cardboard manufacturer in Orange, member of the PPF, and an informer to the Palmieri gang, who wanted the "Jewish" agricultural property of La Gardine. Charrasse then became the target of schemes by Bonjean, who proposed as a buying partner, his own brother-in-law, Roger de Bimard, land owner, president of the Legion at Châteauneuf du Pape, and a member of the de Camaret network. The ploy did not work. Probably under pressure from Bonjean, the prefecture of Vaucluse refused to grant Charrasse a permit to farm, because he did not have professional experience.

After Charrasse complained, Jean Lebon was assigned to investigate. Indignant, he wrote in his report of September 30, 1943: "*Monsieur Charrasse, Aryan, known and respected and with money behind him, looked like a serious buyer.*"[5] In fact the cardboard manufacturer was so drawn to the property that he promised to change his profession and become a wine-maker for the rest of his life. Jean Lebon, a hoodlum from the SEC, came forward as a guarantor of Charrasse, an accomplice of Palmieri. But the Domaine de la Gardine was already sold in July 1943.

Charrasse, the cardboard manufacturer, did not measure up to the new buyer, Gaston Brunel, the descendant of a long line of wine-makers since 1670. On May 28, 1943, Jean Lebon was charged by the CGQJ of Marseille to investigate Brunel, domiciled at 1 Impasse de la Gravière in Avignon, *"candidate to buy the following Jewish asset: Domaine of La Gardine, Châteauneuf du Pape (Vaucluse)."* Jean Lebon delivered the result of his investigation in June 1943:

> Monsieur Brunel is well known in Avignon and enjoys an excellent reputation; he would be desirous of buying the property of La Gardine, in order to develop it. He has the money; half of it is his own, half would be lent by the Comptoir National d'Escompte de Paris with the Crédit Foncier.
>
> However, it should be noted that this eventual buyer does not seem prepared to buy this property <u>for fear of being subsequently dispossessed;</u>* these are his words.

Jean Lebon underscored the hesitation of Gaston Brunel, who was clearly in the know as a buyer. Was he hesitating in order to be asked twice, and thus lower the price? The fact remains that on July 10, 1943, the Domaine de la Gardine passed from the hands of the state, which had confiscated it, to Gaston Brunel for the amount of 1,250,000 francs. One can understand the anger of Charrasse when he realized that the coveted bargain had slipped through his fingers.

In the office of the Conservation des Hypothèques,† the property was described as follows. It spanned *"61 hectares, 10 of which planted with vines, appellation contrôlée of Châteauneuf du Pape, four hectares of arable land and 47 hectares of woods."* It included *"master houses with all modern conveniences, central heating, telephone, electricity and running water; a farmer's house, shed, hanger, stable, sheepfold, cellar, and vats."* In the cellar, there were *"18 casks of wine,"* equal to 4,104 liters, at 228 liters per cask. The vineyard was already productive. La Gardine was already in the land registry of 1763, which mentioned the *"Maitairie‡ de la Gardine."* Its wine was awarded a prize in 1868 in Montpellier where it was granted *"a silver medal…for a wine which had four colors, 13° of alcohol and which was mellow, very fine and very distinguished."*[6]

Everything was fine until Liberation, and exactly as Brunel had feared, the Jewish owner returned. Things should have gone like clockwork for the legitimate owner because *"on January 5, 1943, 17 allied governments and the national committee of General de Gaulle signed a solemn declaration which held as null and void all the transfers of properties or rights carried out in occupied countries"* and on November 12, 1943, an ordinance in Algiers reiterated this declaration.[7] Moreover, a new ordinance of August 9, 1944, prescribed the immediate

---

* Underlined by Jean Lebon.
† Repository of Mortgages.
‡ Smallholding.

restoration of republican legality, as the territory was liberated. The laws of Vichy were cancelled. Only a "small" problem remained: the decrees of application of the ordinances would drag because of the "complications" linked to restitution in a case like the Domaine de la Gardine. It had been easy to dispossess the Pereire family. But the new owner was handled with kid gloves, although he was well aware that La Gardine was snatched from a Jew, as it was recorded in the bill of sale at the Conservation des Hypothèques on July 10, 1943.

After having put in place the application decrees for the simplest cases, the government finally promulgated, on April 21, 1945, an application decree canceling the dispossessions carried out by the Germans and the Vichy government, including commercial real estate placed under provisional administration, and then sold.

This ordinance adopted a very simple solution. Article 17 gave the plaintiff the choice between the Civic and the Commercial Court. The procedure was an accelerated one, the référé or summary proceedings, gave the judge the power of decision on form and content. Any appeal had to be filed within 15 days from the date of the decision. The president of the tribunal could designate any useful expert, and all this at no cost to the plaintiff.

Article 4 stated *"The buyer or the buyers are considered as possessors in bad faith with respect to the dispossessed owner. They can in no way invoke the right of retention. They must return the natural, industrial and civil fruits starting on the date of the nullification…"* The "bad faith" clause was automatically assumed in this article because the buyer could not have ignored that the assets had belonged to a Jew. This was clearly the case of Gaston Brunel.

For that matter, the general report of the Matteoli mission had qualified the spoliation of Jewish assets as "civil theft"—an expression that was both eloquent and surprising.[8] As soon as the decree-law was promulgated, the Civic Court of Orange was requested to settle the La Gardine case. The buyer had to return the property *"whose origin he could not have ignored"* and reimburse the profits wrongfully made. The law allowed the buyer to recover the amount paid at the time of purchase, namely 1,250,000 francs in this case. However (Article 6), *"… Out of the amount to be returned to the buyer, there will be, for the benefit of the Treasury, a deduction of 10 p 100 of its acquisition* [price]*, when it was made in bad faith."*

Article 6 also stated that *"…the brokerage commissions paid either to advertisement agents, to real estate agents or to business agents of any kind by the CGQJ or by provisional administrators, will be reimbursed by these after deducting gross fees for which they are required to provide justification… The same will apply to honoraria received by experts, architects or others, who have lent their help to these preliminary expert operations and hence have permitted or facilitated the despoiled assets being put up for sale."*

Article 16 specified that the state would reimburse the salaries of provisional administrators, because they were designated by the state.

Who are the "table companions" of the spoliation of La Gardine? Of course, Bonjean, the AP who received a salary from July 1942 to July 1943, de Camaret and Lebon who supervised the process, Rivollier, notaire in Châteauneuf du Pape, André Pochy, furniture appraiser in Avignon, the printer of the auction posters, the newspapers, etc. The ads were placed in *L'Eclair*, the newspaper where de Camaret worked, in *Le Nouvelliste*, in *Les Tablettes du Soir*, and in *Le Bulletin du Palais*. The costs of publicity amounted to 11,000 francs, and the fees of M. Rivollier to 1,500 francs, but there are no traces of such reimbursement. Perhaps the state had other fish to fry than to render unto Pereire that which was Pereire's.

As to Gaston Brunel, he had to pay the owner 280,000 francs, which corresponded to the exploitation of the estate and a lump sum for the use, according to the principle of Article 4 and 6 of the law of April 21, 1945.

Then, an amicable agreement took place between Gaston Brunel and Esther Marie Gommez Pereire. In a final agreement, the property was sold back to Gaston Brunel by Mme. Pereire for 1,250,000 francs, the same amount as the original purchase of 1943. This was surprising for two reasons. The first because the value of the property at the time of the initial sale from the state to Brunel was probably significantly higher than the sale price, given that the estate had been auctioned with only one competitor who stopped after an offer of 1,200,000 francs against a starting bid of 1,000,000 francs. The buyers weren't exactly queuing up at M. Rivollier's office. The second reason is that, between 1943 and 1945, the franc had lost approximately 45% of its value, which brought the 1945 price to 687,500 francs of 1943[9] (see Appendix A).

It looked like a bargain for the buyer. He took care of his vineyard himself, and did not have to face the difficulties of the landowner of the Parable of the Tenants.[10] Did Brunel know the rest of the parable, citing only the beginning? Indeed, after having erected the tower, the master:

> … let his vineyard to laborers, and went to a far away country. And the time of the fruit drew near, he sent his servants to the laborers that they might receive the fruit of it. And the laborers took his servants, and beat one, and killed another, and stoned another. Again, he sent other servants more than the first time, and they did unto them likewise. But last of all, he sent to them his son, saying: They will revere my son. But when the laborers saw the son, they said

among themselves, this is the heir; come, let us kill him, and let us seize his inheritance. And they caught him, and cast him out of the vineyard, and slew him. When the master of the vineyard comes, what will he do unto those laborers? They say unto him, He will miserably destroy those wicked men, and will let out his vineyard unto other laborers who shall render him the fruits in their seasons.

Jesus said unto them: Did you never read in the Scriptures: The stone which the builders rejected, the same is become the head of the corner; This is the Lord's doing, and it is marvelous? Therefore say I unto you, The kingdom of God shall be taken from you, and given to a nation bringing forth the fruit thereof. And whoever shall fall on this stone shall be broken, but on whomever it shall fall, it will grind him to powder.

And when the chief priests and Pharisees had heard his parables, they perceived that he spoke of them. But when they sought to lay their hands on him, they feared the multitude, because they took him for a prophet.

"He will miserably destroy those wicked men, and will let out his vineyard unto other laborers who shall render him the fruits in their seasons." Was the Holocaust written into a parable?

The Château de l'Hers

Again in Châteauneuf du Pape, the domaine de l'Hers and two of his residents, Henri and Victor Goldblum, attracted the attention of the small network of vigilant notables. Neighbors of the Domaine de la Gardine, in an out-of-the-way area of the village, the Goldblum brothers were two more undesirables in the eyes of the "guardians of the land," Mayor Rivollier, de Bimard and Louis Raynaud,* the eyes and the ears of de Camaret in Châteauneuf.

The fact is that, on August 25, 1941, Autrand's office was preparing a *"list (established after verification of the census provided by the municipalities of the département) of the individuals presumed Jewish who have not registered according to the law of June 2, 1941."*[11] The list in question included 22 names; among them Henri and Victor Goldblum, designated as Jews by mayor Rivollier, according to Autrand's request.

On September 12, 1941, the director of the CGQJ in Vichy asked the prefecture for an explanation to be provided before October 1. On September 30, one day before the deadline, the Autrand division reported that 6

---

* Louis Raynaud, a wine grower from Châteauneuf du Pape and a member of de Camaret informers network.

people, including the Goldblum brothers, "have signed a sworn statement, stating that they are not Jewish."[12]

The CGQJ reacted quickly, and on October 8, the answer was clear: *"…the sworn statements provided by the individuals…Henri and Victor Goldblum…attesting that they do not belong to the Jewish race are insufficient to excuse them from the registration mandated by the law… They need to justify that two of their grandparents and they, themselves, belonged to a religion other than the Israelite religion before June 25, 1940."* That ended the discussion, since the Goldblum brothers did not have a single Gentile grandparent, and so they were recorded in the first census of the Vaucluse.

On November 14, 1941, Henri Goldblum informed the prefecture that his brother Victor had left the village, but this did not prevent Autrand and his successor from keeping Victor Goldblum in the census until its last update in May 1944.

This was not the end of it. The Domaine de l'Hers, a beautiful wine-producing estate, next to La Gardine, caught the eye of de Camaret who pursued the issue with Lebon. In a letter of August 12, 1942, about the issue: *"Investigation of the property of the Jew Henri Goldblum, Domaine de l'Hers in Châteauneuf du Pape,"* de Camaret asked Henri Goldblum for the date he bought the Domaine and for the name of the notaire, and whether he farmed it or gave it in tenancy.[13] On August 14, 1942, Henri Goldblum responded and mentioned the Terrier family as owners, a fact confirmed by de Camaret on August 19. In spite of the mention of the Terrier family, de Camaret wrote his boss in Marseille, on March 18, 1943, that he continued his *"Investigation about the properties of Jews—Domaine de l'Hers,"* this time without mentioning Goldblum or Terrier:

> Monsieur Lebon, inspector of the SEC, has compiled a report concerning this property, where he concludes that it must be put under provisional administration.
>
> I am proposing to designate M. Georges Bonjean (3, avenue de la Violette, Avignon) who appears particularly qualified to take care of this Domaine which is adjacent to the Domaine de la Gardine, which he is already in charge of.[14]

But this case did not move further, and the property did not change hands.

We know today that several plots that make up the Domaine de l'Hers had been bought between October 21, 1937, and March 1, 1940, by Stanislas Terrier in the name of his underaged sons—Christian, Bernard and Georges, born in Switzerland in 1918, 1920, and 1922, respectively. Stanislas himself was born in Geneva on November 1, 1890. The purchases had all been concluded at the office of the almighty Charles Rivollier.[15]

But actually, Stanislas Terrier was the brother of Henri and Victor Goldblum.[16] He kept the Goldblum name until the beginning of the thirties, when he arranged for an "adoption" by the Terrier family of Geneva. He also converted to Christianity at that time. Nevertheless, the laws on Aryanization of Jewish assets applied to Stanislas Terrier and his sons. This information probably came from Rivollier who knew the relationship between Stanislas, Henri and Victor; then it must have made its way amongst the members of the Châteauneuf establishment, and from there to de Camaret, always on the lookout for a good opportunity to serve the notables.

However, a small problem came up: the legitimate Jewish owners were Swiss citizens, a fact that limited the reach of the anti-Jewish measures. A Swiss provisional administrator could eventually be designated, but the property could not be sold.[17] It was quite possible that the CGQJ of Marseille was backing down from a complicated procedure which would not yield any benefit or that it did not want to touch assets it knew were protected. The fact remains that the Domaine de l'Hers was untouched throughout the duration of the war.

The Issue of Provisional Administrators and "Certificates of Deficiency"

The frustrations of Henri de Camaret's bosses, the administrator of the provisional administrators, and later, a provisional administrator himself, were probably linked to the number of properties for which no buyer could be found. Despite the relentlessness of de Camaret, d'Ornano and Lebon, a significant number of seized Jewish properties remained under provisional administration for too long and were finally declared unsellable. A "certificate of deficiency" was then issued. This "unfortunate" situation, which was the cause of stress between the CGQJ of Marseille and that of Avignon, was not limited to the Vaucluse and seems to have become widespread, to wit several letters, the first one dated at the beginning of April 1943, and sent by Louis Pimpaneau, the assistant general director of the CGQJ.

> Generally speaking, I had the opportunity to notice that, except for a few unfortunately too rare cases, too large a number of provisional administrators still consider their mandate as a sinecure and do not meet my expectations.
>
> They are losing sight of their mission which is not to restrict themselves to managing a Jewish business, but to get it Aryanized.

As a result, the Aryanization trails behind and for the remunerations being calculated for an Aryanization performed within normal delays, the amount pocketed reaches numbers out of proportion with the work done and the responsibilities involved.

In order to remedy this state of affairs, I have decided to take the following measure:

"Starting with the seventh month of management, every remuneration will automatically be reduced by 50%, being clearly understood that the provisional administrator must, in accordance with my instructions, draw the entire amount and deposit the difference to account 611 at the Caisse des Dépôts et Consignation in Clermont-Ferrand"...[18]

Pimpaneau pinned the problem on the provisional administrators, who of course had everything to gain in letting the sale drag, as long as they were paid and not compelled to too big an effort. This circular memo was intended to whiplash the team into action.

A letter from Lebon's boss dated February 16, 1944, revealed the hidden motive of the "rush for provisional administration."

As a follow up to our recent conversation, I would be grateful if you would send me—marked "Private"—the documentation allowing me to take on the case of the APs who have been dismissed in Vaucluse for the benefit of people from the Gard (name, address, business name, date of their dismissal, official reason invoked, for whose benefit, eventually also family ties or friendship relations with who you know).

Finally, I most interested in the cases of unsold enterprises.

I understand, indeed, the profit that may result, for some, from the method, and I am desirous to narrow down the origin of the "light that will enlighten you."*[19]

"Family ties or friendship relations" of the APs—rather than competence—were not expected to encourage speedy sales of Jewish assets. Robert Carayol, subordinate of Pimpaneau and director of the CGQJ for the free zone (regions of Clermont-Ferrand, Limoges, Lyon, Marseille, Nice, and Toulouse) also noticed a "conspiracy" of *notaires* regarding the Aryanization of Jewish assets.

In numerous cases, Aryanization is delayed by the lack of good will of the notaires designated by the President of the Chamber of Notaires.

---

* We left the original insinuation where Lebon is asked for names.

This obstruction has sometimes been a systematic and generalized characteristic… It often looks like it is the response to a watchword.

Consequently, it is recommended that the regional directors end without
delay the procedure currently used in the selection of notaires.

Are we really witnessing a conspiracy of the *notaires*? A small number, like
M. Geoffroy, did their best to help some Jews, who had been their clients
before the war, by hampering the sale through procedural maneuvering. But
this small number doesn't explain everything. Did the *notaires*, who were
cautious members of the establishment, simply realize that it was not easy to
sell Jewish assets? Indeed, the inability to buy some of the properties with
cash-in-hand and the eventual return of the victims discouraged potential
buyers who were careful with their money.

During the session of the CDL regarding the Chamber of *Notaires* on
January 27, 1945, M. Geoffroy, named president of the Chamber of *Notaires*
at Liberation, declared: "*In their majority, the notaires, without displaying a collaborating spirit towards the Germans, remained favorable to the Pétain regime.*"[20] Of
course, their fees might have had something to do with it.

This situation, prevalent in the Vaucluse, was also found on a national
scale, if one believes what the CGQJ circulars say.[21]

The Garson Apartment Buildings

According to a report by Jean Lebon dated April 1, 1943, Samuel Garson,
born in Oran in 1888, was married to Zohara, née Bettan, in 1890. They had
four children, and they jointly owned a ready-to-wear garment store for men
at 60, rue Carnot in Avignon, and they lived at 26, rue du Chapeau Rouge.
They also owned "rental and business buildings" at 22 and 24, rue Carreterie,
at 26, 28, and 30, rue du Chapeau Rouge, and at 67, rue Bonneterie. Except
for their store and home, the other buildings were rented out; they yielded a
gross revenue of approximately 50,000 francs per year. They paid 6,000
francs per year for the rental of their store at 60, rue Carnot.[22]

The report concluded: "*The investigation has revealed no infraction to the Statute
of the Jews by Garson, he is known as an honest tradesman, his war wound and his
pension justify no exemption, it is imperative to place his business and his buildings under
provisional administration.*"

De Camaret was chosen as provisional administrator (*administrateur provisoire* or AP) on May 17, 1943.[23] On May 26, 1943, he warned M. Marchais,
building manager, about the new dispositions: "*You will have to contact me for all
questions related to these buildings, and to pay only to me, the amounts of the rents.*"

These rents were feeding the checking accounts opened in the name of the CGQJ by de Camaret, and contributed to paying for the expenses incurred by the provisional administrators, in the same way as revenues from other buildings.

In February 1944 Bonnet, a man from Nîmes, became AP of the Garson store at 60, rue Carnot. Was Bonnet one of those from the Gard, favored by *"family ties or friendship relations with who you know,"* as mentioned in the afore-mentioned note by Lebon's boss?

The fact remained that the assets of the Garson family remained unsold, and a deficiency was declared on June 5, 1944. However, in the Garson case, as in most other cases, de Camaret "had just done his job" a fact for which the court expressed little interest.

The Aryanization of René David's Assets: The Administrators Line Their Own Pockets

René David owned a canned food plant in Carpentras.[24] On February 14, 1942, Louis de Serre de Saint-Roman was named provisional administrator by decree in the Journal Officiel. On September 5, 1942, he was replaced by Jean Gaugler who remained in that position until April 28, 1944. On October 20, 1944, René David wrote:

> Due to the size of my sales, their salary was 7,400 francs per month; of course, as soon my business was taken over by these individuals, my sales dropped to zero, because I had refused to collaborate.

The manufacturing plant had sales of 3,391,706 Francs in 1941! René David added *"My business was put up for sale by Gaugler, but it could not be sold due to the lack of buyer."* A note of April 28, 1944, in the Registry of Commerce by René David informed that "Jean Gaugler, provisional administrator, declares in the name of René David: the Cessation of all professional activity."

René David also owned 50 or so shares of the Société Anonyme des Etablissements Sautel in Mazan. These shares, which entitled him to a posi-tion of delegate-administrator of this company, were sold to Sautel himself by Gaugler for the amount of 50,000 francs. At Liberation, Sautel did not release his grasp that easily, and on September 16, 1944, he wrote to René David *"These shares are kept at your disposal in exchange for the payment of the price which Monsieur Gaugler must have provided you with an accounting for, if the sale which was effected has been nullified."* If René David wanted to recover the shares that were stolen from him, he could always buy them back!

In his declaration of despoiled assets, René David wrote:

> On the other hand, Gaugler never accounted for the proceeds of this sale
> and kept the money for himself, probably in order to pay his own salary which
> amounted to 7,400 francs per month.
>
> Consequently, I demand the immediate restitution of my shares, as I deem
> with good reason that it is scandalous to see how buyers of dispossessed assets
> keep for themselves assets which they could acquire only by becoming receivers
> of stolen goods and accomplices of the thieves of dispossessed assets.
>
> While I hope for a speedy answer, I must express my saddened feelings.

While René David was going to great lengths to recover what belonged
to him and to restart his ransacked business, Gaugler was already on the run.

Cattle Trade

In the rural France of those days, where the cattle trade was closely tied to
farmland culture, the Statute of the Jews raised the hope of eliminating competition. Monsieur Jean Bonafous, manufacturer of fruit and vegetable
packaging in Cavaillon, "veteran 1914/1918, Legionnaire No. 213 278," expressed this sentiment when he wrote on December 5, 1941, an inflamed
four-page letter to Xavier Vallat, General Commissioner for Jewish questions.
Bonafous advocated in favor of his son-in-law, "*Jean Gaubert, a native of the
Ariège, of French extraction, Catholic. Before the war, he was practicing modestly with his
father who continues it, the trade of dairy cows.*" He added:

> I did fix up for him in one of the facilities at my business: a stable where he
> set up his trade of dairy cows, and modestly shuttling between Cavaillon and the
> Ariège, he would bring every time 3 or 4 cows which he sold at reasonable prices
> that were far below those set by the Jews in the area. This was a severe mistake
> which prompted these gentlemen whose fiefdoms are the Vaucluse and the
> adjoining départements to focus their hatred on him.
>
> Then a law was enacted to regulate the profession. On October 21, 1940, he
> applied for a professional card… It was refused for no known reason…
>
> In the mean time, Monsieur Charles Levy, a schemer refugee from Belfort
> associated himself with the Chabran brothers, sheep traders in Cavaillon…
>
> Neither had been authorized to add to their trade of sheep that of cows, but
> [they] carried on anyway without being bothered… they were able to sell 181
> cows and 66 calves.
>
> In such a state of affairs, my son-in-law continued his small trade, which
> lasted until June 10 [1940], the day when the intervention of the Jew Walch, the
> grand master behind the stage at the Purchasing bureau for cattle and meat

sharing in Vaucluse (GARBVV), forbade my son-in-law from continuing his trade and seized four cows and three calves…

On October 20, 1941, I confirmed to the prefect…that Charles Levy was continuing to exercise his profession and had carried out his audacity to the point of settling in front of the gendarmerie…

You see, Monsieur [Vallat], in Vaucluse, the Jews still are the masters and they make it known. If one does not put it in order, they will continue for a long time…

According to statistics, 97% of the trade of dairy cows is occupied [*sic*] by Jews. I think that after the enforcement of the law, there will be room for French men without any distinction of département and that to your kindness I am calling on, my son-in-law will be indebted for having his place.[25]

In fact, Charles Levy had been authorized on November 12, 1941, by the regional delegate of the CGQJ to transfer his business from Belfort to Cavaillon. He was practicing his trade legally, whether Bonafous liked it or not. However, the law had just changed. On December 11, 1941, Xavier Vallat wrote to the prefect:

I have the honor to let you know that, by application of the law of November 17, 1941, modifying Article 5 of the Law of June 2, 1941, the person in question will have to immediately cease his activity in this branch which is henceforth forbidden to him.

The modified article 5 indeed contained a new interdiction, that of "Trade in grain, cereals, horses, cattle." Among others the law touched Samuel Mossé of Orange, and Bigard and Walch of Avignon. These two companies were rapidly put under provisional administration and sold.[26]

The Small Businesses of the Stallholders

On February 3, 1943, Lebon took on the Sokolowski family. In his report about Icko, the father, he wrote: "*SUBJECT: The Sokolowski is brought to our attention as an agent of Anglo-Saxon propaganda and as an important trader of dry goods against food supplies.*" A few paragraphs later, he reported the failure of his investigation: "*The inquiry has not allowed to verify the veracity of the information provided about the activity of Solokolowski both on the national level and on the economic level. This verification would require a pretty long tailing. Nevertheless, it is appropriate to think that the frequent travel which his stallholder's job allows him, could uniquely facilitate his trade and black market operations.*" In spite of the absence of any proof, Lebon concluded in the report which he sent to the prefecture of Vaucluse:

> From the aforementioned explanation, it appears:
>
> 1. that Sokolowski is a Polish Jew
> 2. that he was naturalized in November 1938
> 3. that his commercial activity is suspect
> 4. that he and his family constitute undesirable elements within the French nation
> 5. that it is not with a turnover of 120,000 Francs, (with a profit of 15,000 Francs) that he can maintain such a family where 3 children are studying and that he has found the means to buy a 50,000 Francs property.

> Consequently, I am asking the prefect of Vaucluse, with copy to the regional prefect, that the decree of naturalization of Sokolowski be reversed, that this Jew be brought to the attention of the economic police and that his circulation beyond the limits of the city of Avignon be immediately prohibited; at the moment when restrictions are becoming progressively more cruel, it is unacceptable and dangerous that Jews are able to find supplies as they please.[27]

In a new sign of disagreement with the SEC, Aimé Autrand, the addressee for the implementation of this request, wrote with a pencil "?Why?" with two question marks, next to the third conclusion.

On April 22, 1943, Lebon wrote a report about Saltiel (Jacques) Yenni. He proposed to cancel his registration on the Registre du Commerce and his travel permit, and to enlist him in a *Groupement de Travailleurs Etrangers* (GTE or Camp for foreign workers). A few days earlier it was the turn of Moïse Yaffe. Under his influence, the CGQJ wrote at the same time, on April 22, 1943, to the prefecture of Vaucluse (Division D1-B2 of Autrand) a note reminding him of the objectives of the law of November 17, 1941:

> "In order to eliminate any Jewish influence on the national economy, the General Commissioner for Jewish Questions can designate a provisional administrator to any enterprise…"
>
> By virtue of this text, I have already provided provisional administrators to a number of Jewish stallholders, and the investigations which were carried out by my services on this occasion revealed that by their type of activity, they were important agents of black market and antigovernment propaganda.

I have decided to get all the Jewish stallholders erased from the Registre du Commerce [Business Registry] and to ask you to be kind enough to carry out the retrieval of their professional cards.

… I will be obliged to you if you send me with the shortest possible delay the list of all the Jewish stallholders, who have received a permit in your département.

These Jews will immediately be provided a provisional administrator…

On May 5, 1943, all the regional offices received a general circular from Pimpaneau in the same vein. Since the prefecture laid low and did not respond, Lebon's boss sent him a reminder on June 12, 1943:

… the application of the measures ordered by the CGQJ could be implemented only if the list of Jewish stallholders were communicated to us by the prefect of Vaucluse, as it was required by the letter from Vichy mentioned as a reference. It is up to you to have this list sent to us as quickly as possible…[28]

Lebon finally received the list he had asked for form the prefecture, strangely dated May 17, 1943, a few weeks before the reminder by Lebon's boss. Was the earlier date given to the list or was the list ready to be sent if Lebon were to insist? Anyway, it contains the names of 64 foreigners and 22 French men.

De Camaret who had been named AP of Yenni's business, wrote to the regional manager on June 21, 1943:

In agreement with M. Lebon who had notified you about Saltiel Yenni, I have the honor to specify:
- that this is about a stallholder
- that I have not been appraised of anything unfavorable about Yenni
- that there are in the département around one hundred stallholders like him, whose list has been sent to the SEC in Marseille
- that M. Lebon had asked to erase them from the Registre du Commerce
- that this global step would have eliminated their possible influence
- that most of them have a relatively small quantity of merchandise
- that this merchandise can easily be concealed and could in numerous cases elude the investigations of AP

Consequently, I would like to ask you to tell me whether I must, in accordance with my mission, take control of the Yenni business as a normal enterprise. If I am expected to limit myself to get him crossed off the Registre du Commerce, and in this case, am I empowered to do it directly or am I supposed to ask the prefecture to do it? Or do I need to wait for a global crossing off? ...[29]

There was no response from the Marseille offices, but the facts on the ground were: Jewish stallholders practiced their profession on the open market of the place Pie in Avignon, despite the cancellation of their permits. To get by, they had to stay put, prisoners of their stalls, until the upsurge in the arrests of Jews in March 1944. This clear threat of deportation made fleeing a necessary option.

The CGQJ did not spare efforts in dealing ruthlessly with the owners of the largest enterprises placed under provisional administration. The other small businesses which managed to take advantage of the confusion at the CGQJ for drawing, like the stallholders, some meager profits, were nevertheless harassed. This pushed a number of Jewish merchants into semi-clandestine activity, like Jean-Michel Dreyfus among many others.

> Having moved away to Avignon... he employs workers already employed by other leather craftsmen and who work at home for him after hours... Dreyfus goes by himself to sell to various stores the goods manufactured in this way; the very small volume of these goods allows them to be manufactured with the greatest ease...

This is how de Camaret described the activity of Dreyfus on May 22, 1942, and he added *"Herclich and Janover (unregistered Jews in the Vaucluse) are also said to clandestinely produce goods, a portion of which is said to be distributed by Dreyfus... Janover has 11 children."*[30] This report was communicated by the regional director of the Aryanization service of the CGQJ in Marseille to the heads of the PQJ in Marseille and Vichy.

All the documents discussed demonstrate that the dispossession process had not been absolute. A significant number of businesses were not aryanized. The Bernheim-Lyon and André Levy families continued renting out their buildings and apartments until 1944, contrary to the Statute of the Jews.[31] Were the victims of choice those who had, for one reason or another, attracted some attention, while those less visible managed to escape, for a time, the grip of the CGQJ? Was that because of the envy of competitors or opportunists taking advantage of the Statute of the Jews to swoop down on their prey?

The Guiding anti-Semitic Ideology

Excerpt from the monthly report of the regional director of the SEC on December 31, 1943:

Region of the Vaucluse

This département is particularly important with respect to Jewish questions. Indeed, my thorough investigation in the region provided me with the opportunity to observe the following facts:

The region of Avignon is home to what it would be appropriate to call "the old Jewish nobility," which has settled there in Vaucluse since that time; therefore, this has constituted actually created an organization for protection and camouflage of the Jews.

Next to them, and in parallel, there is in Vaucluse a significant leading group of freemasons, which is holding the reins of all administrative services, hence a very visible opposition to the action of the CGQJ in this region.

Our service is not the only one to suffer from this opposition. Indeed, the Milice, the Légion Française des Combattants, the Services of Information and Propaganda, are being boycotted by all possible means.

The Jews are being protected by the entire justice system.

Because of its importance, the "covert" action in the département of Vaucluse should fall within the competence of the government rather than that of our services; the principal directives given to the terrorists emanate from the Vaucluse where numerous important personalities of the "ancien régime"* reside, in the shadows: such is the case of the active Monsieur Dautry.†

In the same report, the regional director added:

… because of the importance of the activity carried out by the Jews in this region, an activity which tends to sponsor terrorism, to organize it by using individuals from the maquis and foreign workers, that are very numerous in that area.

A similar investigation in the region of the Var, the Vaucluse and the Bouches du Rhône led us to discover that this tight cooperation also exists in the southeast between all these elements whose headquarters are in the Vaucluse.[32]

This report attests more to fantasy than to a sense of reality, if one takes into account that the resistance counted only a very small fraction of the population and that the number of Jewish resistance fighters was even smaller, even if their percentage was higher than average; it gives an insight into the viewpoint and the anti-Semitic strategy of the CGQJ leaders, and in

---

* The expression « ancient regime » to qualify le republican regime before the war is a bit ironic in the mouth of a true supporter of the Ancien Régime.
† Raoul Dautry (1880–1951) was an engineer, former minister of armaments from September 10, 1939, to June 16, 1940, who lived in silent retirement in Lourmarin during the entire war.

particular of the SEC director. Their ideology is clear to all broken down into three parts:

1. The French Jews have kept the privileged position they enjoyed under "l'ancien régime"
2. The French Jews have formed an alliance with the prefectural administration through the "tentacles" of freemasonry
3. The French Jews are protecting the foreign Jews who are frequently the source of terrorism, black market and higher prices

The specter of this alliance of the French Jews with the prefecture caused an intensified effort by the SEC in the dispossession of their assets, the symbols of a harmful taking of roots. The government's reluctance to see them deported reinforced this phantasm. As for the foreign Jew, responsible for every ill and less protected by Vichy, there was no hesitation to give their names out to the SiPo-SD.

The CGQJ at the Service of the German anti-Semitic Strategy

By tracking down any violation of the Statute of the Jews, the two Vaucluse employees of the CGQJ, de Camaret and Lebon, and their helpers did not demonstrate any real imagination. Their mission was dictated by the anti-Semitic program of Vichy, which was in line with that of Berlin, although it did not advocate extermination.

But in defining themselves as hard-liners in the application of the Statute, de Camaret and Lebon were the actors of a preliminary step, necessary for the policy of extermination. They placed the Jews of Vaucluse in such a vulnerable situation that it inevitably led to deportations.

Justice sentenced those two men. But after examining the procedural files, we conclude that many permanent or occasional contributors of this network deployed over the entire *department*—indispensable to the good functioning of the CGQJ—were never called upon to account for their action.

Chapter 6

Régis d'Oléon, President of the "Légion Française des Combattants" of Vaucluse

The Shadow Prefect In-Waiting

Régis d'Oléon and his organization exemplified the new order established after the defeat of 1940 and the collapse of France. His collaborationist activism created an atmosphere conducive to the persecution of the Jews. More radical than the prefecture, he provided an ideological base for the staunchest anti-Jewish elements. He kept his ideological constancy until the end of the war.

Created on August 29, 1940, by Xavier Vallat, the Legion was the largest mass organization of the Vichy regime; several personalities were appointed to head over time. The Vaucluse was a good example of its national importance. In 1942, there were 102 local community sections including mostly military officers, landowners, industrialists and professionals. On its first anniversary, it boasted 15,000 members. Just for the town of Carpentras, the membership of the section[1] reached 650 veterans-legionnaires, and 400 Volunteers of the National Revolution, who had not fought in the war. The law of November 19, 1941, had opened the doors of the Legion to this last category, thus significantly enlarging its membership. It must be said that the oath of the Legion allowed for it to cast a wide net:

> I promise to continue serving France with honor in peace as I have when I was called up.
> I promise to dedicate all my strength to the homeland, to my family and to work.
> I commit to friendship and mutual aid towards my comrades of the two wars, to remain faithful to the memory of those killed in action.
> I freely accept the discipline of the Legion for all orders I will receive in view of this ideal.[2]

However, the Legion was not a homogeneous organism in either ideology or action. Quite the opposite, it spanned a wide range of opinions and attitudes.

Barely rid of the parliamentary regime and its "old partisan struggles,"[3] the Maréchal imposed the Legion rather than giving in to the temptation of a one-party system and the elections that would have ensued. In the hands of the notables, the Legion served the authoritarian regime of the Maréchal all the better since it was supervised by the old subordinates of the victor of Verdun. And for the demobilized men of the "Phony War," the Legion substituted patriotic fervor for the shame of defeat.

The Maréchal used the Legion as a rampart against challenges to his authority from those who felt nostalgic for Parlementarism or from the ultra-collaborationists. It is possible that Pétain also saw in the Legion a roadblock to the collaborationist schemes of Laval who in turn was not fooled.

In any case, the Legion of Vaucluse did not disappoint the hopes of the Vichy ideologues. The elimination of the Jews from the economy was an integral part of it duty as guardian of the order. Under the d'Oléon presidency, some of its members went even further in their anti-Semitic collaboration in the name of the Révolution Nationale.

A Member of *l'Action Française* in Charge

Régis de Bonet d'Oléon[4] was born in Avignon; he had a good secondary education at St. Joseph High School, followed by four years at the St. Geneviève School,* then he attended the Marine Engineering School in Paris, and had a few industrial internships in England to put the finishing touches on his training as a consulting engineer, a profession he practiced for five

---

* Four years at the St. Geneviève school, a preparatory class for Engineering School, seems to be a very long time.

years in South America. He earned a Military Cross (*Croix de guerre*) in 1914–1918, was a reserves captain in 1920, and was awarded the Legion of Honor in 1929. This was a beautiful career path at juncture of industry and arms manufacturing, with politics not too far removed.

From 1923 to 1929, he served as elected mayor of Rognonas, a village in the Bouches du Rhône at the edge of Vaucluse, in practical terms a suburb of Avignon. Both a land owner and an engineer, he was an active member of *l'Action Française*.

In 1939, he was posted at the light cavalry depot No. 15 in Orange; he served as its squadron chief until the armistice. Demobilized in 1940, he settled in Avignon, where prefect Valin appointed him president of the benefit plan. In 1941, he enrolled in the Legion with a head office located at 3 bis, rue Violette in Avignon. He was then named by decree president of the special delegation and mayor of Rognonas, a position he kept until 1944.

An Appointment Imposed From Above

At the request of General Emile Laure, inspector general of the Legion, d'Oléon accepted an offer to become its president for the Vaucluse in 1942, replacing Ferdinand Bec, former president of the Avignon Bar Association, former mayor, and president of the Vaucluse federation of the League of Large Families.* The report that de Camaret sent on March 6, 1942, to his boss in Marseille about Ferdinand Bec was probably the determining factor in the change of leadership of the Legion.

> … It is particularly as Département President of the Legion that his action has proven unfortunate. Indeed,
> - He has not shown himself to be motivated by the spirit of the Révolution Nationale, and on several occasions, he has demonstrated a lack of faith in its success through some careless comments.
> - As a result, his attitude, suspect in the eyes of the most fervent legionnaire, has sparked much dissension within the Legion.
>
> Several reports were sent to Vichy and the principal authorities, asking for his replacement… I am bringing to your attention the most recent of these reports which was just sent to Doctor Bouyala, Regional President of the Legion, through the channel of the police for Secret Societies…

---

* The Leagues of Large Families (*Ligues des Familles Nombreuses*) were private organizations declared beneficial to the general public which started operating at the end of the 19th century in defense of empoverished large families. Their importance grew with the demographic problems cause by the 1914–1918 war. The Vichy regime enhanced their importance and federated them under French Families Federations (*Fédération Française des Familles*).

As for the Jewish question, Mr. Bec has become in a way the defender of the Jews, who appeal to him precisely because of the authority conferred to him by his title of Département President of the Legion...[5]

It is not surprising that d'Oléon, a great friend of de Camaret, became the successor of Ferdinand Bec.

On May 1, 1942, Bouyala proposed d'Oléon to prefect Henri Piton and asked him to receive two of his collaborators, M. Kellerhals, general secretary, and M. Paillas, inspector of the documentation service, for a discussion about the matter.[6] On May 11, the prefect responded with his own list of candidates.

- Jean Farget, construction engineer
- Lucien Bonnet, lawyer, former president of the Bar
- Ferdinand Tartanson, general practitioner
- Raoul Fabre, coal trader, deputy mayor of Avignon

Visibly, d'Oléon, who did not appear on the list, was imposed by the hierarchy of the Legion, against the refusal of the prefect to accept as he wrote: "this candidate who is not from Avignon," a barely veiled pretext to reject d'Oléon. The story of this nomination already promised a brewing conflict between the prefecture and the Legion.

The confrontations during the demonstrations of July 14, 1942, a few weeks later, radicalized the relations between the administration and the population, and induced the prefect to take action. Like many other parts of the southern zone, Avignon had responded to the appeal of the Resistance and the Free France representatives in London. The next day, in a letter to the head of the government and minister secretary of state, Pierre Laval, the prefect described the excesses of the Legion and the SOL, its independent policing service.

In Avignon, around 6:30 p.m., the City Hall and the Monument, both on place de l'Horloge, had been chosen as a rallying spot by the Gaullist demonstration.

The area of the square in question is very busy, especially on public holidays. Yesterday at 6:00 p.m., it was busier than usual. The police superintendant, in the view of the increasing number of people decided to clear the square and forbid its access, starting at 6:15 p.m.

Under these conditions, the demonstration could not therefore take place at the planned location.

But, as early as 5:45 p.m., the Legion des Combattants, whose club is located on the second floor of a building overlooking the square, started a broadcast with loudspeakers. After having picked out some lies of the British radio about the chief Darnand*, they announced that the British have sent to France a railroad car full of chocolate which the Jews and the Gaullists are invited to take delivery of at the train station…

Around 7:30 p.m., the crowd which had remained close by was slowly flowing through the rue de la République, where a police unit on bicycles was maintaining order. This crowd, swollen with spectators who exiting the movie theaters, was composed of strollers. Among them there were several groups of pretty noisy young people. One of these groups, which other people immediately joined, started again to sing the Marseillaise. There were approximately one hundred demonstrators followed by numerous onlookers. The demonstrators marched to the train station and left a short time thereafter, intending to march again towards the center of town reversing their previous itinerary. A roadblock was immediately established next to the Hautpoul barracks. It was broken, and a second one was set in front of Hotel Crillon, which is occupied by the Italian Commission of Control of War Industries and a German liaison officer.† After the intervention by the Gendarmerie which had been called in as reinforcement, the demonstrators finally scattered while blowing whistles and pouring out hostile screams against the head of the Government. Ten arrests were operated at that time, and four of them still stand.

I must underscore the facts that during the afternoon of July 14 members of the SOL had crisscrossed, in small groups and in uniform, the main artery of the city and the neighboring area of the location for the planned demonstration.

Moreover, the unexpected broadcast done by the Legion, did not particularly contribute to calm people down…

Finally, without having been asked to in any way, neither by me, nor by the Chief responsible for the police, the same SOL, with approximately 20 individuals, intervened and carried out arrests.

I must take note that the agreement that had been reiterated even very recently, about using the SOL during demonstrations, was not respected on this occasion. The public willingly accepted police intervention, but is having difficulties with this group, it is to be feared that should such acts be repeated it may result in unfortunate consequences.

I have shared these observations directly with the Chief of the Legion in the département, M. d'Oléon, but I believe that it is necessary that orders, issued by the Government, be given directly to the Heads of the Legion to the effect that any intervention of the SOL should take place only at the request of the Prefects

---

* Joseph Darnand (1897–1945), leader of the Legion and, later, head of the Milice at its creation.
† The prefect mentions in passing that German and Italian representatives were at the Crillon hotel. Before the occupation of the free zone, these individuals probablement had intelligence functions, under the cover of their coordination role. A prelude to a carefully planed invasion?

or the Police Chiefs responsible for public order, and finally, that they should not be allowed to intervene on their own initiative.

In his trial, d'Oléon claimed:

> The members of the SOL escaped my command. With the Milice, my relations were limited to a few repeated interventions in favor of people arrested either by the Milice or by the Germans.

Who is the Boss?

Following the demonstrations of July 14, the prefect had contacted d'Oléon, which proving that the link between the Legion and the SOL had not been broken, as d'Oléon claimed.

After complaining to Laval, the prefect, Henri Piton, sent a circular note. It was addressed to "The Mayors and Presidents of the Special Delegations of the *Département.*" He reiterated that the mission of the Legion consisted in supervising the veterans, and he accepted the possibility that its members might be called upon to render some services to the authorities. The prefect encouraged the mayors to be attentive to their advice and to establish with them a "*loyal and trusting collaboration.*" But he underscored that...

> ... the agents of the Legion... cannot forget that the representatives of the Central Power are the only trustees responsible for the constitutional authority of the Central Power...

The arm-wrestling with the prefecture continued. In his circular note of October 23, 1942, d'Oléon replied by sending his own instructions to the Presidents of the Municipal Sections of the Legion.

> ... external and internal events lead us to seriously contemplate the possibility that public order may be disrupted... Consequently, I am issuing the following imperative orders:
>
> 1. Each section president will study which are the vital points of his municipality that need to be maintained in the hands of the guardians of order at all costs: post office, city hall, train station, power station, food warehouses, etc.
> 2. Once this study is completed, they will estimate the size of the force necessary to occupy these locations, to be entrenched inside them, and to keep control over them at all costs.

3. After having so determined the number of men necessary for the fulfillment of their mission, they will draw up <u>the list of names</u>* of reliable Legion members, capable of playing the role assigned to them. …
4. Do not count on the SOL that would be used on the outside…

   …

6 … I am requesting that a report be sent to me informing me that the aforementioned orders have indeed been implemented and that the section is ready for its role.

Two weeks later, on November 7, d'Oléon sent a copy of these directives to the prefect who had probably already obtained them from the RG (Renseignements Généraux). The president of the Legion was using a lofty tone:

> … As I had told you before, this note does not have any indication related to liaison with the Gendarmerie brigades and with the mayors. This additional information has been and will be dealt with by oral instructions on my part, this in order to avoid misunderstandings.
>
> This will allow you to come up with your own instructions to the sub-prefects and the mayors, in a coordinated manner…

On January 26, 1943, d'Oléon stayed the course in his report about the collaboration of the Legion with the authorities:

> The prefect… reaches his decisions alone.
> But at his immediate side, the Chief of the Legion of the département is:
> - an informer
> - an advisor
> - an intermediary between the administration and those administered
> - an agent of dissemination of information and directions emanating from the power
> - a political controller of the agents of power

As in most totalitarian regimes, d'Oléon assumed the function of "political controller of the agents of the administration" and of shadow-prefect in-waiting.

Ideas and Actions

A note by the RG about the Legion meeting of June 6, 1943, in l'Isle sur la Sorgue reveals what d'Oléon really thought about collaboration with the

---

* Underlined by d'Oléon.

Germans. In his examination of the situation in front of the members of the section, d'Oléon picked up on a classical theme of nationalistic illusion:

> Thanks to its prestigious past, France will almost have the advantages of a victorious nation. It will keep its integrity. If it must lose certain regions and a few clippings, it will be largely compensated in the north. Moreover, on the other side of the Mediterranean Sea, the territories which are facing it will be considered as an integral part of metropolitan France. She will keep the other colonies and if the general economy is operated jointly, at least the French flag will fly again alone on these lands.
>
> … Some think indeed that Germany has no strength left and that soon it will be useful to join the fight on the side of the Anglo-Americans with the weapons provided by them.
>
> It is unnecessary to qualify this idea as it is fallacious. And if, at any point in time, French people were to act this way, this must be said, they would assassinate France and would be the cause of its irrevocable ruin.

D'Oléon went far beyond the intentions of the Maréchal, when he presented this argument well attuned to the collaborationist line of Pierre Laval. Things went even further. Thus, during the meeting of the Federal Council of the PPF on September 18, 1943, François Séraphin (responsible for information and head of the Avignon district of the Legion) made the announcement that

> Régis d'Oléon, chief of the département Legion, and doctor Bonnefoy, chief of the départemental Milice, have taken identical steps to arm certain members of the Legion and the Milice.

Pierre Bonnefoy—a medical doctor in Sorgues, and a member of the special municipal delegation, within the leadership of both the SOL and the Milice, volunteer in the Waffen-SS on the Eastern front—was sentenced to death in absentia. He was never caught.*

Still in 1943, and in the office of the prefect during a meeting with Stehling, head of the Manpower German office, d'Oléon promised all his help to facilitate the departure of the class of 1942 to Germany for the STO.† Everything converged, most notably in his speech to the Milice constitutive assembly, held at "Le Palace" movie theatre, and reported by "Les Tablettes du Soir" of March 1, 1943.

---

* After several postings, in August 1944, he served in Galicia as medical officer, ending up with the rank of Obersturbannführer (Lieutenant Colonel), in the first battalion of the 8th SS Assault Brigade (Charlemagne Division) of French volunteers.
† The class of 1942 were the 20 year olds, who would have been drafted for the military service under normal circumstances.

D'Oléon claimed that the most profound friendship, the most complete camaraderie unites the Legion and the Milice. We are not only allies but combat comrades. The Legion has been a mother. It has taken its youngest sons to make them the forefront of a vanguard, but when these sons came of age, it has given them their freedom. The Legion is extremely proud of you and you have its entire support. Do not let people say that the Milice and the Legion may oppose one another, because on both sides, we are the soldiers of the Maréchal.

This article demonstrated the link between the Legion and the Milice, that d'Oléon would later deny.

Finally, the tribute paid on May 2, 1944, at the funeral of Bonadona, executed by the Resistance on April 29, 1944. About this chief of the French Guards* in Carpentras, d'Oléon said "He gave his life for France." At his trial, d'Oléon blamed himself for not having known that Bonadona was a member of the PPF; another transparent attempt to minimize his own responsibility. This famous Bonadona was accused post mortem by Gaston Barbarant, the district chief of the PPF in Carpentras, of having made a quid-pro-quo deal with Wilhelm Müller, the Avignon head of the German police: the list of Carpentras Jews in exchange for not being sent to the STO[7].

The CDL is Alarmed

D'Oléon's rantings against the inertia of officials did not fall on deaf years. A police report dated February 10, 1945, confirmed that at the CDL, they remember *"the public meetings at the municipal theater of Avignon where he underscored the benefits of the Révolution Nationale and his praise of Laval's politics. In one of his speeches, he even spoke about the purges which had to be conducted relentlessly in the administrations against the government officials hostile to the regime."*[8]

The news that d'Oléon was to be judged in Civic Court rather than the Court of Justice spread like wildfire in Avignon. Alerted by the *département* section of the national union of government officials and agents of the prefecture, which thinks that *"this decision* [avoidance of the Court of Justice] *could only have originated from the lack of proof and testimony against the accused,"* as the president of the CDL immediately wrote on June 14, 1945, to the president of the Court of Justice.

Already during the session of the CDL of April 21, 1945, Resistance fighter Georges Laudon was very concerned, to the point of going public about the preferential treatment given to the prisoners d'Oléon and his good friend de Camaret. He stated:

---

* PPF groups armed by the Germans in case of uprising.

At the Court of Justice I have learned a fact that I intend to publicize, in spite of the requests I have received to keep silent about it. On the 21st of last month, two distinguished prisoners have been taken out of Ste Anne and transferred to the camp at Sorgues. Moreover, they have never been placed under committal order at the Ste Anne prison. I am talking about Messers. de Camaret and d'Oléon, whose schemes you are aware of. The first was president of the anti-Semitic Legion,* and the second was recruiting Miliciens under the cover of the Legion. This is absolutely unacceptable... this is due to interventions from above and not to the work overload of the government commissioner.

In their session of June 20, 1945, the members of the CDL of the Vaucluse were stunned, when they were told that d'Oléon would be brought in front of the Civic Chamber, thus escaping the Court of Justice.[9]

On June 23, the CDL was informed of the response of the president of the Court of Justice, Judge Pierre Burgède.

In response to your letter of June 14, received today (June 20), related to the Régis d'Oléon affair, I have the honor to inform you that whether to refer a case to the Civic Court or the Court of Justice is for the government commissioner to decide. However, the members of the jury of the Civic Chamber have the opportunity, if they deem the case serious, to declare themselves incompetent, and to send it back to the Court of Justice.

Paul Faraud, the CDL president, thundered forth.

This beats everything we had seen so far. I think that we need to stand our ground. D'Oléon has done so much propaganda, he is, in my mind, far more guilty than an ordinary milicien who has been brainwashed into signing a piece of paper.

The anger was genuine. The case of d'Oléon was symbolic of a period when conflicting interests were colliding in the purge process.

To Judge But to Spare

During his trial, d'Oléon described his functions as innocently as possible:

- passing on to the prefect the complaints about malfunctions of the services
- informing Vichy about the malfunctions of the services, the unfortunate measures...
- helping prisoners and their families
- provide all possible services in the social area

---

* M. Laudon was referring this way to the CGQJ, by using a descriptive expression of the times.

In front of the court, he took pride in the creation of his mutual aid restaurants to feed all kinds of refugees—and he specified "including Israelites."* Here is a man who quite simply did only good things!

When it comes to the persecution of the Jews, d'Oléon's Legion had been the main Vaucluse source for de Camaret's network of informers. In the Vaucluse, seven presidents of local sections and numerous active simple members volunteered for this network, which also supplied provisional administrators to the CGQJ. The presidents of twelve district and local sections were brought to trial in front of the Court of Justice. This role of d'Oléon did not come up during his trial. Who then was the real Régis d'Oléon?

The fact is that his leadership role as a collaborator was minimized. Even his participation in the infamous Tribunal d'État in Lyon from September 22, 1943, to June 20, 1944, the crowning achievement of his career, went off without a hitch.[10] D'Oléon sat on this court as a nonprofessional judge in company of Joseph Darnand—head of the Milice, officer in the Waffen-SS, chief of police and secretary of state for the maintenance of law and order at the request of the Germans—who had recommended him for his titles and his 9 children family, as greatly valuable to Vichy.[11]

In spite of all of this, on July 11, 1945, the Civic Chamber found d'Oléon solely guilty of *indignité nationale* (national indignity) and sentenced him to *dégradation nationale à vie* (national degradation, i.e., loss of civil rights, for life):

> The accused is guilty of having, in France, after June 16, 1940, either by his words or by his actions, knowingly provided direct or indirect assistance to Germany, or damaged the unity of the nation, the freedom of French people or the equality between them. After he committed the crimes retained by the court, he has not rehabilitated himself.

There was no mention that the institution he had been the president of had provided a wealth of anti-Jewish activists, except the rather subtle mention "*damaged… the equality between them.*" A justice barely symbolic in the name of national reconciliation? One senses in this verdict a reluctance to add on any further accusations against this soldier of the Maréchal.

There was even a Jew to defend him. René Gutman, a medical doctor at Hotel Dieu hospital in Paris, claimed that "*d'Oléon had intervened several times in favor of arrested Jews.*" He cited Dr. Albert Lesbros, and for himself, "*d'Oléon has intervened several times with the organism for Jewish Questions for my file to be hidden*

---

* Two are in Avignon, and one in Carpentras, Cavaillon and l'Isle sur la Sorgue.

from the Germans." So d'Oléon had helped a "good Jew," but is that sufficient to exonerate him? René Gutman states: "*Finally, I know that Mr. d'Oléon declared several times that the anti-Semitic persecutions triggered by the Vichy government were disgusting and unacceptable.*"

Would d'Oléon have provided to de Camaret a long list of reliable correspondents in the towns and villages, as well as administrators of Jewish assets, if he had really deemed the persecution of the Jews "*disgusting and unacceptable*"? Or maybe he had "his own Jews," as we have seen in the case of Aimé Autrand? The fact remains that René Gutman, a convert in 1914 and close to d'Oléon, needed this help, because in the eyes of the Nazis and of the CGQJ, he was still Jewish as he did not have at least two Christian grand-parents, as specified in the Statute.

In fact, would Gutman have felt offended by the correspondence of Bernard Faucon to his "Dearest Guigui," as he was so sweetly calling his wife?[12] Faucon, an Avignon insurance agent, who resided in Villeneuve lès Avignon, was the chief of a hundred (*chef de centaine*) in the Milice.* He had participated in several expeditions and was sentenced to hard labor for life. During a reception at his home in Villeneuve, he conversed with his friends Max Knipping and d'Oléon. These people respected and understood one another without having to spell it out. They belonged to the Avignon establishment of the "dark years."

On July 9, 1943, while on a business trip on the Côte d'Azur, Faucon wrote to his wife, the mother of his six children:

> The sky was stormy, but this did not prevent me to have a delightful swim. There is nobody in Cannes except a few Yids. Without them, it would be marvelous.

As Faucon notices, the Jews felt safe in Italian occupied Cannes.

The denials by d'Oléon were barely veiled attempts to disclaim any responsibility. But it is also possible that d'Oléon did not understand, at the time of his trial, how disgrace could have been brought upon the social establishment he had been part of. Moreover, he had not fled as the allies were closing in, maybe because of his trust in the establishment, whose downfall he could not conceive.

The national degradation for life of Régis d'Oléon apparently did not preclude him from being honored after his death. The city of Rognonas made sure we are not disappointed, when it expressed its gratitude to its former

---

* See Appendix B (Organization of the Milice).

mayor of 1923–1929 by dedicating two streets to him, boulevard de Bonet d'Oléon and the alley d'Oléon. The street signs do not mention that in 1941–1944, he had been mayor and president of the special delegation directly appointed by Vichy. There was to be one more street to his name than Aimé Autrand.

On the other hand, de Camaret got nothing.

To Top a Résumé

The arrests of September 16, 1943, aimed at disciplining the French institutions did not succeed in getting the prefecture in step and shake its inertia. Prefect Benedetti, appointed on December 16, 1943, and in the eyes of the Germans, no more docile than his predecessors, was arrested on May 11, 1944. The SiPo-SD became impatient, since the case of the Vaucluse was not unique. On May 27, 1944, Colonel Helmut Knochen, head of the SiPo-SD, sent a proposal for reorganization of the prefectures to his superior infantry General Heinrich Von Stülpnagel, supreme military commander in France. Knochen described the malaise:

> The current crisis in the prefectural administration has the striking result that neither Laval nor Lemoine are in a position or have the will to accept the strict execution and supervision of the orders given by your authority.[13]

He then proposed to replace 14 *département* and region prefects with trusted individuals who were not from the traditional administration. However, this is an approach that von Stülpnagel would oppose. In fact, the supreme commander had penciled a question mark next to the paragraph in question.

For the Vaucluse, Knochen nominated Jean Lombard, subprefect in St. Julien en Genevoix (Haute Savoie). Régis d'Oléon apparently suited the taste of the SiPo-SD, since he was meant to take over as regional prefect of Montpellier.

Régis d'Oléon had definitely crossed into the circle of trust of the heads of the SiPo-SD in Avignon and Marseille.

Had Knochen's letter been revealed to the court, would it have made a difference?

Part Two

The Germans and Their Associates

The "German Solution" to the Jewish Question in the Vaucluse

On November 11, 1942, the Germans crossed the demarcation line taking over the free zone, as they broke the Armistice and put an end to Vichy sovereignty.

If the military presence was rapidly felt, the German police, whose missions required a good understanding of the local French population, seemed to move slowly at first. As early as April 1943 the German police carried out targeted arrests of Jews in Carpentras and Avignon. These arrests continued sporadically, and in the following months were mostly focused on a few notables; a very striking contrast with the collective arrests of the foreign Jews in August 1942. Was this a Vaucluse anomaly or part of a more generalized phenomenon?

An appropriate answer may be found in Marseille, where the section of the German police in charge of Jewish affairs, under the direction of Sergeant major Willy Bauer and his boss Rolf Mühler, shows a clear interest in the arrest and deportation of Jews as early as March 1943, but here as well it was in a small proportion relative to the total Jewish population.

At the beginning of May 1943 a conflict occurred between Bauer and Mühler, on one hand, and Raymond Raoul Lambert, the director of UGIF for the free zone, and Robert Andrieu, Regional Intendant of police, on the other hand.[1] Following an assassination attempt on May 1, 1943, when two SS were seriously injured, Bauer tried to impose sanctions; he demanded from Robert Andrieu a list of people to arrest, and from Lambert a list of 200 Jews and 10% of his personnel. Both refused to comply; Andrieu had the support of Vichy. As to Lambert, he argued that the arrests were contrary to the armistice agreement and that no French law allowed to bypass it.

The German reaction was not long to come, and on May 6 Bauer turned up, with a German police unit, at the offices of the UGIF, 58, rue de la Joliette in Marseille. They arrested the personnel, as well as refugees, men, women and children, caught in the mouse trap. Bauer stated that he had orders to arrest 100 Jews without any distinction of nationality, but he released a few Italian and Turkish Jews. Bauer seized the pretext of the assassination attempt to send a message: there was no point in protecting French Jews any more.

On May 18 Lambert, who was at the prefecture for a meeting with Robert Andrieu, found himself face to face with Rolf Mühler also visiting Andrieu. There is little doubt that the question of Jewish hostages, a major point of contention between them, came up on this occasion.

Lambert and Andrieu were both arrested after a noble but clearly futile struggle. Were they able to save a certain number of people by delaying the fatal outcome? Raymond Raoul Lambert, his spouse and their three children were deported on convoy 64. Robert Andrieu was freed.

Despite sporadic actions and the broadening of the arrests to French Jews, the German anti-Jewish activity remained limited. It is in this context that the roundups of April 19, 1943, in the Vaucluse must be placed as well as two prefectural behaviors, discretely supported by Vichy, must be considered. On one hand, a passive resistance to the measures against the Jews, in particular the French Jews; on the other hand, the delivery, in October 1943, of a list of foreign Jews to the Germans, who had unsuccessfully requested the list of all Jews, seven months earlier, in March 1943.

But, while German intentions were clear, there was a big difference between their wishes and reality. The German police had other fish to fry, they were understaffed, and they were not completely deployed in the southeast, largely covered by Italian occupation troops. Moreover, the implementation of an efficient network of French auxiliaries, which the Germans badly needed, required a lot of time and effort to set up.

The Italian capitulation in September 1943 and their evacuation of southeastern France created new demands placing a heavy burden on an already overextended staff, but they also provided the opportunity for the Germans to take full control of the region. This coincided with the arrival of Aloïs Brunner, the Berlin envoy of the SD in charge of accelerating the deportation of the Jews from France. Changes were about to take place.

Finally, the "negotiations" between French and Germans about the denaturalization of a new segment of the Jewish population were not progressing. Vichy still resisted giving its agreement for the deportation of French Jews. The Germans were becoming impatient, and at least formally they tried to obtain the collaboration of the French so as not to offend public opinion. It seems though that by the fall of 1943, the Germans had lost their illusions about collaboration and were to care less and less about public opinion.

Chapter 7

The Purest Riffraff Around

Alfred André, Georges Parietas, and the "blue collar" agents of the GFP

The file of Alfred André, a fanatical leader of the persecution of the Jews of the Vaucluse, could not be found either in the archives of the courts of justice of the Vaucluse or the Gard which took over the Vaucluse judicial system on July 15, 1945. The court of justice of the Gard had effectively sentenced a certain number of collaborators for acts which had taken place in Vaucluse. Why was that specific file missing? Had it been lost, destroyed, stolen or simply requested—and never returned—by another court of justice investigating closely related issues in another département? Everything was possible.

Alfred André can be found nevertheless. Even though his biographical information and civil status are also missing, enough information about him is available in files of the Vaucluse, Gard and elsewhere. Alfred André was described as an "agent of the Gestapo," but he was actually a French member of the GFP (Geheime Feldpolizei), secret military intelligence, which had settled at the Avignon Hotel "la Cigale," 11, rue Bancasse.

The official role of the GFP, described as "protecting the back of the Wehrmacht," is misleading, since it also was one of the nerve centers of the persecution of the Jews of the Vaucluse. There are clear indications of the collaboration between the GFP and the SD (security police) both in the fight against the Resistance and in the hunt for the Jews across all French territory.[1] These tight links between the two groups in the Vaucluse are apparent through some testimonies. For instance, Gaston Mouillade, an active member of the SD, an individual sentenced to death and executed, related during his interrogation the circumstances that followed his fortuitous encounter, in a restaurant in Cavaillon, with Blaise Bounias,* a member of the Resistance, accompanied by two women:

> Faced with this providential encounter and considering the extreme urgency, I went straight to the GFP, rue Bancasse. I alerted these services which, after a phone call to the SD [avenue Monclar] and after agreement of the inspector on watch, have arrested Bounias and the two women, according to my information.
>
> M. Poutet[†],very happy about my decisiveness, asked the SD to continue on this case by arresting Mme. Jacotet and two police inspectors of Cavaillon who are said to have fabricated the forged identity papers of the two Bounias companions arrested with him.[2]

The GFP submitted the matter to the SD of avenue Monclar before taking action. The Avignon situation presented at the same time some autonomy and a local collaboration amongst the various German police forces; for the witnesses of that period, this was the source of confusion between the "services of rue Bancasse," the headquarters of the GFP, and the "services of avenue Monclar," the headquarters of the SD and of the Gestapo. The name Gestapo was anyway often used as a general term to designate all the police services, distinct and coordinated at the same time.

In their numerous testimonies, the Jews arrested often declared having been taken to the "Gestapo" of rue Bancasse, before being taken to the Ste Anne prison, even if their arrest was carried out by the squad of the avenue Monclar, a clear indication that these two offices were not as distinct as people thought.

Other names were to surface associated with Alfred André, the local Avignon boss. The French team of the GFP was composed of 5 main operatives compared to some 20 Germans,[3] according to Georges Parietas, *aka* Georges Boyer, alias superintendant Boyer, the official leader of the French components of the Avignon "Gestapo" from November 1943. On June 2,

---

* Blaise Bounias was executed on July 9, 1944.
† Jean Poutet, a registered milicien et head of the PPF in Lisle sur la Sorgue (3U7/255, Procédures de la Cour de Justice du Gard, Archives Départementales du Gard). His name will come up again several times.

1945, two gendarmes of the Sorgues brigade, Charles Martin and Gabriel Chabannis, informed the investigating judge in Marseille:

> … Among the agents of the Gestapo who were crisscrossing the region, the best known is a man named Boyer.[4]

Alfred André, seemed to be Boyer's alter ego. Antoine Cappe, another "founding member" of the unit, incarcerated and transferred to Marseille on February 16, 1945, to be judged there,[5] generously awarded to Alfred André the medal of "*top chief of the Gestapo.*"[6]

Alfred André and his Victims

Alfred André was 47 at the time of his arrest; he was a native of Aigues-Mortes and resided at 30, rue du Rempart St. Lazare in Avignon.[7] Officially a stallholder—a strategic profession to catch Jews—he had, upon the arrival of the German police until his flight to Germany in August 1944, played a key role in the arrest of Jews, who were often his competitors on the open air market. Although he did not leave a systematic report, and all the circumstances are not known, what we learn indirectly from other files suggests that he was very busy and had very little time left to lay out his merchandise on the market.

One of his brave deeds was the arrest of the Jews in Bollène in March 1944. He admitted to his participation in the raid during his interrogation of June 15, 1945:

> While I was at the offices of the Geheime Feldpolizei in Avignon, a man named Titien* Feroldi, département inspector of the Milice, came and stated that he knew the hiding place of a German deserter, hidden near Bollène. With Feroldi, there was another milicien, around 27 year old, blond, domiciled in Bollène who had provided information about the case.† I do not know his name. The Germans asked me to accompany them to conduct the arrest. We left with two cars. In the first, was Feroldi, two miliciens and one German; in the second, myself, a sergeant, and two German soldiers.
>
> The young milicien who accompanied Feroldi gave us directions, but he did not accompany us. We arrived in front of a castle which I knew later belonged to an Israelite named Rosenberg. Feroldi entered the yard through the large gate. We heard people running and the lights went off in the castle. Shots were fired by the Germans accompanying us. Feroldi and I, entered the corridor and we

---

* Titien is the French name for Tiziano.
† We have established circumstancially the identity of the informer, but we do not have a positive proof.

were rejoined by two miliciens and a German flanking the owner of the castle, M. Rosenberg and three daughters.* All had been arrested in the park. I stayed in the living room to guard the four people. Meanwhile, the others went to the castle wing inhabited by the farmer and arrested the German deserter we were seeking. Two Alsatians were also arrested, but outside the castle.

On the following day trucks arrived. The seven people arrested sat in one of them. The furniture, paintings, etc. were looted in this castle. In the course of this operation, the miliciens looted all the rooms. One part was kept by Feroldi, rue des Lices, Caserne des Passagers;** the rest at the headquarters of the Milice, rue Joseph Vernet. The Germans took away all the wine: 250 liters. Personally, I did not participate in the plunder because I was guarding the defendants [*sic*]. I swear to you that I did not receive from the Milice anything from this pillage.[8]

The manhunters were seeking a deserter from the German army and ran into the Rosenberg family. André's deposition clearly indicates that, in addition to the Rosenbergs, the Nazis had found the deserter in question and several other persons of interest. Of course, it is possible that they found the Rosenberg family by accident because the deserter was hidden in their farm. But it may also be possible that, from the time of their departure from Avignon, they had in fact intended to arrest the Rosenbergs.

In this affair, André accused Feroldi,† a milicien who was largely in the same class, but no longer available to account for his deeds, since he escaped justice. Today, the veil over the circumstances of the arrest of Szlama Rosenberg, his daughter Marceline, and two refugees, Marie and Suzanne Melman, who were also unfortunately Jewish, is lifted. All were deported on convoy 71.

On that day, the entire family would have been arrested, but Jacqueline Rosenberg, now Mme. Haby, and her little brother Michel, who had been hidden by their parents at a woman's home in Bollène, were saved. It is a miracle that the mother and Henriette, the eldest daughter, were able to escape by hiding in the garden. The Melman sisters who happened to be present at the wrong time were captured with Szlama Rosenberg and his daughter Marceline.

In 2008, in her autobiography, *Ma Vie Balagan,*‡ Marceline, an Auschwitz survivor, recounts the circumstances of her arrest. With some minor exceptions, her story sadly echoes Alfred André's confession.

---

* One is actually Marceline Rosenberg, but the two others are friends, Marie and Suzanne Melman.
** Literally, "barracks for the passengers"; subsidized lodging offered by city hall to distinguished personalities on "temporary" assignement in Avignon.
† We will return to the Feroldi case later on.
‡ My Chaotic Life.

On the morning of February 28, 1944, my eldest sister, Henriette, who belonged to the Resistance, came to warn us not to sleep in the château that night. So, during the day, my father had carried some of our belongings up the mountain, to an abandoned house, full of bugs... At home, that night, there were two girls, two sisters, Marie and Suzanne [Melman]. Since they had not found a place where to flee, my parents had offered them to hide with us in that abandoned house, in the forest.

It was in winter. It was very cold. My mother had cooked a pot-au-feu. She said: "We are not going to leave tonight, I have a terrible headache"...

The memory of that day has not faded away:

I remember it's getting darker. I remember the last pot-au-feu prepared by my mother. I remember our fatigue, the migraine of my mother, and the insistence of my sister [Henriette] pushing us to leave. I remember the decision to stay... one more night. I remember, I am the first to go to bed on the second floor, and I fall asleep. I am 15 years old.

I remember: I am suddenly awakened by my father "Fast, fast, Marceline, they are here"... I remember, completely in the dark, the yells "Open, open," the screams, the gate of the internal yard being opened by M. Roussier, our tenant farmer, who lives right behind.

I remember the violent knocks on the doors, the submachine gun shots, and of my frantic flight amid yells, screams, "Open, open, you are finished."

I remember running from one stairwell to another; I remember that I do not succeed in coming downstairs, as the shots become so much precise.

I am alone in the house. I must get out at all and reach a hidden door, at the end of the park, leading to the woods.

I remember: with fear in my stomach, I succeed in leaving the house. My father, mad with worry, is waiting for me behind a tree, at the beginning of the park.

I remember I saw only him; we run like mad towards the edge of the park, in the darkness.

I remember, I am ahead of him, I unbolt the door, I say "That's it, Daddy, we are safe."

Behind the door, a man, a French milicien, revolver in hand, a flashlight in the other hand. He tells us "Halt, or I shoot!" He violently hits my father on the head with the butt of his gun.

I remember our return to the dining room; the pot-au-feu is still on a corner of the wood stove. It is midnight, they are a dozen, French miliciens from Bollène, from Avignon, Germans in uniform, from the Gestapo, dressed in black, all armed.

I remember their violence, the brutality of the interrogations.

I remember the looting of the château, the truck arriving, the furniture they are moving, the despondency of my father who is suffering from the blows he has received and the slaps that come my way, the milicien who wants to rape me. I remember my cries.

I remember this German officer, rushing in and screaming: "It is forbidden to touch this dirty race."

I remember this dreadful phrase that saved me.

I remember the evasive look of M. and Mme. Roussier who witnessed it all.

I remember the next day at noon, the departure on the trucks, crammed and sitting on chairs from the château...

From the château, the prisoners are taken to the St. Anne Prison, from there to the Grandes Baumettes in Marseille, then to Drancy. Marceline had noticed an unusual German officer:

> There was a German, a very classy one. He told me "I am a member of the Fifth Column. The Fifth Column was an intelligence organization already present in France before the war. I was a German teacher at the lycée Lakanal, in Sceaux."[9]

This man probably is Wilhelm Wolfram, *aka* Gauthier, a subordinate of Wilhelm Müller, the head of the Avignon German police.

The man hunters were seeking a deserter from the German army and they ran into the Rosenberg family. André's deposition clearly indicates that, in addition to the Rosenbergs, the Nazis had found the deserter in question and several other persons of interest.

The testimonies lead to the first question: "Who knew of the existence of the Rosenbergs?" Of course, the farmhand and his family were aware, but they were not the only ones. Moreover, we know from several sources that the Rosenbergs were well known in Bollène; well-off families indeed do not go unnoticed in small towns. They had been registered in the census of 1941, 1943 and 1944; their names had been collected by the Bollène town hall and the prefecture of the Vaucluse. We also know that the list of foreign Jews they were a part of had been communicated to the Germans in October 1943. Moreover, we also know that, on January 28, 1943, Georges Cruon, a violent and greedy anti-Semite, forwarded to de Camaret the list of 38 Jews of Bollène, amongst them the Rosenbergs.[10] Self-appointed as the chief supervisor of the Bollène Jews, Cruon surely gave away this information to whoever asked for it. Finally, on December 7, 1943, the SEC of Marseille transmitted to Jean Lebon *"... for execution... letter No. 38200 from the CGQJ relative to the Bollène Château du Gourdon affair (the Jew Rosenberg)."*[11] Apparently, like many other Jews, the Rosenbergs lived out in the open.

The second question is: "When did the members of the GFP learn of the existence of the Rosenbergs?" According to the deposition of Alfred André, the raid on Bollène was first and foremost motivated by the arrest of the German deserter whose hiding place was known to the GFP. Besides, a police report[12] relates that, on March 3, 1944, "*... at M. Jean Roussier's home,* [the German police seizes] *a radio set, linen and money in the amount of 20,000F...*" It is thus possible that the German police had become aware of the Rosenbergs on their arrival at the home of the farmhand, whom they roughed up, but it is equally possible they had known all along who were the owners of the Château and the farm.

There is no obvious way of determining the scenario that led to the Rosenbergs' arrest.

Another aspect to this case, hidden by Alfred André, was disclosed by his friend Jean Costa, who became acquainted with André at the penitentiary in Nîmes (they had shared a similar prison experience). They reconnected at the Hotel "La Cigale"[13] where Costa was interrogated by the Germans for arms trafficking, before he was hired by them at the GFP. Costa shed light on the raid in Bollène during his deposition on June 28, 1945.

> I did learn that André had participated with the Germans in the arrest of the three Israelite girls. Later, the mother who had fled through the garden was put in contact with André, without the knowledge of the Germans, through the intermediary of the owner of the Crillon, Paul Biancone. André wanted 500,000 francs to get her three daughters out. This woman transferred the amount in question, but her children were nevertheless deported.

Jacqueline Haby testified that in fact her mother had to pay double the amount cited by Costa. One way or another, the money at stake was considerable, and one can easily imagine how the money was split among all the intermediaries.

Biancone ran the bar "Le Crillon," one of the meeting places most prized by the hooligans of the Vaucluse collaboration. Alfred André did not stop at the arrest of Szlama, Marceline and the Melman sisters; he jumped at the opportunity to demand a ransom from the family. Mme. Frenata Rosenberg did not disappoint him in her desperate hope to snatch her husband and the three girls from the clutches of the criminals.

Marceline continues:

> I remember the arrival at the Auschwitz train station, the opening of the cattle cars, the screams, the SS, and a few rare French words, meant to be reassuring, which we could not grasp: "Give the children to the elderly, do not get up on the trucks..."

I remember the hunger which gnawed at us day and night, the blows, all the humiliations, the cold, the roll calls, the selections for the crematorium, our cheeks which we were pinching to look well before walking in front of Mengele, the camp doctor in chief, the wounds which we attempted to hide to survive, the kapos, the roads we were paving, our skinniness, my father whom I saw by chance, who held me tight against his chest. I remember the SS who beats me to death in front of him while he called me a whore, and I fainted. I remember being happy that my father was alive.

I remember: Birkenau, Bergen-Belsen, the death of Simone Ragun's mother, Theresienstadt, Prague, the return, the Hotel Lutétia in Paris. My father will not come back. I would learn later about his long forced march from Auschwitz to Gross Rosen in Germany, the liquidation of all the survivors by the SS, the Russians arriving and finding only corpses…

An Auschwitz survivor, later married to Joris Ivens, the famous documentary maker with whom she created a large cinematographic body of work, Marceline Loridan Ivens produced in 2003 *The Little Meadow with the Birch Trees*, a film with Anouk Aimée inspired by her own deportation.

A Sordid "Entente": German Police and Local Scoundrels

The association between French collaborators, Costa, André, and the German police reflects a familiar scenario in the Vaucluse. The Germans were fond of ex-convicts whose services they sought and loyalty they secured. They fished out their future collaborators from the hands of the French police; or they hired them with the knowledge they were wanted by the French authorities; or they arrested them on their own after being informed of their criminal record or to crack down on an "alleged" crime against the Germans. These shady individuals worked for the Germans on all fronts of repression, intelligence against the Resistance, arrests of STO dodgers, procurement of all kinds of merchandise, struggles against the black market, arrests of Jews—in short, whatever the German police was after.

In all cases, they benefitted from a number of privileges in exchange for their services; they received protection certificates from the German authorities or German police cards—often renewable on a monthly basis to remind the gangsters of their duties, the right to bear arms, and in some cases, a monthly salary and bonus for good performance. The Germans often turned a blind eye on extortions and looting of many victims "on the side." These crooks will reappear in a significant number of raids as "bogus police," their lucrative parallel activity.

The French hoodlums in turn used similar tactics: they also recruited criminals and turned them into loyal subordinates who in return owed them their freedom as well as the opportunity to fill their pockets with impunity. The "grateful" hoodlums also shared the proceeds of their loot: everyone had a hand in the till.

The Unification of the German Police

To better understand the situation in occupied Vaucluse, it is necessary to take into account what happened during the occupation of northern France, before the invasion of the free zone. Jacques Delarue gave a detailed view in 1962.[14]

As soon as he took control of the Gestapo in 1934, Heinrich Himmler, already head of the SS, campaigned to increase his police powers. He created the SD, Security Service of the SS, which worked hand in hand with the Gestapo. First he took control of civilian life through the German police forces and created the RSHA (Reich Main Security Office) in the October 1939; then he attempted to get the military in step. When the Germans occupied the northern zone of France, the military command of the Wehrmacht opposed direct intervention by the SS in French affairs: the Germans would provide the direction and issue decrees, and the French would execute them. This was more effective and would prevent a counter-productive reaction on the part of the French population. The only exception was the Jewish section under Theo Dannecker, formerly from the Gestapo and reporting to Adolf Eichmann's section in the RSHA. But the French dragged their feet, and the Germans began losing their patience.

Since the military method was yielding no results, on August 22, 1941, General Von Stülpnagel ordered hostage executions that only made things worse the following year. All along, Himmler's group remained in the shadows, while increasing their control under the direction of Helmut Knochen. At the same time, they linked up with the shadiest element of French society, including outlaws and members of the most extreme political parties. Little by little, the GFP was overtaken by the pressure of events and its inadequacy, and was forced to allow the Gestapo to come in, at the beginning as an auxiliary, thereby increasing its influence.

After long negotiations between Knochen and the military command, the solution to the problem finally came from Berlin, where Himmler obtained from Hitler in April 1942 the control of all police organizations. The GFP was dismantled; some of its members were picked up by the Gestapo; others were transferred to regular military units. Most of the separate police organizations were finally integrated into one unit, the Sicherheit Polizei-Sicherheit Dienst or SiPo-SD.

Oddly enough, the GFP was not considered a criminal organization during the proceedings of the Nuremberg International Military Tribunal. Therefore, the senior commanders of the GFP were not charged, although it was recognized that a large part of its members had committed war crimes and crimes against humanity on a considerable scale;[15] this is definitely the case for the Vaucluse.

The exoneration of the senior commanders of the GFP is surprising, if one considers that most of them were members of the Nazi party, the SS or the SD. Before their mobilization, many had been members of the police often with a high rank. Their good fortune can at least be explained in part by the fact that after the unification of the police forces under Himmler in April 1942, the focus for the atrocities was put on the SiPo-SD, while, after the war, the senior leadership of the GFP played up the rivalry that existed between the two organizations. It is undeniable that the GFP committed atrocities before the unification, especially against Jews and Gypsies on the eastern front.[16] This did not change after April 1942, for the member of the GFP who joined the SiPo-SD as well as for those who remained under separate GFP command. The tightening of the grip of the SD on the police forces after April 1942 may have served as a shield for war crimes the senior officers of the GFP committed before and after that date along with their subordinates. This will come to light in the case of the Vaucluse, although on a smaller scale.

The new Himmler representative in France, General Karl Oberg, enjoyed a quasi independent status for his police organizations which in fact received their orders directly from Berlin rather than from the German military command in France. Himmler's delegates had even quietly infiltrated their agents into the free zone under the cover of armistice commissions or military liaisons.* Their discreet network preceded the invasion of November 11, 1942.

Oberg's complete control of all police forces reached down at all levels of the hierarchy, in Paris, in the regions, in the départements, and eventually, in the municipalities. With the invasion of the free zone, he only needed to extend his police system by leveraging the "moles" set up before the invasion and now ready for action. Kommandant Rolf Mühler reigned over Marseille and its prefectural region from January 3, 1943, to July 18, 1944, and Second Lieutenant Wilhelm Müller on Avignon and the Vaucluse, assisted by Second Lieutenant Wilhelm Wolfram, *aka* Gauthier, and a team of around 10 to 20

---

* Such a delegation, residing at the Crillon Hotel, was mentioned in the reports about the Avignon demonstrations of July 14, 1942.

active subordinates in charge of various files.[17] This unified police command all the way down to Avignon and the Vaucluse explained the tight collaboration between the rue Bancasse and the avenue Monclar. It is also because of this unified command that several German police officers dealt with members of the Resistance as well as with Jews, depending on the needs of their boss, Second Lieutenant Wilhelm Müller. The German police were nevertheless significantly understaffed, a fact which required, as with have seen during the raid on the Rosenbergs, a lot of additional forces.

This confusion about the affiliation of the German police was not limited to Avignon. From the beginning, even the military court of justice in Marseille designated the members of the police as SS, while Ernst Dunker, *aka* Delage, a GFP subordinate of Rolf Mühler, the head of the SiPo-SD of Marseille, provided the court with the correct information. In his deposition of May 7, 1945, Dunker gave a list of section heads where we counted 7 SS, 10 GFP, 1 Gestapo, 11 Gestapo SS, and 16 members without a precise affiliation. Dunker added 15 members whom he knew only by sight. Apparently, the members of the SiPo-SD remained posted with their original units, independently of their missions within the unified police.[18]

The errors made by the courts of justice may be explained by the early sources of their information. At the beginning, they drew on the "London files," a body of reports from the Resistance rank and file that used SS, SD and Gestapo interchangeably.

The Avignon unit was small, but Müller and Gauthier, two sadists, were surrounded by a small number of German subordinates in their image. Some of them, in particular Oberscharführer* Willie Schultz and Hauptscharführer† Fritz Hachmann had turned Ste Anne prison into a living hell.[19] Witnesses also mentioned Oberscharführer "Perrine" who could not be found in any list of the SiPo-SD and was probably an assumed name of Schultz himself.

Gauthier was transferred to Digne on April 1, 1944, and mortally wounded by the Resistance on June 6, 1944, at Vergons in the Basses Alpes. He died a few days later in the Digne hospital.

The Auxiliaries of the rue Bancasse

Before we follow the tracks of Alfred André and his acolytes within the GFP, we should clarify and discuss once and for all the thesis often repeated by local historians who claim that the "Gestapo" moved on February 4, 1943,

---

* SS rank equivalent to warrant officer.
† SS rank equivalent to chief warrant officer.

from 11, rue Bancasse to 32, avenue Monclar, thus implying that there was no more German police activity at the Hotel de la Cigale.

Actually, it is the leadership of the SiPo-SD that settled in avenue Monclar, with Wilhelm Müller as its boss. He was the number one in the German police in Avignon (including the GFP, which remained in rue Bancasse). The confusion which already existed between the names of the police units—GFP, Gestapo, SD, SS, and SiPo-SD—could have been compounded by several moves that occurred in February 1943. The Kommandantur left the Hotel du Palais des Papes to go to 35, rue Joseph Vernet. Similarly, the troops stationed in the Palais des Papes and the vehicle parked in front of the Palais rejoined the Chabran and Haupoul barracks.

In a letter dated April 19, 1943, the prefect wrote to Gauthier in avenue Monclar to forward a baptism certificate of the gentile wife of Henri Dreyfus, the former mayor of Carpentras. She was arrested with her husband, Henri, and her brother-in-law, René Dreyfus who was deported.[20] Wolfram, *aka* Gauthier, was sometimes referred to as chief of the GFP, and on other occasions as second in command of the SD. On May 17, 1943, referring to himself as department head of the service of 32, avenue Monclar, Gauthier informed the prefect of the arrest of some Jews. Gauthier, who could alternatively be found in rue Bancasse and in avenue Monclar, seemed to serve as a liaison between his boss, Wilhelm Müller, and the members of the GFP, and probably kept an eye on them. The presence of Gauthier simultaneously at both addresses can be explained in part by the recent unification of the German police units.

Joseph Grunstein, who resided in Valréas with his wife and two children, was arrested on February 9, 1944. Four days later, Deborah Grunstein, having not heard from her husband, traveled to Avignon. She did not return. On February 14, Maurice and Pauline, the two children, were summoned to 11, rue Bancasse. Another indication of the continuing activity of rue Bancasse: in May and June 1944, a 20-year-old man named Roger Leonetti, with a long police record (robbery, possession of stolen goods, illegal carrying of firearms, former reform school inmate) was called twice to the rue Bancasse because his papers were not in order. His closeness with Biancone, the boss of the Bar Crillon, his uncle who was hiding him, eventually got him released.[21] Finally, on March 15, 1945, the deposition of Georges Parietas, *aka* Commissaire Boyer, judged in Marseille, left no doubt:

> I was an agent of the GFP at the Hotel de la Cigale from December 1943 to June 15, 1944. At that time, I was transferred to 348, boulevard Michelet in Marseille, the GFP of the air force. I have participated on my own and with

other comrades in numerous bogus detective jobs and the blackmail of Jews. In my capacity as head of the French service of the GFP, I had several people under my command: Alfred André, Vial *aka* Bouboule, Cappe from Arles, Jean Costa whose primary role was informer, Nicolas Raineroff, Orloff *aka* Nicky (might have been arrested in Paris), Boyer "from Mondragon" killed by the Germans, Robert Bonhoure *aka* Le Moël (might have been arrested in Paris), Lassia from Entraigues (found dead on the Rhône riverside), Charles Isnard, *aka* Le Toulonnais (executed in Villeneuve), André Moreau, Grimaldi from Arles, Pic also from Arles, Frasson from Chateaurenard, Villard, and the Arab Simon Seghir.[22]

There were many more than five people involved, but the hard core was composed of Boyer himself, André, Cappe, Nicky, and Costa. The additional names of people coming from different locations showed that the activity of the Boyer gang, connected to rue Bancasse, extended beyond the boundaries of the Vaucluse. The agents of higher caliber—those that a man like Etienne Bravi, 30 years old, called "inspectors of the Gestapo"—all had their own paid or volunteer informers, and kept looking for more. If we include the associates of the hard core, the network becomes much larger. Etienne Bravi, a plasterer by trade, but in reality a pimp and ex-convict, was a man under police surveillance and threatened with being sent to a labor camp; he asked Boyer for protection and was hired by him. In exchange for information about Jews, Boyer succeeded in letting him stay in Avignon. Previously chased out of town and forced to reside in Isère, he had indeed secretly returned to Avignon.

Alfred André, Boyer's "lieutenant," outdid his own boss. Amongst his acquaintances, we find Victor Bruni, his official informer, according to Boyer.[23] Bruni, 44 years old, a stallholder like André, ex-convict from before the war (theft, illegal carrying of firearms, pimp), will eventually be sentenced to forced labor for life for "*intelligence with the agents of the Gestapo, serving as an informer and taking part in this capacity in arrests, searches, looting and extorting money.*" In spite of the multiple testimonies piled up against him, Bruni admitted to only one raid which he carried out in the company of agents of the Gestapo against the Jew Maurice Stora in Villes sur Auzon, and netting 35,000 francs.

Among the documents of the Bruni trial, one indicates that Sophie Tcherkes, née Cherkaski, domiciled 72, rue Joseph Vernet, testified that "*five of her family members were arrested on March 13, 1944, because they were Jewish.*" Léon, Gilbert and Ginette were deported in convoy 71. Ginette survived. Sophie added that she has "*learned from M. Millet, secretary of the Union of Stallholders, who himself learned it from a French employee of the OPA, that they were denounced by Bruni and another man who is said to have been executed.*" Gisèle

Guillermin, née Zizerman, a relative of the Cherkaskis, knew Bruni. Like him, she owned a stall on Place Pie. She remembered her conversation with Bruni in front of the Bar Léon: "*I have a great friend at the Gestapo; if you have a large sum of money, we can get them out.*" Jean Guillermin confirms his wife's testimony: "*After learning that my wife was Jewish, Bruni contacted her and informed her that, if the Cherkaskis had one million at their disposal, he could get them released thanks to his friendship with Müller.*" In recent testimony, Ginette Kolinka, née Cherkaski, remembered that her sister got in touch with this influential person on the German side in a house of the rue de la Bourse, at the time the disreputable neighborhood of Avignon and a nest of pimps.[24] Wilhelm Müller really knew how to choose his friends.

Denis Teyssier, 21 years old, married, one child, for a while employed at the locomotive depot, made Alfred André's acquaintance in the bars of place de l'Horloge, as he described it in his deposition of October 24, 1944:

> One day that I needed money, I informed Alfred André about a Jew. The Jew lived at 11 chemin de Bonaventure. For this denunciation, I received 5,000 francs. As for the other [French] members of the Gestapo, they first extorted 40,000 francs from this person and afterward, they arrested him and delivered him to the Germans. I do not remember the name of this Jew, I can only tell you that he worked at the leather goods shop behind the court of justice.[25]

He stated that he had split the 5,000 francs with his "work" colleague, Aimé Delorme, whose profession as a waiter must have facilitated the gathering of information.

The address at 11 Chemin de Bonaventure gives a clue about the person denounced by Teyssier—a person whose name he did not remember. This was where David Kreikeman was living with his family. Besides, the denunciation of David Kreikeman was attributed to Teyssier a few weeks later, on November 12, 1944, in a report of the Screening Commission.

As to the Kreikemans, they were arrested in May 1944 by Palmieri and his gang.* This indicated that Teyssier did not work exclusively for Alfred André or that André himself collaborated with the Palmieri gang or simply that the extortion took place long before the arrest of the family. In all cases, it showed the multiple links of the Avignon networks.

At André's request, Teyssier attempted to get rehired at the locomotive depot of Avignon—a center of Resistance—to provide intelligence to the Germans. He was rejected. But of course, he could still deal with the Jews.

---

* See Chapter 9 about the Palmieri gang.

The rest of his story conveys the distrust, probably justified, that existed between the gangsters:

> I denounced the Jew Amar, place St. Lazare; the agents of the Gestapo told me that he is clean and I got no money. I informed Alfred André about the Jew Jacques Birman, greengrocer at Chemin des Sources in Avignon. A few days later, the André gang told me that they did not find him. I did not believe them, but I said nothing because they let me understand that my job was to help, no less no more. Alfred André was constantly reminding me: look for good deals that bring in money, especially the black market and the Jews.

The Birmans—Jacques, his wife Jacqueline, and their three children, Anne, Catherine and Marie—were arrested on July 17, 1943, at their villa in Villeneuve-lès-Avignon, and deported 6 months later in convoy 68. On the same day, the Germans visited their neighbors next door, the Arokas family. Salomon Arokas and his son Maurice were arrested and deported in convoy 59. Two days later, it was the turn of Ida Arokas and her daughter Denise who were taken to the prison of les Beaumettes in Marseille. Eleven years old Denise became feverish and was moved to the Hopital de la Conception. She was able to escape and survive, while her mother was sent to Drancy and from there to Auschwitz by convoy 60. In 1951, Denise Arokas fortuitously became a nurse for ailing Henri Matisse and served him as a model.[26] The family of Julien Lévi, the neighbors of the Arokas and the Birmans, was also targeted on the same day, but they fled just before the arrest.[27]

Teyssier's deposition provides us with two timeline data points, the arrest of the Biermans and the Arokas in July 1943, and the arrest of the Kreikemans in May 1944. This indicates that the André gang was working for the Germans at least during that time frame. André probably made contact with the SiPo-SD, and particularly its GFP contingent, soon after their settling in rue Bancasse.

During his interrogation, Teyssier "exonerated" his friend Poutier who had helped him find Jews, but he was never paid for it. Well, as long as it is pro bono… He concluded:

> I admit I had told my wife that I was a member of the Gestapo, and that I had moved around every time in the Gestapo car. Occasionally, I went to the Hotel de la Cigale, where the services of the Gestapo GFP resided, to provide Alfred André with information. All in all, I worked for the Gestapo during a month and a half under the orders of Alfred André.

On September 3, 1945, Teyssier, Delorme and Poutier were sentenced to hard labor for life and 5 years and 8 months in prison, respectively.

Anecdotally, we even know the automobile that Teyssier was using. It was Georges Parietas who is very precise about it:

> I owned two cars, a front wheel drive Citroën and a Matford. Cappe was the driver. Alfred André personally owned a front wheel drive. The license plates of one car, the Matford, were 2613 ZA 5. As for the other two cars we had a set of license plates which allowed us to swap them for our operations.

The life of Jean Costa took an unexpected turn toward the rue Bancasse, when he caught sight of Alfred André, Georges Boyer, and Nicky inside one of these cars. At least this is what he claimed. He probably knew them before his first arrest. Otherwise, they would not have hailed him to join them for the arrest of a Jewish dentist on boulevard Raspail in Avignon.

We found the information in the file of Maurice Pardini, who was completely exonerated in this case. In his deposition on May 11, 1945, Pierre Aizen provided all the details of his arrest:

> Alfred André, Georges Boyer, Nicky and a man named Costa came on March 28, 1944, to arrest me at my work place, the dental clinic on boulevard Raspail. They told me that they had to arrest me as an Israelite to send me to a concentration camp. They took me to my home after a two hour discussion in my office. During that conversation, I bargained to get them to release me and I was able to sway them. They offered me to work for them, namely to provide them with good deals in exchange for a percentage of 25%. I pretended to accept et they asked me for a "security deposit" of 250,000 francs. I took Alfred André and Georges Boyer to my home to give them the money. Since I had approximately 500,000 francs and that Boyer who had come upstairs saw them, he grabbed a hold of them. They later returned to my home where they did a search in front of the mason who happened to be in the house. I went to hide at a friend's house in Avignon and later in Villeneuve.[28]

For just hanging out with them, on the evening of this achievement, Jean Costa received 7,000 francs from Alfred André at the Bar Carnot;[29] a modest beginning for this 45-year-old house painter, born in Marseille, who had been sentenced in his youth in Aix en Provence to a five year restraining order. His father, a mechanic at the PLM,* facilitated his employment at the Marseille streetcar company. He might not have been thrilled with the prospect of a working class life. So he alternated between truck delivery and burglary. In

---

* The PLM (Paris-Lyon-Marseille) is the company which operated the railway line between these three towns.

1936, he seemed to settle down; he set up his own house painting business in Avignon. But in 1938, he was sentenced for non-declaration of weapons. Then, the war broke out. After demobilization, he ended up as a technician at the Grégoire pharmacy in Avignon. To supplement his modest salary, he resorted to the black market, then arms-dealing got him to rue Bancasse, where he again met Alfred André, his old Nîmes jail mate.

Costa was very forthcoming about the "financial" operations of the gang, but proof of their true extent can be found in the file of Antoine Cappe, who was tried in Marseille. We know that looting brought in large, and even very large, amounts of money, because rue Bancasse had become a center of theft, looting and extortion. Its reputation reached far beyond the city limits.

As with the Rosenbergs in Bollène, loot was a "by-product" of the persecution of the Jews and their arrest, and had to be disposed of. This is when Simon Seghir came into play. A member of the gang according to Boyer, and a grocer in the rue de la Carreterie, Seghir owned a warehouse at 7 rue Rempart de la Ligne, a stone's throw from the hoodlums' roost. A coincidence! This is where Seghir kept his food supply, but also where Boyer put his stolen goods in storage, before reselling them on the market of Place Pie and elsewhere. Did Seghir surrender to intimidation and terror or did he simply want to make easy money quickly? It may be for both reasons. Boyer's watchful eye was safer than a padlock to look after Seghir's food.

As to Costa, in August 1944, he blackmailed the Jewish director of a Monoprix department store, M. Franck, who had to pay 47,000 francs for his freedom. Business was still going on a few days before Liberation. The conclusion of the police report of January 13, 1945, wraps up the Costa affair best:

> To conclude, Costa, blessed with the title of member of the Gestapo, turned to the search for Jews because he saw in it a way to increase his budget. Moreover, he has participated several times in break-ins for the same reason, knowing full well that these raids would go unpunished.

This greed of André's gang was well known to the Jewish population of Avignon and its surroundings.

The Boss Who Came from Paris

As to Georges Boyer: no file about him could be found, but there are many depositions scattered throughout several other files ([Roger] Boyer[30] "from Mondragon," namesake of Georges Boyer, Jean-Baptiste Cabagno,[31] Antoine Cappe[32]). Paraded from trial to trial, Georges Boyer appeared to be a high-class prisoner. Arrested in Lyon in the fall of 1944 and executed by firing squad on December 17, 1946, he had enough time to talk. He did not spare any detail on his career, even if he tried hard to reduce the scope of his activity to high robbery; he denied having arrested Jews or members of the Resistance on his own initiative, but always acting at the behest of the Germans.

Before the war, Boyer, age 30—his real name was Parietas—was a minor gangster in Paris who had done time for a number of offenses such as possession of stolen goods, swindling, and gambling. His parents were hotel owners and coal merchants and he managed a hotel in Levallois, and worked as a waiter in many restaurants and cafés. He mostly lived by his wits and was a gambler for ten years after his imprisonment in Fresnes, in spite of an order, in 1923, to stay away from Paris, which he clearly didn't abide by.

With the 1939 draft, because of his criminal record, he was sent to the Camp of Caylus (Tarn et Garonne). In March 1940 he volunteered for the combat duty and was sent to the Light Infantry Battalion in North Africa. Discharged in Marseille, he returned to Paris and went to the racetracks where he resumed his "profession" as a bookie. Suddenly, Boyer was hit with some bad luck: he was summoned by the Clichy police commissioner for guard duty on the railroad line. As a result, he left Paris to escape his obligations and set out to the city where organized crime was well-established.

> Upon my arrival in Marseille, I got acquainted with the underworld. At the beginning, I often used to go to the bar "Le Gaulois," rue de la Darse, managed by Mathieu Costa and also to the bar "Mistral" managed by Jeannot Carbone. I was broke and they noticed that I was jobless. A man named Bauer (a pimp), who visited Carbone often and had a day and night pass delivered by the Germans, introduced me to a man named Nau. This man asked me to enter the Gestapo's service. After I accepted, he took me to Avignon, rue de la Bancasse, in his personal car. Nau introduced me to the German services in Avignon where he was very well-known.
>
> I was greeted by a German lieutenant named Rupp, who started with a questioning and hired me after I gave him my photographs. I was expected to work for the German military security (GFP). I was not supposed to get a salary, but lieutenant Rupp had told me to manage with "the others," namely to participate in the looting organized against the Jews.
>
> For my job, I had received a card that said: "The man named Georges Boyer is attached to GFP service no. 27203 in Avignon, rue de la Bancasse." This document was signed by Lieutenant Rupp, written in German and bearing the stamp with the swastika and the German eagle. As a precaution, this certificate was renewable on a monthly basis, because I knew that the Germans

had provided similar documents to others for periods of 6 months and that some of them had fled after using the certificate for committing wrongdoings or fraud as "bogus cops."

In December 1943, I started my job in Avignon under the orders of Rupp himself.

This testimony underscores an essential element, the freedom granted by the Germans to practice looting, and as a natural consequence, to organize raids as bogus cops. But in addition, Lieutenant Rupp, cited here as head of the Avignon GFP, does not appear in the membership of the SiPo-SD of the region of Marseille. This establishes a dual hierarchy with joint operations.

Boyer dated his hiring to December 1943, but in his deposition about Gautsch von Sachsenthurn[33] (Hungarian agent of the GFP), he situated his own arrival at the Avignon GFP in November. Several other statements confirm that Boyer, Cappe, Nicky and André were ready to get down to the job as early as November. The description of the gang members is quite precise.

- André Vial: common law criminal, brothel manager in Fréjus, domiciled in Nice. Hired by the Avignon GFP at the end of December 1943.
- Nicolas Raineroff, *aka* "Count Orloff," also called Nicky: a Quartier Latin student in Paris, Russian born with French nationality, fluent in German as well as English. We learn from the Cappe file that he was indicted in Paris at the Liberation.
- Antoine Cappe. He was recruited by Nau (A German national in charge of recruiting for the Gestapo). Hired by the Avignon GFP with the help of Georges Boyer, but he had known Alfred André earlier in Arles where he lived. According to his file, he was known as a member of the PPF, responsible for propaganda in the "groupe Collaboration." A foreman at the Coinard enterprise in Nîmes, he became a driver for the organization Todt, that fired him after he was caught selling gasoline. Sentenced to death by the court of justice of Marseille on July 17, 1946, his punishment was commuted to hard labor for life by the decree of November 20, 1946.
- Alfred André was recruited at the same time as Cappe.
- Roger Boyer, so called "Boyer from Mondragon," was named by his peers after the village he came from to avoid any confusion with the boss, Georges Boyer. He was liquidated by the Germans around August 18, 1944, before their departure from Avignon. They had decided to get rid of him after he had received money for a "Jewish deal" and greased the palm of a German captain. The captain in question had him executed to eliminate an embarrassing witness. A local member of the gang, Roger Boyer had probably been in the area from the beginning.

As to Kurt Gautsch von Sachsenthurn, former agent of the French intelligence before the war, he was hired around September 10, 1943, by the Avignon GFP:

> My job consisted in translating denunciations provided by the PPF, the Milice, or anonymous letters, so that investigations could be launched. I was in charge of initiating these inquiries, conducting the interrogations and recording the minutes…

Although much testimony exists about gangsters working for the GFP, Von Sachsenthurn did not mention them specifically. The probable reason for this omission is that people like Alfred André and his associates were considered permanent members of the GFP. They were not seen as informers.

In the course of 1943 the head of the German police, Wilhelm Müller, who had operated from the villa at 32, avenue Monclar, surrounded himself with a growing number of very efficient French agents like Pierre Terrier and Robert Conrad. As a growing number of such individuals joined in, the persecution reached its peak in March 1944 with the takeover of the operations by Palmieri, who had started infiltrating the Vaucluse a few months earlier.

The Crime Villas

Today, the "Hôtel de la Cigale" in the rue Bancasse, two minutes away from the Place de l'Horloge, is called "L'hôtel de Blauvac" that was the marquis de Blauvac's home in the 17th century. In the presentation booklet of this very well restored hotel, there is understandably no mention of its function during the war that could disturb the customers.

The villa at 32, avenue Monclar, is a beautiful impressive house, outside the city walls but very close to the train station, it remains untouched by time. Before the war, it belonged to Albert Carcassonne, a Jewish lawyer. In April 1940 his widow Madeleine and his daughter Andrée sold it to Doctor Gayraud. Interestingly, Andrée Carcassonne was married to Doctor Georges Pons, a Resistance figure, and the future mayor of Avignon after Liberation. Pons had his office in the villa, and at some point, even a clinic. Did he continue using the villa as his office after the sale? It is indeed possible. Anyway, the sale's agreement stipulated that Gayraud would take possession of the property in August. Was there a tacit agreement so that Pons could continue using it? And did all of this play a role in the decision of the German police to settle there? It remains a possibility.

As for the French members of the GFP, they lived, according to Georges Boyer "*at 2, rue Rempart de la Ligne, in a beautiful building belonging to the Jew Naquet, whose assets were confiscated by the Germans.*" To get a better understanding, we need to go back to Jean Costa's file.[34] In his deposition, young André Naquet stated that "*his father and several members of his family had a close call and escaped arrest by the French agents of the Gestapo who belonged to Boyer's gang.*" We also learn that the house was looted; paintings, fabrics, rugs disappeared from 2, rue du Rempart de la Ligne. After that the Germans decided to allocate it to Boyer's gang providing him with sumptuous lodgings as well as offices for his "commercial activity," focused on black market purchase and sale, and the disposal of stolen property.

Today, the Naquet residence has been replaced by the "La Cardère" condominium building, named after the thistle plant used for the carding of textile fibers; the enterprise of the Naquets, adjacent to their home, specialized in the treatment of the thistle that they sold in the textile industry. But the address is important: 2, rue Rempart de la Ligne is at the end of rue de la Banasterie, a stone's throw from the Ste Anne prison. It was very handy for the arrests. On the other hand, if help was needed, one could always call upon Alfred André who lived at 30, rue du Rempart St. Lazare, in the immediate continuation of rue du Rempart de la Ligne. These two short streets run along the inside of the walls.

André Naquet testified that on October 28, 1943, the day of the operation against his family, he and his parents were absent. Only his cousin, Lily Meyer, née Amado, and her mother (Achille Naquet's sister) were on the third floor. Two individuals who showed up to arrest the Naquets introduced themselves. The first, a young man, stated that he was a White Russian who spoke several languages. The other one was a paint salesman in Avignon. Probably, these two men were Nicky and Costa, whose personal data from their files matched their statements. Fortunately, Lily and her mother succeeded in escaping through the attic by pretending to go and fetch some clothes.[35]

This was at the end of October 1943, and the French gangsters were already on the job. Georges Boyer was probably not yet in town, and we do not know whether he had a predecessor. However, his arrival coincided with significant criminal escalation.

The Money of the Jews

During his questioning by Superintendent Fafur from the Squad for the Surveillance of the Territory (Direction de la Surveillance du Territoire) in Marseille, Alfred André described the blackmail of André Mossé:

In November 1943, while I was at the Bar Central in Avignon, I overheard the conversation between the owner and a customer about an Israelite whose name I have forgotten. The client was saying that this Israelite was well hidden in Mollèges [Bouches du Rhône] and that he was rich. I carefully wrote down the name and the village. I told Boyer, and the next day, we went to that Israelite, Boyer, Cappe, Nicky and me. We asked around in the village, and we found the man in the company of his wife and a maid. Boyer showed his German police documents and announced that he had come to arrest him and his wife. The Israelite then proposed a deal and offered 40 pounds sterling in golden coins. We accepted and left him free. The sharing out took place during the trip in the car. Everyone got 8 pounds, because one share was kept for Vial who had provided the car. The Israelite told us he had decided to look for a hiding place in another region.[36]

Questioned on May 31, 1946, André Mossé identified the photograph of Boyer without any hesitation. Boyer, who did not deny the accusation, added: *"After this expedition, we did not say a word about the deal to the German services."*

Then, there was the raid at Marie Riz' restaurant, "le Coq Hardi":

In November 1943, Cappe, together with Raineroff and André went to the woman Riz, an Israelite, took her in the car to Parietas, and under the threat of arrest, obtained a payment of 60,000 francs, from her given to Raineroff.

Then there was the Stora case in Villes sur Auzon, on June 3, 1944, which is also in the Cappe file. This was another instance of blackmail that brought in 180,000 francs in cash for freedom. The victim, Maurice Stora, an antique dealer living at 32 Bd Haussmann in Paris, testified on July 24, 1946:

It is correct that in 1942, more precisely in December 1942, I left Paris without my family to escape the reprisals against the Israelites. I sought refuge in the vicinity of Avignon, at Villes sur Auzon, where my brother-in-law Paul Cartoux still owns a villa. In that village, I first stayed at the hotel, then I rented a villa as soon as my family joined me.

In Villes sur Auzon, I had no problems until June 3 or 4, 1944. On that day, I received the visit of two individuals accompanied by M. Mus, a garage owner in Villes; he used to drive me to the dentist in Avignon… One of the individuals was hiding behind Mus… I immediately opened the door, the individual in question came in, gun in hand, and said "German police! Don't breathe a word! Don't make a move! You are Jewish, and I am going to arrest you and carry out a search…" He said that his boss was coming in a few minutes; he added that his boss had already made deals with several people and that there was no reason why he could not come to an agreement with me. Naturally, he said that after seeing the contents of a leather briefcase which contained my money, because I had asked to take it with me.

As I realized that he was impressed by the money in the briefcase, I asked how much I had to give him. He answered that he wanted it all, and that I would be better off in Villes sur Auzon than in a concentration camp.

At that moment, his boss arrives and introduces himself as "German police," but he did not show any document… As they insisted on arresting me, I asked whether there was a way to strike a deal, as the first individual had suggested… The so-called chief refused. I insisted and he ended up accepting. I gave them the entire content of the briefcase, namely 180,000 francs approximately. This so-called chief asked for the authorization to take a new tie by Lanvin and a pair of pig skin gloves by Hermès, from a chest drawer. Naturally, I shrugged and did not even answer. He then took the two objects on top of the 180,000 francs. This happened on a Saturday morning. When they left, they said they would be back on the following Wednesday.

Stora did not wait for his due; he immediately left for Paris.

"One-armed Simon" was a name given to a man named Simon by those who had come to arrest him.[37] A tip from Albert Sauvet and "Boyer from Mondragon" indicated that Simon and his wife were hidden in a farm in Morrières, on the road to Montfavet. Georges Boyer suspected that the man was very rich, so he needed to show class. He introduced himself as "Commissaire Boyer," and after a thorough search, "Simon" understood clearly the reason for his arrest. Boyer continued with his deposition:

> Simon proposed one million for his release and I accepted. In the meantime, my comrades had discovered the jewelry of Madame Simon in a safe, at the very least worth three million. They wanted to take the jewels. I objected because Simon agreed to leave the area on the very next day and not say a word to anybody about what happened. Moreover, my comrades had made a mistake when they drove the cars into the farm yard. I knew that the witnesses would write down the license plate numbers and I was afraid we would all be arrested the next day. Therefore, I insisted on leaving the jewelry. Simon paid 800,000 francs in banknotes and 200,000 francs in gold coins—louis and dollars. When we left, we said to the farm people that our investigation was a mistake and that Simon was in order, so that no news of the affair would get out. Simon confirmed in our presence. Then we drove to André, at 30, rue du Rempart St. Lazare in Avignon, where we divided immediately.

Here too, we have the victim's testimony given on December 20, 1944. "Simon" was in fact André Himmelfarb, 46 years old, business manager, domiciled in rue d'Armény in Marseille. He indicated that he took refuge in the Gard with his wife and estimated the damage to three million and a half, a much larger amount than acknowledged by Boyer.

Finally in another expedition to demand a ransom from a couple staying in a hotel at Fontaine de Vaucluse in February 1944. On December 2, 1944, Georges Boyer claimed that it was Cappe who had been tipped by a third party:

> Around 3 p.m., the four of us arrived at the hotel and learned that the couple in question was staying on the second floor. We went to their room, we presented our police documents from the German service, and threatened to have them arrested. We immediately carried out a search and discovered a pack of securities worth about one million. Pursuing our search, we found a metal box containing gold coins of different origins (dollars, pounds, sterling, and Louis). For his part, Nicky Raineroff had found two rings that he had kept in his possession.
>
> We seized the box with the gold coins, and the Israelites asked whether they could leave immediately. We agreed to their request; however, we returned the securities that bore their name. We stayed a few more minutes in the room, but having not found anything of interest, we went down after them.
>
> Nicky showed me the two rings he had stolen from the woman's bag. He told me that we should share these two pieces of jewelry only between the two of us and leave Cappe and André out. The first, a platinum ring with a diamond, was worth about 150,000 francs, the other, of lesser importance, could bring in about 50,000 francs; it was also a platinum ring with a diamond. In agreement with Raineroff, I removed the diamonds so that I could easily hide them and sell them later. I sold the platinum, around 10 grams, but I do not remember who bought it.
>
> The metal box with the gold coins was in the hands of Nicky, who shared the contents equally among us. This yielded a value of about 75,000 francs per person. As to the informer from Avignon who had tipped us off, we told him that our raid was negative and that the Jews had left the area.
>
> While I was in Marseille around May 1944, I sold the two diamonds to a man named Max, an assistant jeweler, expert in the trade, for a sum of between 200,000 and 250,000 francs. I split the proceeds of this sale with Nicky without informing Cappe and André.[38]

It is during another questioning of Boyer, on December 29, 1944, that the victims' names came to light; they were Robert and Martha Fischer, the parents of Max Fischer, the co-founder of the Maquis Ventoux.* Boyer did not know this family link. Actually, they were targeting another couple who had left the village. And, in Boyer's words, "*in order not to come back to Avignon*

---

* The Maquis Ventoux, a Resistance group in Mount Ventoux, was founded by Fischer and Beyne.

with an empty bag," they made do with another hotel where the Fischers were staying. Boyer gave one more detail: "*During the search, Raineroff threatened Mme. Fischer with his gun, because she had come to see what he was stealing.*"

The sharing on the sly of the money coming from the sale of the rings opened a crack in the often romanticized "code of honor" of the mob. An anecdote by Boyer himself brings us back to reality. Under the mediation of his Marseille agent, "Lou from Toulouse," Boyer had received in his warehouse at the Naquets' villa, the delivery of 500 kg of green beans of coffee at 1700 francs a kilo by a Spaniard from Marseille. When he was about to pay the man, two "policemen" who were in fact Boyer's accomplices, burst into the luxurious office of Boyer pistol in hand; they arrested everybody and "confiscated" the coffee beans. They finally released, only issuing a warning, the Spaniard who was only too happy to get off so lightly. Later, Boyer and his men split the proceeds of the sale of 500 kg of coffee beans. However, Boyer's acolytes did not know that, in reality, the trusting Spaniard had delivered 1000 kg of beans and that Boyer had pocketed the money from the remaining "undeclared" 500 kg. Stealing from other thieves!

The Arrest and Deportation of the Jews

Of course, all these thefts, ransoms, extortions went in the same direction. And if we take them to the letter and forget the raid at the Rosenberg's in Bollène, the facts can be misleading, as if it was sufficient to pay in order to pull through. Freedom in exchange of money worked in some cases, and Boyer and his gang provided ample details about them. But they kept the other cases under wrap. If we believe them, they limited themselves "*to numerous instances of bogus police raids or blackmail of Jews.*" They certainly had hoped that eventual prosecution witnesses would be rare or non-existent. Fortunately, several witnesses blew apart their defense and underscored their responsibility.

On May 4, 1946, Fanny Bleines (registered in the 1944 census at 4, rue Molière in Avignon) provided an insight in her deposition given to Inspector Dominique Felce, superintendant of the DST* of Paris:

> In September 1943, while I was visiting one of my friends, Mme. Cohn, 1, impasse de l'Oratoire in Avignon, where I had been invited to a tea party with other ladies, five individuals introduced themselves by announcing "German police!" while showing their police badges. They immediately carried out a

---

* Direction de la Surveillance du Territoire, French equivalent of the FBI.

search in Mme. Cohn's apartment and took away jewelry, linen, a brand new woman's bag, two pairs of shoes, several perfumes and a radio set.

During the search, one of these individuals asked me to accompany him to my home, 4, rue Jacob, while the others continued searching the home of Mme. Cohn... He again verified my identity, did a cursory search, then asked me to pack my suitcase, to take a blanket and to follow him; he made it clear to me that he was taking me for deportation as an Israelite. Before leaving, he told me that he would set me free if I gave him the names of several Israelites that I knew were not in order... I told him that I did not know anybody in default. At that moment, he became very forward, and proposed that I sleep with him. I refused and left my apartment in his company. We went back to Mme. Cohn where he was supposed to discuss my case with his boss, "Superintendant Boyer." I want to report that he grabbed my radio set when we left my home.

At Mme. Cohn's home, these gentlemen caucused about our case, then they left with the loot only but without taking anybody.

A little later, in March 1944, my parents who did not feel secure in Paris, came to my apartment, to stay with me. My father, Salomon Lerner, is 69 years old, and my mother Sarah Lerner, 58.

Since the arrival of my parents, I stopped sleeping at home, because of the threat of arrest. For the same reason, my parents stayed there intermittently. Finally, during the night from March 28 to 29, 1944, a raid was carried out in Avignon, my parents were arrested and taken to an unknown destination and I have had no news from them. According to information I gathered, the arrest of my parents was carried out by a German assisted by a French team who claimed they belonged to the Gestapo. In my apartment, they engaged in real burglary and looted jewelry, linens, money, etc...

I insist on the fact that my parents were unknown in Avignon and that nobody knew my address, except the gang that came to Mme. Cohn in November 1943. Consequently, these individuals are the only ones who could have been at the origin of my parents' arrest and deportation.

Among the pictures that you are showing me, I recognize clearly the men named Alfred André, André Vial, Antoine Cappe and Georges Parietas, *aka* Boyer, as the individuals who came to the home of Mme. Cohn where I was invited in November 1943. I do not recognize among the photos the individual who took me to my home, 4, rue Jacob, to search my apartment and took my radio set. I believe without being totally sure that his name was Nicky Orloff...[39]

During the confrontation that followed with Boyer, Cappe and Vial, Boyer confirmed that Nicky accompanied Fanny Bleines to her home. He admitted having participated in the raid on Mme. Cohn's home. He provided however, a different angle claiming that "*he carried out the search at Mme. Cohn's home following an investigation by the German police about counterfeit rationing cards trafficking imputed to her husband. After making a deal with Mr. Cohn at his office, where he recovered the ration cards, he promised to leave him alone and advised him to hide.*" On the other hand, Boyer made no mention of the arrest of Salomon and Sarah Lerner, deported on convoy 72. He was very talkative about the morals of the thugs, but silent about the deportees. The bottom line is that the hidden Jews with enough money were not necessarily safe. They too were vulnerable behind an imaginary shield.

On June 26, 1945, Jacques Senator, deported on convoy 76, who survived Birkenau and Monowitz, testified in the same vein as Fanny Bleines, before Charles Bonnet, Police Superintendant:

> I used to live at 54, rue Bonneterie in Avignon, when I was arrested by three miliciens on May 30, 1944, around 2:30 p.m., at the bar of the Brasserie des Arts, on the Place de l'Horloge.
>
> I did not know anyone of the three individuals who carried out my arrest. Here is how it happened: I was having a drink at the bar when a black Citroën front wheel drive, stopped in front of the café suddenly putting on the brakes. The three associates came out and accosted me. They surrounded me, asking whether I was Mr. Senator. Upon my confirmation, they forced me to go with them.
>
> Once in the car, they asked me where I lived; since I could not refuse, I gave them my address.
>
> In my apartment, they carried out a thorough search and turned everything upside down to find money… They found 7000 francs in my vest pocket. As they insisted and threatened to beat me, I told them that they could find under a pile of laundry another 20,000 francs, which constituted all of my savings. They attempted a blackmail maneuver by promising to let me free in exchange for another ransom, but I categorically refused, because I knew they would arrest me anyway.
>
> Driven to the Gestapo of the Hotel de la Cigale in rue Bancasse, they made the same blackmail attempt which I resisted again, and after written questioning, they sent me to the Ste Anne prison… Before my departure [for Drancy], they took 3500 francs out of the 7000 that I had given; I had hidden my last 19,000 francs inside the lining of my coat.
>
> … After my return to Avignon, I mentioned my arrest to Mme. Tourel, I think the owner of the Brasserie des Arts; she said that she recognized "Superintendant Boyer" as one of the three individuals.[40]

Charles Palmieri, an agent of the SiPo-SD in Marseille, a central figure in the hunt for the Jews in the Vaucluse, gave undeniable proof that the members of Boyer's gang did not limit themselves to extortion; they did not hesitate to deliver their victims to the Germans, their masters. Only the hope of additional gain could make them to delay an arrest.

In his deposition of March 15, 1945, Palmieri declared:

> In Avignon, I had several agents: Bergeron, Mouillade, Lucien Blanc, Pierre Josselme. Bergeron and his colleagues come often to Marseille to provide information and reports about the activity of the Resistance. They also brought the list of Jews to be arrested. I organized a few operations in Avignon. The first one was in the company of Thomas Ricci who brought around 15 of his agents while I brought 10 of mine. Bergeron, Mouillade, Blanc and Josselme* from my service as well as Georges Boyer, Alfred André and Nicky took part in it. On that day, we arrested 44 Jews who were transferred to Marseille by bus...[41]

The various gangs were able to collaborate when numbers were needed to hunt down the Jews leading us to the conclusion that Boyer and his gang had several modes of operation. If their employers were out of sight and their victims had significant liquid assets, they vigorously used extortion in exchange for freedom. Of course, discretion was the rule. If the victims had modest means, the gangsters stole whatever they could and delivered the victims to the Germans to make the quota. Finally, when the German police "needed Jews," they asked Boyer and his men, as well as other auxiliaries to join forces with them or to deliver their own designated victims. If the victims were rich, it was more difficult to appropriate the loot without arousing the suspicion of the German police that had seen it all.

Everybody wanted something in return: the Germans wanted Jews and some of them were interested in their money; the gangsters wanted money and the opportunity to continue making money. To stay in business, Boyer had to find a balance: not an easy task. The use of the mob by the Germans produced conflicting results. It contributed to the death of hundreds of Jews from the Vaucluse, but the greed of the gangsters allowed many of them to save their lives.

At the beginning of the summer of 1944 the gangsters from Avignon were not the only ones hunting the Jews. In his report of July 31, 1944, the director of the SEC for the Marseille region, Raymond Guilledoux, informed his bosses in Vichy:

> Increasingly, the Jews or their friends are being swindled, often outrageously, by individuals who pretend to have been sent by the German authorities to arrest them... and who agree to a delay of 24 hours in exchange for 25, 50 and even 100,000 francs.[42]

---

* Palmieri is probably mistaken about the presence of Josselme, who was gunned down by the police on February 28, 1944, while the first operation byPalmieri in Avignon took place at the end of March.

As illustrated by the SEC's track record, it is unlikely that this report of Guilledoux was motivated by ethical considerations.

Boyer's "Exile" to Marseille

In May 1944, Albert Sauvet joined the GFP team. He ran two brothels, one in Avignon and the other in Nimes. He also owned a hotel in Nice in his wife's name. But this month of May stands out because of Boyer's serious problems with his employers. He described his own tribulations:

> In May 1944, the Avignon police superintendant received several complaints about our schemes, and he informed lieutenant Rupp… The [French] authorities had decided to arrest my entire team, but I must tell you that the Germans were not keen on having us booked by the French police. However, a certain Major von Bock* decided to have us arrested by the Reich's military, more specifically, units of the Brandebourg regiment. Informed ahead of time, I fled in company of Raineroff and we took refuge in Marseille, while Cappe, André and his wife, Boyer from Mondragon and Albert Sauvet were apprehended by the Waffen-SS and taken to Pont St. Esprit.†43

Technically unemployed, Boyer and Nicky renewed their contact with Rupp from Avignon who declared that they *"can no more be of any use to him,"* but he gave them a note recommending them to Lieutenant Walter from the Marseille GFP at 348 boulevard Michelet. Their remuneration, was the same as in Avignon: it was agreed that they would manage on their own. Looting Jewish assets was clearly an integral part of German strategy as long as the French did not complain. The "firing" of Boyer was merely a smoke screen for the French police.

Boyer began his Marseille episode in June 1944. He rebuilt a new spider network around himself and relied on the occasional help of his Avignon friends, who were soon released from Pont St. Esprit and returned to serve under the orders of Lieutenant Rupp. Boyer, who didn't drive, hired Cabagno as his driver.

Jean-Baptiste Cabagno's file is replete with information about this petty Marseille gangster, a member of the PPF who avoided the STO and worked for the Gestapo in 1943. He got into trouble after the heist of a jeweler, Paul Eyssantier. The loot was estimated at one million francs. Boyer succeeded in

---

* A German officer, who was based in Aix en Provence and served as a military liaison to the GFP of Avignon and Marseille.

† The fortress of Pont St. Esprit was the base for units of the Brandebourg Waffen-SS regiment.

setting Cabagno free and hired him as his driver. The prosecutor's statement was unambiguous:

> The man named Cabagno, together with the man named Georges Parietas, agent of the German police, who employed him as his driver, participated in Marseille in the arrest of several Jews and several patriots. In addition, he would also loot the apartments of the people he was arresting.[44]

Although Cabagno denied having officially been a member of the Avignon or Marseille GFP (a fact confirmed by Boyer), he nevertheless maintained contact with the GFP until October 1944, even in Germany where he had fled. The Germans attempted to use him after sending him to a radio course at Tübingen in preparation to parachuting him back into France. Finally, *"taking advantage of the allied advance, Cabagno succeeded in entering a camp of French prisoners where he pretended to have been sent to Germany by the STO. Repatriated under a false identity, he reconnects in Paris with a former member of Boyer's gang, Robert Bonhoure, who informs him about the warrant for his arrest in Marseille."*

Bonhoure was no small fry. His questioning, gives a good picture about the type of person he was. Back from the First world war, he managed his own café in Paris, a gift he had received from his father, a dairy producer from Seine et Oise. If we believe his interrogation of December 27, 1944, for 25 years he had lived the colorless life of a small businessman.[45] He bought and sold several businesses, always cafés and restaurants. *"In addition to my activity in business,"* he added, *"I was taking care of race horses. I even owned a racing stable at Maison Lafitte before the war in 1939."*

Boyer was at least more direct:

> One of my old acquaintances, the man called Robert Bonhoure who also called himself Robert Le Meur* had just arrived at the service in boulevard Michelet†. He was an ex-convict and had been a bookmaker with me in Paris.

Bonhoure explained his arrival in a discreet way:

> In 1943 and 1944, I had no job, but there was a warrant for my arrest coming from Epinal,‡ and I considered it a good thing to leave the capital and get some distance in Marseille. In the past in Paris, I had known the man named Georges Parietas with whom I was dealing at the races, and I learned that he was

---

* In a document already cited, Bonhoure uses the alias Le Moël. Le Meur is yet another alias. He has also used Chausaudme and Amouroux.
† Address of the GFP offices in Marseille.
‡ This was a French warrant.

working for the GFP in Marseille. So I wrote him from Paris to inform him that I was being sought by the Germans after a heist and to ask him whether I could seek refuge in Provence. On Sunday, June 18, 1944, I arrived in Marseille. Boyer stated that he was going to get me into his [*sic*] Avignon service and in the meantime, I would be his driver… On July 1, 1944, he gave me a certificate signed by him, stating that I belonged to the GFP.

Boyer helped out his friend in need, and on June 18 1944, they met at the "Brasserie Le Gaulois" as agreed. But in his questioning of December 28, 1944, Boyer became very explicit:

> He told me that he had worked in Paris in the German police services of the rue Lauriston under the orders of Lafont. During a mission in Epinal, he grabbed assets belonging to Jews which had been sealed. This was a large amount in Treasury bills that he had later disposed of on the black market. But the certificates had been stopped and Bonhoure had to reimburse the buyer. In the meantime, the German services of rue Lauriston had become aware of the matter and Lafont summoned him to his office demanding an explanation. He was relieved of his German police badge and he was threatened to be turned over to the French authorities, who effectively issued a warrant for his arrest after he had fled to Marseille.
>
> During the first week of July 1944, I introduced Bonhoure to Rupp at the office of the GFP in Avignon. He received a badge similar to mine under the name of Le Meur.

Boyer had a good opinion of his friend: "*He has executed all the missions that were assigned to him.*" But he was seemingly not aware of Bonhoure's entire itinerary. Before joining the gang at the rue Lauriston, Bonhoure had been a member of Rudy von Mérode's gang, also known as the "Neuilly Gestapo" which had amassed hundreds of millions of francs. This gang represented a formidable competitor for Lafont who succeeded in having their German police badges canceled and their network liquidated.[46] As it was customary, Lafont picked up a few men from his former rival's gang, among them Bonhoure, who used this opportunity to make a few bogus cop operations on his own. In Tulle, he also took part in several lootings, one of which degenerated into a machine-gunning[47].

During his Marseille period, Boyer clearly did not break his links to the rue Bancasse, in spite of his "dismissal," since he got Rupp to hire Bonhoure. It is useful to know that, at the beginning of August 1944, Boyer resumed active service in Avignon. Several raids and hauls against the Resistance—one of the headaches of the GFP—demonstrated that a link did exist between the GFP of Avignon and that of Marseille. Therefore, the residual GFP kept a separate hierarchical chain of command aligned with the army after the SiPo-SD absorbed some of its staff, but it continued collaborating with the SiPo-SD, among others in the hunt of the Jews.

The Fall

From this partnership between Boyer and Bonhoure sealed at the Paris race tracks, one can infer a high probability that Boyer also collaborated with the SiPo-SD in Paris area—perhaps under yet another alias. He left the capital at the end of 1943 and did not seem surprised at Bonhoure's mention of the rue Lauriston. It was as if he had heard it all before.

Boyer's account of how he and Bonhoure fled ahead of the allies is worthy of a film scenario:

> I did not want to leave with the Germans because I could tell that in their retreat they would drag me along to Germany and could get rid of me by executing me in cold blood. So I stayed with Bonhoure in Avignon. During the German retreat, a SS unit seized my car, and when time came to leave the city to evade the allies, I was without transportation.
>
> While in Avignon on August 14 or 15 near the PPF headquarters, four vehicles arrived from Marseille. One was a commercial truck completely closed with Jeannot Carbone, Charles Palmieri, Olivier Charles as well as others I knew only by sight (a total of approximately 18 people). Palmieri, alias Merle, was in command of the group, and I went and asked him for a space for Bonhoure and me.
>
> It was agreed that he would take us with them in the direction of Paris, but I would have to provide the gasoline and split with Bonhoure the cost of the meals for everybody. I accepted and provided 100 liters of gasoline and 200 liters of diesel fuel that I was holding in reserve in my garage. The roads were congested and for fear of bombing, we drove only at night. Once in Lyon, three days later, and because of the excessive expenses run up by the group, that I did not intend to follow anyway, I decided not to continue and to abandon them.[48]

The two fugitives succeeded in taking refuge in Trévoux (Ain) for one month. Bonhoure found a way to reach Paris where he was employed on probation for a while by American intelligence. We know this from Cabagno who found Bonhoure again in the capital in May 1945. For his part, Boyer got into gambling to make his last francs work for him; until he was arrested.

In his deposition of December 22, 1944, Palmieri mentioned the escape of Alfred André toward Germany, but he placed Boyer in Auvergne, where he *"had a friend, a man named Maurice, an agent of the SD of Paris and collaborator of*

Bony Lafont.'* In the underworld, one did not lose track of one another, even during a rout.[49]

A long time had passed since the Naquet's house at 2, rue du Rempart de la Ligne had become a hub for all kinds of trafficking and a memorable torture chamber, as André Naquet testified in front of his visitors. He remembered the changes to that effect in the bathroom, and if one needed exhibits, it was sufficient to examine the two clubs abandoned by the gangsters on top of a wardrobe. André Naquet had kept them to this day.

The violent Alfred André also resurfaced. Like Boyer, he was deeply enmeshed in the arrests of the Jews. Alfred André was part of the regulars of the Bar Carnot, probably established by François-Henri Blanchard, a member of the Resistance collecting information about the French agents of the Gestapo, miliciens, and PPF. Next to André's name one reads the mention "The killer." In the file of Marcelle Véran, a dancer and hostess at the Troubadour cabaret in Paris, also a Gestapo informer and André's mistress, a police report dated September 4, 1946, described her life style in Avignon: "*She carried on with him and his friends openly in public, in the large cafés, bars and restaurants of Avignon, where she gave herself over to uninhibited debauchery.*"[50] Well in the spirit of the times, the police reporter railed against the "temptress" who probably limited herself to benefiting from the money taken from the Jews, while her lover took care of sending them to their death. An aside in the same report indicated: "*Alfred André was arrested, sentenced to death, and executed by firing squad in Nimes, together with the milicien from Avignon, Lucien Blanc.*" Before kicking the bucket, Alfred André burned the candle at both ends. There was a lot of money, and André and his men spent it as if there were no tomorrow.

One can imagine the reactions of the French police, powerless in the face of the excesses of Boyer's gangsters, who, confident in their immunity, must have thumbed their nose at them. There may also have been some admiration for these passing tough guys, who had succeeded in turning the tables on them.

As evidenced in the court files, the willingness of the gangsters to talk freely in court about the money of the Jews may have been a defense strategy. By admitting to bogus cop operations, they risked prison terms at the most. However, the arrest of Jews to deliver them to the Germans fell into the category of intelligence with the enemy, a capital offence. As for the manhunt of members of the Resistance, it would have sealed their fate.

---

* The "Bony Lafont" gang is in reality the gang of Lafont whose lieutenant was former police inspector Bony.

The Vaucluse Model

Georges Boyer had established a network loosely connected to Paris through close friends from Henri Lafont's gang. The network was composed of concentric circles around a nucleus of tough guys at the head of which he had appointed Alfred André for Avignon and the Vaucluse. André's main customer on the German side was Wolfram, *aka* Gauthier, a fanatic according to testimony. His boss Müller put him in charge of the Resistance, draft dodgers or the Jews, depending on the needs. Gauthier behaved as a jack of all trades, and Müller delegate with full powers to the GFP, whose independence he was wary of.

The men Boyer and André used were mostly ex-convicts, purposefully snatched out of the clutches of French justice by the Germans and turned into loyal servants, while allowing them to work for their own profit under the nose of the French police. That technique proved to be an excellent strategy for the Germans on two levels. On one hand, they had turned them into allies whose prosperity depended on their good will. On the other hand, part of the loot was making its way up to the head of the SiPo-SD, Wilhelm Müller, a man with a misleading gentlemanly appearance.

Several witnesses, among them those of Charles Palmieri we already cited, indicated that the network of Georges Boyer, Alfred André and Gauthier occasionally collaborated with other networks also controlled by Wilhelm Müller. The head of the SiPo-SD diversified his repression enterprises by simultaneously betting on several horses and encouraging competition between his various sub-networks.

Although the study of occupied France in its entirety goes far beyond the scope of our research, we may state on the basis of multiple testimony and documents that the activities of the Vaucluse gangsters extended far beyond the department and reached the Gard, Bouches du Rhône, Isère and Drôme; that they had links with Auvergne and the Paris region, and that their bosses were covering a large part of the Marseille prefectoral region.[51] Moreover, it is likely that the members of the German police were a party in looting by the gangsters, to the point that the discretion of one side ensured the tranquility of the other.

After Liberation, Captain Gervais shared his observations in a report to "M the Commander of Military Security XV":

> It is already clear that the Merle enterprise [Bureau Merle], constituted along the principles of the Gestapo, was not unique in France.

In Toulouse, the Marty brigade, and in Tunisia, the Saffy brigade have a strange resemblance with it.[52]

Apparently, the "Merle Enterprise" (Palmieri gang) was not unique either in Avignon or on the national stage, as we have just seen. Of course, this raises a question which cannot be answered in the context of this work: what role did the underworld play in the execution of the Holocaust in France?

The study of the Vaucluse leads us to believe that the German strategy was to put in place a similar model in the whole country, for several reasons. First, the small workforce of the German police was spread too thin, especially after the invasion of the southern zone, and they had to seek the services of ten times more "loyal" collaborators.[53]

It cannot be said often enough how indispensable it is, for the understanding of the persecution of the Jews, to take into account the manner in which it was carried out on the ground and its motivations, often a mix of ideology, evil and greed. The history of the Holocaust cannot forego the grassroots level.

Chapter 8

Wilhelm Müller's Favorites

On February 22, 1944, Wilhelm Müller, head of the Avignon SiPo-SD, sent a telling request to his Marseille boss, Rolf Mühler, through the head of the liaison service at the Avignon Kommandantur:

Sicherheitpolizei – SD Avignon outer station
In re: List of agents and informers, who will need a special pass in case of an Americano-British landing.

56 861	Karl Uhl - Avignon, rue Flammarion 16
72	Laurent Josef Idlas – Avignon, Av. St. Jean prolongée
83	Pierre Terrier – Avignon, Bd des Villas 5
94	Victoire André – Avignon, Place des 3 Pilats 10
56 505	Simone Pillet – Avignon, rue de la République
16	Titien Feroldi – Avignon, Caserne des Passagers rue des Lices
27	Jean Poutet - L'Isle s/Sorgue
38	René Yves Louis Le Flem - Orange
49	Yves Thesmar – Avignon, 71, rue Josef Vernet
510	Vahan Sarkissoff – Avignon, avenue Monclar 31
56 611	Robert Conrad – Avignon, Impasse Moline

Signed: Lieutenant – SS and Station Chief

According to the RG of the prefecture, the German original of this letter was found at Liberation in the premises of the "Gestapo," which, in the language of the time, meant the villa of avenue Monclar. Each individual had an identification number which implied official employment at the SiPo-SD.

The procedural files "Wilhelm Müller's favorites" includes SiPo-SD employment index cards found on the premises of the German police in

Marseille. The charred corners of these cards indicate that they had barely escaped the incineration of compromising documents organized by the fleeing Germans.

The worry about an allied landing was in the air and was not limited to the German police. In June 1944 the national director of the SEC, Paul Besson, wrote a memo[1] on this topic to his subordinate of Marseille, Raymond Guilledoux:

> … Congratulations on your initiative to requisition a building in the area of Avignon in case you need to evacuate the archives. I do not think that I can obtain a means of transportation. On this matter too, your initiative is key…

Among the members of his herd of collaborators from Avignon, Wilhelm Müller had undoubtedly chosen those who provided him with the best help in discharging the tasks he was responsible for (struggle against the Resistance, dislodging of draft dodgers, repression of the black market, hunting down the Jews, pursuit of Gaullists, propaganda for collaboration, infiltration of collaboration groups, etc.).

When Müller, an accomplished calculator, offered special passes to his closest French collaborators, it was likely killing two birds with one stone. While he assured their protection, he was also sending eventual embarrassing witnesses across the Rhine, in case he would be caught before he had the time to drive off. He may also have received orders from high up to shelter his most important informers in the eventuality of retreat. He may also have needed body guards in case of a rough time on his way to the northeast. In exchange he offered them protection.

Among the eleven persons in the list of "favorites," two women did not leave any clue: Victoire André and Simone Pillet; informers, spies, or simply "confidents" of Müller the warrior? The nine men were judged in person or in absentia. Among them, five belonged to the PPF, where some had been leaders in the PPF Vaucluse federation and were on the frontline of the hunt for the Jews. Most of them stood out in their ability to network.

In his deposition of May 11, 1945, Ernst Dunker, member of section VI in the SiPo-SD of Marseille, particularly focused on the Resistance, shed some light about the importance of some of the individuals in the list of the "favorites of the Germans." Among his collaborators in the Vaucluse—Louis Bergeron, René Yves Le Flem, Louis Blaise Fournier, Jean Garbarino, Laurent Idlas, Constant Kobahdkidze, Raymond Le Cam, Karl Uhl, and Roger Alphonse Villard—three individuals, Le Flem, Idlas and Uhl were Müller's "favorites."[2]

Pierre Terrier and Robert Conrad
Two Hoodlums of the Bar Carnot

INVESTIGATION ABOUT A GESTAPO AGENT DESTINED
TO THE FREE GROUPS[3]

GESTAPO SD (secret police) 32 Bd Monclar - French personnel
PIERRE TERRIER
Pierre Terrier, 23-24 years old, born in Monaco where his father serves in the police, has done an internship in the officers school in Uriage for the benefit of the Legion, was then hired as a secretary-interpreter at the SD due to the influence of his cousin Jean Terrier, as he was a low-level employee and lived with his mistress … *aka* M…, at 5 boulevard des Villas.

DESCRIPTION: 1 m 80, blond, blue eyes, fair complexion, hair combed back, has a quaff starting at the base of the hair on the forehead, looks like a Nordic athlete, friendly face, inspires confidence.

He has been involved in sugar trafficking, was in a French prison, was the only one to get out thanks to the intervention of the German authorities, then enlisted in the 8th Waffen SS company in Pont St. Esprit (civil section) where he did a one month internship; following that he is again employed by the SD and adopts a working technique: he pretends to be a draft dodger or to have been parachuted in; he has in his possession a card from the IS* in the name of Pierre Tessier asking for assistance from all our services, he gets himself invited by one of the groups, studies it for some time, reports to his bosses of the SD and sets up an operation against [them].

His known operations are [Fontaine de] Vaucluse, Gordes, Petit Palais, L'Isle sur Sorgue.

In addition to these operations, he participates in questioning both as an interpreter and as an inquisitor [*sic*]. The torture inflicted is terrifying according to a listener.

At the moment, he lives in St. Ruf† with his current mistress. He wants to break with… and he is courting the daughter of the owner of Bar Carnot; he now only goes to this café which is visited only by the Gestapo.

His schedule: Arrives at the prison around 8:30-9:00 a.m. after he stops at Bar Carnot, leaves around 12:00-12:45, returns to Bar Carnot, comes back [to the prison] around 2:30 p.m. after his stop at the bar, and exits around 6:00-6:30 p.m. and he stays then at the bar until around 7:20 p.m. Times and habits pretty regular during a 15 day check.

---

* Intelligence Service (probably British).
† A neighborhood of Avignon outside the ramparts.

This Resistance document is a tailing report probably aimed at preparing Pierre Terrier's summary execution or at least his trial after Liberation.

The summary execution did not take place. The court of justice sentenced him to death in absentia on June 14, 1945. He was found *"guilty of having, after June 1940, undermined the external security of the state and maintained intelligence with the enemy, as an agent of the German police SD in Avignon and an informer of the Gestapo, and as a participant in numerous arrests, house searches and lootings."*

The last person who could give information about his presence in Germany after Liberation, was again Palmieri in his deposition of March 15, 1945: *"I also know that Pierre Terrier, agent of the Avignon SD, and another individual, whose first name is Ernest, a former volunteer of the LVF, were also in Germany, at the Radio-Stuttgart school."*[4] Terrier was an old acquaintance of Palmieri who had put him in touch with Feroldi several times at the SD of boulevard Monclar.

Terrier's file confirmed the essential information in the investigation of the Resistance.

From November 5, 1941, to June 20, 1942, Pierre Terrier did an internship in the youth camp of Poyol in the Drôme. Then, after an internship in the Milice officers' school of Uriage, he emerged with an equivalent rank of second lieutenant, a nice position for his age. Born on November 18, 1921, in Monaco, he was barely 20.

On December 10, 1943, he was arrested by the Avignon police for theft, complicity and possession of stolen property. The file of Jean-Daniel Michon contains more information about the event.[5] An entire gang stole sugar in Apt: Michon, Terrier, Roger Giraud, Jean Tichit, Robert Rieu, and last but not least, Avakinian who lived in Apt and had prepared the heist.

The closeness between Michon and Terrier may have caused confusion in the mind of Resistance witnesses. On December 1, 1943, Michon returned to Avignon on leave from the STO in Germany because of his mother's illness. He immediately engaged in criminal activity and was indicted a few days later, approximately at the same time as Pierre Terrier, receiving a six-month suspended prison term. When he was freed, he had already done two months prior to his sentence. He was taken to the de Salles barracks (probably to be sent back to the STO), and from there to the offices of the OPA, where he met Beaufrère and Pierre Kuhling, two of its employees. Both had been kicked out of the Milice before being hired by the OPA. In order to evade the STO, Michon accepted their proposal to enlist in the 8th company of the Waffen SS in Pont St. Esprit, the same unit as Terrier.

However, contrary to the Resistance's investigation, Terrier's court file did not mention his enlistment into the Waffen SS in Pont St. Esprit:

He had already been working since early October 1943 for the SD whose headquarters were at 32, avenue Monclar. Following his arrest and upon the request of Müller, he was released to Müller who had reserved the right to refer him to German justice. But two hours later, Terrier was walking around free in Avignon.

Did the Resistance report confuse Terrier with Michon? Anyway, Müller had once again picked up an ex-convict.

Terrier's case file also mentioned a crime that was not picked up by either French or German occupation court systems. Terrier was involved in the theft of furniture and fabrics at the home of Elias,* a Jew sought by the Gestapo, and the resale of the merchandise to a certain Rinck through an intermediary, Camille Evangelista.

After Liberation, the description of Terrier was broadcast. "*1 m 80, blond, blue eyes, has the body of an athlete, a very pleasant demeanor, easily earns people's trust. A very daring mindset, he hides ferocious brutality under his airs of almost juvenile shyness.*" He had the right qualities not only to fool the Resistance organizations but also to unleash his fury against his victims. It is clear why he was sought by the police ahead of his trial.

At this stage, we gain a useful perspective about Terrier through the Conrad file.[6] Conrad, a young Alsatian who knew German, was hired by the SD as an interpreter, under the recommendation of Terrier.

During questioning, "*the* [German] *investigating judge did not hit the accused. That job belonged to Pierre Terrier and Leo Isnard.*" In his deposition, provided on October 4, 1944, and added to Terrier's file, Conrad stated "*that after the massacre of the maquis of Séderon, Pierre Terrier became the right hand man of Müller, even according to the Germans themselves.*" It is also stated that Terrier was able to find the location of the Maquis. We know that "the massacre of the Séderon Maquis" or more exactly of Izon la Bruisse, on February 22, 1944, happened because of the treason of two members of the Resistance of the Maquis Ventoux, Cyprien Bono and Namin Noiret, who were identified by a witness and gunned down,[7] immediately after the massacre. Did Terrier play a role in first obtaining information and then turning the two members of the Resistance round? We have no clear cut answer. However, he was probably present among the Frenchmen who participated, alongside the Germans, in the attack against the Resistance camp.

The Conrad-Terrier team was also tracking the Jews. In Conrad's interrogation on December 1, 1944:

---

* This is probably Elie Elias from Avignon.

One night, at a date that you cannot specify, you followed Merle*, an agent of the Marseille Gestapo, to pick up Jews. You were accompanied by Blanc and Bergeron, former miliciens and four agents of the Gestapo of Marseille. You went to M. Valabrègue, rue Bancasse at the "Coq Hardi," and to other Jews whom you arrested and took to the Hautpoul barracks. Several Jews escaped and you arrested only 5 or 6 of them. That evening, you heard that Merle was accusing Blanc of establishing incorrect lists. You admit having stolen from a wallet in Mr. Valabrègue's home 8,000 francs that you split with Terrier. You are claiming that, during that night, your role was to serve as an interpreter for Merle, if he ran into German patrols. You state that, on two occasions, you had met German patrols to whom you explained that you belonged to the Gestapo and that you were in the process of picking up Jews.

Pierre Terrier fit the usual profile of an ex-convict hired by the Germans to conduct actions against the Resistance and the Jews, while continuing his side business. The file of his cousin, Louis Terrier, a patrolman in Monaco who visited him in Avignon, does not give the impression that Pierre was the black sheep of the family.[8] Louis' brother, Raymond Terrier, was handling merchandise trafficking between Spain and France. At Liberation, his nephew, Jean Terrier, was detained in Carcassonne as a Gestapo agent. But with Pierre, we are dealing with pure savagery. His tally of kills makes us shudder.

In a letter to the owner of the Bar Carnot, dated September 1, 1944, Marcel Idzkowski, the manager of this nest of Gestapo vipers, wrote: "*Terrier has 39 dead Frenchmen on his conscience.*" No other information is provided, but the number of victims leads us to believe that he may mean the massacre of Izon-la-Bruisse which was publicly rumored to have been caused by Terrier. Anyway, his file shows a number of actions taken against the Resistance.

There were several women around him, mistresses or just informers. Josette Castagneau, about whom Odette de Saint Oyant, the cashier of the Bar Crillon, said that "*every day at the Bar Crillon, she used to drink abundantly, had a lot of money… spoke about sleeping with men to get them caught by the Gestapo.*" Josette was the bait, and it is not surprising that Terrier used her. But the testimony does not specify whether they were trying to catch Jews. However, in the file of Marie-Claire Jean[9], we learn that Josette had denounced Jean Valabrègue when Terrier asked her whether she knew any Jews. It is likely that Terrier and Conrad used this information to rob Mr. Valabrègue at the "Coq Hardi," as mentioned by Conrad in his the previously cited questioning.

---

* Merle is the pseudo name of Charles Palmieri, whom we will meet again in Part Two, Chapter 9.

Mr. Valabrègue was not registered at the prefecture, and his first name cannot be confirmed.

With Marie-Claire Jean—her file describes her as a "registered prostitute"—things were different: *"She was the mistress of Gestapo agent Terrier, especially in charge of finding Jews. She denounced her lover, the Jew Weimann of Vaison against whom she had a complaint and the Jew Sayas, who was hidden in Sablet and whom she accused of having swindled her out of money and jewelry in Nice. Both Israelites were arrested by Terrier and his gang."* This testimony does not give more detail, but it clearly indicates the interest of Terrier for the Jews. As we can see from this report, the Vichy terminology, "The Jew Weimann" and "the Jew Sayas," was still in use after Liberation.

Marie-Claire Jean denied having been Terrier's mistress, who, according to her, *"preferred someone younger"* (she was 35 years old at Liberation). In the police report of November 6, 1944, she confirmed *"that she has asked Terrier to arrange for the arrest of Weimann* who lived in Vaison, and that a few days later Terrier told her that he* [Weimann] *would not bother her anymore, 'I had him arrested'."* During her questioning on December 12, 1944, she backed out, stating that she had not denounced that Jew, since he did not exist! As to Sayas, she claimed having met him at the casino of Nice and that he had bought her jewelry at a very good price after an evening of gambling losses. And Terrier told her: *"If he is Jewish, I will find him, there can't be 36 of them in Sablet!"* There was indeed a Doctor Sayas who came with his family from Marseille to Sablet. But the secretary of the town hall, Henri Bastet, testified: *"The doctor and his family left for Caromb. His brother, a book store owner, has also resided in Sablet. Neither one was bothered by the Germans in Sablet."*

The answer of Terrier has a powerful ring to it: *"If he is Jewish, I will find him, there can't be that many in Sablet!"* Many Jews left the cities for villages away from the main communication routes, especially during the spring of 1944. However, the countryside was not necessarily safe because a stranger would easily stand out there. To be safe you would have to live on a farm, never to go out, and be able to trust the neighbors.

Eluding the Jew hunters was close to impossible, especially since every act of daily life could be dangerous. There was nothing to prevent Terrier from finding Sayas, who was probably on the village list of Jews. Anyway, he was known at the town hall. As to Marie-Claire Jean, during her trial, she had a fit of dementia, which she possibly faked. She received a death sentence, commuted to life imprisonment, but her file raises many questions and her testimony does not seem reliable.

---

* We also found the spelling Wiedmann.

The Jews appeared in a different relationship—probably a platonic one—of Terrier with Gisèle Guyon, the daughter of the bar Carnot manager.[10] What happened in this bar adjoining the St. Pierre Church, across from the Avignon Synagogue, is both incredible and hair-raising. "*On July 14, 1943, M. Boré de Loisy, a hotelkeeper in Marseille, 24 quai du Maréchal Pétain, bought the bar Carnot whose management he entrusts to Denise Guyon Idzkowski; the business was to be run by husband and wife.*"

Rapidly, the bar becomes one of the nerve centers of gangster collaboration. Using a black pencil on a small card, a member of the Resistance (probably Blanchard or a member of his group) had established, in short hand, the list of regulars of the bar Carnot. This card appears in Guyon's file:

Georges Boyer
Nicky, also called Orlof
Alfred André (the killer), tel. 832 Arles, see the bar place Voltaire
André Vial, also called Bouboule
Albert Sauvet, see Nîmes
Mathieu Costa, owner of brasserie Gaulois intersection of rue Molière and rue de la Darse
Robert, tall, strong, very irritable
Blonde, secretary of the funeral home
Paul, very short, hairless, from Chateaurenard
Pierre Terrier
Walter, from Nice, Italian origin
Léo, Spanish origin
Feroldi
Roger Villard, rue Arc de l'Agneau
Raymond Bravy (Renée Estellon)
Docteur Guidoni
Jean-Paul
Félix Olivier
Victor, he is a friend of the woman who owns the hôtel Lucy, he has bought a café in Romans for Ginette
H Jedamzik, torturer of the Gestapo [Hotel de la] Cigale
Bébert, boss of [l'Hotel de] l'Oustallet
Paul Hilhouze, lives at l'Oustallet, Bar de l'Olivier, Gestapo informer

Those specialized in the persecution of Jews made up the list. The bar Carnot was open house for the cream of the crop of rue Bancasse and the Parietas gang. Doctor Antoine Guidoni[11] was present with Terrier, an agent close to Müller. Guidoni, a Marseille businessman, a former military doctor, had been recommended by Simon Sabiani, the head of the Marseille PPF, as "*a convinced militant and a great champion of the collaboration with Germany.*" Following numerous house searches and thefts, Guidoni was picked up by Müller and assigned "*to the surveillance of the great cafés and of the bourgeois classes.*" He ended up with a death sentence and was executed.

Walter, another friend of Terrier, was in fact Walter Garattoni, an Italian who belonged to the fascist Milice in Nice.[12] "*Witnesses have seen him in Avignon in the company of Gestapo agents who were looking for Jews to arrest.*" He declared that in Avignon he met Terrier who "*forced him to denounce the Jew Bernard.*"

Several individuals on the list remain unknown. We do not know who H. Jedamzik was. He may have been a torturer of rue Bancasse. As to Paul Hilhouze, the indication "bar de l'Olivier" refers to a bar on the place Pie, where the French members of the Gestapo were also regulars.[13] The "bar de l'Olivier" was the ideal location to watch the stallholders on the place Pie open air market. Finally, Léo was probably Léo Isnard, the torture partner of Terrier during the interrogations mentioned previously. In closing this review, let us remember that Villard had long been an administrator of Jewish assets before joining the rue Bancasse team.

The "freelancers" working for Müller, like Terrier, Guidoni and Feroldi (head of intelligence in the Milice of Vaucluse), provided, voluntarily or not, through the bar Carnot, a link parallel to that of Gauthier, between Müller, Boyer's gang and Alfred André. A keen sleuth, seasoned in underground activity, Müller seemed to cultivate multiples routes to his victims. Can one indeed fully trust any hoodlum? Anyway a lot of paths crossed one another at the bar Carnot.

We continue this story through the court file of Gisèle Guyon, who was 18 at the Liberation. She went out with Terrier, without being his mistress. But at Liberation time, a past flirt with Terrier wasn't just a mistake; it was high treason. Avignon was in turmoil. People were being executed without trial. Dead bodies were being thrown out just about anywhere. The court of justice was set up quickly, and the public at large was thirsting for revenge. In such a climate of reprisals against "horizontal collaboration"—the sexual insult to the country's purity—a flirt with Terrier required an arrest and a police file, even if it was to be closed without an indictment.

How did this happen? Gisèle's mother, Denise Guyon was married to Marcel Idzkowski, a Jew and a member of the Resistance. Marcel pleaded with the court:

In August 1943,* we received the visit of Georges Boyer from the GFP, at the hôtel la Cigale. Alfred André, Marcel Cappe, André Vial and Nicky were his friends. As soon as I became aware of the appalling activity of this gang, I got in touch with the rebels [members of the Resistance]. First, I wrote two reports and gave them to Mr. Pinto, 3, rue Grande Fusterie, who asked me to give a statement at his home in front of Superintendant Schlinger. In November, I became acquainted with Bonin, Pierre Bataille and Guy Planchenault who belonged to the rebellion and transmitted the reports I wrote to their chiefs, Beyne and Fischer....

Gisèle went out with Pierre Terrier, but she did not stop helping the people I was passing the information to. Seven weeks of prison will be enough—I think—to satisfy public opinion which had made its judgment on the base of appearances, because I was unable to disclose neither my secret activity nor my religion, because I had been hunted since 1940 by the Gestapo of Paris, Marseille, and finally Avignon. The discriminatory laws that struck me and forced me to manage a bar with dubious customers caused Gisèle to be exposed by my fault to a despicable environment and I beg to request the dismissal of this case.

When Marcel understood what he was into and the advantage he could derive from the situation, he made contact with the Resistance. Isaac Pinto was a refugee from Dunkerque. He was arrested on May 17, 1943, and immediately released. Did the Germans suspect his Resistance activity, and was he under surveillance? This was not out of question. Claude Bonin, a nephew of the painter Pissaro, was the curator of the Javon Museum† which served as a storage for the provincial museums. He was an intelligence officer in the Resistance. Guy Planchenault was a 20-year-old member of the Resistance who would be killed on July 1, 1944, near St. Saturnin d'Apt, together with several comrades during an attack on the abandoned farm they used as a shelter.[14] Philippe Beyne and Max Fischer were the co-founders of the maquis Ventoux. All had been in contact with Marcel Idzkowski.

It is possible to verify Marcel's statement *"Gisèle went out with Pierre Terrier, but she did not stop helping the people I was passing information to."* In a letter sent on October 20, 1944, to Max Fischer, then sub-prefect for the purges, Claude Bonin, who was in Paris, confirmed Marcel Idzkowski's version: *"The information provided about the Avignon Gestapo came from the most part from the bar Carnot."* He asserted that *"Gisèle, who can be criticized only for her escapades, provided no information to the Gestapo and continued to inform me after the attack on the Javon camp where Guy Planchenault was killed."* Bonin, who specified that he used to

---

* The date is incorrect since Boyer arrived in Avignon in November.
† The castle of Javon (15th century) is situated in the village of Lioux in the Vaucluse.

meet Gisèle in Caumont, a small town 10 km away from Avignon, concluded *"The secret activity of the Idzkowski and Guyon family deserves recognition on the part of the Resistance."* Colonel Beyne added: *"Idzkowski's information about the Gestapo agents was very precious and proved to be accurate."*

In the letter that he wrote to superintendant Georges on August 28, 1944, Marcel shed light on his action for the Resistance. He wrote that he had been an informer working for Bonin and Planchenault from February to June 1944. Marcel's recorded testimony mentioned him in the third person: *"When, for the second time, he* [Marcel] *attempts to contact the FFI on July 2, 1944, Planchenault had just been savagely gunned down by the Germans and the miliciens, and Bonin, who feels he is being hunted down, leaves for Paris. Unable to get the help from his two friends, he* [Marcel] *leaves to hide away in the FFI group of the Mt Ventoux."*

But above all, he explained the cause of his family's inferno:

> Gestapo agents had a file on me and they ceaselessly blackmailed my wife who, after the massacre of my family, feared for my safety... Managing the bar was beyond her capabilities and she thought that she would save me through her customers [the gangsters]. It was a woman's idea and a selfish thought, but how was it possible to stand up to regulars who shoot into the window pane when one refuses to open the door at night?

How could the family possibly get out of the trap when Terrier even threatened Denise Guyon to get her husband, Marcel Idzkowski, arrested, if she prevented her daughter from going out with him? The bar managers were rendered powerless. The gangsters were holding all the cards to turn the bar Carnot into a lair for their criminal activities. They did not know that the Resistance was actively listening in.

Evidently, they didn't expect Marcel Idzkowski's joining the Resistance under their pressure, and yet, Marcel felt the need to apologize for Denise's clientele at the Bar Carnot and for Gisèle's outings in the company of Pierre Terrier. There remained the issue of their mutual feelings. In April 1945 Gisèle, who was living in Besançon, was interrogated by the gendarmes.[15] She didn't hide the fact that she had left her Besançon address with Terrier and that he promised to visit her after the war.

Robert Conrad's Fate

At first glance, his association with Terrier proved fatal for Robert Conrad. The 26-year-old Alsatian had been sentenced in October 1943 by the Avignon tribunal to 6 months in jail for theft and tobacco trafficking, and, after serving his sentence, he probably met Terrier, who got him into the SiPo-SD.[16]

A radio operator in the navy from 1937 to 1942, then a technical inspector in the post office (PTT) in Marseille, he found a job at "La Gauloise," a tobacco and cigarette factory on the road to Sorgues. This is where he got into trouble with the law. Out of prison on January 27, 1944, and visibly without a job or any resources, he became acquainted with Terrier who did not have to push him very hard: Conrad applied for a job with Müller, who was looking for an interpreter.

With a salary of 4,400 francs per month, it was not for translations that Müller gave him a 7,65 mm pistol. He participated in searches, arrests and looting. One more ex-convict who is "put on the right track" by Müller.

On the subject of the hunt for the Jews, his file of course mentions the looting at the "Coq Hardi," the Marie Riz restaurant, and the theft of Jean Valabrègue's wallet containing the 8,000 francs he split with Terrier. However, his confession concerning the "collection" of the Jews one night with Palmieri and his men gave him a completely different dimension.

Arrested immediately at Liberation, Conrad was accused of intelligence with the agents of Germany; as an agent of the Gestapo, he had participated in searches, arrests, physical abuse against detainees, and looting. He was sentenced to death. In these early days, the court of justice was far more severe, and his chances to escape execution were slim.

Indeed, the Nimes court of justice rejected his appeal, and the Minister of Justice his plea for pardon. He was executed in Nimes, but the files do not offer any date.

Yves Thesmar,
Chief of the Vaucluse Milice

Müller had no time to size up the head of the Vaucluse Milice before placing him on the list of individuals eligible for special passes. Indeed, less than one month had passed between his arrival in Avignon and the establishment of the list. Others higher up than Müller certainly had enough knowledge about his commitment and his loyalty to the occupier. He was probably already known at the Marseille SiPo-SD because of his past record.

On January 25, 1944, Thesmar began his new task in Avignon, appointed by Paul Durandy, the regional head of the Milice in Marseille. His court file had little to say about his prior history.[17] Born in Tlemcen (Algeria), a store manager for the Radio Star company in Nice for 12 years, he had climbed the ladder up to "chief of thirty," and deputy head of the Milice in that town. He did not distinguish himself by a flamboyant attitude, but his actions on the Côte d'Azur must have been significant since he suddenly found himself at the head of an organization that included several individuals well known on the national level for their loyalty to the Germans.

But during his questioning, he only stated his support for the politics of Pétain, the Bolshevik threat and his training at the school of Uriage. He was almost portraying himself as a white knight: *"As soon as I arrived in Avignon, I dismissed four men who were working for the Gestapo, namely, Layet, Lucien Blanc, Bergeron and Albert Goldstein."*

He knew how to keep his distance and impose a stern brand of morality: *"I got in touch with Müller who did not get along with me. He dealt only with actions against the Jews to steal their money… I forbid my men to have any contact with him."* It's an order that Feroldi, the subordinate of Thesmar, did not follow. Feroldi's boss added a little later: *"In June 1944, I fired the head of the second service, Feroldi, because of his police activity with the Germans."*[18] Thesmar was clearing his own name on Feroldi's back.

In avoiding money belonging to the Jews by his "reprimand" of the links existing between Müller and his subordinate, Thesmar built a defense which protected him from being seen as in the pay of the Gestapo.

> The GFP was headed by captain Hunsch of the Wehrmacht. He wanted to organize operations against the Maquis but I refused to provide any men. It was agreed that I would take care of the arrested French people and would give my opinion about their situation. After earning his trust, I could later, thanks to my influence, get many French people freed.

In simple terms, unable to deny his contacts with the SD and the GFP, he alleged that he had limited them to the strict minimum and drew a flattering picture of his strategy. But, then, how to explain his request to Jean Lebon of the SEC, around March 22, 1944, to inform him of *"any obstruction by the Police, the Judiciary, the Prefecture, and others"*?[19]

The mention of Captain Hunsch of the Wehrmacht is noteworthy. Thesmar placed him as the head of the GFP, possibly the part that had remained attached to the Wehrmacht. Was this a maneuver by Thesmar to distance himself from Müller?

The head of such a sinister organization as the Milice had to be taken seriously.

Created by Joseph Darnand in January 1943, the Milice was operational in the Vaucluse as early as February with the establishment of the Union Départementale. A former air force officer, Max Knipping, the first head of the Milice of Vaucluse, and the lawyer Georges Gras, chief of the 3rd service (security), made immediately every effort to open a departmental school of officers at the de Salles barracks in Avignon. As early as April, Pierre Louis de la Ney du Vair, the director of the Uriage national school, visited Avignon to give 4 talks at city hall.[20] The teachings and the conclusions of the Milice leaders deserve to be examined.[21] They went back in time to the Roman Legions in tracing the Jewish problem, and observed that three solutions had been tried and failed in France:

Expulsion – but the Jew comes back
The Statute – but the Jew works around it
Equality – but the Jew becomes the master.

In their frenzy, they saw no other way than the most severe application of the Vichy legislation, which, by the way, they deemed too soft. The constitution of the Vaucluse Milice was seen very favorably by Prefect Darbou. In his report about the state of mind of the population in July 1943, he observed:

The Milice maintains good relations with my administration which it does not want to hinder. Its intelligence allowed us to arrest a leader of the STO draft dodgers. In my department, I consider that I can personally rely on its chiefs, as well as on the Legion's chiefs.[22]

The committee of the Union départementale of the Vaucluse Milice was established in the summer of 1943. At the beginning of September, the RG issued an opinion:

> The Union départementale of the Vaucluse includes around one thousand members. However, all are not trustworthy, and according to opinion polls, it seems that a very small proportion of miliciens would respond to the call of their chiefs, in case of serious events. According to reliable sources, there might be differences of opinion among the ranks of the miliciens. Some, one hundred percent collaborationists, support the policies of union with Germany, and the others, called moderates, believe the allies' military successes and the Russian advance to be an indication of the decrease of German power and the defeat of its armies. The fear of reprisals in case of an allied victory is said to be the cause of these differences.[23]

The thorough study by Christelle Fageot reduced the numbers significantly.[24] She did count 311 registered miliciens including 22 women. These numbers are based on the available archival information, and are probably lower than the true count, but very far from the one thousand cited by the RG. However, the RG seemed better informed about the internal crisis. Their bulletin for the period of September 5–11, 1943, showed significant discrepancies:

> Many miliciens want to leave. Some are already attempting to connect to the opposite groups in order to get people to forget as fast as possible their recent activity in favor of collaboration... Darnand is expected to come on September 6–7 to try and resolve the crisis.

Prefect Darbou, who would later become Laval's chief of staff, came up with a similar assessment in his bimonthly report[25] on October 5, 1943:

> The Milice appears to be going through a serious internal crisis. Several miliciens have resigned or were forced to resign. The principal heads of service have left Avignon at the beginning of last month under the pretext of taking a few days of vacation. The chief Darnand came to Avignon on September 6 in an attempt to unravel the crisis. Doctor Bonnefoy, chief of the department's Milice, a volunteer for the Waffen-SS, left for Vichy to take the mandatory medical checkup.

Bonnefoy was then replaced by Raymond Bonnabel as the head of the Vaucluse Milice.

Of course, the execution by the Resistance of the Avignon lawyer, Georges Gras in his own home, on October 28, 1943, was not likely to boost their morale. This prompted Idlas to say at the November meeting of the Vaucluse PPF bureau: *"There are chickens everywhere since 25 Vaucluse miliciens resigned on the wake of Georges Gras' assassination."*[26] This caustic remark illustrates the ambivalent relations between the Milice and the PPF. Idlas' words often conveyed a sense of rivalry, while his assistant Jacques Tricon, who belonged to both organizations, insisted on taking common actions, particularly the surveillance of homes to avert possible assassination attempts. At the meeting of the Vaucluse PPF bureau on January 5, 1944, Tricon bemoaned these antagonisms:

> Tomorrow, the Milice and the PPF will perhaps fight side by side. Their ideas are less conflicting than those of the radicals and the communists, who nevertheless came to an understanding in the Popular Front.[27]

As for the help given to the Germans during operations against the Resistance, discretion was imperative. The issue was never raised during the official meetings of the Milice leadership. Only the French initiatives against terrorism were mentioned, like that of Carpentras, where a committee for revolutionary action had been created, led by a triumvirate: the chiefs of the Legion, the PPF and the Milice. The objective was to gather political intelligence.[28]

Thesmar's installation in the Vaucluse practically coincided with the entry of Darnand in the government as General Secretary for the maintenance of law and order. The new prefect, Jean Benedetti, appointed on December 16, 1943, provided a view of the Milice in his bimonthly report of February 3, 1944:

> The chief of the Milice, Mr. Bonnabel, was assigned to new duties in Paris. He was just replaced in Avignon by Mr. Thesmar, who is arriving from Nice. The appointment of Mr. Joseph Darnand to the post of General Secretary to the maintenance of law and order has not been received with the expected enthusiasm. The miliciens are indeed afraid that their chief might be inclined to make certain concessions in the application of the Milice program, by taking part in the government. Locally, the Milice still hopes in the creation of a corps of free guards.[29]

The prefect's description testified about the state of mind of the miliciens who had overcome the 1943 crisis, namely the hard core with the strongest ideology.

Milice Priorities

Thesmar who estimated his own forces at around 400 people—a number that was closer to reality—was quite straightforward. The account of a press conference on March 4, 1944, was clear about his mindset:

> Thesmar says that the Milice must fight:
> 1- Against the "Francs-tireurs et partisans," a movement of communist inspiration
> 2- Against the "Armée Secrète," composed of former officers and NCOs
> 3- Against the STO draft dodgers
> In the Vaucluse, he adds, it would be sufficient to get around 60 big chiefs arrested and shot for the Maquis to be wiped out.
> The collaboration between the Milice and the German army is necessary, Thesmar claims, because it is aimed at exterminating common enemies.
> He proclaims that most of the terrorists are foreign Jews and not French people.[30]

His estimate of the size of the hard core of the Resistance was not far from the number given by Maxime Fischer.[31] Anyway, Thesmar was a man who had perfectly integrated anti-Semitism as a key element of his political propaganda. This may also provide an explanation for his anti-Jewish activity: look for the Jew so that you can find the Resistance. In his report of April 3, 1944, the prefect observed:

> As soon as the new head of the Milice, Mr. Thesmar, arrived, the organization became very busy. His efforts are entirely aimed at the struggle against terrorism, and if the department is calmer than at the beginning of the year, his action has been a big part of it. Recently, the terrorist organization in the département has been unmasked and its chiefs responsible for the sabotage that destroyed locomotives at the Rotondes depot have been arrested.[32]

As for his direct role in the persecution of the Jews, the sources available do not convey a criminal image to begin with. The testimony of his former employer was more than understanding. On October 25, 1945, Camille Barreau, manager of the Radio Star company wrote:

> His departure for the Milice [in Avignon] was not motivated by economic interest, because his financial situation with us was excellent. His closest colleagues tried to hold him back, but he seemed to have been led by external influences. From the beginning of the Legion, his desire to distinguish himself

led him to accept a first promotion, and step by step, he was pushed toward the SOL and the Milice.

I had never noticed any hatred or political or racial sectarianism in his words or his acts. I want to give a specific example. In 1942, before the occupation, the regional office of Jewish affairs asked me to fire two Jewish employees. Thesmar helped me a lot in all the steps I took which finally allowed us to keep these two people.

On the surface, he had nothing in common with Bonnefoy, his predecessor. Indeed, in July 1943, Marthe Angel, née Arokas, went to the headquarters of the Milice, because she erroneously believed that they arrested her father Salomon, her mother Ida and her brother Maurice.[33] She hoped to get them freed. Bonnefoy turned her away with this explanation: "*For the Jews, no mercy!*" Salomon and Ida were Salonika Jews, established in the city for a very long time. Maurice was born in Avignon in 1923. All three were deported, Ida on convoy 60, and Salomon and Maurice on convoy 59.

Thesmar's Men

During the trial of René Caprio, both a milicien and PPF assigned to the surveillance of the Jews, René Zarade, owner of two stores in Avignon, remembered the night of September 1942, when a flock of bullies was daubing slogans over the windows of Jewish shops throughout the city. Once the job was done, they all returned to Caprio's house. Zarade added that Kraskourine, a man linked to Caprio, had told him that "Caprio was assigned to the liquidation of Jews, freemasons and Gaullists."[34]

Another milicien, Pierre Kuhling, a fanatic SOL, leading ten men, armed and in uniform, was specifically assigned to gather intelligence about Jews.[35] After committing various swindles, he was employed by the OPA (Office de Placement Allemand).* While managing the convoying of French workers to the Reich, he too was in charge of locating dodgers and in particular Jews. The list of his activities was very long, but once again an ex-convict was active in the repression.

Mary Lévy, the spouse of Jean Lévy, from Carpentras, reported[36] that the milicien Paul Desjardin and his brother-in-law Barbarant, chief of the Carpentras PPF, denounced her husband to the Gestapo. Jean Lévy was deported on convoy 64.

---

* Office of German Placement, a German service in charge of securing a French work force to cover German needs.

Among the miliciens, some anti-Jewish activists were ready to take things to the bitter end. The Gandon case illustrated this hatred.[37] In his deposition of June 15, 1945, Kurt Leppien, the husband of Suzanne Ney, who was deported on convoy 72, declared:

> My name is Kurt Leppien, 35 years old, laborer, Quartier des Confines in Sorgues.
>
> I was a neighbor of Auguste Gandon. In the course of several conversations from 1941 to 1944, we were able to notice, my wife and I, that Gandon expressed antinational views, disgraceful for a French man. We were able to retain a few sentences verbatim, as he said them:
>
> "Winning this war would have been a calamity for France. Fortunately, we lost it. I got the Military Cross because I was able to run faster than others. I believe that we will have to fight once again, but I sure hope that this time it will be side by side with Germany against England. It is about time that the Germans occupy the southern zone of France to put some order and rid us of the Jews and the Resistance groups."
>
> Gandon advised me several times to work for the Germans, because, with the knowledge of their language, I could make a lot of money, as he would have done himself, if he had the capacity and the necessary skills.
>
> After he realized that our thinking was different from his, he ended up threatening us several times and said that he would get us sent to concentration camps. He uttered the same threats toward our neighbor, Gil.
>
> During the fall of 1943, Gandon joined the Milice. We saw him in uniform and he boasted that he owned weapons and that he would gun me down on the first occasion.
>
> At the beginning of 1944, he told us "I have you now under my control. I cannot do anything against you, because you are a French soldier like me [Kurt Leppien had obtained the French citizenship after volunteering in the Foreign Legion], but I have learned through M. Baudière that your wife is of Jewish descent and she will be soon in a camp and deported to Germany."
>
> Although we do not have positive proof, we have no doubt that it is Gandon who attracted the attention of the CGQJ, who visited us soon after. It is following this incident that my wife was arrested by the Gestapo on March 21, 1944. I was also arrested by the German Feldgendarmerie in Avignon on March 22, 1944...[38]

Kurt Leppien cited the "German Feldgendarmerie" which probably was helping the German police. It is also possible that he meant the GFP. He also linked his wife's arrest to the CGQJ, which, at the time, was represented by Jean Lebon, inspector of the SEC.[*]

---

[*] Once again, we note the approximation of functions in a contemporary testimony.

The Horn Affair: a Specific Interest in the Jews

Did Thesmar merely cover his men and once in a while rein in their anti-Semitism to get them to deal with his first priority, namely the struggle against the Resistance? Indeed, the Government Commissioner enumerated a long list of charges consisting of raids against the Resistance, at times together with German units, interrogations accompanied by torture, arrests and even executions. Every time his responsibility was emphasized, but nothing was mentioned about the Jews.

Yes, but there was the Horn case. Henri Horn was Jewish; he was born in Nancy on April 30, 1904. After his arrest on March 14, 1944, he was deported on convoy 73. Since he was not registered, there is no way to know how long he had been in the Vaucluse.

He lived with his companion, Clairette Grely, who testified that in April 1943, he obtained a permit to sell fabrics on the open markets after managing the "Restaurant de la Banque."[39] He had a stall on the Place Pie and a former police inspector, Durand, was providing some help in exchange for a cut of the profits. She added that Horn had false papers that were sent from Paris. She knew of no link to the Milice. In the context of the times, there was nothing unusual.

But, at the Liberation, she accused her jealous husband, Jules Gondoin, a plumber and zinc worker from Avignon, of having denounced Henri Horn. Gondoin, after a 5-month jail sentence for theft, then volunteered as a worker in Germany. She remembered his threats in a bar: "*I know he is Jewish, he will pay dearly, with his life.*" In her mind, her husband must have known at that time that Horn had just been arrested and deported by the Gestapo. During his trial, a man named Le Lorrain affirmed that Gondoin was probably an informer of the German police; Gondoin rejected emphatically this accusation and denied having denounced Horn.

The investigation took a completely different dimension with the declaration of Moustrou, who was in charge of special intelligence operations for the Resistance:

> In March 1944, I came across information about Henri Horn, a fabric merchant in Avignon. One day, I recorded a conversation involving Villard, a Gestapo agent who was shot at the Liberation by the Resistance in Buis les Baronnies. Villard was saying that Horn was an informer for the Milice and the Gestapo and that he mainly provided information to get Jews arrested. He is said to have given his information by using little notes inside cigarette packs; he would give the packs to Germans or miliciens who acted as ordinary customers. Villard had added that Horn was playing a double game and that "his cover got

blown." He was accused of having warned a Jew after denouncing him and having received 50,000 francs for this services.[40]

A nasty business with a Jew playing the role of the traitor, but it did not yet reach Thesmar personally; he was only implicated because he was the boss. However, a note from the RG of Avignon to the Director of Sûreté Nationale in Paris, dated December 23, 1944, brought the head of the Milice straight into the heart of these events:

> The man named Henri Horn, domiciled at 50, rue Banasterie in Avignon and a stallholder, was a member of the Milice. Very cautious, he was giving information personally to Thesmar. For his services, he was getting fees between 1,000 and 10,000 francs, depending on the importance of the cases. He was specialized in the denunciation of Israelites. Arrested in March 1944 at the behest of Thesmar whom he had double crossed; the chief of the Milice accused Horn of having warned a person about to be arrested and of having received 50,000 francs in exchange. Horn was deported to Germany because he was a Jew. This was a dangerous individual; capable of accomplishing missions on behalf of the enemy in whose service he had probably entered, if he has not been killed.

But a research report, compiled by Pierre Bonvallet[41] and found in the Musée de la Résistance in Fontaine de Vaucluse, offers another point of view. Bonvallet cited a list of members of the Resistance provided long after the war by Philippe Beyne, the chief of the Maquis Ventoux. Henri Horn was named in the list of "dead, missing and deported members of the Maquis Ventoux." Was Horn then a member of the Resistance who was turned around by Thesmar? During these times of unbridled violence, everything was possible under pressure and threats.

Thesmar was not just a man wearing a uniform, whose responsibility was in line with his rank. He was at the leading edge of the network. This fighter against greed who supposedly shunned the persecution of the Jews collaborated with the German police.

Strangely, the court of justice left out one side of his deeds. The prosecution did not look for the arrest of Jews; therefore the persecution of the Jews did not appear in the list of charges. In particular, the assassination of Schlema Medvedowski, the Jewish doctor of the Resistance, was one of the charges against Thesmar. But nobody asked whether the fact that he was Jewish had anything to do with his summary execution.

The Medvedowski Affair

Before Liberation, Thesmar's declaration of July 6, 1944, gave the facts as he saw them.

Doctor Medvedowski was arrested by us in Cucuron on June 16. We brought him to Vinon because of the requirements of our investigation. He disappeared during the night of June 17-18, and on the 18th we were unable to bring him back with us to La Tour d'Aigues. His car, which had a breakdown, was towed; at some point, the tank was fueled to start the engine, but following a short, it caught fire and we left the burned-out car on the side of the road. Later, I learned that the car had been brought back to La Tour d'Aigues.

A report about Doctor Medvedowski is going to be sent by the Milice to the regional Prefect. I think that doctor Medvedowski left for the Maquis unless he was arrested by the German units which, at that time, were performing a regional police operation. I will try to get information and see whether he was arrested by the German Autorities.[42]

This declaration took place two weeks after the event, but also after a popular protest demanding clarifications about the arrest of the doctor from La Tour d'Aigues as well as his liberation. On June 17, praising the dedication and competence of Medvedowski, a letter signed by 101 people from the village of Grambois "*begs the responsible authorities to return him as soon as possible.*" On the same day, La Tour d'Aigues' mayor wrote to the prefect:

Doctor Medvedowski, who practices medicine in the [medical] center of La Tour d'Aigues, was arrested on June 16, 1944, in Cucuron by the French Milice.

Sir, our doctor knows only one duty, his doctor's duty. He rushes up even at night where he is needed without worrying about the distance. He has said many times that a doctor is like a priest and he has taken care of his patients irrespectively of their ideas or opinions.

Sir, before taking any measures, we are asking you to investigate this case.

Attached, are the signatures of all the people who have benefited from his dedication.

(220 signatures follow)

On June 18, a third letter with 91 signatures from the people of St. Martin de la Brasque asked the prefect to intervene with the Milice to obtain the doctor's liberation.

On June 19, it was the turn of 31 citizens of la Motte d'Aigues. The tone was the same: praise for the caregiver and respect for his "French qualities."

Doctor Medvedowski's tragic end was revealed much later. His body was discovered on November 20, 1944. His son, Jean-Louis Medvedowski described the circumstances in his book.[43] If Thesmar was not the executor, he was the one who gave the order, according to Gaston Turcan's testimony, cited by the author.

In July 1944, confronted by the impressive solidarity of the people for their doctor, Thesmar had to resort to a travesty of reality. Had he tried to justify the action as part of the struggle against Jewish terrorism, his argument would have fallen on deaf ears.

On June 22, 1946, Thesmar was sentenced to forced labor for life, but his life sentence was commuted to 20 years. He got off easy, considering the charges: "*As a chief of the Milice, his responsibility is found in all the operations and wrongdoings attributable to this organization.*"

Thesmar had first fled to Germany "*where he was assigned to the Charlemagne brigade as a lieutenant, then as a political instructor at the Etville parachuting, spying and sabotage school.*" In the Charlemagne brigade, he had named the group he was heading after "Philippe Henriot"—in memory of this Pétain's fervent propagandist who was eulogized by the archbishop of Avignon, Mgr. Gabriel de Llobet, after he was gunned down by the Resistance. As the allies were closing in, he fled to Italy like many others. "*Unmasked and arrested in Milan under the name of René Euch, he had succeeded in getting hired as a secretary at the French consulate.*"

Tiziano Feroldi
The Head of Milice Intelligence in the Vaucluse

Sentenced to death in absentia on June 14, 1945, Tiziano Feroldi was never found by the court of justice.[44] His tracks were lost right after the general mobilization order of Darnand's Milice, more precisely in Mulhouse and Belfort where Charles Palmieri was the last to see him.[45] He was fleeing in the direction of Germany like the others. But during his questioning of March 13, 1945, Palmieri had some doubts about his destination: "*I know that Tiziano Feroldi intended to settle in northern Italy where he has relatives.*" Was he successful?

Born on July 24, 1904, in France in Sathonay (Ain),[46] Tiziano Mario Feroldi was 40 at the Liberation. He was the divorced father of a little girl. Just before his departure, he picked her up and took her away from the places where he had brought death. The gendarme Aimé Bourguet confirmed it in his report of March 17, 1945. A man and a young child are less likely to attract much attention. On March 19, 1945, police headquarters in Nice (Alpes Maritimes), on the Riviera, reported that it had "*looked for him to no avail following a warrant for his arrest.*" Some tips and Palmieri's deposition had probably situated him in Nice, on his way to Italy.

Before the war Feroldi had been a maître d'hôtel, then a musician and a band leader in night clubs.

When Pétain came to power, he joined various political movements (they are not specified) before landing in the Vaucluse. In 1941 he headed the "Companions de France" in Pertuis, and in November 1942, he becomes department inspector for the SOL, where he manages recruiting, propaganda and new members. He continued in that position, even after the transformation of the SOL into the Milice in February 1943, in addition to the intelligence service. He became the head of the Milice 2nd Bureau.

Feroldi had an office on the third floor of Milice headquarters, at 71, rue Joseph Vernet in Avignon. He almost always wore a uniform and carried a side arm. His closest friends were Georges Cruon and Albert Marin, who "*always ride in the first car, in the company of Thesmar, during raids against the Resistance.*"

Feroldi's Associates

Georges Cruon was an obsessively anti-Semitic Milice chief. He was a member of the Bollène establishment. Since he owned a bus company in Bollène, Aimé Autrand used his services on August 26, 1942, to drive the foreign Jews from the northern part of the Vaucluse to the camp of Les Milles. He was constantly focused on arresting Jews. He drew up the complete list of the Jews in Bollène; he had identified 38 of them through the Legion, and on January 28, 1943, he sent the list to de Camaret.[47] At the end of the list, Cruon added a comment: "*You doubtless know the harmful influence of this race, and I am sending you this report for your information.*" After a raid against the Resistance, he was seen in the company of Marin in a hotel-restaurant of Baumes de Venise, where he demanded to see the list of patrons so that he could identify the possible Jews among them.[48]

Cruon was sentenced to death in absentia on October 5, 1945, but he surrendered of his own free will on June 7, 1951, to settle his situation in the Marseille military court.[49] On the eve of his trial, he was living as a free man at the home of a certain Mme. Eliette's, 35 place Jules Guesde, in Marseille. The testimony against him was overwhelming. Let us cite a few witnesses.

M. Joffre, Mayor of Seynes (Gard), 49 years old:

> I am unrelated to the defendant
> - In June 1944, I was driving a car, when a group of armed miliciens ordered me to stop and to get out of the car
> - The car was searched
> - Mr. Cruon was armed, he had a pistol in his hand. He seemed to be the chief. He interrogated me about my actions. He checked my wallet, which he then returned to me. I recognize Mr. Cruon without any doubts.
> - It is Mr. Cruon who signed my release document
> - There were no arrests in the village

Mr. Jean Prince, 59 years old, farmer, Noves:

> I am not related to the defendant
> - I was arrested in Noves on July 19, 1944. There were Garros, Ferret, Sartin, and Mr. Cruon, the driver.
> - Cruon was holding a sub-machine gun and aimed it at me.
> - The gang stole 250,000 francs from me.
> - In Avignon, I was tortured with the electricity in a dreadful way. It left me crippled. My hand is now paralyzed
> - Mr. Cruon did not torture me. I do not know whether or not Cruon did participate in the search [of my home]
> - Mr. Michon told me after Liberation that Cruon was the driver during my arrest.

M. Vincent Michon, 52 years old, farmer:

> - I was arrested on July 19, 1944, at 9:30 a.m. at my home

- Cruon, among others, Garros, Perret, and Santini were present
- Ferret tortured me with electric current
- Cruon was holding me in sight and ordered the others to search my house
- They stole 350,000 francs in banknotes and gold coins. They ate in my place and stole cold cuts. They rummaged through everything in my home.
- I must mention that Cruon gave the order to set my house on fire. They did not do it, but they burned an empty shed a little further away.
- I was dropped at the school in Noves, and then driven to Avignon. Cruon was present during the tortures in Avignon. He did not intervene to stop the tortures.
- I was never asked for information about the Resistance. I stayed in Avignon until August 24. Then, I was handed over to the Germans and released when Avignon was liberated.
- I recognize Cruon without any doubt

Cruon denied everything.

With the exception of the death sentence I was given in absentia on October 5, 1945, I have no criminal record:
- … I only held a passive function in the Milice. I did not participate in any arrest. I was the head of transportation of the Avignon Milice. I have not arrested anybody.
- The witness Jean Bruce is lying brazenly. The only true details are that I was the driver—although I do not remember having been in Mr. Bruce's home. If I went, I stayed in the car. I definitely never owned a weapon.
- Mr. Bruce is lying. It is not at the Milice of Avignon that he lost the use of his hand. He had polyarthritis.
- With respect to Mr. Roche's deposition, I must say this. One day, I heard screams, and I saw that Mr. Roche was being tortured. I interceded with Mr. Thesmar so that he stopped the beating. Immediately, the beating stopped. When he was freed, he thanked me, he held out his hand, and said "No hard feelings!" I never hit Mr. Roche.
- I believe that Mr. Michon's memories are rather vague.
- During the investigation, he did not recognize me. He must have confused me with someone else.

On December 17, 1952, Cruon was sentenced to 8 years in prison and 5 years of ban from the area. His sentence was automatically reduced in 1954 and 1955, and he was finally pardoned. Much later, he reappeared a few times in Bollène; he was rumored to be in Franco's Spain.

Feroldi, the Man of Action

Feroldi was a member of the apparatus, focused on the smooth running of its criminal enterprise. He was active on all fronts.

A propagandist, he made a point to brainwash the young people he wished to recruit. A 19-year-old farmer from Jonquières, Michel Mercier, mentioned the influence of the village school teacher and above all that of Feroldi, who succeeded in getting him to sign up for the Milice "*by giving him a long-winded speech about the repression of black market and the maintenance of law and order.*"[50]

An organizer, he regularly visited Antignac, the parish priest of Chateauneuf de Gadagne, who was also a registered milicien. With the priest, he prepared the imminent arrests of the opponents in the village.

A torturer, Feroldi used a pickax handle to get information out of prisoners from the Resistance, at the farm of the Roussets, a family of miliciens.[51]

A henchman, he assassinated a café-owner from Bollène with his own hands, following an order from Raymond Bonnabel, Thesmar's predecessor as the head of the Vaucluse Milice.[52] This murder was carried out in retaliation for the execution by the Resistance of the Avignon lawyer, Georges Gras, a milicien and a visceral anti-Semite.

As a back-up for the Germans, he was side-by-side with other French men, miliciens and Waffen-SS from the 8th Regiment of the Brandeburg division, during the expedition against the Maquis Ventoux.[53] The 35 members of the Resistance, who were stationed around the village of Izon-la-Bruisse, on the hills of Séderon (Drôme) were the victims of a bloody massacre. Among others, Alfred Epstein,[54] who had escaped arrest and deportation in August 1942, was executed during this operation.

The report of March 1, 1944,[55] documenting the meeting of the federal board of the Vaucluse PPF, offers a sampling of Feroldi's role:

> Augusta Vernet,* the delegate for cultural affairs, reports that she has learned from the militant Adrean from Ménerbes, that a few days ago, in the area of Sault, Feroldi, one of the chiefs of the Milice, has killed an armed car driver and captured two of his comrades. The two were British nationals, representatives to the terrorists.

---

* In her neighborhood, Augusta Vernet was called "the Kraut."

The testimony of Albert Coupon of February 13, 1945, in the context of the investigation of Judge Albert Leyris, was not just eloquent about Feroldi himself, but also suggested the existence of informers working for him.

> On March 22, 1944, around 6 a.m., six plain-clothes individuals knocked on my door, and told me they had come to arrest a member of the Resistance they suspected to be hiding in my home.
>
> I noticed two armed German guards in front of the door and in the corridor of the apartment building. One of these individuals who were all speaking French correctly asked me who was coming to sleep in my home… They were referring to my cousin, a member of the Resistance who was sleeping in my apartment at every visit he made to Avignon. The way they searched my home, I understood that they were well informed and that my cousin had been denounced.
>
> After being treated harshly for a good while, I was taken to the offices of the hotel de la Cigale and from there to the Ste Anne prison where I was held for 53 days.
>
> During my absence, my home was looted and I strongly suspect—I am even certain—that a man named Feroldi participated in the looting…
>
> Because of this abuse, the damage amounted to about 130,000 francs in clothes, jewelry, linens, etc., they stole.
>
> Mr. Barras and the owner of the Pavillon de Flore, rue de la République, as well as Mr. Paturel assured me that it was indeed Feroldi who did it.

Every opportunity was too good to miss.

As for the Jews, an examination of the court files does not provide any information about arrests, except for those in Bollène, in the company of Alfred André.[*] Of course, this did not mean that it was the only case. In general, we are far from being able to associate a perpetrator with every Jew arrested. The small number of surviving deportees has limited the availability of testimony, and the survivors did not always know the names of the perpetrators. It has only been possible to determine that the Vaucluse Milice had a contingent of individuals involved in crimes against the Jews.

The Looting of the Store "Les 200.000 bas"[†]

The usual actions of the miliciens consisted of operations against the Resistance, denunciations and arrests. On the margin and behind the shield of the ideology of law and order, the profit generated by blackmail, theft and looting was a powerful motivation in the hunt for the Jews.

---

[*] This episode is described in Chapter 1.
[†] The 200,000 stockings.

Feroldi was just such a case. Henri Gardiol, director of the Roblot funeral home, 23, rue Carnot in Avignon, testified on March 6, 1945. A former officer in the Legion, he kept his distance at the creation of the SOL which signaled the criminal drift of the Legion. He did not change his mind because of the expressions of anti-Semitism, but because of the letters of threats and denunciations against some war veterans. This aspect added to value to his testimony.

In response to the information requests published in the press, I am honored to make the following declaration, relating to two miliciens in Avignon: Titien Feroldi, former department inspector of the Milice, and Marin, former employee of the department transportation team*.

Here are the facts: on April 4, 1944, a dark red Peugeot-5 cv [horse power], stopped next to the store of Mr. Imberton, a tailor at 21, rue Carnot, in front of my offices. Marin, the driver, and a passenger, unknown to me, came out of the car. Shortly thereafter, Feroldi whom I knew well and Layet, executed since then, arrive on foot. The four of them entered the building of the food store "Le Casino," 19, rue Petite Saunerie. They asked the manager, Mme. Béraud, where the warehouse of the "200,000 bas" belonging to Mr. Nahoum was located.

Without losing her cool, Mme. Béraud, who was suspicious of the individuals she was dealing with, told them that she was not the manager of the building and that she had no information for them. Feroldi, who had found nothing came back aggressively, and threatened her, he pressed Mme. Béraud for information while showing a card with red, white and blue stripes; she believes it read "Milice Française" [French Milice]. In any case, Feroldi stated that he belonged to the German police. With the threat hanging over her head, Mme. Béraud had no choice but to give him the information he wanted.

As soon as they heard, the four individuals broke the door open, and entered the warehouse which they burglarized from top to bottom. You can still see the state in which they left the place.

They loaded the car over and over again for two days openly and publicly. In addition to the vehicle, Layet and Feroldi, who had helped load it, left on foot, carrying packages full of merchandise, stockings, coats, etc. Everything was stolen.

At the same time, a pickup truck was operating at the residence and store of Mr. Nahoum, 2, rue St. Jean le Vieux. The house was practically emptied; the German were operating at that location. Besides, the teams of miliciens and Germans seemed to be operating under the same orders.

Everyone in the neighborhood was distressed and helpless at witnessing this organized burglary. I was able to understand exactly what happened from my

---

* According to Thesmar who was impressed by his administrative competence, Marin, the Département secretary of the Milice, had been requisitioned by the Prefect for the maintenance of public order.

office, which is a perfect observation post; this is why I can absolutely assure you of the truthfulness of my statement which I sign in all conscience.[56]

Raymond Layet, the third man cited by Gardiol was not a newcomer. He was a milicien and the owner of the Central Bar. His café on the Place de l'Horloge was not a place for choirboys. In her deposition of December 2, 1944, Denise Layet declared:

> I was a shopkeeper; I was managing the Central Bar... I have been jailed since August 23, 1944. On that date, I was arrested by the Avignon police together with my husband. When I asked why, I was told it was a security question since my husband was a milicien.
>
> People of the underworld were the main patrons of the Central Bar; among others: Marcel "the doctor," who managed a brothel, rue Favart, Mimi Poggi, and many others whose names I do not remember. I can also cite MM. Marin, Feroldi, Bouillon, and Mme. Gras. These people would come to the bar about 2 or 3 times a month.
>
> I knew Conrad very well; he had a girlfriend, Mme. Schmidt who was a waitress in my bar. I also knew Pierre Terrier and Max William, as well as René Boyer, who used to come, sometimes in company of Jeannot Ricard, the owner of a dance hall in the rue St. Jean.[57]

Henri Gardiol was very specific about the date of the looting. He said "*on April 4, in the morning.*" He did not say, or did not know, that Moïse, Sarina and Isaac Nahoum (one of the Avignon families from Turkey who at the time formed the majority of the Jewish community) had been arrested on March 29, 1944, and later deported; Moïse on convoy 74, Sarina and Isaac on convoy 71. And it just so happened that the looters operated on April 4, namely 6 days later. Of course, this could have been the result of postponed looting. But this two step action was not necessarily conducted by the same perpetrators. The looters could also have been tipped by a discreet informer. It must be noted however that Germans and hoodlums were all sharing in the loot.

What did Feroldi do with the booty? A few weeks earlier, during the looting of Château de Gourdon in Bollène, after the arrest of the Rosenbergs, Feroldi unloaded part of the property at his domicile at the "Caserne des Passagers," and dropped the rest at the Milice headquarters. For the Nahoums, we do not know. Did he sell his "war trophies" and to whom? The full knowledge of this lucrative underground trade network escapes us, because of the lack of full documentation. But it will be possible, here and there, to establish clear complicities in selling the proceeds of the looting.

Many indications point toward the Villa Monclar, where Wilhelm Müller had a finger in the pie. Thesmar assured us in his testimony that he had forbidden his men to have any contact with Müller; this is an order that Feroldi did not obey. His boss added a little further into his deposition: *"In June 1944, I fired the chief of the second division, Feroldi, for his police activity with the Germans."*[58]

All of this puts financial interest at the center of anti-Semitic violence.

One can't help but notice that Thesmar "dumped" his subordinate Feroldi rather late, just at the moment when the allies were pouring onto the beaches of Normandy and when the noose was tightening around the south of France through northern Italy and the Mediterranean coast.

Feroldi's Connected Networks

Feroldi did not operate on his own; obviously he did so with other miliciens, but also with the upper crust of the French agents of the German police. He was listed in the Blanchard list of the bar Carnot, the headquarters of the French GFP gang of the rue Bancasse. This is also where other right-hand men of Müller stayed, like Pierre Terrier and the PPF Antoine Guidoni, *aka* the doctor, *"in charge of the surveillance of the large cafés of Avignon and the bourgeois classes."*[59] It is more difficult to determine his relationship with Palmieri, but they knew each other, and Palmieri was quite open about it: *"I have known Feroldi the milicien through the intermediary of Pierre Terrier, an agent of the SD in Avignon. I have met this Feroldi at police headquarters, boulevard Monclar."*[60] This placed Feroldi in two centers of the Avignon German police, Gauthier's domaine at the rue Bancasse, and the offices of his boss, Wilhelm Müller, at boulevard Monclar.

Feroldi's greatest strength was his ability to establish contacts outside the Milice and to cooperate through informal networks with members of other organizations. This networking was also the strength of Georges Boyer— Parietas, Alfred André, Lucien Blanc, Gaston Mouillade, Palmieri himself, and so many others. Moreover, Feroldi was no stranger to Parietas, who reported on March 15, 1945:

> I know Feroldi very well; I know he was head of the Milice in Avignon. I saw him often at the Cigale when he brought information to the German inspector Rupp. I never worked directly with him.

… or Emile Gratian, 50 years old, sports instructor, who declared on March 13, 1945, during his detention at St. Anne prison:

I got acquainted with Feroldi when he was department inspector of the Milice in Avignon.

He was often going out with Georges Cruon,* Albert Marin, and Jiovani, three miliciens from Avignon. At every outing, the four of them organized expeditions against members of the Resistance or communists.

I heard from Feroldi himself that he was a pillar of the fascist Revolution in Italy. By the way, this is the reason he had earned a high rank in the Milice.

When the general mobilization of Darnand came, Feroldi was already working for the Gestapo, at the Hôtel de la Cigale, rue Bancasse. I am not aware of his activity on the side of the Germans. However, I know that this individual was extremely mean to the people he arrested.

Feroldi was not a newcomer in the extreme right militancy. When he arrived in Avignon, he had already been active within Italian fascism. However, his action in the Vaucluse went far beyond the more moderate—should we say less malevolent?—action of the Italian fascism described by Renzo de Felice in his *Storia degli ebrei italiani sotto il fascismo*† (1961); an image that was reinforced by a less brutal, and often protective, attitude by the Italian occupation forces in the southern zone.[61]

To carry out his mission, Feroldi needed intelligence, and he drew it from any source. It was the testimony of Ferragut which had placed him at the home of parish priest Antignac from Châteauneuf de Gadagne, who was also an organizer of miliciens' meetings: *"Feroldi came to visit me after leaving the home of the priest. Feroldi used to have his meals at the priest's home. He already had a complete list of people to arrest."*[62]

Feroldi was not going to confession when he was visiting with Antignac, the parish priest who stoked the anger of the population of Gadagne at the Liberation. The archbishop of Avignon, Gabriel de Llobet, alluded to it in a letter to the prefect on September 27, 1944, to thank him for his *"intervention in favor of the priest of Gadagne, who will be assigned elsewhere after some rest."*[63] Justice did not touch the clergy, which appeared to be a state within the state. Moreover, the letter attested to the ambivalence of Archbishop de Llobet. In 1940–1944, he was satisfied with the privileged position the Church held within the anti-secular Vichy regime; he was first and foremost a convinced Pétain supporter, who preached the cult of the Maréchal. But he was however uncomfortable about the persecution of the Jews, to the point of denouncing *"the materialistic doctrines based upon race"* in a Lent sermon of 1941. Although some members of his clergy remained forcefully anchored to the

---

* Here, Georges is the first name of Cruon; elsewhere it is Pierre. Are we dealing with two individuals?
† *The Jews in Fascist Italy. A History.*

anti-Semitic traditions of the Church throughout the war, a large segment of public opinion was nevertheless strongly influenced by the protest of Cardinal Salièges, soon joined by Théas at Montauban, Gerlier at Lyon and a few others, before switching to Gaullism, and a small group even went into active résistance. The resistance of several Avignon Catholic institutions (St. Joseph High School, the Sacré Coeur Convent, and the Immaculate Conception Convent) must have been known at the archdiocese.

After the stress of the war period, de Llobet readjusted his position and practiced *realpolitik* toward the new order at Liberation, even if this new order did not offer the Church the same promises as the previous regime.[64]

The Deep Dive

In April 1944, Jean Poutet, the all-powerful milicien and PPF chief, took his leave from Thesmar.[65] He was leaving for Paris to a posting as colonel in the line guards. Before his departure, Poutet came to say good bye to Thesmar, and he did not forget to inquire about Feroldi. In his testimony, Poutet stated that Feroldi had also applied for a job in the line guards and communications, an organization where Poutet would have an influential position. Was Poutet advising a friend to clear out before it was too late or was he promising to pull some strings? At the time of this visit, Feroldi was still the chief of the second bureau (intelligence) of the Vaucluse Milice, according to the certificate from Thesmar on May 14, 1944:

> I, undersigned, Yves Thesmar, chief of the French Milice of the Vaucluse, certify that Titien Feroldi, holder of the food card No. 21 854 category T* is still in the permanent service of the French Milice where he occupies functions that require significant physical exercise.

Then, Feroldi, who expended a lot of energy, disappeared at the last minute a few days before Liberation. After his departure, his name was mentioned several times. On January 29, 1945, the Avignon police superintendant broadcast his description:

Particulars	Individual information
40 years old	Titien Feroldi
1 m 75	Nationality: French
Black curls	Born on 7/24/1904 in Sathonay (Ain)

---

* Category T: Persons of both sexes from 12 to 70 years of age who hold a difficult job requiring a great expense of muscular energy.

Exposed forehead	Domicile: rue des Lices – Avignon
Hooked nose	Profession : former orchestra conductor and
Average mouth	maître d'hôtel
Prominent chin	Married
Dark complexion	One child
Oval face	

Information

Former assistant to the chief of the Compagnons of France in Avignon

Former chief of the SOL of Avignon, then Département Inspector of the same organization

Member of the PPF

Chief of the Département Milice

Agent of the Gestapo, informer of the German services

Very dangerous individual – a killer

In case of arrest, inform the government superintendant at the Court of Justice of the Vaucluse.

Then, the trail went cold. Much later, on February 21, 1952, Feroldi's file was sent to the Government commissioner at the court of Marseille, in relation *"to the procedure against Raymond Bonnabel."* On December 6, 1957, the State Public Prosecutor told the Public Prosecutor at the appeals court of Nîmes that "… *Tiziano Feroldi… is still wanted.*" Finally, on January 1964, a document sent to the appeals court in Nîmes repeated that he "*is still wanted,* like Jacques Bouchet *and Suzy Pommier, all sentenced to death.*"[66] This woman's file indicated that she had taken part in operations against the Resistance and that she had married an industrialist from Milan in 1945. The State Public Prosecutor warned that the sentences were to lapse between the end of June and the beginning of July 1965, because of the statute of limitation.

So, did Feroldi survive in another country or even a different continent? In any case, he was one more criminal who evaporated in the chaos of Liberation. But with Feroldi, we are in for another surprise.

Feroldi Reappears

By sheer coincidence, the story of Tiziano Feroldi came to a dramatic ending. We were able to locate with the help of Internet an actor named Tiziano Feroldi who played bit parts in four movies: *Grand Prix*, by John Frankenheimer (1966), as the doctor on the Monza race track, *Revenge*, by Pino Tosini (1969), as the commander, *A Woman Against Arsene Lupin*, by

Tony Blaad (1971), as the police chief, and *True Life*, a remake of *Revenge* by Alastair Reid for the BBC (1972).

We found no other movies before 1966 or after 1972. Feroldi however played a few theatre roles in Italy, in particular in "Maman Colibri" under the direction of Anton Giulio Majano and in "Partita a Quattro" under the direction of Raphael Meloni.

At first glance, the doctor from Monza was about 60 years old—the age of Feroldi from the Vaucluse. In his last film, he looks 65 to 70 years old. Everything fits, his age, his disappearance until the statute of limitations in 1965, and his profession in show business where he started before the war in night clubs. There is no biographical data in any actors' data bases. We are in the presence of a man who "did not exist" before his first film at a late age. We found one exception though: Feroldi played a secondary role in "L'Anaspo" at the Milano Picolo Teatro, on March 2, 1964, just before the end of his 20 years run. Did he think that he was not taking a great risk with this role in an avant-garde show?

The actor of 1966 had a large build, and was rather stout. With his physique, he could have played the role of the harmless and easy going neighborhood storekeeper. Who would recognize the Feroldi of the dark years? However, in a photograph found in his file, he had the same profile, the same nose, and the same chin, in spite of the intervening years; and most of all, the same chilling eyes.

So, respectability was at the end of the road for Feroldi, one of the most accomplished figures of the collaboration in the Vaucluse. He took his secrets with him, including the reasons for the missing 20 years in his biography. One does not disappear that long without help.

In 1864, after fleeing the Austrian persecution of northeastern Italian nationalists, Tiziano's grandfather, Louis Feroldi from Brescia, and his wife Monica Brusaferri had settled near Lyon, where Louis created a silk business. As soon as Italy was finally unified in 1861, he set up headquarters in Milan[67]. His son, Charles, took over the business; three children were born from his marriage with Helene Gippet: Monica, Tiziano and Garibaldi. The first names of the two boys were not just an empty expression of Italian pride, and after World War I, the family returned to northeastern Italy, where Tiziano Feroldi joined the Fascist Party.[68] This strongly suggests that the Milan region was where Tiziano found help during his "missing years."

Feroldi's story offers some resemblance to that of Paul Touvier, a graduate of Uriage, a murderer, an intelligence specialist in the Lyon Milice, and later its chief, who disappeared before his death sentence in 1946. In his flight, Touvier was helped by the Catholic Church which provided him with hiding places, until he is arrest in 1989 near Nice where he lived quietly away from the limelight. Touvier knew well that, even if his original death sentence lapsed after 20 years, the crimes he had committed fell in the category of crimes against humanity, without statute of limitation, as defined by the law of December 26, 1964.* As to Feroldi, he seemed to not realize that, by coming out of the shadows in 1966 under his real name in a film with mass appeal, he exposed himself to the death sentence, until its cancellation on October 9, 1981, and to life in prison thereafter.

---

* The single article law states: "The statute of limitation does not apply to crimes against humanity, as they are defined by the UN resolution of February 13, 1946, adopting the definition of crimes against humanity, as it is stated in the charter of the international tribunal of August 8, 1945."

The "White Collar" Agents of the "Collaboration" Group

1.

Charles Uhl
The founder

The 60 year-old Swiss born, Charles Uhl—Karl for the Germans— obtained French citizenship in 1930.[69] He was the thinker of the "Collaboration" group, although "thinker" may be a big word. He was a sales representative in southeastern France, of Baignol et Farjon, the pencil manu- facturer, and his thinking was centered around the spirit of collaboration aimed at moving France from the camp of the vanquished to that of the victors.

"Collaboration," a group created before the symbolic encounter at Montoire between Pétain and Hitler, liked to think of itself as an echo chamber for the old Maréchal. Its motto was borrowed from the call of the great military man: "*It is not sufficient to trust me; I need your help.*" Fernand de Brinon, the plenipotentiary ambassador of the Vichy government in Paris, took the organization under his wing. The clearly stated objective was for "*France to seize upon the unique chance of recovery by participating willingly in the irresistible movement which drives Europe toward its unity.*" A statement that defined the framework.

The instructions were well defined: "*In each town where you will create a movement or a sub-committee, you will make sure that the individuals called upon are of unquestionable morality and you will require them to give their word that they are Aryans and do not belong to freemasonry.*"

In Avignon, Charles Uhl was on a roll. The recital of the facts in his court file described him accurately.

He has been a member of the Collaboration group from early June 1941 until Liberation. He was a vice-president from 1943 and worked intensely in favor of collaboration with Germany. Under the assumed name of Charles Sonat, he published in "l'Union Nationale," a weekly of New Europe, and in "le Petit Vauclusien," articles in favor of rapprochement with the enemy. He created posters for lectures by notorious collaborators, Georges Claude, Grimm and others. He even went so far as to say that the French had harmed Germany more than the Germans had done so to France. He wrote enthusiastic letters to Doriot and to the Gringoire newspaper.

Basically, his "love" letter of December 31, 1940, to Jacques Doriot was a statement of his intentions:

> Your movement is the only one capable of implementing in France at the same time the social and national renewals, and by a loyal collaboration with Germany, the indispensable integration of France at one of the first places in a Europe united against plutocracy and fake democracy which must be made powerless at all costs.
>
> I subscribe heartily to the editorial of your newspaper of the 21st of this month, "Yes, Monsieur le Maréchal!" and I am asking you to kindly accept me in your ranks, and if so, to accept my pledge to fight, body and soul, for the realization of your program.

The exposition of the facts by the prosecutor stated:

> In Avignon, he was in constant contact with Stehling, the chief of the OPA; he had regular contacts with chief of the Gestapo Müller, and his name is on the list of special passes which the Germans were supposed to provide to their informers in case of an Anglo-American landing.
>
> Uhl claims that he considered collaboration in a spirit of equivalence and mutual respect. He pretends to have been able to help several people arrested by the Gestapo, thanks to his connections. He maintains that he never was an auxiliary of the Gestapo, and explains the presence of his name on the list of passes by Stehling's positive feelings toward him.

What set Uhl apart from the other leaders of "Collaboration" in Avignon was first and foremost his knowledge of German (he translated article by Goebbels "War and the Jews" in the newspaper *Das Reich* of May 9, 1943). In addition, his closeness to Stehling was nothing but puzzling.

His correspondence with Stehling in German seemed compromising. First, he gave 500 francs to the German Red Cross. Then, he put his own car at the disposal of Stehling for 100 francs a day. They signed a proper contract to that effect. Finally, a note from Stehling to the Gestapo of Konstanz spoke very highly of Uhl as an enthusiastic and leading supporter of collaboration. But his speech in the name of "Collaboration" at the reception given by Stehling at the Hôtel Crillon on November 13, 1943, one year after the invasion of the southern zone, exploded with "Uhlian" terminology:

As soon as you arrived in our town and from our first contact with you, we were won over by your constant kindness and impeccable behavior. During the weeks and months that followed, our sympathy for you, Mr. Stehling, did not stop growing, and for some of us it turned into a feeling of sincere friendship. This feeling is all the more valuable for us that we see in you, dear Mr. Stehling, the representative of new Germany, of National-Socialist Germany, in short Adolf Hitler's Germany.

Stehling was not just anybody in the German occupation system in the Vaucluse. He was the one who banged on the table when the efficiency of the STO was not as it should be, and who demanded a higher contribution of workers. The tracking of dodgers was in itself of the highest importance, since the considerable German mobilization had taken a high toll on human reserves in Germany. We already know that Kuhling was leading the tracking of the Jews in the STO.

On the national stage, "Collaboration" was the descendant of the France-Germany committee from before the war (1935–1939) and had the strong support of Ambassador Otto Abetz. Created in 1940 by the writer Alphonse de Chateaubriant, it was authorized in February 1941 and was specialized in the indoctrination of the French, through a multitude of speeches on diverse topics, but all linked to collaboration with Germany. Its recruits, anti-democratic and pro German, all belonged to the intellectual elite and to the conservative bourgeoisie.

The local Avignon group had been created at the end of 1941. On January 9, 1942, Philippe Dreux, director-founder of the weekly *L'Union Française* (the official newspaper of "Collaboration") came to establish a sub-committee in Avignon.[70] The kickoff started with a speech and a discussion at the Café-Glacier on the Place de l'Horloge. This was the beginning of a sustained period of activity at the headquarters of the Avignon collaborationists at 11, rue St. Charles. They held monthly meetings with undeniable attendance peaks. Uhl was in the forefront of the preparation and organization of these encounters, where speakers, French and German alike, blathered on. The announcement of the upcoming speech by the propagandist, Dr. Manfred Zapp, reads:

The lectures-discussions will be extremely interesting, given the extensive knowledge of Dr. Zapp about the vast contemporary political problems, and more specifically about the politics of the United States, Roosevelt and the Jews. In our judgment, they will have a deeper and effective influence directly on our propagandists and on people who already have training and culture strong enough to easily absorb this information. They will then be in a better position to take advantage of it, broadcast it and contrast it to the stupidity and lies so brazenly spread by the Judeo-Gaullists.

According to several reports, during the lecture tour of Professor Hans Grimm in the unoccupied zone, 4000 people gathered in Avignon on June 5, 1942. Assembled inside and outside city hall, they came to hear the eminent jurist from the German academy of law, and the author of the book *Hitler and France,* published in 1938. The preamble to his Avignon lecture reminds the listeners that:

> Grimm argued against the Jews in Cairo, in Switzerland when Wilhelm Gustloff was assassinated by a Jew,* in France when the German diplomat vom Rath was assassinated by the Jew Grunspan.†

The court sentenced him to 10 years in prison. Why only 10 years? Even if it is hard to believe, the reason was that the charge of being affiliated with the German police was dropped.

Possibly, the certificate he received from his employer, the pencil company "Baignol et Farjon," on October 30, 1944, had some influence with the court.

> No one among the customers he visited in the southeast reported any behavior or talk against France. Quite the opposite, two out of his three sons have served the country; one of them was in the air force for 6 years. He was our very loyal representative in the sale of our products in fierce competition with German products.

Did the presence in his file of the letter from Mgr. Salièges, the archbishop of Toulouse, who reminded that the Jews belong to mankind, contribute to those extenuating circumstances?

2.
Jean Gaugler
The chief and his network

Although Jean Gaugler was not on the list of Müller's "favorites," he is very important to understand the network. An antifascist on the eve of the war, pro-German after the armistice, he was a Legion militant, and at the

---

* Wilhelm Gustloff, the German leader of the Swiss Nazi party, was assassinated on February 4, 1936, by a Jew, David Frankfurter.
† Ernst vom Rath was assassinated on November 7, 1938, by Herschel Grynszpan (and not Grunspan).

end of 1942, the département delegate of the "Collaboration" committee for the Vaucluse. In the following year, he became its president, and remained in that position until Liberation and his flight to Germany.

During those years, the activity of "Collaboration" was not limited to ideology. Its ranks included some key figures. Another "favorite" of Müller, Laurent Idlas, a manufacturer of sanitary equipment, served as general secretary to "Collaboration" before he resigned in April 1943 to dedicate himself fully to his job as chief of the local PPF. Idlas received the death sentence in absentia.[71]

Other PPF activists became founding members of "Collaboration." With Charles Uhl,[72] the salesman, who was the true initiator of the group, we find a lawyer from Orange, René Le Flem,[73] in the Milice and member of the anti-Bolshevik committee of Joachim Gatto,[74] the architect Maurice Riety.[75] Riety, sentenced in absentia to national indignity for life, retreated to Germany in the bus carrying the members of the PPF,[76] and was killed in an allied airplane raid near Loriol in August 1944.

The accountant, Raymond Bonnabel, chief of the Vaucluse Milice in 1943, was also a member of "Collaboration" before moving on to higher postings in the Milice.[77] Sentenced to death in absentia by the Vaucluse court of justice on June 30, 1945, Bonnabel surrendered voluntarily to the Marseille court of justice in 1951, and his sentence was commuted to 30 months in prison on February 24, 1953.

Dr. Passelègue, a war veteran and convinced Pétain supporter, was president of the Vaucluse "Collaboration" group in 1942. This lightweight president did not last very long and left in October 1942. He went on to help the resistance, and was rehabilitated thereby lifting his sentence to national indignity.[78]

The membership of the "Collaboration" group peaked in 1942 in the département. It seemed to benefit from the influx of a certain number of renegades of the "Amicale de France,"[79] an organization of Pétainiste propaganda created in the Vaucluse by Jacques Petit, a lawyer from Villeneuve-lès-Avignon, and dissolved at the national level on July 23, 1942. Idlas and Gaugler for example were members of l'Amicale before joining "Collaboration." In 1943, "Collaboration" shrank from 300 to 200 members. Gaugler claimed the same 200 members in 1944 and announced only two resignations during membership card renewals.

But beyond the size and the ideology of "Collaboration," it is particularly interesting to examine Gaugler's case in order to open a window into the persecution of the Jews. Gaugler did not just appear in de Camaret's file.[80] He was a candidate to a position as provisional administrator on December 11, 1941, stating that he was the recipient of the Legion of Honor and of the Military Cross. An engineer by profession, he was also an architect and an expert at the court of Avignon. He boasted about his competence in the strength of materials, making him a prime candidate for the rehabilitation of a number of buildings confiscated from Jewish owners.

The Statut des Juifs and the CGQJ gave him a new opportunity for social promotion. Like all the candidates for provisional administration, he provided references meant to impress the recruiting commission. Gaugler cites Michel-Béchet, the doctor of the Milice and deputy mayor of Avignon, Caurel, the delegate for the propaganda in the Vaucluse, and Knipping, chief of the Avignon section of the Legion, later chief of the SOL for Vaucluse, then head of Milice in the Bouches du Rhône, before he was called to higher functions in Paris. Knipping was sentenced to death by the Paris court of justice in 1947,[81] in part for the assassination of Georges Mandel, Jewish Interior Minister under Paul Raynaud. Knipping was obsessed by visceral anti-Semitic hatred, to wit his letter to Knochen where he suggested providing the list of Jews from the entire northern zone while the SiPo-SD commander was asking only for the Jews of Paris and surroundings.

With all this support, Gaugler became the provisional administrator for the Vaucluse. He destroyed the businesses belonging to René David, and as a reward, received a generous pay and looted the assets of the victims under the cover of the law*.

As an informer and a denouncer of Jews, Gaugler went even further. In its session of September 23, 1944, the CDL studied his case, with evidence in hand: "*Berger, a stallholder in Avignon, joined the Collaboration group in July. On that same day, he gave Gaugler the names and addresses of his colleagues whose status was illegal vis-à-vis the social laws* [the Statut des Juifs]. *Gaugler decided to hand over the list to de Camaret, because he did not trust the Gestapo who, according to him, sometimes gave away the names of their informers.*"[82]

Gaugler returned the favor to de Camaret who received extensive information about the Jewish stallholders; on that basis 68 names were sent later to Marseille by Jean Lebon.[83] In exchange, Gaugler could count on de Camaret in his function of provisional administrator. Cautiously, Gaugler kept his distance from the rough French agents of the Gestapo. At "Collaboration" in Avignon, members sported good manners; one could find an insurance agent, Jean Grégoire, sentenced after the war to 4 years in prison; or an engineer, Marius Ribière, 15 years of forced labor. These were

---

* This is found in Part Two, Chapter 7

people who enjoyed discussions and philosophical debates about "*the grouping of French energies toward continental unity,*" for instance.

But sometimes it may be necessary to descend from the clouds. During the monthly session of January 22, 1944,

> Gaugler advises the members of Collaboration to join the Milice as Free Guards, if they are young, and as simple miliciens, if they are older or female. Incidentally, he is very pleased with the presence of Darnand and Philippe Henriot in the government. He hopes to see Marcel Déat[*] take an important position soon. During that same meeting, Gaston Mouillade rose up against the fact no one mentioned the action of the PPF, the movement the most feared and the most hated by the Gaullists and the communists; all the more since Doriot[†] is the only party chief in combat on the eastern front. Gaugler[‡] assures him that he respects Doriot, but by acting too often as a free lance party, the PPF stood in the way of a movement of national unity. Clearly, Charles Uhl builds consensus among the parties by wishing to see the government of the 3 Ds: Doriot, Darnand, Déat.[84]

A few lines added in a neat handwriting on the typed record of the court session of May 24, 1945, when Jean Gaugler was sentenced to death in absentia,[85] specified that "*the military tribunal of Marseille acquitted him on January 9, 1952.*" In fact, he appeared voluntarily on November 17, 1951, as he had probably been assured that his risk was minimal. It had been worth waiting for! Less than seven years later, nothing remained of the membership in "Collaboration," the Milice, the PPF; nothing of the accusation of intelligence with the enemy, or of having asked Knipping to impose sanctions against Gaullist magistrates, of his collaboration with the Germans; nothing either of the list of stallholders which made its way to the SiPo-SD by transiting through Jean Lebon. Times had changed and the general amnesty was not far away.

---

[*] Founder of the Rassemblement National Populaire.
[†] Doriot was the head of the PPF.
[‡] Gaugler was considered as a "non militant" member of the PPF.

Müller's Assistants

1.

René Le Flem, an Ambitious Young Man

A Breton from St. Brieuc, living in Orange since 1936, must have found it advantageous to accumulate memberships.[86] Member of the "Collaboration" group in 1941 and 1942, he was also a member of the Legion, and SOL, then chief of hundred in the Milice. He claimed he was not a milicien since September 1943. However, he scrupulously renewed his PPF membership from 1940 to 1944. Of course, there was also his membership in the anti-Bolshevik committee.

This 34 year old lawyer was not born with a silver spoon in his mouth. He came from a modest family and became a lawyer through the shortcut of a two year diploma, which was not the most prestigious road. He took an internship with a lawyer and finished his studies while on the job. His court file is not very eloquent about this penniless hard worker, but his career path demonstrated a strong desire to emerge from his social class. This ambition was confirmed by an RG note of August 30, 1945, which mentioned that "*he was hoping to be appointed sub-prefect of Orange, when Caprio, the PPF secretary for the Vaucluse, would become the prefect, under the reign of Doriot.*"[87] His strategy of social advancement, anchored in political activism and power through allegiance to the winning side, made a lot of sense.

His forced labor 20-year sentence of May 17, 1945, was based on his "*membership in anti-national groups and his collaboration with those organizations by engaging in propaganda and recruiting.*" He was also accused of having "*maintained relationships with the Gestapo with the goal of denouncing French people or providing information to the enemy.*" His presence in the list of the "favorites" appeared in the findings, but it did not lead the court to begin any investigations. Le Flem played the role of someone who did not understand why he was on the list and even claimed that "*this list is a fake.*" Of course, one can understand his desire to elude justice, but shown previously, the documents of the Bouches du Rhône archives confirmed that those on the list probably were recognized informers.[88] Some, including Le Flem, were agents of Ernst Dunker from

Section IV* of the Marseille SiPo-SD. When working for Dunker, Le Flem was rubbing shoulders with members of the Palmieri gang.

The case of Le Flem was troubling for another reason. His sentence was rapidly commuted to a one-year prison term;[89] this caused considerable discontent among members of the Resistance. Was that the result of an attempt to limit the damage with a "favorite" of Müller who boasted that he went to avenue Monclar to intervene in favor of arrested fellow countrymen? Strangely enough, he was not asked for any names. All of this did not fit a leader of this caliber, who attended the funeral of Georges Gras, his professional colleague, a visceral anti-Semite executed by the Resistance on October 1943. This was not the last time that justice takes a back seat.

2.

Jean Poutet, the Industrialist

According to Palmieri, the all powerful Jean Poutet worked directly with Müller.[90] He also had a record at the Marseille SiPo-SD with the code letter Z (Zutrager or informer). Socially he was of larger stature than his colleagues of the PPF, and his relations with the Germans earned him high esteem within the collaboration circles. The German guards would stand at attention when Poutet entered the Kommandantur in l'Isle sur la Sorgue.

An engineer, he was known as the administrator of the "Plâtrières du Vaucluse" (Gypsum manufacturing of the Vaucluse)—founded in 1906 by the merger of the businesses belonging to three families, Poutet, Char and Rieu. Jean Poutet was both a PPF member and a milicien. In October 1940, as president of the Legion in l'Isle sur la Sorgue, he denounced the poet René Char (his colleague on the board of directors of the company) for Gaullist activity. What followed for the writer was being under surveillance and the checking of his mail. But, with the arrival of the Germans, his arrest was about to take place and Char fled to the Basses Alpes where he was in charge of the Landing and Parachuting section of the Resistance.

Poutet was also targeting another share holder of the same company, a friend of Char, François Papelon, a member of the Resistance, who would die for his political choices. His name was listed among the "undesirables"

---

* Initially, Section IV-J was the Jewish Section in Berlin; later, it became IV-B-4. Section IV-B was the Jewish Section of the Marseille KdS.

from l'Isle sur la Sorgue, established by Poutet on April 30, 1943. The list included members of the Resistance, British citizens and Jews. Poutet identified 16 Jews, including Georgette Goldstein, the wife of René Char. Four Jews were deported: Jules and Jeanne Israel, on convoy 75, Hedwige Mayer and Jacques Weiss on convoy 61.

In the case of René Char and Francois Papelon, their ousting from the "Plâtrières" for political reasons was bound to serve Poutet's business interests.

Poutet's collaboration with Mouillade, the close ally of Wilhelm Müller, through the steps leading to the arrest of Jews in l'Isle sur la Sorgue left absolutely no doubt. In the court documents, one cannot find a testimony about the Jews more precise than that of Jean Légier, a local chief of the Resistance, who claimed that Poutet was the instigator of the arrest of "21 patriots." According to a report of the Criminal Investigation Department on June 20, 1945, Poutet *"is congratulated by Idlas for the information destined to the Gestapo about Gaullists, communists and the Resistance."* But how many Jews, whether members of the Resistance or not, were among his victims? In the heat of Liberation, focusing the interest on Resistance patriots was the norm.

Generally, Poutet did not stop halfway. At the beginning of 1944, when he was designated as commissioner of the French Guards[*] by the PPF leadership, he drew a plan to deal with street fighting and snipers on the roofs. But was this 47-year-old man, who loved action on the side of the German forces, suddenly losing his courage? Did he fear for his life when he ran away, in April 1944, from the volcano about to erupt and left for Paris to become a colonel in the Line Guards and Communications for the Paris region? Or was he simply abandoning the management of the "Plâtrières" to "see how things are elsewhere" and "have a whitening treatment," ahead of the allied advance?

In his presentation of the facts, the government commissioner revealed:

… that he held his post in Paris until August 17, 1944. The investigation proves that in Paris Poutet was frequently visited by German officers and miliciens… Around August 20, he arrived in Nancy accompanied by people in uniform. On August 31, 1944, he resigned from his post in the Line Guards.

---

[*] In its process of militarization, the PPF sets up the Gardes Françaises in 1943, both as a response to a growing string of terrorist attacks and as an expression of radicalization.

What follows came as no surprise: after Nancy, he went on to Germany. His file mentions that he became an officer in the Waffen-SS but Poutet claimed during his trial that three lectures for the PPF were his only activities. As for the accusation that he participated in arrests, he denied everything altogether.

His trial took place late, because he surrendered to the American troops in Innsbruck on May 6, 1945. He was first imprisoned at the prison of La Santé on October 15, 1945, and then transferred to Nîmes on November 2, 1945. Sentenced to death on November 6, 1946, he nevertheless eluded the execution squad and his sentence was commuted to forced labor for life.

3.

Vahan Sarkissoff, the "Servant"

It is almost unbelievable that the court of justice did not wonder why Vahan Sarkissoff was on the list of special passes. However according to his file and the resulting "closing without further consequence" that is what happened.[91]

Sarkissoff was an Iranian and a refugee from Alsace-Lorraine. He was *"apparently forced by the Gestapo to become a jack-of-all-trades, to run errands, to open the doors at the villa of avenue Monclar… He was arrested by Gestapo agents due to a libelous denunciation in August 1943 as an Israelite. Even after he proved it wrong, the Germans forced him to work in the Gestapo building."* This servant of Müller was seemingly paid as an unskilled worker and his name was on the city hall list of employees paid by the "Occupation Authorities." According to rumors, he was particularly abused by his employers and some witnesses stated that he was pro-French.

Why would Müller have delivered a special pass as an informer to a servant whom he treated like a dog, and moreover who had not performed any collaborationist service? Could it be that, as a doorman, he knew too much?

Laurent Idlas
and the Activists of the PPF

Louis Bergeron joined the PPF in 1936, as soon as it was set up in the Vaucluse. During the occupation he was in charge of maintaining order, but his role was merely as an agent of Palmieri.

At the time of the Front Populaire, Raymond Verguier, a country doctor from Goult, was its president with Maurice Renier, a brick-layer who had been a communist, as his deputy and typically for the Vaucluse, one of the few working class militants who joined the local PPF. During the war, Renier became a member of the leadership group. He even held a secretary function at the national level. In April 1944, just after the move of the Vaucluse PPF headquarters to "Marisse," the requisitioned "Jewish store" at 7, rue de la République, he expressed the wish that *"the PPF blow up the synagogue, if a terrorist attack is launched against the new headquarters."*[92] Did Renier get his idea from the reprisals against the Marseille Synagogue at rue de Breteuil, a little earlier in January 1944?[93]

It was also in 1936 that René Caprio, owner of the store "Aux Belles Fantaisies," rue des Marchands, joined the PPF.[94] He served as secretary for the Vaucluse from the beginning of 1942 to April 1943. During his interrogation on November 13, 1944, he displayed surprising candor:

> During my time in the party, I was a convinced anti-Semite like all the militants. At every meeting, we used to talk about the Jewish problem and like all the other comrades, I was sure that this race had to be eliminated.

The significance of this declaration is somewhat mitigated when he added that he used to mingle with Jews at the Avignon Sporting Association.

In 1936, the PPF recorded Gaston Barbarant, as a member;[95] he was an engineer and owner of a manufacturing plant of slippers in l'Isle sur la Sorgue, and then in Carpentras. In 1938, Barbarant presided over the party, with Dr. Gaillard from Vaison la Romaine as the secretary. Dr. Gaillard later became an agent of Palmieri.[96]

Jean Poutet was another militant from the early days along with the members from before the war, François Séraphin, an electrical engineer, future delegate for information and member of the Vaucluse board. In a note of April 4, 1945, about him, the chief of the RG from Avignon informed the National Security services *"that he proposed executing Jews in reprisals for executions of collaborationists by the Resistance."*[97] The administrative secretary was none

other than Augusta Vernet, the woman called "the Kraut" in the streets of
Avignon. She too had been a member since 1936, and held the position of
delegate for culture, then of delegate for French workers in Germany. She
was a fanatic who kept a photograph of Wilhelm Müller in her handbag and
loved to write "Power to Doriot, PPF will win" on banknotes. Concerning
the Jews, she proved "moderate," as she proposed to just demand a ransom
from them in response to the *"terrorist offensive,"*[98] namely the action of the
Resistance against the PPF.

The size of the PPF membership before the war was not known with any
precision and its organization remained unclear. Barbarant indicated that the
Vaucluse PPF was divided into two sectors in 1938. He was the chief of the
southern sector which included Avignon, Cavaillon, Apt, Pertuis... while the
northern sector was headed by Dr. Gaillard from Vaison. In 1938, the two
sectors merged and Gaillard took up the responsibility for the entire département. We know that the sole section of l'Isle sur la Sorgue had 15 members.
This probably brought the entire département to somewhat more than 200
members.

Everything collapsed when the war ended in a French defeat. A note
described the situation:

> ... Just after the armistice of 1940, the PPF of the Vaucluse was completely dis-
> organized. Only the section of Cavaillon had some activity. Dr. Gaillard under-
> took as département secretary to restart the PPF. Gaston Mouillade, the sole
> member of the Avignon section, was designated Gaillard's assistant. In January
> 1941 there were already 120 members. A duty office was set up at 21, place
> Crillon.[99]

However, by the end of 1941, Mouillade "displeased" the leadership and
was dismissed from his functions as deputy federal secretary. In the following
years, it cannot be said that the PPF grew in numbers, although it is undeniable that it maintained a high level of activity until August 1944. The list
of members found in the documents seized at the Liberation amounted to
about 100 individuals.[100]

Gaillard lobbied intensely in favor of recruiting for the LVF; he even
volunteered personally in 1941, but remained in Vaison "under the orders of
the party leaders." However, he did not renew his membership, and in 1944,
he became an agent of Palmieri in the same way as Mouillade and Charrasse.

A note attached to the procedural file against Charles Palmieri sheds
some light about the tensions around Gaston Mouillade. Indeed, *"as he was
trying to get closer to the PPF in order to collect information for the Gestapo, two members*

of this party, François Séraphin and Albert Sicard, led a campaign against him, stating that they did not want to rub shoulders with an ex-convict, who is also an agent of the Gestapo…"[101] These tensions continued all through the war, but they did not end up in a clear cut split, at least as far as the hunt for the Jews is concerned.

After the demotion of Mouillade, Charrasse from Orange—the man who applied in July 1943 for the purchase of the la Gardine property in Château-neuf du Pape*—became federal secretary of the PPF with René Caprio, deputy federal secretary, at his side.

At the beginning of 1942 Caprio took the leadership after the resignation of Dr. Gaillard. On December 14, 1944, testimony by René Zarade, a Jewish merchant at Place du Change in Avignon, accused Caprio of having personally directed actions of vandalism against Jews in September 1942—daubing their store fronts and smashing their shop windows. Denunciations to the German police and arrests would soon follow.

The period of Caprio's leadership was unstable probably because of strong rivalries. The Vaucluse seemed to be awaiting a chief but Caprio complained of the arrival of *"questionable individuals, recruited by Mouillade, notably pimps."*[102] When he decided to give up the reins of power in October 1942, agents of Sabiani came from Marseille and threatened him. He was forced to go back on his resignation. The Vaucluse PPF seemed to become more and more lined up along the national model and in particular that of Marseille—where Sabiani had been trying for more than a decade to find himself a spot on the political spectrum while relying heavily on the violence of the underworld. The ideology did not matter as much as power, money and influence.[103] In that sense, Sabiani looked more like a godfather than an ordinary party boss.

In March 1943 Caprio finally succeeded in making way for someone new. Laurent Idlas, a businessman in sanitary equipment in Avignon, one of Müller's "favorites," became the leader of the PPF federation of the Vaucluse.[104] A renegade of the local "Collaboration" group, where he was the federal secretary, he put all his energy into his new job. Idlas headed the PPF during most of the German occupation period.

Very soon, in May 1943, he organized the département conference in the presence of Sabiani at the Hôtel des Sources in Avignon. The conference was held in private because the French authorities had forbidden all public meetings. Idlas put a federal board in place, and until the end, he held regular leadership meetings. During that time, the RG did not stop reporting on this activity for the benefit of the prefecture and of Vichy. During the summer of

---

* Part One, Chapter 5.

1942, they noticed that a slogan was circulating in Avignon: "*Down with Laval, and Doriot, come back from the eastern front to seize power!*" This was probably due to the influence of the collaborationist press, which accused Vichy, and in particular Laval, of helping the Jews. This was indeed the period of fruitless continuing "negotiations" between Vichy and the Germans for further denaturalization of Jews where the national context played a key role.

Vichy and PPF Tension in Avignon

Jacques Doriot, the national leader of the PPF, pushed more and more toward total collaboration with Germany. After a falling out with Laval, probably for propaganda purposes, he volunteered for the Russian front at the head of the first contingent of the LVF in September 1941; this was not to Vichy's liking. Henri du Moulin de Labarthète[105], Pétain's personal secretary, described the repugnance of the Maréchal during a Vichy visit of Doriot who had just returned from the front.

> He stopped in Vichy, in December 1941. The Maréchal, who could not forget that the chief of the PPF, the former lieutenant of Abd-El-Krim,* had worn the German uniform, refused purely and simply to meet him. But Admiral Darlan put up with it, and asked me to keep him company…

The relations between Doriot and Pétain's immediate entourage were truly tense. The gripes of Vichy against Doriot did not stop at his wearing the German uniform. They suspected that he wanted to create the political conditions conducive to a putsch against the government, while seeking German support.

Doriot's quarrel with Laval and the Maréchal's refusal to meet him certainly coincided with the radicalization of the PPF and its leader. This had evidently also reinforced Vichy's hostility toward an element which was going too far for its taste. Vichy firmly intended to steer a delicate course between both extremes, on one side Doriot and the ultra-collaborationists, and on the other, the ultranationalists—including those in the government—who accepted no concessions to the Germans.

The schism between Vichy and the ultra-collaborationists suited the Germans nicely, as they played brilliantly on this division. By using the ultra-

---

* During his communist period, Doriot and the Communist Party had taken sides with Abd-el-Krim, the rebel of the Riff war, against the French government. Doriot had not literally been the "lieutenant" of Abd-el-Krim, but as Labarthète shows it well, this past "treason" stuck to the founder of the PPF even after he veered toward fascism.

collaborationists when it was in their interest, without actually favoring one or the other, the Germans were obtaining from Vichy increasingly important concessions, with a truly French seal. If the Germans had imposed their will directly on the country while going around the government, they would have run the risk of accelerating the drift of the population toward the Resistance. Paradoxically, maintaining the division between the various collaborationist ideologies was one of the few points of full agreement between Vichy and the occupation authorities.

The PPF clearly aroused the interest of both the RG and the Resistance.[106] Their informers provided information from the end of 1943, long after the break between Doriot and Vichy. At that time, the PPF was already radicalized and war was declared between the party and the government. From then on, the party leadership was going to gravitate increasingly toward the occupying power. On February 4, 1944, two contributors to the *Cri du Peuple* were the guests of the PPF of the Vaucluse.

> Ralph Soupault,* a cartoonist for the collaborationist newspapers, and Camille Bryère, an editor for *Le Cri du Peuple*, were conducting a survey for Le Cri du Peuple among the militants; they interviewed various officials about their activities.
>
> Once the survey was finished, Ralph Soupault spoke, and let it be known that, in Paris, the PPF was looked at with less hostility. The bourgeois did not hide that they wanted the defeat of the occupier, but they are afraid of Bolshevism. So they start turning toward Doriot with sympathy…

The next day, Soupault attended the meeting of the Avignon section of the PPF where feelings against Laval exploded. The head of the Cabinet became a lightning rod for the antigovernment sentiments of the PPF.

> Ralph Soupault declares "the true revolutionaries cannot trust Laval, since he is of the Jewish race, because his mother is a moghrabite [*sic*]. Moreover, on photographs, he looks more like Abd-el-Kader than Vercingétorix. Thanks to the events, his fortune now reaches two billions…"
>
> Maurice Riety says that Laval is indeed of the Jewish race, because Dr. Montandon, the specialist in ethnology, has concluded as much. He adds that he is a saboteur anyway, because he has forbidden the delivery of "Je suis partout"† for the subscribers of the southern zone.

---

* Ralph Soupault, a cartoonist turned nationalist and fervent member of the PPF, put his talent at the service of *Je Suis Partout* and *Le Pilori*, and published violently anti-Semitic drawings.

† *Je Suis Partout* started in 1930 as a neutral newspaper for international news and progressively veered toward fascism and anti-Semitism. Authorized to continue appearing during the war, its tone became

Here, Riety was alluding to Dr. Georges Alexis Montandon, a communist sympathizer who veered to the right and developed "anti-Jewish ethno-racism," the French version of Nazi racism. In 1940, Doriot appointed Montandon president of the ethnic commission of the PPF. In March 1943 he became director of the Institute of Jewish and Ethno-racial Questions, attached to the CGQJ. It was Montandon's role to rule on individual questions of "non-belonging to the Jewish race" in conjunction with the application of the Statut des Juifs.

The diatribe against Laval showed not only the hostility of PPF members toward him, but also a fantastical style which is the trademark of most fanatics. But this was only a starting point for an even more significant drift. The hunt for the Jews by the PPF mobsters was governed by a dynamic that was practically independent of Vichy.

The Radicalization of the Vaucluse PPF

During May 1943, one of the first targeted arrests of Jews took place in Carpentras. Barbarant, a member of the PPF federal board and a direct link to Müller, provided an account of this event. The presentation of the facts by the government commissioner can be found in Barbarant's court file:

> In May 1943, Bonadona (chief of the French Guards in Carpentras) was required to leave for Germany. To avoid leaving, Barbarant sent him to meet Müller at the Gestapo. Müller accepted to intervene, but asked in exchange for the list of Carpentras Jews. Bonadona, Laget (chief of the Carpentras PPF section) and Barbarant put the list together and the first two men took it to Müller. As to Barbarant, he put five people on the list. Three of them are still in Germany…

The three Jews mentioned in the commissioner's report were Adrien, Gaston and Marcelle Naquet, deported to Auschwitz on convoys 59, 58 and 59, respectively. But, Barbarant himself provided a second version of this event, which appears as plausible as the first. In his interrogation of January 11, 1945, he stated:

> Concerning the Jews, it is not the Gestapo which asked us for the list but the PPF. Idlas asked Laget for the list. Laget came with Bonadona to talk about the list and I gave a few names of Jews I knew, but they knew better than me… After the list was established (I think that Mouillade did this), I do not know

---

collaborationist. Its final drift took place in September 1943 with its new editor, Pierre Antoine Cousteau, who aligned the newspaper with Nazism; hence the opposition of Pierre Laval.

who used it. Practically speaking, the consequences were not that terrible since only Jews were arrested and freemasons and communists were not bothered by the Germans…[107]

No need to comment on "the consequences that were not that terrible," but let us look at the initiator of this list, which apparently was not limited to Jews. It is impossible to incriminate Idlas with any certainty, but the head of the PPF did not remain on the sidelines of the hunt for the Jews. Palmieri implicated him in his deposition of March 13, 1945: *"I have known Idlas while I was a member of the PPF. Later, I saw him two or three times and I know that I was giving information to Josselme."* Pierre Josselme was a grassroots PPF and also an agent of Palmieri, and as such, one of the most effective Jew hunters. But more importantly, the piecing together of various testimonies unveiled a scheme whereby Idlas, the political chief, became the informer of Josselme, the simple member but mostly an individual without scruples; anyway, a proven scheme to erase any fingerprints.

In June 1943, during a meeting of the federal board, Idlas admitted publicly having made contact with Müller, and the RG note provided the details:

> From this moment on, he held weekly talks with Müller and his agents. Jacques Tricon, deputy federal secretary, also attended. As the Doriotists of the département were often bringing information to Idlas about political enemies, the federal secretary hastened to bring them to Müller.[108]

While it is likely that information about the Resistance was one focus of these meetings, it is more than likely that the hunt for the Jews was another very good reason. Moreover, in the mind of the protagonists, the Jews held a prominent place among the "political enemies."

On August 8, 1943, PPFs from all over France gathered for a march in Paris. Idlas had succeeded in sending about sixty militants from the Vaucluse. Later, some of them remembered this parade as the high point of their demonstration of strength and bitterly regretted that the party had not attempted to seize power then. On his return, Idlas raised his level of energy, and wanted weapons for his most combative men. The RG bulletin for the week of September 12–18, 1943, indicated:

> Idlas announces his intention to create a shock team of 15 militants. These will be chosen among the members of the federal board, the men of the police contingent, and several militants whom Idlas trusts. The list, established by Jacques Tricon, chief of the PPF police, will be communicated to the German authorities to eventually obtain the authorization to bear arms and to travel under any

circumstance. In the event of a landing on the coasts of France, these 15 militants would be grouped and serve as back up police to help with maintaining order in the streets. Idlas added that the most dedicated Doriotists in the département would be asked to play the same role.[109]

Idlas obtained the weapon permits from Müller for 15 members of the PPF, but this agreement was suspended in January 1944. It is likely that the Germans backed out because of the discontent of the French authorities, who rightly suspected the Doriotists of planning to take power by force under the pretext of civil disorder. In the face of this set back, Idlas reassured his troops:

> The Doriotists can continue carrying their revolvers but at their own risk. Nevertheless, in case something happens, an intervention will take place anyway to prevent legal repercussions.

Idlas must have received assurances from Müller. But it is impossible to clearly know whether Idlas wanted to arm his elite forces out of fear of the Resistance, to join the German army in case of allied landings, or to help in a coup by Doriot; maybe all three reasons together.

The end of the summer of 1943 marked a peak in the self-confidence of the Vaucluse PPF. As time went by doubts began seeping in. Indeed, it was not easy to maintain the goal of leading a national revolution intended to establish a totalitarian regime. Idlas tirelessly continued to encourage his troops to not be influenced by the news about the change in the fortunes of war. The belief in a German victory was as imperative as the conviction that Doriot would finally be anointed by the Germans; this would put an end to the Laval government, that held far weaker beliefs and was seen as a traitor in the Doriotist mindset.

At the end of 1943, "*Idlas asks the militants to fill information sheets about the Resistance, Gaullists and communists, the police and the gendarmerie. These sheets, prepared for the upper echelon of the Gestapo by the intelligence services of the party, were taken to Lyon by Albert Sicard, delegate for the press and propaganda.*" In reality, the PPF of the Vaucluse encountered significant difficulties in preparing this information about the "anti-France," because of the insufficient presence of the party at the grassroots.

The PPF fell short of its political goals of building an intelligence network, readying for the ultimate fight against the partisans, to provide maximum help to Germany, through the STO on the German home front and through the LVF on the war front. It was not for lack of trying. But, the resistance was growing and the PPF militants realized that their lives were threatened. As for Germany, the likelihood of an allied landing, increasingly eagerly expected by the French population, made any chances of victory unrealistic.

And yet, in the middle of this storm where all predictions jostle each other, obsessions still remained. The RG recorded that during a meeting of the federal board on February 5, 1944, the département PPF inspector Salobert...

> ... recommends to return to virulent politics toward the Jews and the freemasons, who have been left alone for several months, because the party was focused on terrorist acts. Salobert then informs the people in attendance that the PPF proposes to allocate all the Jewish assets to the victims of bombings.[110]

The meeting of the federal board of March 1, 1944, showed a PPF full of verbal energy and going nowhere.

> ... Edmond Baptiste would want to see the PPF raid the Villeneuve city hall to seize a bust of the Marianne painted in blue, white and red. Idlas promises to organize the expedition. Augusta Vernet volunteers to participate in this raid...

Even if the organization was not ready to fight on the eastern front, the boss was confident he could assemble enough courage to attack the tricolor Marianne of Villeneuve across the river Rhône.

Barely three weeks had passed since the great roundups of Avignon, and at the meeting April 23, 1944, of the Avignon section, Mouillade asked *"the PPF to make use of its authority to force the government to take severe action against the Jews and the freemasons"*; to which Idlas responds that...

> ... the PPF has no influence on Vichy. To see anything new, one must wait for the advent of the State of Doriot which is anti-Jewish and anti-Masonic in its essence.[111]

It seems thus that the complete disengagement of the prefecture pushed the PPF more and more toward one alternative: either wait-and-see or collaboration with the Germans. One should not be fooled though by the saber rattling of Idlas against the Villeneuve Marianne. He was not only a man with whom Müller was dealing personally, but he was also a partner of the Kommandantur, in the Hôtel Brancas, 35, rue Joseph Vernet, the Feldgendarmerie, in the Hôtel St. Yves at the corner of the Place Pie and rue Thiers, and the OPA, in the "Jewish store" Parisette, 8, rue de la République, a stone's throw away from his own offices, in another "Jewish store" Marisse.

This man, ready to take things to the bitter end, still presided over a public meeting in the salons of city hall.

Idlas had a file at the SiPo-SD of Marseille as an informer, and evidently, his information was valuable enough to earn him a spot in Müller's list of special passes.

It is not clear whether it is his admiration or servility toward the German masters, or his personal taste for culture that induced Idlas to actively sponsor the Franco-German Institute which organized two lectures: one about music and the other about poetry—both German of course.[112]

During the night of August 23, 1944, Idlas left Avignon, and after him, the fleeing Doriotists embarked in a bus. The information note of December 12, 1944, specified *"He was never seen again."* There was good reason for it: he died during his escape, probably in a blind machine-gunning during an air raid. As late as October 4, 1946, the city hall of Macon issued a death certificate. His wife indicated that he died in that town on August 23, 1944. In the meantime, the court of justice had sentenced him to death in absentia on June 21, 1945.

As to Tricon, a note from the Avignon Central Police, under the heading "information," described him as follows on January 29, 1945: *"Member of the PPF, former SOL. The mind of a killer. Deputy Secretary and chief of the policing service. Intelligence agent for the Gestapo."* He was sentenced to death in absentia on June 19, 1945, but was acquitted on October 23, 1951, after surrendering voluntarily.[113]

Chapter 9

The Palmieri Gang:
Serving the SiPo-SD

Fearing Neither God Nor Man

The best known crime shall serve as an appropriate introduction. Estréa
Asseo, an Auschwitz survivor, told Superintendent Victor Roton:

> On June 6, 1944, I had just come out of Mr. Seguin's store in rue des
> Fourbisseurs, when I noticed a Gestapo car that I knew well. I also noticed that
> some of its occupants had entered a shoe store.
>
> I did hesitate for a few seconds, because, as an Israelite, I was afraid to be at
> the Gestapo's mercy. After a few steps, Lucien Blanc whom I knew very well
> caught up with me. Blanc, my husband and I, had worked together at the
> "Bouchara" store.
>
> At the time, I did not know that this man was working for the Gestapo and
> I greeted him. Lucien Blanc nodded to one of his acolytes and I immediately
> understood that I would not be able any more to escape.
>
> Nevertheless, without losing my head, I walked swiftly toward rue
> Bonneterie, as I felt the presence of an agent of the Gestapo behind me. A few
> seconds later, this individual stopped me and I showed him my documents. He
> brought me back to the car still parked in front of the shoe store, and there I
> started a discussion with Lucien Blanc and a man named Merle. I was unable to
> convince them, all the more so since Blanc perfectly knew my situation as an
> Israelite.

They grabbed hold of me and pushed me into the car. On the way, I begged Blanc to let me go in exchange for a certain amount of money, namely all of my savings, because I was not rich. He answered that the money I could give him would not be sufficient. He also asked me where my husband and children were, I am sure, so that he could arrest them.

We arrived at my home, and Blanc and his acolyte whom I did not know searched my apartment in the hope of discovering money or jewelry. Blanc himself prepared a small suitcase with clothes for me and we came back downstairs to the car where Merle was waiting for us.[1]

It was Palmieri, *aka* Merle, the gang leader form Marseille who supervised Estréa Asseo's arrest. One of his henchmen, Lucien Blanc from Avignon, did the dirty work. In June 1944, the process put in place by Palmieri to hunt the Jews was still running smoothly.

In any case Estréa Asseo was not the only Jewish person arrested around June 6. During a short period, Palmieri and his Vaucluse team conducted multiple raids in the département. The result was 68 Jews packed in a cattle car that left the Avignon train station for Drancy on June 13. Only one person, Raymond Brahinski, succeeded in escaping through a small skylight in the boxcar, before reaching Drancy. Most of them, including Estréa, were among more than 1,000 Jews sent to Auschwitz on convoy 76 on June 30, 1944. Estréa belonged to a small group of survivors.

The Marseille Connection

The link between the Marseille gangsters and the hunt for the Jews in Avignon has already been established in a previous work.[2] In his deposition of March 13, 1945, Palmieri offered details:

> I had both my office and my home at 8, rue Paradis [in Marseille]. I had in my possession a protection letter signed by the authorities of the German police accrediting me to the French authorities and giving me the right to bear arms. I was under the orders of a lieutenant named Kompe whose office was located at 425, rue Paradis. My mission consisted of looking for Jews and gathering intelligence about the Resistance.[3]

After providing the names of his agents and recalling his first operation in Avignon, he provided specifics about his second operation:

> … again with my team from Marseille and that of Avignon, I carried out the arrest of about 10 Jews who were on a list prepared by Mouillade and Blanc.

And he added:

> The other operations have been conducted similarly on the basis of information provided by my agents at Avignon. I do not remember exactly the number of arrests carried out. I must tell you that I also came pretty often to Avignon to pick up Jews arrested by the Germans.

The operations mentioned by Palmieri spanned the period from mid-March to July 1944, although his presence had been documented much earlier. Palmieri continued:

> My salary was 10,000 francs per month, paid by the Germans. As to my agents, Bergeron, Blanc, Mouillade, and Josselme, they were making 5,000 francs per month. I know that these agents were carrying out looting operations for their own benefit. Besides Blanc has been arrested by the French police because one of these affairs and he left for Germany where he may still be.

The Boss's Guide in Avignon

The reasons for Lucien Blanc's departure for Germany are unclear. The explanation given by his wife who talked about mobilization for the STO and a departure for Austria on July 6, 1944, does not hold. The Germans would have exempted him. Lucien Blanc preferred to blame a bad business decision as the cause of his drift and misfortune. Indeed, in the spring of 1943, he bought a lignite mine in Mondragon, in partnership with a man named Salvador. Blanc's share of the investment amounted to 225,000 francs—no small change for an ordinary salesman at Bouchara. When asked about his profession, Blanc described himself an engineer. We know through the testimony of Mr. Nicollet, a former employee, that the company, called Les Lignites de Provence, *"has always operated in the red and that it has not been possible to continue production due to a lack of capital."*

When interrogated on October 2, 1945, Blanc stated that *"since he did not have the permit to operate his mine, he has engaged in some illegal trade and got involved in a deal involving tires."* This is how he got connected to Palmieri who arrested him for this violation and made him an offer: *"I know that you have national views and that you are anti-Semitic... If you agree to work with us, this matter will have no consequences."* Blanc went into the terms of the agreement: *"It was agreed that I would have to accompany him during the operations he conducted against the Jews. I was supposed to guide him through the streets of Avignon, because Palmieri did not know the city."* And he added *"I have indeed acknowledged to the gendarmerie that the anti-*

Semitic struggle corresponded to my political ideals, but I deny having provided any in-formation concerning the Jews, because Palmieri already had in his possession the list of Jews which had been given to him by the prefecture."

In short, Blanc described himself as an "ordinary" militant of anti-Semitism who never went so far as to denounce Jews and establish lists. This was pretty clever since Palmieri had actually obtained a list originating at the prefecture among others, but of course, this was a half truth.

Robert Pierre, café owner, 19, place du Portail Matheron in Avignon, declared on October 22, 1945:

> On the night of the arrest of Mr. Elie Cohen and Mme. Eugénie Cohen, I was at home. I have positively recognized Lucien Blanc among the members of the Gestapo who came and conducted these arrests. When I saw that these individuals were arresting Mr. Cohen, I made them aware that this man's son was a prisoner of war and that he deserved some consideration... I have to say that these individuals knocked on my door, and when he saw me, Blanc declared "We are not interested in this one; he is not a Jew."

Elie and Eugénie Cohen were arrested on March 29, 1944, and deported on convoy 71. Apparently, Lucien Blanc was not content with proclaiming his anti-Semitic "ideal"; he also took action.

In his final interrogation on December 1, 1944, Robert Conrad, interpre-ter and agent of the SiPo-SD, remembered that night when he followed Merle, who had come to Avignon to pick up Jews. His interrogator summarized the facts:

> You were with Blanc and Bergeron, former miliciens, and four agents of the Gestapo of Marseille. You went to Mr. Valabrègue, rue Bancasse, at the "Coq Hardi" and to other Jews whom you arrested and took to the Hautpoul barracks. Several Jews succeeded in escaping and you arrested only five or six of them. On that evening, you heard Merle criticizing Blanc for having established inaccurate lists...

This action probably took place on May 16, 1944. This was the date of the second blackmail of Marie Riz in her restaurant "le Coq Hardi." Contrary to the testimony of Robert Conrad, Marie Riz did not escape: she was released in exchange for money.

Who was Lucien Blanc, a 28 year old man, who claimed to be an engineer? In his investigation report, police Superintendent Roton indicated that Marc Asseo, the husband of Estréa, had worked with Blanc at Bouchara's in Avignon and that after he was demobilized in 1940, Blanc was broke. Asseo had provided him with some help. Later, he knew him as a member of the Legion and the SOL, and an "active milicien*" and Blanc confided that he was making a lot of money from the traffic in gold and foreign currency. This was probably how he got the money for his share of the lignite mine in Mondragon.

The documents show nothing before his salesman job at Bouchara's, and after that, the trafficking episode which pushed him into Palmieri's arms. He was not an angel caught up in the system.

Before his accusers, Lucien Blanc seemed confident that his statement *"the anti-Semitic struggle corresponded to my political ideal"* would not be very damaging. But what was the nature of this "ideal"? His wife said that he had been an activist at *l'Action Française* since he was 17. Practically speaking, he did not have the profile of active member. After the defeat, like so many others, he joined the Legion and the SOL, but he was seen only once in uniform. There was no trace of his participation in the Milice either as a regular member or as an officer. Anyway, his advancement in the criminal ranks did not require it.

A more likely profile would be that of a young man barely making ends meet as a low level employee at Bouchara's, this humming fabric business managed by Jews, where he did not see any prospects. The Statut des Juifs may have presented him both as revenge and the promise of a good life.

Also his hatred of Jews should not be overlooked, and the help he got from Marc Asseo apparently did not change his mindset, since he did not spare Estréa Asseo, but it cannot be separated from his greed. Of course, the payments Palmieri made to his agents for catching Jews were too good to miss. The deposition of Rodolphe Bride, a medical student and agent of Palmieri in Marseille, provides an insight about Blanc:

> Lucien Blanc had a card in the Merle file. He owned a weapon, a small pistol 6.35 caliber which he carried on his belt... Blanc was put in charge by Merle of gathering information about the Jews in the Avignon region. I saw Blanc give Merle such lists. Merle was paying Blanc his travel expenses, as he was saying. I even noticed that Blanc was evaluating them every time at 500 francs per day; Palmieri commented that he was overdoing it.
> Blanc made something extra on the side on every occasion.

In his deposition of February 8, 1945, Bride peppered the facts with personal opinions:

---

* It must be noted again that "milicien" is here taken in the broad sense of a "Nazi collaborator" and not strictly speaking a member of the Milice.

Blanc claimed to be the director of the lignite mines of Mondragon. He asked me once to type a whole file concerning the operation of those mines, specifying that he wanted to ask the government for permission to put them in service. He claimed to be an engineer. Unlike the other members of the Merle enterprise, I feel that Blanc and Mouillade acted out of a sense of political and racial conviction.

And in his report of March 1, 1945, he wrote:

Blanc has a file as an intelligence agent. He lives in Avignon, and brings information to Charles Palmieri on a weekly basis… He appears to be sharply anti-Jewish. Owns a few revolvers and gave two of them as a present to Charles. However, he does not reappear in June and Palmieri states at that time that he "messed around" in Avignon and that the Germans have sent him to Germany. He is a great friend of Mouillade and Bergeron.

Concerning this "messing around," Palmieri clarified the issue during his interrogation of March 16, 1945, when he introduced his Avignon team:

Pierre Josselme, domiciled in Montfavet (Vaucluse)
Louis Bergeron, *aka* "Toto," 23, rue Bonneterie
Lucien Blanc, rue Banasterie, deported to Germany because of a fake police raid
Louis Mouillade* route Nationale in Montfavet

Thanks to his "strategic" position, Etienne Petrucci, the boss of the "Café Glacier" on the Place de l'Horloge, was better equipped to help define the personality of Lucien Blanc. Superintendent Victor Roton recorded the deposition of Petrucci on May 1, 1945:

Lucien Blanc was a customer at the café belonging to Petrucci, who was aware that Blanc was an agent of the Gestapo. Blanc did not hide this fact and he even proclaimed that he went to Paris and asked for the creation of an Avignon office which he would manage. Petrucci adds that he had amassed a good amount of money (about one million francs) by selling vehicles hidden by the French military at the moment of the armistice in June 1940 to the Germans. He summarizes his view of Blanc as an unscrupulous individual capable of anything to make money.

Although the Germans were usually tolerant of this kind of "business deal," at some point, they did not wish to excuse Blanc for his greed any-

---

* The real first names of Mouillade are Gaston Frédéric.

more. Was this because of the sloppiness of his work for the SiPo-SD, like the "inaccuracies" in the search for the addresses of Jews, made him less valuable?

The Avignon Team

With his circle of associates, Blanc was in good hands.

Mouillade, a 45-year-old native of Carpentras, a long-time city council-man, had a lot of acquaintances, many of them Jewish.[4] He personally par-ticipated in the arrest of Henri Dreyfus, the former mayor of Carpentras, who was sent to Drancy, and his presence during the arrest of other Jews of the town, where he was born, was mentioned in the file of Gaston Barbarant, the chief of the Carpentras PPF.[5] It must be said that all the preparation work, done as we have seen by his fellow Barbarant who provided the list of vic-tims, made things much easier for Mouillade. Barbarant, the leader in estab-lishing lists, received the death sentence, soon reduced to forced labor for life.

The testimony of Henri Dreyfus, on October 4, 1944, provided a window into Mouillade's soul.

On April 12, 1943, at about 10:00 a.m., at the moment I was leaving "l'Hermitage," my property in Pernes where I was usually residing, I saw a German car stopped in front of my entrance. Two officers came out while a civilian remained inside.

After inquiring whether indeed I was Mr. Dreyfus, the two officers asked to speak with me, under the pretext of getting some information. They followed me into my living room, and there, without any other explanation, they stated that they were arresting me and taking me to Avignon. My wife, Mme. Dreyfus, and my brother, Mr. René Dreyfus, who were also present, were arrested and taken to Avignon at the same time as I was. When I came out to take a seat in the car that had brought the officers, I met the civilian who had come out. He was wearing a fedora hat lowered on his eyes, as well as dark sun glasses; his face was in the shadows, but I recognized nevertheless that he was Mouillade. I shouted at him "You, Mouillade, are doing such dirty work!" He answered "I was not speaking to you." I got into the car with the two officers, my wife and my brother, while Mouillade remained to guard the place.

On my return [at Liberation], my employees appraised me of the conduct of Mouillade after my departure. This is how I learned that this individual had ordered lunch to be served to him, had forbidden the servants to leave the rooms he was in, and asked the farmer to tell him the location of the weapons I own…

I wish to add that during the conversation that Mouillade had with my personnel, he stated that his nationality was German. Following this arrest undoubtedly caused by this individual who knew me well, my wife was detained in Avignon for two weeks, my brother was deported to Germany, and I was interned for 8 months in a concentration camp.

Mouillade was incapable of appearing without a disguise before the former mayor with whom he has had political connections before the war. But this momentary uneasiness did not spoil his appetite, once Henri Dreyfus had been arrested. Very early—a few weeks after the beginning of the occupation, Mouillade volunteered with the Germans in the hunt for the Jews.

Mouillade confirmed in a report to Palmieri that he was about to receive the list of Jews of Lisle sur la Sorgue from Poutet whom he held in high esteem. Seven of them were deported; Edwige Mayer and Jacques Weiss, on convoy 61, Ernestine and Maurice Herzog, on convoy 74, and Jeanne and Jules Israel and Maurice Spitz, on convoy 75. In addition to the Dreyfus brothers, Mouillade took personal responsibility for the arrest of Adrien Naquet, arrested on May 15, 1943, in Carpentras and deported on convoy 59. On the same day, three other members of the Naquet family were arrested in Carpentras and deported, Gaston, to Auschwitz on convoy 58, Marcelle, to Auschwitz as well on convoy 59, and René to Aurigny on convoy 641.

For 1944, Mouillade acknowledged only the arrest in May of Leonore Stern and her daughter Maidy in Le Thor; they were deported to Dresden.

In the spring 1944, he went into a frenzy. The ministry of internal affairs reported that *"during that period, he was gleaning everywhere information to locate Jews. After taking a seat in a car of the Gestapo, he shows the Germans two stallholders who were arrested shortly thereafter."* After Liberation, a member of the CDL, Lucien Grangeon, accused Mouillade of being at the origin of the arrest of the Hanania family from Vaison la Romaine, David, Myriam, Rachel and Vitalis, all deported on convoy 76.

Although Mouillade had been active very early on the Vaucluse scene, he was seen by the investigating judge as Palmieri's lieutenant. His methods were well tuned. He practiced extortion, for instance when he proposed to Georgette Bloch, the manager of a newspaper kiosk in Avignon, to get her husband back if she provided him with lists of Jews, communists, and STO dodgers; Moische Bloch was deported on convoy 70. Mouillade also stole for his own benefit. To justify his dispossession of Jews, he decreed openly: *"In this revolutionary period, the law gets done instead of being written."*

Before his judges, he did not hesitate to adopt an indignant style. As an elected representative of the people, he chose not to run away from the Germans. *"His duty was to stay in Carpentras."* In his deposition of September 25, 1944, he went one step further:

> I never accepted a salary from the Gestapo, because that would have turned me into their slave, but I admit having received 3,300 francs per month as an interpreter for the Luftwaffe. I wish to specify that, if I have had relations with Müller, Gauthier and Hans Bach* at the beginning, it was on a political and racial level. Twice a month they needed to establish a report about the fluctuation of French public opinion. They used to ask me according to current affairs: Was denkt das Volk—what do the people think? This was a kind of Gallup institute.

In short, he was only a specialist in "opinion polls" who brought information about Jews every time he went to the Merle office in Marseille, introduced himself with the Hitler salute and called Palmieri "the boss." It is enlightening to observe that Mouillade did not hesitate to acknowledge his own "racial" attitude, because, in his own mind, denouncing Jews was less serious than denouncing members of the Resistance. It was a trifle on the scale of crime. An individual card, probably prepared by a member of the Resistance during fall 1943, described him:

MOUILLADE – Ecole de Cantarel - Avignon

> Former communist, then Trotskyite. In 1940, he joined the PPF on the advice of Riety who served as his mentor on matters of racism. After having been designated as a party chief, he was dismissed at the end of 1941. In the spring 1942, he volunteered for the anti-Bolshevik Legion, but he was rejected in Versailles because of his age. Signed a contract to work in Germany and returned for a few days in Avignon, saying he was leaving for Ludwigshafen. Resurfaced only in September 1942…
>
> Mouillade claimed he belonged to the "Front Franc" of Boissel† and to the "Institut d'Etudes Juives."‡ Holder of a permanent [German] pass, he was rolling in 1,000 franc banknotes. When the free zone was occupied, he came back to the area. His villainous activity was interrupted during summer 1943 by an illness requiring him to check in to the Sanatorium of Lauris. Unfortunately, he was about to resume his activity.
>
> Mouillade, an ex-convict, is an embittered man, who wants to take revenge on society. We know the despicable ways he uses to harm honest people.
>
> Agent of the Gestapo. Very dangerous.[6]

---

* Hans Bach was a subordinate of Wilhelm Müller.
† Jean Boissel was the founder of the "Front Franc," a small far right anti-Semitic group.
‡ Institute for Jewish Studies.

In the same file, an additional information note gave added precision:

> On Thursday, February 10, 1944, at about 11:30 a.m., Gaston Mouillade came to the Tourist office to inquire about the prefect of the Vaucluse, whom he suspects of supporting the terrorists... On this occasion, Mouillade gave a real speech against Mr. Mayer, the director of the Roquefraiche sanatorium, near Lauris; he accused him of being a camouflaged Jew who is spending his time stealing food rations from his patients and hiding Jews and Red Spaniards in his institution.
>
> He expressed his great pleasure about the arrest by the secret police of two Jews hidden in this institution (these two arrests are surely attributable to him).
>
> ... Augusta Vernet: served as a liaison officer between Mouillade, when he was in the Sanatorium of Lauris, and the offices of the Avignon Gestapo.
>
> She is a fanatic and very dangerous.

Mouillade, who proclaimed his great admiration for Josselme (he identified himself as his secretary), was not choosing a paragon of virtue as his role model. According to Palmieri, Josselme was the coordinator of all the information about the Avignon region. However, there is no Josselme file, but first-hand information in the file of his wife, Rose Chauveau, who was suspected by the judiciary police officer at the Vaucluse court of justice of *"enjoying the use of assets which are the result of her husband's treason."*[7] How many of these ill-gotten gains have melted with impunity into the French fabric?

Josselme managed to make his commercial relations with the Germans work to his advantage, to the point of acquiring a magnificent property in Montfavet, where he received among others, the heads of the German police, Müller and Gauthier. A note by the Resistance described his dealings.

> ... PPF, former SOL, milicien. Last year, he was involved in illegal carrying of firearms and resisting arrest. Was not prosecuted thanks to the Milice.
>
> Became very rich by selling trucks to the Germans. Recently, lists of arrested people were in his possession.
>
> Very dangerous.[8]

Josselme was under surveillance by the Resistance that was planning to kill him. At the meeting of the PPF federal board on January 26, 1944, Renier shared a worry with the members in attendance:

> Pierre Josselme got a warning from the terrorists, as a result of the publication of his obituary in the "Petit Marseillais." Besides, a lady's mourning hat had been sent to his wife a while earlier. It would be a shame if he was gunned down,

because he lets the PPF largely take advantage of the millions he has made recently.[9]

These threats by the Resistance were no longer necessary. A few weeks later, on February 28, 1944, Josselme was gunned down by the French police during a bar scuffle between him and Bergeron, when a policeman was wounded. At the following PPF board meeting, on March 1, 1944, Idlas *"states that Josselme fell with a bullet in his gut and that the police who were furious about the wounding of their colleague, finished him with several bullets at close range in the head…"*[10] This explained of course the absence of any legal action against Josselme. As to Bergeron, he was severely wounded during the settling of scores with his colleague.

On June 6, 1944, Bergeron participated in the arrests of Jews in Le Pontet, in company of Blanc, his childhood friend, Palmieri, and Billarz, a subordinate of Aloïs Brunner. As a result, there were seven deportees in convoy 76 from Drancy to Auschwitz: Moïse Benyacar, his wife Lisette, and their baby, Sylvain; Sarah Levendel; Esther Kramer and her son Georges; Anna Bitran. On July 29, 1945, Palmieri was confronted with Moïse Benyacar, the sole survivor, and admitted having made these arrests.[11]

Since the scuffle with Josselme, Bergeron was given a weapon before leaving for a raid. He did not own one anymore, because his own Luger had been seized by the police in Avignon. But, since Bride liked to be precise, he added some more information in his testimony of February 8, 1945:

> I wish however to specify that his index card carried the mention "Has a firearm permit." Bergeron is a former member of the anti-Bolshevik Legion and he still has in his possession the cloth-covered military booklet, bearing his picture stamped with the German Eagle. He explained that he had spent one year in German uniform on the Russian front… During a conversation in the Merle bureau, Bergeron said that his parents owned a factory or an enterprise in Avignon, and that he had a brush with their workers in 1936.

This certainly shows where his sympathies lay, but does not show a lasting commitment to the hatred of "Judeo-Bolshevism." Most likely, Bergeron was simply like the rest of the gangsters who had chosen the Nazis.

The Avignon hardcore of the Palmieri gang was surrounded by other individuals, informers of benevolent sub-contractors, like Fournier and Pontarelli* from Graveson, Léopold Fosco from Chateaurenard, who distinguished

---

* Pontarelli was assassinated in April 1944, and his body was found after the Liberation.

themselves in the Avignon surroundings.[12] Fournier and Pontarelli were occasionally seen in company of Blanc and Mouillade, in particular during *"the arrest of a Jew in Boulbon (Bouches du Rhône) by Lucien Blanc."*[13] The network around that nucleus spanned the entire Vaucluse and its surroundings, where the gangsters used their PPF membership to recruit voluntary informers. The beginning of the insurrection against the occupiers and their collaborators (early June 1944) put the gangsters on the defensive. An information note about Bergeron illustrates the situation.

> … PPF since 1936, he was a "protection guard" [in the PPF] at the end of 1940, SOL in 1942, left as a volunteer worker in Germany, he returned rapidly and never went back. Miss Augusta Vernet claims that he gave great political service there.
>
> Bergeron, who is considered as a killer, recently went to Buis les Baronnies for several days to guard the Achard family, whose father, a PPF, was wounded during a terrorist attack. Very dangerous.[14]

The network of gangsters was present in Buis les Baronnies (Drôme), very close to the position of the Resistance in the Maquis Ventoux. On the other hand, Bergeron, Deluermoz and Blanc went far beyond the Vaucluse, in lending a hand to Palmieri, their boss from Marseille. The report of Superintendent Castellan of October 7, 1946, placed them among other members of the Palmieri gang, on the side of his brother and right-hand man, Victor Palmieri, in the Basses Alpes during the arrest of 12 Jews on May 5, 1944. Castellan's report of December 2, 1949, described the assassination of Fraim Slobodzianski in Mane (Basses Alpes), perpetrated by four members of the Palmieri gang on April 29, 1944.[15] The gendarme Dailly recognized Deluermoz as one of the four gangsters. The assassination was corroborated by Nadia Karczmar, the daughter of the victim.[16]

Jacqueline Payeur, the wife of Charles Palmieri, also testified that Bergeron was in Cannes at her husband's side.

The German Police Settles in, the Mob Follows

Immediately after the arrival of German troops in the southern zone, the German army occupied the territory west of the Rhône and also took control of a narrow strip along the eastern side of the river. The remainder of the southeast—except the Marseille area and a narrow coastal strip up to Bandol—remained under Italian control until Italy's armistice on September 8, 1943. Italian troops occupied Orange and Carpentras.

The German military units were accompanied by an Einsatzkommando (special detachment) of about twenty police officers under the command of Heinz Hollert. This small group formed the embryo of the future SiPo-SD of Marseille.

Hollert established his regional center in Marseille at 425, rue Paradis. Reinforcements quickly followed and set up offices in the neighboring buildings. Building numbers 401, 402 and 403 soon accommodated the offices of the SiPo-SD (Sicherheit Polizei—Sicherheit Dienst). During this initial period, the Marseille group created two "antennas," one in Avignon, the other in Nîmes.

Hollert did not remain in the service long. On January 3, 1943, he was transferred to Lyon, where he died during a bombing. He was replaced in Marseille by Rolf Mühler who provided a view of the coexistence with the Italians in his deposition of January 25, 1947.

> The presence of the Italians complicated our work in the Marseille region a lot. There was a line along the Rhône from Lyon to Avignon which left the Rhône in that town and reached the [Mediterranean] sea between La Ciotat and Toulon. We did not have the right to carry out searches or arrests on the east of Toulon… For every arrest East of that point, we needed an Italian authorization for each one.[17]

It may be complicated. But this did not prevent the subordinate of Rolf Mühler, Wilhelm Müller, and Mouillade, the auxiliary, to *"carry out the arrests"* of the Jews of Carpentras on April 12, 1943, as shown in the testimony of Henri Dreyfus. The separation line between Germans and Italians was relatively porous.

Soon after the Italian defection, the Einsatzkommando in Marseille broadened its activity to the seven départements of the Marseille region: Gard, Vaucluse, Hautes Alpes, Basses Alpes, Alpes Maritimes, Var et Bouches du Rhône. This territorial expansion immediately triggered deep transformations. A new organization was set up, the KdS (Kommando der SiPo/Gestapo und des Sicherheitsdienstes) of Marseille; in short the command of the unified German police.

The antennas of Nîmes and Avignon were renamed Aussendienststellen, literally "external service stations," and the grip of the German police was expanded with the creation of Aussendienststellen in Toulon, Digne and Nice as well as Aussenposten ("External posts") in Draguignan, Brignoles, Cannes and Monte Carlo. Temporary units were sent to Aix-en-Provence, Orange, Hyères and Briançon. The Aussenposten of Cannes and Draguignan were eliminated on June 1, 1944, before the total retreat of the KdS on August 15,

1944, through the Rhône valley. In its stable state, the SiPo-SD network was more or less parallel to the organization of the French government, even if an occasional presence of the Marseille KdS could be found in some départements outside the Marseille prefectural region (Drôme, Isère, Ardèche). All these regional extensions strengthened the KdS grip.

Rolf Mühler, who had been the chief of the Lyon KdS before his assignment to Marseille, held his function until the end of June 1944, and Wilhelm Nolle replaced him until Liberation.

The KdS had multiple responsibilities: repression of the Resistance, black market, hunt of STO dodgers, military security, intelligence functions, operational functions, etc. With the growing opposition to German occupation, the struggle against the Resistance consumed an increasing proportion of the KdS scarce resources. This is why French auxiliaries became critical to its operation.

It is important to observe a significant parallel structure between the network of the German police and that of the French collaborators. The French auxiliaries were "accredited" to Charles Palmieri from Marseille, who was himself accredited to the organization of Rolf Mühler, the boss of Wilhelm Müller from Avignon. When Palmieri came to Avignon, his close association with the Marseille SiPo-SD gave him, in the eyes of his Avignon gang, the prestige expected of a big boss.

The chiefs of the German police, Müller and Gauthier, sealed their "professional" relations with their auxiliaries with the help of the carrot and stick approach. Conversely, the hoodlums picked up very fast whom they are dealing with, and they made sure that their masters wanted for nothing.

Should we be surprised by a true symbiosis between the SiPo-SD and the underworld?

The German Scoundrels

Ernst Dunker was a perfect example of the "rehabilitated" German ex-convict in the SiPo-SD. He became a key sergeant major of the Marseille KdS. Philippe Aziz has reconstituted his path.

> ... he was born on January 27, 1912, in Halle (Germany), in the modest family of a postal worker... The family lived in a state close to poverty... In 1927, the father died, Dunker finds himself an abandoned orphan at the age of 15... He worked at small jobs, barely making ends meet; he pilfered here and there... Dunker steals and poaches; in 1931, he is sentenced to four months in prison; once released, he is sent to a reformatory until his coming of age. When he

comes out, Hitler is in power. Dunker settles in Berlin… He spends his time in the slummiest parts of Berlin…[18]

He was recruited by a Nazi and became a party militant. He was known in the underworld as a pimp, the manager of the bar "Blaue Engel"* and an enthusiast for raids at the service of the Nazis. He was drafted in February 1940. Later, he was sent to the Altenburg school in Thüringen when he was trained in spying and intelligence techniques. He was then assigned to Paris at the Hôtel Duquesne, headquarters of the 11th GFP group. His mission was not that exciting: a few searches and a meager salary. In April 1942, his encounter with Lafont, the boss of the French Gestapo of rue Lauriston, put him back in money, and "freshened" him up. Their similarly tormented youths sealed an immediate friendship between them. Lafont *"introduces Dunker to Boemelburg[†], one of the great masters of the Paris Gestapo, and warmly recommends him… Under the protection of Boemelburg, Dunker neglects his strict German police duties and takes up the black market. He meets Abel Danos and Joanovici… and gets rich…"*

But he was hit by a new hard blow.

On December 15, 1942, the Hotel Lutétia[‡] discovered the trafficking of Sergeant Dunker… He was jailed during one month. Once freed, he got his job back, thanks to the intervention of the Boss. He was demoted and transferred to Marseille; he chose a truly French pseudonym: Delage.

On January 28, 1943, Delage arrived at the St. Charles (Marseille) train station in the company of Abel Danos, *aka* "Mammoth," a lieutenant of Lafont. Marseille which had been recently occupied was a town where gangs ruled the streets. Because of his mobster's past, he understood the underworld, even if it was different from the one he had known in Berlin. He had the right instincts. His personality and his alliance with the Paris underworld would help him settle in and do a better job in Marseille. The Paris underworld had connections with their Marseille "colleagues" (Carbone, Spirito[§]). They knew one another at both ends of the PLM railway line.**

---

* Blue Angel.
† At the time, Karl Boemelburg is the head of Section IV, in charge of Gestapo, sabotage, terrorist attacks, Resistance, counter-espionage, communists, and Jews.
‡ Headquarters of the intelligence services of the Abwehr.
§ Spirito disappeared in 1944 thanks to his relations with the mafia. Reappeared in the US in 1948. Was extradited in 1954 and acquitted for insufficient evidence. Died in Marseille in 1967.
** Paris-Lyon-Marseille railway.

Dunker remained under the explicit pressure of his Paris SS chiefs who must have forwarded his file to Rolf Mühler. He would be either totally dedicated to the SS cause or return to prison, if not worse.

Dunker earned a reputation commensurate with his bosses' expectations in Marseille and gratified his direct chief, Lieutenant Paul Kompe. He linked up with various gangs who shared the territory (arms trafficking, black market, prostitution), and with their help, his first priority was to tackle the Resistance networks. In particular, his offensive against the Ajax* resistance network of the police earned him the sympathies of the mob which saw in it a way to neutralize the police, their "class" enemies. Help was readily available. Not only did Dunker promise to protect "his" mobsters from the police, but in the case of the Ajax network, he ironically sent them to fight it. Dunker harnessed more than 200 active collaborators in the Marseille underworld.

In his deposition of May 11, 1945, Dunker emerged as a coldblooded killer, who had all that it took to get along very well with the other mobsters.[19] Erick,† a man parachuted into France to teach the new Resistance recruits, had proposed his services to Dunker in exchange for considerable payments. A few weeks later, Erick became worried that two officers parachuted with him were suspecting him of treason; he asked the Germans to kill these two officers. Instead, Dunker cold-bloodedly executed Erick in early August 1944 and got rid of his body on a deserted road; then he called the French police anonymously and told them where to pick up the body. He explained to his court interrogators: *"I must tell you that the way Erick operated had already started making me sick…"* Dunker's anonymous call to the French police created the perception in Erick's family that he had been killed by the French police.

Dunker provided the names of his Vaucluse collaborators; three of them, Bergeron, Fournier, and Garbarino, were lent by Palmieri. It is with this gangster, this killer in uniform, that Palmieri would cut his deals.

Charles Palmieri in the Wake of Simon Sabiani

Dunker recruited Simon Sabiani to his cause. Sabiani was a former communist deputy (1928), turned socialist, and now the leader of the Marseille region PPF.[20]

---

* Centered on Marseille, the Ajax network extended to the bordering *départements*, in particular the Vaucluse.

† Erick is the assumed name of the double agent who is in fact a member of a Marseille family.

Charles Palmieri was a Marseille *Sabianiste* from the beginning, as early as 1933, and he became a protégé in exchange for a few electoral "services" jointly with famous bosses, like Paul Carbone and François Spirito, as well as other members of the Corsican underworld. One must realize that political supremacy comes with geographic supremacy; he who chases the opponents from a Marseille district and keeps them out wins the votes of that district. Hence the importance of employing a contingent of tough guys.

It was the period when Sabiani, a populist with left leanings, still was the *éminence grise* of Marseille city hall with a chance at becoming mayor. When the electoral wind turned against Sabiani after 1934, and city hall slipped away, he got closer to Doriot, and in 1936 became a member of the PPF, which the grateful Palmieri brothers also joined on their protector's heels. Sabiani had no cause to be jealous of his new PPF boss, as he already had his army of shady characters even before his "conversion" from Sabianism, his self-serving ideology, to Doriotism.

After the 1940 defeat, the leader of the Marseille PPF strengthened the presence of these shady characters in its ranks. Doriot designated him as the General Secretary of the LVF for the southern zone.

In his December 22, 1944, deposition before an inspector of the Brigade de Surveillance du Territoire* in Paris after his arrest, Palmieri described his Sabianist autobiography:

> I have been sentenced three times... I left the Marseille public schools when I was ten to sail with the Compagnie de Navigation PLM.† I did my military service at the fleet depot in Toulon as a seaman; demobilized in April 1933, on the recommendation of Sabiani, I was hired at Marseille city hall. Since my salary was low, I lived by my wits until 1936, which is the date of my enrollment in the PPF, that had just been established in Marseille, under the direction of Sabiani.
> ... I was discharged in September 1940, and decided shortly thereafter, to go Paris where I hoped to find work much more easily.[21]

When he left, his criminal record already included two sentences for car thefts and acts of violence. Once in Paris, he married Jacqueline Payeur. With his "savings," he bought "Le Mirliton," a bar which was also a meeting place for influential members of the PPF. In 1942, he was sentenced to a 1,200 francs fine and a prison sentence for "*violation of the laws about food supply*," in

---

* Brigade for the Surveillance of the Territory, analogous to the FBI.
† Palmieri probably means La Compagnie de Navigation Nicolas Paquet, PLM being a railway company.

simple terms, the black market. His spouse was interrogated on September 23, 1944:

> When he came out of prison after the intervention of Doriot who had his sentence lowered to one month, Charles sold his share in the bar to a man named Jean... I must say that my husband had been a member of the PPF since the creation of the party.
>
> The Mirliton was a meeting place for influential members, Doriot, Jean Le Can,* [Victor] Barthélémy, General Secretary of the party, [Marcel] Marchal, mayor of St. Denis,† Maurice-Yvan Sicard,‡ Sabiani...

So Charles Palmieri was a regular of Jacques Doriot[22] who was also surrounded by an additional number of gangsters: François Spirito, Paul Carbone, Marius Manuelli, Auguste Ricord, Paul Alessandri, Serge Laurent, Pierre Fettu, Henri Jourdan and Guy Lavigne;[23] and in particular three brothers, Alfred, Michel, and Laurent Palmeri, whose last name was very close to that of the Palmieri brothers, Charles, Alfred, and Victor. At times this similarity caused confusion for the investigators after Liberation. All members of Doriot's "entourage" were Nazi collaborators, and some of them became familiar figures in the Marseille arena. This evidently contributed to tightening the links between the Paris and Marseille gangsters and the Germans.

Palmieri was divided between Doriotism and Sabianism following tensions between the Paris leader and his Marseille associate, but he kept his ties to Sabiani for the moment, as he explained in his deposition of December 22, 1944:

> Since I had been a member of the PPF in Marseille, I continued to meet the members of that party who were regular customers of the bar I owned [in Paris]. So I was attending the meetings, as much as my activities allowed me to.
>
> At the conference of November 1942,§ upon the request of Simon Sabiani, outraged to see the exploitation of his son's death by party propaganda and who was being increasingly excluded, I personally intervened to trigger the incident that ended the session. I was congratulated by the man named [Paul] Santolini, the owner of the "Pershing" brasserie, on boulevard Pershing, for this intervention in favor of the man he called his friend and cousin.

---

* Le Can was the owner of a construction company in Bordeaux.
† Marcel Marchal, a Dorit's lieutenant, was St. Denis city councilman and not the mayor.
‡ A journalist, postwar author of several books glorifying the LVF under the pen name Saint-Paulien.
§ He is referring to the famous "Conference Toward Power" organized by Doriot in Paris.

The "exploitation" mentioned by Palmieri refers to Doriot's wish to sell postcards with the photograph of Sabiani's son, a volunteer of the LVF, who had been killed on the eastern front. The repercussion of this tension on the Avignon subordinates of Palmieri was evident, when Mouillade, back from his "attempt to enlist in the LVF," took action:

> Mouillade… reappeared only in September 1942. He went to see the Doriotist militants and urged them to leave the PPF, because "their chief is a phony." His declarations caused a sensation among the local and regional chiefs of the PPF, but he was not excluded from the party for that…[24]

In spite of the diminishing influence of Sabiani on the party at the national level, his network in the Marseille region served him as a major asset with the KdS, after the arrival of the occupation troops in Marseille at the end of 1942. His relations were often dominated by his friendships—with hoodlums, with Gaullists, even friendship with some Jews. Gratitude for services rendered counted often more than ideology in Sabiani's politics.

Palmieri, Director of Human Resources

Shortly after his return to Marseille, Palmieri cut his ties to Sabiani and left the PPF, or more exactly did not set foot there anymore. The reasons of this break are not clear. Anyway, Palmieri found new masters in Marseille. He continued taking good care of his relationships with members of the PPF—established before the war and during his back and forth trips between Marseille and Paris from 1940 to 1942. The PPF remained one of his favorite recruiting grounds.

Palmieri consolidated his network around his direct collaborators:

In Marseille	André Simon*
	[Paul] Giacometti
	Tomasini
	Jean Pozzo di Borgo
	Quinson
	Reynoird
	Ollivier, *aka* "Nettou"
In Avignon	Pierre Josselme
	Louis Bergeron

---

* Albert is often used as Simon's first name.

	Lucien Blanc
	Louis Mouillade
In Orange	Charras[*]
In Vaison la Romaine	Docteur [Victor] Gaillard
In Cavaillon	Vinatie
In Graveson	Louis Fournier

This list does not include his two loyal brothers, Alfred and Victor, as well as other collaborators: Deluermoz from Orange, and Rodolphe Bride, Queudane, Simonnet, Marius Frézet, François Heiter, Jean Gibelin (*aka* Carteron), Guillaume Fasciola, all from Marseille. A few occasional associates also joined his operations: Bonavita, Guenouni, Manguerra, etc.

Frézet owned a map store at 8, rue Paradis, just below the office of the Merle enterprise, in front of his warehouse. His role was to detect members of the Resistance. When a suspect came in to buy maps, Frézet pulled an alarm rope, connected to Palmieri's office, just above. This triggered the tailing of the suspected Resistance member hoping to reach the entire network.

Palmieri found himself at the center of a network of allies, subordinates, profiteers and volunteers, who were often linked to the PPF. Most of them were ex-convicts or professional gangsters. There was a constant concern on Palmieri's part to maintain his political ties to the PPF, His network had a triple objective: serve the German police while lining his pockets and remaining shielded from the French police. On the German side, he had ties to individuals of the same ilk who understood him well.

Jean Gibelin, *aka* Carteron, hired by Palmieri at the end of 1943, specified the chronology of the Vaucluse activity which did not yet target Jews:

> Around January 20, 1944, Giacometti introduced two new members: Josselme and Bergeron. They were accepted by Palmieri and provided addresses for operations in the Vaucluse.
>
> A few days later, towards the end of February, Palmieri left for Avignon where he recovered at the home of a man named Daumas in La Motte d'Aigues, 40 tons of war equipment (Josselme and Giacometti had provided the tip for this deal).
>
> On his return, Palmieri brought in three new agents: Lucien Blanc, Louis Fournier and Mouillade. These three agents had a mission to pinpoint the camps of [STO] dodgers and all the anti-German activities in the region.

---

[*] This is Joseph Casimir Charrasse and not Charras.

Toward the end of February, upon Palmieri's request, I accompanied him to Avignon... We returned to Marseille with numerous tips about dodgers in Pont St. Esprit and Bourg St. Andiol.

A few days later, I learned that Dr. Gaillard had informed the SD of Avignon of a camp in Séderon housing 40 dodgers who are said to have been massacred by the SD of Avignon, helped by the Avignon Milice and the detachment of DCA* of Carpentras...[25]

This was an additional source of information which would have guided the Germans in the massacre of Izon la Bruisse.

However, at the end of 1943 and during 1944, the fight against the Resistance proved dangerous. With the allied advances on all fronts, Resistance groups became increasingly daring and the assassinations of collaborators grew in numbers.

The tragic death of Paul Carbone in a train sabotaged by the Resistance in 1943 must have cast a chill over the gangsters, and somewhat mitigated the satisfaction of seeing him disappear from the Marseille competition. Being at the service of the German occupier in the southeast in 1943–1944 was not the safest job.

Charles Palmieri Sets Up His Own Business

Santolini, *aka* "Paul from Marseille," was an independent mobster specializing in trafficking with the Germans in Paris. He was close to the Gestapo of rue de la Pompe[26] and had more than sympathy for Palmieri. Santolini served as his godfather back in Marseille.

Santolini, a friend of a man named Ottavi, both of them notorious traffickers on behalf of the Germans, introduced me to the latter who offered me to go into wholesale trafficking with them between Marseille and Paris.

With the objective of becoming purchasing agents for the Germans, we all went to Marseille, where we settled at the Hôtel Méditerranée.[27]

It is important to realize that in Paris the Germans had set up a multitude of "purchasing offices" aimed at providing military units with all kinds of products they needed.[28] This mechanism allowed the Germans to obtain supplies outside conventional channels while relying on mobsters who would not miss this godsend. Of course, the gangsters more or less closely affiliated

---

* Défense Contre Aéronefs (Defense Against Aircrafts).

with Lafont took advantage of this opportunity. The link to Marseille allowed them to expand their supply range.

The German purchasing offices in the hands of the gangsters contributed to the black market which the German police were in charge of combating. The same mechanism was found in Marseille. In the first deal recommended by his Parisian allies, things did not turn out that well for Palmieri:

> Our next deal consisted of buying cognac and tires which I wanted to sell to the Germans through the intermediary of a man named Aubert, owner of a café, rue Bernard Dubois [in Marseille]. At the time of the sale, the buyers who were none other than Gestapo agents arrested us, claiming that the merchandise had been stolen from them. With Aubert and three other people, we were incarcerated at the St. Pierre prison, German section. After one month in jail, I was freed through the intervention of Ottavi, who had connections with the German services, as an SD agent of the Hotel Majestic in Paris.

Was this accusation against Palmieri a German maneuver to take control of him? Anyway, Palmieri was well connected and from that point on, his position kept improving. During a trip to Marseille, Santolini introduced him to friends who had come there. Their description says a lot:

> Later, Santolini introduced me to a man named François Wilhelm who was the chief of intelligence for Gegoff in Paris. His entire gang was introduced to me in Marseille where they had come to perform some operations. This is how I got acquainted with Philippe, *aka* "Baron Delanoy," Edmond Brémont, *aka* "Count of Timbuktu," Lucien Scherrer (an Alsatian), *aka* "The Admiral," Cazeau, *aka* "The Doctor," and finally Jacques Lambert, who was introduced as Wilhelm's secretary. I must add that the woman named Annie, an intelligence agent and mistress of Lucien, was among these people.

Palmieri continued to engage in "business deals." In the company of Wilhelm, he requisitioned 40 tons of soap warehoused at the "Agricola" factory, and later 14 tons of soap at the "Rocca, Tassy and de Roux" factory. This last shipment was intercepted by the Gestapo. Palmieri landed in a German prison; then he was sought by the French police following a warrant for his arrest issued by M. Jouin, the investigating judge.

As Palmieri recounts his story:

> After he learned that the French police were looking for me…, Wilhelm introduced me to Keller who also stayed at the Grand Hôtel and told me that he would see to it that I would get away with it. This took place in April 1943.

Then, as he stated in another document:

> As for me, since I was sought by the French police, I got myself hired as an
> SD agent, by a man named Keller, who had been introduced to me by Santolini.
> I received a protection document from the Kriegsmarine and I became the
> general intelligence agent in charge of discovering French stocks. My salary was
> 10,000 francs per month, and I was earning, in addition to the salary, 3% of the
> official price of all the merchandise seized with my help.

Keller, who was about to leave Marseille, introduced Palmieri to
Lieutenant Kompe, chief of Section IV-E of the SiPo-SD, where he met
Dunker. Around September 15, 1943, the purchasing office at Merle was
established to provide a legitimate cover for the intelligence activity. An
apartment and a warehouse were allocated at 8, rue Paradis, and Palmieri also
received a revolver and a submachine gun. Later, Palmieri explained his role:
*"My work consisted of collecting intelligence and more precisely the locations of the Maquis
in the Var. I was receiving this information thanks to the complicity of Dr. Jamin,
secretary of the PPF and SD agent in Toulon."*

Section IV-E was in charge of counterespionage. For Palmieri, this
meant identifying underground radios, seeking information about the Maquis
in the Var, a sore spot for the Germans, locating clandestine equipment. He
also participated in the Dunker-Kompe operation against the Ajax network
of the police; this operation was more or less a failure because most of the
police belonging to Ajax managed to flee; even so, this half-success, to use
the words of Dunker, did probably please his mob subordinates, since they
had caused the police to run away. The arrests of members of the Resistance
continued, accompanied at times by extortion for the benefit of all the
participants.

The Germans had set the fox to mind the geese.

The tightening of the links with the SiPo-SD culminated with the Cannes
episode in June 1944. In that city on the Côte d'Azur, Palmieri became the
chief of the French Gestapo reporting to Bauer.

> Toward the end of June, the services of the SD under Bauer moved, and he
> asked me to move my office to Cannes where the headquarters was established.
> On June 20, accompanied by André Simon, Ollivier [*aka* Nettou], Louis
> Bergeron, Quinson, and my brother Alfred, we left for Cannes where we were
> supposed to settle. The services included two sections, the French one, and the
> other, the German one, was under the high leadership of Bauer. The French
> section, which I headed, was based at the Villa Conchita, boulevard Carnot,

while the German section was at the Villa Montfleury, Impasse Montfleury. In that town, I continued my Marseille activity, namely general intelligence, and more particularly, the arrest of Israélites.

In the investigation of the Marseille military court of justice, Bauer was described as "*a warrant officer, 52 years old, chief of torture, transferred to Cannes in July 1944.*"

The "Jewish Period" of Charles Palmieri

The Jews were weakened by repeated attacks from Vichy propaganda organizations and by government legislation. This made the hunt for the Jews a lucrative activity without any immediate risk. Moreover, the Jews were not protected by the Resistance, which did not consider their security to be a strategic objective. Abandoned by all, they became easy prey.

Palmieri admitted the arrest of 30 Jews in the Bouches du Rhône, 70 in the Vaucluse, 50 in the Basses Alpes, and 18 in the Var. These numbers were probably underestimated since, for instance, his subordinates performed arrests in his absence. The activity of the Palmieri gang spanned the entire Marseille prefectural region and beyond, through a network of agents and collaborators. For instance, they were spotted in the Drôme, in Buis les Baronnies, where they arrested Jewish refugees from the Vaucluse. Their action has been documented throughout the Gard, and the Hautes Alpes.

Palmieri showed his hand in his statement of March 15, 1945:

… I organized a few operations in Avignon. During the first one, I was with Thomas Ricci who had brought 15 of his agents while I had 10 of mine. Bergeron, Mouillade, Blanc and Josselme* of my unit as well as Georges Boyer, Alfred André and Nicky took part in it. On that day we arrested 44 Jews, who were transferred to Marseille by bus.

During the second one, still in the company of my Marseille and Avignon teams, I arrested 10 Jews from a list provided by Mouillade and Blanc.

The other operations were also conducted according to information provided by my Avignon agents. I do not remember exactly the number of arrests. I must add that I often happened to come to Avignon to pick up Jews arrested by the Germans.

… I know that my agents were organizing looting operations for their own benefit. Besides, Lucien Blanc was arrested by the French police for one of those deals…

---

* Palmieri was mistaken with respect to the participation of Josselme, who had been gunned down by the police in February 1944, while this operation took place at the end of March 1944.

I knew a few agents of the GFP, the individuals named Alfred André, Georges Boyer, [Albert] Sauvet, Nicky, Marcel Cappe,* Roger Boyer (from Mondragon).

As I already told you, the lists of Jews were provided by my Avignon agents, but also, at times, by Müller, the SD chief, who himself got them from the services of the Avignon prefecture.

I knew Feroldi, the milicien, through the intermediary Pierre Terrier, SD agent in Avignon. I have met Feroldi several times at the headquarters of the SD, boulevard Monclar in Avignon.

I knew Idlas when I also belonged to the PPF. Later, I saw him two or three times in Avignon, and I am aware that he was giving information to Josselme.

I was arrested on July 31, 1944, in Marseille, by the Germans who held me in custody for questioning about the Ajax network. I was released on August 13, the day of the landing and I immediately left Marseille...[29]

This provides a global view of Palmieri's activity in the Vaucluse: looting, arrests, collaboration with the various gangs to set up and execute large-scale operations.

In the sixth paragraph, Palmieri mentioned that Müller had at times given him lists of Jews from the prefecture. If we take his statement to the letter, Müller may have had a "mole" inside the prefecture. However, we have not been able to verify this possibility.

The second possibility, which does not exclude the first, is that he was speaking about the list of foreign Jews who had transited through Raymond Guilledoux, the regional director of the SEC and boss of Jean Lebon.†

Providing this list would have been for Vichy a compromise that could have spared French Jews. Such a list was found in Palmieri's office at 8, rue Paradis in Marseille. In his request for information of May 29, 1945, Jean Fabre, the investigating judge of the Marseille court of justice, cited Charles Palmieri:

These are list of Jews established by the French authorities during the census of the Jews. They were provided to Bauer [Palmieri's direct boss for Jewish Affairs in Marseille] and were given to us much later. I had sent these lists to my Avignon agents, specifically Mouillade so that he can find out whether these registered Jews still live at the recorded address...[30]

---

* This is Antoine Cappe and not Marcel Cappe.
† Part One, Chapter 4.

In fact, Palmieri's lists were partial copies of the census of foreign Jews. There were only 189 names out of more than 400 names recorded by the prefecture. In addition, he had a list of about 20 French Jews, which may have been a separate pool of potential victims.

For added efficiency, he had the addresses verified. For instance, Modka Korzec was first listed in Avignon at the address of his wife, then stricken out from Avignon, and finally recorded in Lauris. Other names were directly added with the address, where they were "hiding," like Hedwig Delange who was not on the census list. The names of people already arrested were stricken out.

Several testimonies stand out. Some Jews, who had been victims of extortions in exchange for their freedom, were ready to talk after Liberation. Since not all of these cases were willing to come forward, it is impossible to determine the exact number of Jews who were arrested and then released. However, one is left with the impression that the numbers are significant. In a report of May 2, 1945, Police Superintendent Victor Roton wrote:

> ... then in Orange, where, in the absence of the father, I recorded the testimony of Miss Danielle Mossé, age 20, unemployed, living in that town. She indicates that she was arrested on April 6, 1944, by several individuals and taken to the Gestapo, together with her father Samuel Mossé. Among the photographs, she recognizes Charles Palmieri and François Heiter. She adds that she and her father were released in exchange for 120,000 francs.
>
> Mr. Edmond Carcassonne, age 56, businessman in this town. On March 23, 1944, several individuals came to his home. He was not arrested, and for that, he had to pay 130,000-135,000 francs. He recognized Charles Palmieri's photograph without any doubt.
>
> Mme. Valentine Geismar, née Wildenstein, age 68, unemployed, in Orange. She declares that on October 8, 1943, three individuals arrived at her home and stated that they came to arrest her son-in-law Bomsel. They undertook a search of the house and grabbed the sum of 10,000 francs as well as various objects.
>
> Among the photographs, she recognizes without any hesitation Charles Palmieri. He behaved brutally toward her and slapped her.
>
> Later in Cavaillon, where on April 3, I recorded the declaration of Jacques Lévi, age 81, unemployed, living in this town. He indicates that on April 12, 1944, he was visited by several armed individuals who took him to the Police station of the city. They wanted to know the whereabouts of his son Maurice. They grabbed various objects during the search of the apartment. Then he was released two hours later...

On June 8, 1945, it was Samuel Mossé's turn to tell the story of his liberation with his daughter Danielle. The details he provides are worthy of an historical detective novel.

> … After my daughter finished preparing her suitcase, she proposed to one of these individuals to release us on bail. I followed suit by offering the chief the same thing, but he answered "that he was having nothing to do with that."
>
> We were then taken to the Kommandantur, but we never entered the offices.
>
> After entering the Kommandantur, the two individuals came out and took us back to our home.
>
> The "assistant" told me that he was accepting our proposal, namely the immediate payment of 120,000 francs.
>
> They took us back to the Kommandantur; again, we stayed in the car while the chief entered the offices. He came back in company of the German commander who looked at us; they both went back in.
>
> The chief came back a few minutes later and told the driver of the car "Take them wherever they will want, they are free."
>
> I asked to leave in the direction of the Champlain neighborhood, three kms away from town, I asked the car to stop and before giving the agreed amount, I asked my daughter to get off first. After she got out, I paid as agreed, and when it was my turn, I was prevented from getting out.
>
> The second individual who was with the chief at the beginning told me then: "Do not go back to your place and take it into your head that if we catch you again, you will be gunned down, you and your family, because we are doing something that we should not be doing." I was then released.

Palmieri knew very well who among the Germans *"was having something to do with that"*! In fact, during his confrontation with Samuel Mossé on July 24, 1945, before Judge Jean Fabre from the Marseille court of justice, Palmieri stated:

> … The claim of the witness is correct, it is me and Heiter who have arrested Samuel Mossé and his daughter; we had them released in exchange for money.
>
> I left part of this money at the Kommandantur and the remainder went to the coffers of the bureau Merle…[31]

In his deposition before Judge Larat on March 10, 1945, Palmieri confirmed that the Orange Kommandantur affair was not an isolated case:

> … We carried out the arrests, and then, we took the Jews to 425, rue Paradis. At times during a roundup, some Jews would give us money (100,000 or 200,000

francs) and we would let them go; of course we would keep the money for ourselves. Sometimes, we would find jewelry in the apartments abandoned by Jews, but we would give that to Bauer who was the chief of the anti-Jewish section, at rue Paradis.[32]

It must be noted that in the spring of 1944, jewelry seemed more practical than foreign exchange offices.

Palmieri responded cynically to Edmond Carcassonne who accused him of having arrested him on March 25, 1944, together with his wife and mother in law, then released them in exchange of 130 to 135,000 francs:

> I have to say that I was expected to put the seals on the apartment of Mr. Carcassonne and that I did not do it; I even carried their luggage to their place of hiding.

During a later confrontation, on August 7, 1945, with Edmond Carcassonne, Palmieri cited Lucien Blanc as an accomplice in that extortion. We also learn that Palmieri had started the discussion with a demand for 5 million francs. It was possible to haggle with Palmieri who could listen to reason.

In another report of May 25, 1945, Superintendent Roton recorded the following facts:

> Then on March 30, the testimony of Marie Riz, age 40, businesswoman, 27, rue Bancasse.
>
> She states that on May 15, 1944, two individuals whom she has learned since then are Palmieri and Conrad (he was executed since then) arrested her at her domicile listed above. She adds that the individuals named Charles Palmieri, Robert Conrad, Isnard, Pierre Terrier, Félix Olivier, as well as another one she thinks is named Costa, looted her apartment, on the second floor, and took with them fabrics, food, liqueurs and other. Then, they let her go free under the promise that she would bring them 100,000 francs the next morning. On the agreed day, Félix Olivier came to the home of Mme. Riz, but after he could not come to an agreement with her, he brought Charles Palmieri, who, out of his mind with anger, assaulted Mr. Gustave Vonet, a friend of Mme. Riz. Then, he arrested him and took him to the St. Anne prison. Two days later, Mr. Vonet was released in exchange for 100,000 francs.
>
> She recognized Lucien Blanc, Louis Bergeron and Charles Palmieri in the photographs that were shown to her.

Marie Riz had already been ransomed by the Alfred André gang a few months earlier, in November 1943.*

Anything Goes to Increase Revenue

Jean Lebon and the SEC were not the only ones interested in the stallholders. A note about Gaston Mouillade provides an insight:

> Gaston Mouillade had the stallholders on the place Pie arrested on Thursday, March 16.
>
> He was looking for Jews engaged in the black market and owning stocks of merchandise which have been promised to him in payment.[33]

The stallholders on the place Pie were on the list of the Palmieri gang. The shortages at the time made the little merchandise they may have owned even more desirable, all the more so since everyone knew that some of them continued their small trade in order to survive, in defiance of the CGQJ anti-Jewish measures. But there was more to it: some of them were well connected, and this could become useful to street tyrants who were pursuing them.

Victor Roton recorded the deposition of Marthe Angel, née Arokas, given on March 24, 1945:

> In March 1944—I am not able to provide the exact date—my husband told me that the man named Joseph Allemand, stallholder in Avignon, claimed that he can arrange to free his stepfather, Jacques Toledo, at the time detained in Marseille, at the prison of Les Beaumettes, in exchange for 500,000 francs. After my husband, who could not afford that amount, refused he was summoned a few days later at the home of Mr. Yaffe, stallholder, place des Carmes, by an individual whose name I have learned to be "Merle."
>
> This man stated to my husband that he could do nothing for his stepfather, but he strongly suggested that he pay 200,000 francs if he wanted to avoid being arrested. After a discussion, my husband handed over the requested amount to Merle, and on his advice, my husband left for Buis les Baronnies where I joined him.
>
> One month after our departure from Avignon, my husband was arrested by three German soldiers and three French civilians.
>
> Among the photographs you are showing me, I recognize without any hesitation Joseph Allemand, a neighbor of mine, and without being completely certain, the individuals, whose names you gave me as Gibelin, *aka* Carteron, and

---

* Part Two – Chapter 7.

Louis Bergeron, were probably among the people who arrested my husband in Buis les Baronnies.

Marthe Angel did not seem to know that Lucien Blanc had also participated in the Buis les Baronnies operation.

The court file against Joseph Allemand shed light on this strange episode, in spite of a few details that remain unclear.[34] In a statement otherwise rather favorable to Allemand, Moïse Yaffe declared on March 27, 1945, that "...*he was arrested on March 15, 1944, by four individuals who introduced themselves as members of the German police; he recognized Palmieri among these four individuals. He was taken to St. Anne prison where he was brutally beaten, then released the next day because of his Turkish nationality.*"

Charles Palmieri shattered Moïse Yaffe's explanations with his own deposition during Joseph Allemand's trial:

> I am the one who got him released because the Germans were arresting the Turkish Jews. A few days later, Moise Yaffe gave 5,000 francs for the German Red Cross.
>
> Then, Moise Yaffe came to ask me to free a man named Toledo, arrested at the German prison. I was unable to have him freed because there was an ongoing blackmail affair; some people had come to see the stepson of Toledo and were asking for money to release him. I refused to handle this issue any more.
>
> I want to add that, since I learned about an upcoming roundup of Jews, I was keen to tell Yaffe that I did not want him arrested a second time, after having saved him. I posted André Simon [in front of his door] with the instructions not to let Yaffe communicate with the outside, but to let him go after the roundup was finished; that is what happened. At the same time as Yaffe, I bailed out Elie Angel, who had been arrested as I have already explained.

Charles Palmieri was changing into a Good Samaritan in front of our eyes! He was evidently ready to use all means at his disposal to save his skin. As to Moïse Yaffe, he somewhat corrected himself in his next testimony:

> I have been forced to make a gift to the Red Cross. It is true that Palmieri warned me about a roundup and that I would be let free at 5:00 a.m. There were 4 other Israelites in my apartment, my wife, Toledo, Toledo's brother-in-law and Angel. After my departure, there was a search in my home, but I was already gone. After I came back to my apartment building, I was not bothered any more.

With the help of the traditional techniques of the underworld, the gangsters put pressure on their victims to identify through them the most affluent Jews. Then they discreetly contacted the targeted Jews and extorted money in exchange for freedom. Palmieri put around the neck of his victims the same kind of noose he used to get his own subordinates to toe the line; exactly the same way his Germans bosses were able to do with him.

For his victims caught in the spiral of brute force and intimidation, terrorized by the fear of deportation, there were very few choices: either submit or become a destitute runaway. How many others, faced with the same choice, took the same road? What would each one of us have done under the same circumstances?

Although Palmieri had no scruples, he seemed however to keep his word and released his rich victims after a ransom, if he was not being watched or if he was able to bribe his German partners. It was good for business to keep a good reputation, especially among future victims. This "honesty" was apparently not the case for other Avignon gangsters, the Parietas gang, who took advantage of their victims as if there were no tomorrow.* Palmieri and his gang did not neglect smaller amounts, between 5,000 and 35,000 francs, during organized roundups. A good network of informers showed him the path to follow between the rich Jews and the less affluent ones. Palmieri knew how to optimize his business: filling his own pockets while delivering enough Jews for deportation.

Palmieri—the Man

On November 17, 1945, Rousselier, the Marseille court psychiatrist provided an assessment of Charles Palmieri:

> … he has a sharp and intelligent eye, he is in a pretty good general state of health… A good memory, attentive, well balanced, demonstrates judgment and will, shows no psychotic behavior…
>
> About the accusations against him, Palmieri insists that he has always been a good Frenchman, without any intent to damage the external security of the state… PPF since its beginning, he left the party in 1942 "because of Doriot."
>
> … He specifies that his wife has been faithful…
>
> The man claims to have normal sexual activity, to be free of any venereal disease, to drink only one liter of wine per day, to consume a few rare aperitifs, to smoke little, four or five cigarettes a day, to use no hard drugs, not to be an habitual gambler.
>
> The man is very calm, has full self-control, and has not once tried to make any "self-serving statement" nor has he simulated any symptoms.

---

* Part Two – Chapter 7.

Moreover, this defendant, very direct, very precise in his statements, affirms that he has never had any anti-national intentions; and he claims he can explain his acts only because of political convictions, and that it is because of his convictions that he wanted to fight the internationals and the Jews.

Today, Palmieri, who claimed *"to drink only one liter of wine per day, to consume a few rare aperitifs,"* would be considered a "functional" alcoholic. Alcohol may have unleashed his brutality.

Palmieri looked dapper, as confirmed by his photograph in his court file. In his memorandum of March 1, 1945, Bride, his secretary, painted the portrait of a boss and provided testimony against him.

Charles Palmieri was the "director" of the Merle enterprise. The round pink face of a doll, irascible and brutal at times, he never smokes, but he drinks and likes going to bars and night clubs… He loves money, and in my judgment, if he works with the Germans, it is toward a lucrative goal, since I saw him deceive them when it is profitable. And what's more, he liked to say "Everybody likes dough, but you must know how to earn it cleverly." He is always armed, a revolver in his belt and a sub-machine gun at his reach. He loves sartorial elegance and has expensive suits tailored at Severin, rue Paradis… He often brags about his relations with the krauts, in particular Bauer, an officer of the Gestapo in Marseille, Richard, an officer of the Gestapo in Marseille and in Cannes, Bilharz,* another member of the Gestapo… He often goes to the race-track in Avignon† with Bauer… He constantly praises the krauts and the miliciens. He is openly against Sabiani and declares not to set foot in the PPF anymore. He owns a grey family front wheel drive which he claims having bought in Cannes together with Régis Balthazar for 100,000 francs. He owns a covered truck which he uses to transport the Jews he arrests and is driven by Albert Simon… Albert Simon and Queudane take care of his cars.

He displays a violent hatred against the Jews and does not hide that he steals from them and loots whenever he can; he lets them know, especially if they are rich, that he will deliver them to the Germans if they do not pay him off generously. If the Germans approach, he lets the rich Jews escape… He delivers the poor ones to the Germans mercilessly. During my presence at the office, he got several "reprimands" on the part of the Germans who do not want him to take money from the Jews, but only to deliver them.[35]

Palmieri used the language of violence, with snappy formulas. During the arrest of Sarah Levendel, he refused to let her go in spite of her pleas: *"You don't have a heart!"* He replied: *"We do have one, but it is made out of steel!"* [36]

---

* Rolf Bilharz is a subordinate of Aloïs Brunner.
† The race track, Roberty, is located in Le Pontet, near Avignon.

On July 6, 1945, David Kreikeman testified about his own arrest and that of his family, a little more than one year earlier.

> Palmieri criticized me for hiding my wife and my child: "Now we know their address, and we are going to pick them up!" He hit me several times on my shoulder with a cane he had taken in my wardrobe… Jean Pozzo di Borgo and Charles Palmieri arrested my wife in my presence. Palmieri conducted a search and seized a jewel box containing [gold] coins of 10 and 20 francs, a radio set, and a camera. He ordered my wife to take some clothes and he took us to the truck with our two-year old toddler. Then I asked Palmieri what he was going to do with my son and he replied: "Sausage meat and we'll make you eat it!"

He was a tough guy who did not tolerate any resistance. The testimony of the Cavaillon police superintendent, recorded by Victor Roton on April 3, 1945, testified to it:

> The man named Charles Palmieri, who carries a Gestapo badge with the name Merle, conducted operations in Cavaillon several times, often accompanied by Frenchmen, or by Germans, and in particular a man named Gauthier, Superintendant of the Gestapo in Avignon. Concerning the arrest of Levy and Grech, here is what took place:
>
> Merle arrived at the police station at about midnight, accompanied by twenty or so PPF. He tried to obtain the list of all Cavaillon Jews; in particular by pressuring my sergeant who warned me immediately.
>
> As soon as I arrived at the station, Merle demanded the complete list of all the Cavaillon Jews; I refused categorically.
>
> As he insisted, while indicating that he would arrange for Captain Müller of the Avignon Gestapo to order it, I repeated my refusal, and I phoned the prefecture chief of staff, who told Merle that he had no right to ask the police for information. He insisted and ordered the chief of staff to go immediately to Captain Müller who will order him to provide this information.
>
> … I want to specify that he was accompanied by fifteen or so individuals, all armed with sub-machine guns and revolvers; they arrived with two cars and a truck. These individuals were carefully watching my people's every move as well as our telephone exchange…
>
> Merle accused me of having provided Grech with a fake ID card and told me he was a Jew. I intervened several time while vouching for Grech whom I knew very well. Merle consented to release Grech and his wife temporarily, and he warned me that if Grech were to escape from Cavaillon, he would arrest me…
>
> Merle had told me and my services that he was the boss of the entire organization fighting against the Jews in the Marseille region.

Confident of his own power, Palmieri turned the situation round: the gangster threatened the police superintendent.

It is not hard to see the pattern in the archival documents, although he had once in a while been touched by a passing emotion, as in the case of the arrest of the Benyacar—Maurice, age 24, Lisette, age 22, and their baby Sylvain, age three and a half months. Palmieri proposed to Lisette to go away with her baby. Unfortunately, she refused; she wanted to stay with her husband. The result was deportation on convoy 76. Lisette and Sylvain were gassed on arrival, but Maurice survived.

The testimony of Jacqueline Payeur, Palmieri's "faithful" wife shed additional light on the personal world of the boss.

> ... I must tell you that I met Francois Heiter at "Marianne Michel"... He became my lover in August 1943... I rejoined [Charles] at the end of December, and I renewed my contact with my lover. At that time, I arranged for my friend Heiter a position as interpreter for my husband at a salary of 10,000 francs per month.
>
> ... my friend Heiter who had left the Merle office about the end of May [1944] joined me in Paris, where I hid him in my apartment...
>
> ... If I have housed and hidden Heiter, even though I knew that he was the interpreter of my husband, it is because he was my lover and I was pregnant by him...

François Heiter probably did leave the Merle office fearful of Palmieri's anger who was suspicious of his relationship with Jacqueline, but he used his flight for his defense, according to the report of investigating Judge Jean Fabre: "*... this work was making you nauseous and you were about to leave.*"

A Subordinate Worthy of His Master

Queudane was one of Palmieri's Marseille subordinates who participated in the roundups of the Vaucluse Jews. On December 18, 1943, gun in hand, accompanied by Alessandrini, Cabagno and two other acolytes, he ransomed Ernest Girard from Aubignan: 155,000 francs in banknotes, jewelry, gold coins and bearer bonds, in total a 300,000 franc value. The investigating Judge Caralp recorded the testimony of Arnaud, subprefect of Carpentras:

> ... It seems that this theft had not been perpetrated by terrorists or ordinary bandits, but that we had here skilled specialists, who had succeeded in avoiding the severe penalties of French law concerning the use of counterfeit police badges. They did so by betraying the good faith of the German security services and obtaining genuine German police badges, in order to elude the just punishment of their wrongdoings.

Of course, we have noted many times the "good faith" of the German Security services. Anyway, on February 15, 1944, an arrest warrant was issued by a Carpentras investigating judge against the "bogus-real" police.

Cabagno, who had been caught, was released following "*the visit of man named Meyer, introducing himself as an SD agent in Avignon… who warns that Cabagno was attached to the same service.*" A word to the wise was enough.

As to Queudane, he was going a bit farther. Again, the sub-prefect Arnaud testified:

> On June 7, 1944, at about 5:30 p.m., the investigating judge was visited by three individuals introducing themselves as German police; they provided identification on the judge's request.
>
> From the beginning of the conversation, these individuals, among whom Queudane was present, declared to the High Magistrate… that in the case of the Girard husband and wife theft, he had acted thoughtlessly, by ordering the arrest of Queudane…
>
> However,… after the discussion resumed, these individuals forced the investigating judge, under threat and pressure, to sign a letter addressed to "M. Merle, German Security in Marseille," in which the magistrate declared that the man named Queudane was released, because no element in the criminal file justified any legal action.
>
> While leaving with the letter in hand, these three individuals swore at him, and delighted in informing the Magistrate that the president of the court had already been executed, and that the police superintendant, who had launched an investigation against them, was already locked up.
>
> … Let me underscore the significant number of thefts perpetrated in the region under the cover of the protection of the German security services.

Queudane, the gangster, became the judge. It was a scheme that may be found elsewhere in France.[37] Two observations are now in order. The original incident against the Girards, which took place on December 18, 1943, indicates that some members of the Palmieri gang were already operating in the Vaucluse before the boss's arrival as a Jew hunter.

In addition, the incident in the judge's chambers in Carpentras occurred on June 7, 1944, the day following a major roundup by Charles Palmieri in Avignon. A little detour through Carpentras before returning to Marseille was well worth the effort.

This episode was not held against Queudane.

Trickery and Double Dealing?

Palmieri claimed that the Germans jailed him toward the end and Dunker confirmed it. They supposedly suspected him of being a double agent for the

Resistance. Did Palmieri have a last minute change of mind? Dunker provided an insight.

> ... I wish to avoid any confusion that Palmieri has worked for our service, in Section IV-E with Kompe.
>
> A few days before our departure from Marseille, during the first half of August, Palmieri who had played bogus cop and robbed everybody and everywhere, by taking advantage of his functions with us and with Bauer, was arrested under the orders of the assistant of Kommandeur Gustav Meyer.[*] By coincidence, he was put in a cell with the American officer "Lucas"... I do not know what he had told Lucas. Anyway, he must have earned his trust, since this man shared with him secrets that Palmieri rushed to write down and forward—or at least attempt to forward—to Kompe, with whom he was in very good terms. One of these letters missed its destination and landed in the hands of Pfanner,[†] who was taking a jaundiced eye of the friendship between Kompe and Palmieri...[38]

Palmieri knew how to take advantage of every opportunity.

We are faced with another unexpected situation during Palmieri's confrontation with Andrée Pons, née Carcassone, who was arrested on the day following the arrest of her husband, a notorious member of the Vaucluse Resistance.

> <u>Andrée Pons</u>: I recognize Charles Palmieri, although he has lost weight. He is not the one who arrested me. I saw him at the St. Anne prison. I was transferred from the St. Anne prison in Avignon to Marseille by bus. I stayed in the bus and was not taken to the Gestapo [in Marseille].
>
> I spent the night in an office at the end of rue Paradis, near the Place de la Bourse. On the next day ... Palmieri, the man here, came alone and told me I could leave under the condition I do not return to Avignon, in which case I was risking being arrested again.
>
> I gave him the address where I was going to stay, 27, rue Sainte. I was not bothered anymore...
>
> I must specify that Palmieri never asked for any money.
>
> <u>Charles Palmieri</u>: I have been told to transfer Mme. Pons from Avignon to Marseille. Upon the insistence of members of the Resistance whose names I do not want to mention, I freed her... One of them came to see her in my apartment where Mme. Pons had spent the night.[39]

---

[*] Gustav Meyer is the assistant of Rolf Mühler, the head of the Marseille KdS.
[†] Pfanner, who by that time had replaced Nuttgens as the head of Section IV, was the boss of both Kompe (Section IV-E against the Resistance) and Bauer (Anti-Jewish Section IV-B).

The aforementioned transfer was requested by the Avignon or Marseille SiPo-SD. It was impossible to confirm through other sources whether Andrée Pons had really been freed following a specific request form the Resistance or whether this was a gesture taken on Palmieri's initiative. Anyway, the liberation of the wife of this member of the Resistance would certainly serve as an insurance policy in the near future. Apparently, Palmieri had been wise enough to keep a back door open to his enemy, the Resistance.

By rendering some services to the Resistance, hunting the Jews, extracting information from an American prisoner for the benefit of the German police, the man was always cultivating multiple relationships; a good practice in the underworld and an insurance policy for the future.

Palmieri's Last Round of Poker

Let us follow Palmieri's story during the hours that preceded the liberation of Marseille:

> On August 15, I left Marseille under surveillance, accompanied by members of the SD, in the direction of Belfort through Lyon. On our way, I met Kompe, who got me released in Belfort. In that town, I met my brother Alfred, Bergeron, and Kalpadjian…
>
> Since we had been asked to spy on our compatriots, we asked to be relieved and we were sent to Berlin… two individuals told me they belonged to a group headed by Obersturmführer Neyser whose mission was to train agents susceptible of returning to France. At their request, I was introduced to Neyser, who accepted us into his group…
>
> When we arrived at that school, in the presence of the instructors, Captain Winter and Lieutenant Lang, we signed a paper in which we promised not to divulge the secrets of the school. Any failure on our part to do so could get us executed.
>
> … The classes were about explosives… Lieutenant Lang trained us to shoot the revolver and the sub-machine gun, while Captain Winter was in charge of classes about tactics and reading survey maps… At the end of the course, a first group left for the front… A second group left the school ahead of us… Their mission was to attack the pipeline along the Rhône valley…
>
> As for my team comprised of two groups, one formed by three SS and the other by my brother Alfred, Bergeron, Karadjian, and Albert Jeanne, it was supposed to attack the pipeline between Cherbourg and Paris or Paris and Nancy… In addition to explosives and food, we were each given 25,000 francs, 100 dollars, 36 pounds sterling, and for the entire group, four Louis gold coins. My brother and I had 80,000 francs which belonged to us personally. A few minutes before the departure, we were given a vial of poison we were supposed

to use in case of arrest... On the eve of December 14, we boarded an American four-engine plane with German colors...

The flight took place at an average altitude of 3,000 meters and I do not know why we were parachuted in Chemery instead of Marolles (Yonne). At 00:20 a.m., Mer, who was keen to accompany us, ordered us to jump. Once landed, the whole team gathered except Jeanne, whose tracks we never found. On contact with the ground, my brother Alfred dislocated a knee ... I ordered the whole team to leave the bags and the material on the spot. We met in an abandoned house; in the small hours of the morning, two peasants came to our landing area and they were able to identify the landing spots when they saw the bags. Fearing that these peasants would trigger an alarm, the three SS wanted to take them prisoner before fleeing, I objected, and after leaving the explosives and my bag, I left with my brother to get him medical attention. After learning in Chemery that American headquarters were in Blois, I planned to make myself available at their headquarters and to inform them about the objective of my mission and provide them any information they might be interested in. But on our way, between Chemery and Contres, the gendarmes who had been warned by the peasants, patrolled the area and arrested us. Fearing torture by the French police, as the German propaganda had indicated, my brother swallowed the vial he had received when we left. He died a few minutes later. I spontaneously gave mine to the gendarmes and asked my comrades to do the same.

I asked to be immediately given over to French military authorities, to provide all the information I intended to give to the Americans when I left Chemery... I want to underscore, and this pleads in my favor, that I have voluntarily abandoned the bags and their contents on the landing spot, that when I left Germany, I was firmly intent never to accomplish my mission and to contact the American forces...

Bergeron was caught in company of the SS attached to Palmieri's commando. He was transferred to the military tribunal in Orléans, sentenced to death and executed on February 2, 1945. He was found guilty of treason and sabotage attempts against the allies in the Fifth region. Although his activity in the Vaucluse and the Marseille region was considerable, it was not held against him.

Palmieri was handed over to the DST, which at the time was worried about the residue of collaboration, the new crime families and the members and sympathizers of the Communist party. In many parts of the country, the provisional government was engaged in arm wrestling with the left wing members of the Resistance it suspected of seeking a violent power takeover.

A letter from the Paris Criminal Investigation Direction indicated that Palmieri's final gamble of Palmieri was not a success.

Paris, August 25, 1945

Police Prefecture
Criminal Investigation Division

REPORT

The investigation conducted per request of the Investigation Judge reveals the following: Monsieur Briel, Police Superintendent at the DST in Orleans, could not be auditioned.

Monsieur Bernard, Divisional Superintendant at the DST in Paris, who was heard, declares: "Charles Palmieri was supposed to be made available to M. Briel, police superintendant at the DST in Orleans, that was going to use him for police operations, but because of the lack of results obtained in Paris between Messrs. Orabona and Palmieri, this project was abandoned, and Palmieri was handed over to the Marseille court of justice."

Before his transfer to the Marseille court of justice, Palmieri was seemingly free and went back to his usual lifestyle, as we learn from an anonymous denunciation that was ignored by the court as long as the DST kept the "Palmieri project" going.

Monsieur the head of security,

I am writing to you as a patriot who has suffered, I am writing to you to designate to justice four hoodlums of the Gestapo. These are the three Palmieri brothers domiciled at la Madrague Ville; their names are Charlot Palmieri, No. 1 agent of the Gestapo… his brother Alfred Palmieri… as for the third one, he was rejected by the Gestapo because he is a hunchback and an informer for the two other brothers…

These three individuals, dangerous to the population, are still free and parade at La Madrague. The fourth agent whose nickname is Nettou… has just bought the bar Moutier at l'Estaque for 500,000 francs. All this money was stolen from his victims…

P.S. If they are not arrested, I will contact the CDL directly.[40]

The author of this anonymous denunciation recognized the members of the Palmieri gang, but erroneously situated Alfred Palmieri in La Madrague, while he had committed suicide after his unfortunate parachute incident.

After Palmieri's return from Germany, his network of acquaintances, who, for the most part, had worked for the Germans, had been decimated and his friends had become rarer: some had eluded justice and were working for bosses who had helped the Resistance; a few were on the run; others were in prison awaiting trial.

Palmieri himself testified for many months before the courts of the Marseille region; these were the last services he was able to render before his death sentence in May 1946, and his execution on August 22, 1946, at La Malmousque in Marseille.

Cleaning up Palmieri's "Little World"

Ironically, it was Bride, deeply implicated in the Palmieri gang, who gave the coup de grace to his boss's defense. This penniless student, that Palmieri provided with a good monthly income, saved his own skin by using a stratagem concocted shortly before Liberation. At the last minute, he set up a good insurance policy. The investigating Judge Fabre, who was not fooled, reported to the court:

> In the course of a confrontation, Charles Palmieri attempted to knock out Bride with a telephone ear piece.
>
> All the other members of the Merle gang are trying more or less to accuse Bride. It is difficult to determine whether they are sincere…
>
> In summary, Bride has been the denouncer of the Palmieri affair.
>
> He has provided the DGER* and for the court investigation a slew of documents that he had collected during the time he worked in Palmieri's office and that allowed uncovering part of Charles Palmieri's activity. It is important to note that the other defendants who pretend to be in the Resistance (Leca, Quinson, Pozzo di Borgo, Renucci) have provided only insignificant information.
>
> It is clear that, right after Liberation, Bride did not deem it necessary to tell the whole truth to the DGER as a precaution…
>
> Anyway, it is certain that without Bride most of the defendants in the Palmieri case could not have been put on trial, that without the documents he has provided the charges against them would have been minimal.[41]

Contrary to Judge Fabre's statement, it was unlikely that Bride acquired the documents in question *"during the time he worked in Palmieri's office."* The boss would probably have noticed it. He must have picked them up later, during the confusion following the allied landing, at the time Palmieri had clearly become the loser and was locked up by the Germans. *"Bride did not deem it necessary to tell the whole truth to the DGER as a precaution"*? Nevertheless, Bride became a "friend of the court."

Rodolphe Bride was acquitted *"for services rendered to the court."*

Justice had been severe and swift in the first weeks following Liberation, when the CDLs were channeling public vengeance. In the case of Gaston Mouillade, the questions to the jury reflected the haste of the court.

---

* The DGER (Direction Générale des Etudes et Recherches) was formed in November 1944 by unifying all the intelligence services, including those of the Resistance.

1. Is the defendant Frédéric Gaston Mouillade guilty of having belonged to the PPF, an organization aimed at helping all the enterprises of Germany against France, while these two nations were at war?

Yes, by a majority.

2. Is the defendant guilty, as a Frenchman, of having belonged to the Gestapo?

Yes, by a majority.

3. Is the defendant guilty of having delivered or denounced French people* to an enemy organization and of having arrested them or caused them to be arrested by this organization?

Yes, by a majority.

4. Are there extenuating circumstances in favor of the defendant?

No, by a majority.[42]

The first question corresponded to article 2 of the ordinance of August 26, 1944, and implicated Mouillade in the crime of national indignity. The second and the third question fell under the definition of article 1 of the ordinance of June 26, 1944. However, the third question was limited to "French people" in spite of the fact that a large number of his victims were foreign Jews.

Judged and sentenced to death by the Avignon court of justice on October 7, 1944, the prefect rejected his plea for clemency on the afternoon of the verdict and he was executed on October 10, 1944. On October 17, 1944, a note from the Government Commissioner near the court of justice to the prefect evoked the last chapter of Mouillade's life:

> … it is evident that the firing squad in charge of Mouillade's execution was composed of inexperienced recruits. It would be wise to make sure that these recruits be more experienced… We support all the measures which are aimed at sparing the victims an unnecessary ordeal.[43]

At the beginning, judgments were hasty, and executions were hasty. After the government took back control of justice, the interventions of the French minister of justice resulted in a significant softening of the verdicts.

However, Lucien Blanc did not benefit from clemency. Let us go back to Estréa Asseo's story.

> I was taken to the Hautpoul barracks and two days later to the St. Anne prison. Eight days later, I was sent to Drancy, then to Poland at Birkenau (Upper Silesia).
> We were about 15,000 in this camp; we suffered more than a human being can bear, and on arrival, we were tattooed on our left arm, as you can see my

---

* Underlined on the court document.

number is A.8521; on my back I also have a cross made with an acid that ate away at my flesh.

I cannot describe all the suffering without shivering, just at the thought of it. Lucien Blanc and Merle are the only ones responsible for my deportation to the German slave camps. When Lucien Blanc is arrested, my wish is to be confronted with him so that he has the opportunity to justify my arrest.

This statement of Estréa Asseo was given on May 27, 1945. On that date, Lucien Blanc was still at large. He was arrested on September 10, 1945, by the gendarmes of Meyruis, a village in the Lozère, during an identity check. He was holding counterfeit documents. After coming back from Germany, he buried himself in the sticks, or at least he thought so. The immediate verification in the fugitive list of the Mende gendarmerie proved fatal.

Estréa Asseo fulfilled her wish to confront Lucien Blanc. In the hall of the Nîmes court of justice, the defendant's wife, who saw Estréa after her testimony, hurled about: "Bitch!" Estréa Asseo later shared with Isaac Levendel that during her Auschwitz hell, she only wanted one thing: having Lucien Blanc arrested and testifying against him.[44]

Lucien Blanc was executed on February 11, 1946, by a firing squad of 12 soldiers.

The underworld purges in the Marseille region followed the same pattern as the other "professions"; they were limited to a handful of scoundrels— "une poignée de misérables," to use de Gaulle's words.[45] The bigger scum— Palmieri, Parietas, André, Blanc, Mouillade, and some others also implicated with the occupiers—were rapidly eliminated. Others were on the run until they got caught or had tried to "rebuild a good position for themselves" in foreign countries, at the service of other governments or for the own benefit.

For others from Palmieri's inner circle, a new era opened up. Quinson, Queudane, Toussaint Renucci, Pozzo di Borgo, and the likes, were recycled by the new Marseille godfather, Mémé Guérini, who had chosen the resistance side from the beginning and got rewarded for it. Their late conversion to the patriotic ideal threw a veil over their actions against the Jews. Before the court of justice, Guérini "confirmed" their membership in the Resistance. He had "*indeed caught a glimpse of them on the barricades on the day of Marseille liberation.*"

The Berg affair illustrates well the low priority of the crimes against the Jews on the scales of justice at the Liberation. Alberto was a "double agent" in the Mouraille gang at the service of the intelligence network of German

Captain Hans Senner;* Palmieri gave an occasional hand to Mouraille, and vice versa. In particular, Alberto and François Heiter escorted a Jew to Paris to pick up a 500,000 francs ransom. Palmieri rewarded Alberto with a 50,000 francs bonus. In the Berg affair, it was Heiter who reciprocated.

On February 28, 1945, Alberto testified: *"For a few months already, other French agents working for the Gestapo, particularly a man named Charles Palmieri, had started suspecting me… Under these circumstances, I showed a spectacular zeal when I went on missions for the Germans, so that they would think that I was the most sincere agent of the German consulate"*[46]

After Liberation, Alberto landed a job as a driver for the Nice DST. Georges Berg, a victim of looting by Alberto in company of the SiPo-SD, filed a complaint at the gendarmerie of La Turbie which fell on deaf ears. On February 23, 1945, he expressed his feelings in a letter to the public prosecutor in Marseille:

> … Almost one year has passed since Alberto committed this theft; he has not been arrested, he is still free, he even kept his job in the police even after the authorities were informed of his case…
>
> Alberto has admitted the facts. He pretends having informed his superiors who detached him to the Marseille Gestapo before and after the theft. It is incomprehensible that his superiors did not fire him…
>
> I do not know whether Alberto's statements have been verified and whether a search took place in his home; this search would have been fruitful, because the Gestapo was giving significant bonuses in kind, so that Alberto probably owns the objects stolen at my home… Alberto pretends that he could continue working for the Gestapo only if he provided value to them…
>
> I cannot understand why Alberto is still free 6 months later, while he has admitted the action. The size of the theft—a one million franc value—is surely not so small that the guilty person should not be punished.
>
> Possibly, Alberto has rendered services to France by his work as a spy inside the Gestapo… but is it proper that one individual only pay the cost?[47]

Georges Berg's intervention was no more than a small detour toward a dismissal of the charges.

The Economics of Evil

The Jewish trade organized by the Germans and their helpers in the Vaucluse yielded in 1943–1944 three times more Jews than the hunt by the prefecture in 1942.

---

* According to Dnker, Hans Senner was in fact a member of Berlin's SD Section IV, who had established a spy network under the cover of the German consulate, even before the occupation of the southern zone. His network was "recovered" by the Americans after the war.

To accomplish their various tasks—getting supplies of all kinds, searching for STO dodgers, tracking the Resistance, hunting the Jews, etc.— the Germans needed efficient, French speaking and unscrupulous personnel. In order to obtain better results, their choice went to the bosses and their soldiers in the underworld. After recruitment, the German "work permit" gave the gangsters official status along with the power it brought. It guaranteed impunity from the French police, which allowed them to erase past offenses and gave carte blanche for offenses to come.

An economy emerged that worked in a very simple way: the Germans paid, and paid, and paid. They paid comfortable, but not extravagant, salaries which were the basis of that economy. They paid bonuses in exchange for merchandise they coveted—an amount per head for Jews, a percentage for various supplies, or something in each case; they paid for incidental expenses. They also provided the work tools: Gestapo badges, cars, trucks and weapons.

Palmieri's case offers an exceptional window on the trading in Jews, a true market of crime. As long as the gangsters provided a reasonable "yield," black mail against the Jews was tolerated and even welcomed in some cases, since they were a "gold opportunity" which could satisfy everybody along the way. Moreover, Palmieri cared about his reputation as an "honest business-man." During the arrest of Danielle and Samuel Mossé, Danielle already knew probably through rumors that she could ask Palmieri to let them go "free on bail." This "trustworthy" purchase of freedom with cash was the guarantee of considerable future profits from new "customers."

From the German viewpoint, this economy had leaks. Its yield was far from 100%. However, without the prospects of raking in enormous amounts of money, the motivation of the gangsters would diminish and the yield would be even lower. The German police had a good understanding of the economy of the Jewish trade. As long as the yield was reasonable, they did not intervene. On the other hand, when their bosses in Marseille, Paris or Berlin became restless, one worked twice as hard... for a while, by bringing in helpers from Avignon, Marseille or elsewhere. And if the gangsters went too far, they were grounded for a time and lost their privileges.

The trade took on a determining role in the history of the deportation of the Vaucluse Jews under German presence. It hinged on the general condi- tions prevalent in the entire country. The shortages of German personnel grew as the front expanded and the military situation deteriorated. Generally, the French did not have much sympathy for the Germans, those "hereditary" enemies. The language barrier made the situation worse and the allied advances did not encourage much voluntary collaboration. Finally, and very importantly, the scattering of the Jews was not conducive to focused and efficient operations.

But there was a fundamental question which lingered at the end of Palmieri's story. What was the role of ideology in his criminal life? We must acknowledge the increasingly vocal anti-Semitism of the PPF, although it did not have a monopoly on it. The association of the local and national leaders of the party with the mob exploded throughout the documents of the various courts of justice, in Avignon, Nîmes, Marseille, and the military tribunals. These links often preceded the war. A similar scheme unfolded from the activity of the Paris mob under Henri Lafont's rule.[48] So much so that a question cannot be avoided: what was the dominant motivation, ideology or villainy?

Whatever the answer, the Germans had obviously been adept at using the bearers of a gangster ideology in the hunt for the Vaucluse Jews.

As to Palmieri, his last message was omitted from the minutes of his trial; fortunately, a reporter of *Rouge Midi** recorded it on May 23, 1946.

> The president of the court asks: "Palmieri, do you wish to add anything?" Palmieri approaches the witness stand; his face is convulsed; he is shaking. In his hand, he holds a sheet streaked with red markings. "I am not shaking because of fear; I am just angry…" In a fury, he calls cowards those whom he has helped in the past and who wouldn't testify in his favor. "I know I am going to die, but I don't care. I am going to name the men who are holding today resistance credential and higher functions, in spite of their collaboration with the occupier. I am going to read in front of you German documents I was able to steal in the offices of Luchaire, the former Vichy minister of Information… Maljean,[†] Barraud,[‡] Lemoine,[§] former prefects, have established lists of Jews to be arrested… I have never arrested French citizens… As to police superintendants Lefort, Novara, Aquilo, Creysonne, Etienne, I accuse them of having arrested Jews, exactly as I did." Notables from the Vaucluse and Alpes Maritimes are thus implicated. He takes to task the BST[§] and the officers of the second Bureau Bureau whom he calls cowards. "The only thing I did," Palmieri says, "was to collect Vichy's leftovers."

The arrest statistics of Palmieri's gang definitely contradict his assertion "I have never arrested French citizens…" But he is probably not making a legal argument, and is rather expressing his own view of the Jews as strangers in their own country—a common idea of his time.

---

* Communist newspaper in the south of France.
† Emile Maljean, prefect deputy of the Bouches du Rhône in 1944, was exonerated.
‡ Pierre Barraud, prefect deputy of the Bouches du Rhône in 1943, was exonerated.
§ Marcel Lemoine, regional prefect of the Bouches du Rhône in 1943, was exonerated.
§ Bureaux de la Surveillance du Territoire (Office of Territorial Surveillance).

France divided into zones of occupation and Vichy following the armistice of June 1940.

The Pétain-Hitler meeting at Montoire in 1940 inaugurated official collaboration between Vichy and Nazi Germany.

Pétain with local Avignon women in traditional costumes.

Heinrich Himmler, Reichsführer SS and head of the German police.

Reinhard Heydrich, Head of the RSHA Reich Security Main Office of the SS and SD and in overall command of the extermination operations.

Xavier Vallat, the first Commissioner of Jewish Affairs under Vichy.

Karl Oberg Chief of the German Police and SD in France (left) in conversation with Joseph Darnand, head of the Milice, July 1944.

Jacques Doriot leader of the PPF parades down the Champs Elysées in 1943.

Louis Darquier de Pellepoix, the second Commissioner of Jewish Affairs in 1942.

Pierre Laval who returned as prime minister in April 1942.

Adolf Eichmann, head of Amt IV B 4 of the SD in charge of Jewish affairs and the Final Solution.

Theodore Dannecker, SD officer and Adolf Eichmann's man in France from 1940 to July 1942.

German soldiers in front of the Palace of the Popes in Avignon.

Rolf Mühler head of SiPo-SD in the back row, behind René Bousquet, head of the Vichy police (in fur coat) and Marcel Lemoine regional prefect of Marseille in January 1943. The occasion was the destruction of the Vieux Port district.

Lufwaffe soldiers sightseeing at the Avignon medieval bridge.

Change of the guards at Hautpoul Barracks in Avignon.

German vehicles near the Palace of the Popes.

Avignon population lining up to buy food in 1944.

German OPA office in Avignon.

Public auction poster of the Goetschel property.

ENTREPRISE JUIVE

DIRECTION ASSURÉE PAR UN ADMINISTRATEUR PROVISOIRE ARYEN, nommé en application des lois du 10 Septembre 1940 et du 22 Juillet 1941.

Aryanization notice posted on the window of a store owned by Jews.

The French collaborators: Albert Marin.

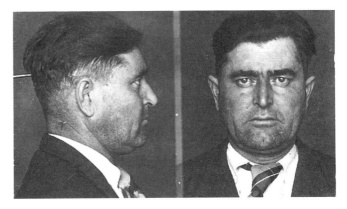

Alfred André.

Antoine Cappe.

Tiziano Feroldi.

Charles Palmieri.

Victor Palmieri.

Alfred Palmieri.

Baptiste Cabagno.

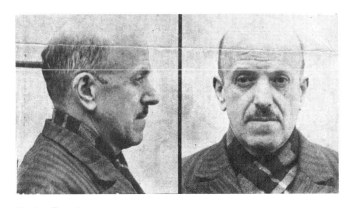

Marius Frezet.

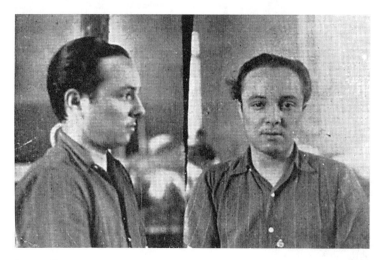

Pontarelli.

Queudane.

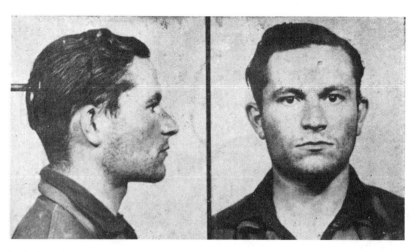

Louis Fournier.

Gaston Mouillade.

Victor Gaillard.

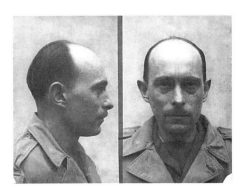

Yves Thesmar.

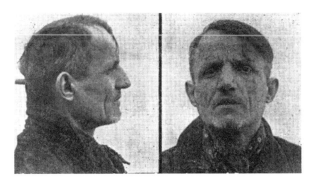

Joseph Allemand.

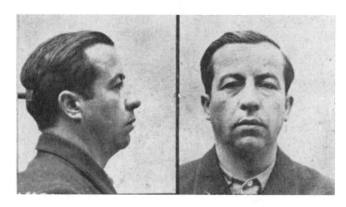

Charles Vincent.

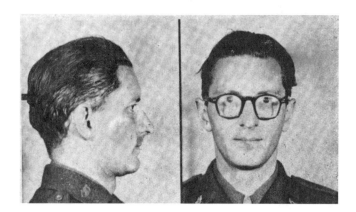

Rodolphe Bride.

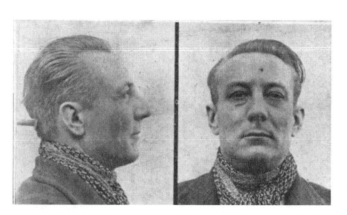

Deluermoz.

Part Three

Shades of Gray

Fifteen Cases

As we delve deeper into the court documents, the comforting thought of the righteous confronting evil to save as many Jews as possible no longer holds true.

Picking fifteen files at random is meant to focus our attention on cases which cannot be resolved unambiguously. At the same time the aim is to examine those cases that reflect the state of mind and thinking of a period that can't be painted in simplistic black and white. The past is filled with many shades of gray.

Those involved acted, often for the best or the worse, but they were not hardened criminals. However, their "moderation" does not make them "average Frenchmen," because anyone who took a position—in one direction or even in both directions—remained a minority. Although it is difficult to identify individual motivation in every case, it is clear that some key events played an important role in helping the ambiguities to come to the surface.

The arrival of the Germans in November 1942 created a break in the Pétainism of the southern zone. The prefecture, the government's listening post and official disseminator of information in the province, had clearly changed course. The progressive withdrawal and the often passive resistance of a number of its officials becomes clear. Of course this change accompanied—and probably contributed to guide—a drift in public opinion.

The French were massively hostile to the STO, and dodging it had become the norm. The perspective of leaving the area was often unthinkable, all the more so since it implied a lack of willingness to doge and hence an excessive alignment with the Germans. This pushed the population toward Gaullism and resistance—at least passive and at times active. The German military setbacks and the prospect of an allied victory accelerated this evolution. Armed resistance was becoming a symbol of national rallying, even for those who were not ready to do much of anything.

Parallel to this, covert information raised the public's awareness about anti-Semitic persecution which in turn motivated humanitarian feelings in some individuals.[1]

Jews were not saved exclusively by decent people. At times, a helping hand could be held out by cowards, by half-hearted individuals, by members of the administration, by accomplices, and in some cases, even by the most implacable oppressors.

Focusing on the details of the "black" period will unquestionably expose the ambiguous, the disconcerting, and the gray. We, humans have the stunning capacity of living at peace amid striking inconsistencies.

1.
Edmond Autran

E dmond Autran owned a vineyard in Sablet, and became mayor of the small town in 1934. He was a registered member of the Radical Socialist party, then lead by Edouard Daladier. After the armistice, he became a member of the Friends of the Legion. In 1941, he is maintained as head of the municipal council, and president of the Special Delegation. He resigned from that position in 1943, but remained a member of the Special Delegation until Liberation.[2]

At that time he had some trouble with the court of justice. In 1941, he had informed the Regional school inspector about the "attitude" of Mme. Bonfils, a teacher in Sablet. Such matters were not forgotten, and the Bonfils couple launch a complaint at the Liberation. Autran was accused of having collaborated with the Vichy government and the Germans.

In presenting the facts, the government commissioner found no political or even antinational goal, and added: "*No precise fact has been found to justify the claims of Mme. Bonfils. If one takes into account that the main accusations are made by a personal enemy of Autran, Bonfils, whose animosity went as far as denouncing a milicien who was hiding Jews, one is forced to admit that this is a purely local quarrel which should not find its epilogue before the court of justice.*" However, during this "purely local quarrel," nobody seems to be concerned by the Jews caught in the crossfire.

Two testimonies confirmed the help Autran provided to the Jews. In her letter of February 21, 1945, Hélène Valabrègue, who was registered on the census of the Jews of the Vaucluse, the daughter of Roger Valabrègue, president of the Jewish community before the war, writes:

> I, undersigned H. Valabrègue, widow of Sidi-Leon, domiciled 6, rue de la Croix in Avignon, certify that M. Autran, mayor of Sablet, helped make every-thing easier when I arrived in his municipality, both from the point of food supply and of lodging.

On April 11, 1943, while my parents had just been arrested by the Gestapo, I went to ask for help.

He promised to warn me in case some would come to arrest me, then, the next day, he strongly advised me to leave for the Savoie, because he thought I was not safe in Sablet, and he gave me the address of one of his friends who was a member of the Resistance; he told me to mention his name and that his friend would help.

I only have good things to say about all that Mr. Autran has done for me.

This behavior favorable to persecuted Jews is confirmed by J. Saias, who is not registered in the Jewish census, but his presence in Sablet was documented in the Terrier file[3] by the municipal secretary of the village, Henri Bastet. Saias was a doctor from Marseille who found refuge in the Vaucluse. His letter of January 14, 1945, to the wife of Edmond Autran, whose arrest he had just learned about, speaks very highly of the mayor of Sablet:

His humanity and liberalism became apparent on our first contact while fleeing form a despicable persecution, I was in the presence of a mayor full of understanding who did not stop comforting me by his attitude which went straight to my heart.

This pretty ordinary case which will be dismissed nevertheless triggers some reflection. Did Autran play a double game? Probably not, since there was no testimony in his favor from the Resistance. Perhaps, he was even a mild Pétain supporter? As a Friend of the Legion, he must indeed have been close to Vichy and its ideology. This is why, like many others, he was appointed president of the special delegation. But the man showed empathy toward Mme. Valabrègue and Dr. Saias.

However, like all the Vichy appointees, he transmitted the list of Jews in his village for the 1941 census, out of which the prefecture extracted the list of foreign Jews targeted for deportation on August 26, 1942. Armed with the list, the gendarmes in Sablet, arrested Brucha and Osias Tieder who were deported on convoys 33 and 30, and perished in Auschwitz. The court of justice did not show a particular interest in those foreign Jews, who, in the spirit of that period, were not "the Jews of the mayor."

But one episode remains unclear and turns things round. Bonfils denounces the mayor to a milicien "*because the mayor was hiding Jews.*" It is difficult to imagine more shades of gray.

2.
Edouard Badier

W ho was Dr. Badier, the president of the Apt* Legion?[4] The October 4, 1944, report by the FFI 2nd bureau (intelligence) states: *"In the Apt Legion meetings, he took a clearly collaborationist line. He has praised the policies of Pétain and Laval."* The report however stresses that *"according to his neighbors' opinion, he was pressed by his wife who never forgave his failure to be elected to parliament and saw in an all-out collaboration a way to achieve his ends."* Then, the report focuses on specific accusations: *"Badier refused to give several young men medical accommodation certificates so that they could avoid going to Germany; they had to ask Dr. Morizet. Badier had frequent conversations (about twice a week) with a PPF member, Lataste, executed in Cavaillon."*

In the exposition of the facts on May 23, 1945, the government commissioner was far more lenient to the doctor who was being held prisoner in Sorgues: *"The man named Badier is a right wing politician who is well known in Apt. He was president of the Legion. He is accused of having shown a certain inflexibility while examining young men summoned for the STO. Many certificates show the opposite. His case falls within the authority of the Medical Association and not the jurisdiction of the court of justice. Being that this inquiry against Edouard Badier domiciled in Apt, did not yield sufficient charges to the effect that he committed the crimes he is accused of, we declare that it is appropriate to drop the charges, except that the file could be reopened in case new charges come up."*

During his interrogation on May 11, 1945, we find out that Badier belonged to the Croix de Feu group,† that in 1936 he was a candidate to the parliament as an independent Radical Socialist, then that he was a member of the special delegation in Apt from 1941 to August 1944, and that he did not belong to any anti-national group.

Badier defended his role simply:

> When the STO was created, I thought that the goal was to replace with young people the French [soldiers] who had been prisoners of war for three years. I thought it was my duty as a doctor to deliver no accommodation certificates, but over time, when I realized that the "relief" ended up providing young people without bringing back prisoners, every time I was asked I provided medical certificates where I did not hesitate to give false information. I provided certificates to help people elude the departure to Germany. Moreover, this got me arrested on January 8, 1944, by the Germans who kept me at Ste Anne

---

* Apt is a small town in northeast Vaucluse.
† Between the two wars, the Croix de Feu (Cross of Fire) was a far right group, led by Colonel de la Rocque. It was dissolved in 1936, and its members were absorbed into other far right organizations.

prison for three days and released me as a result of the intervention of the prefecture and the Medical Association.

He specified that he had seen Lataste only twice in his entire life.

The first time, he came to Apt to thank me for the medical care I had provided to a relative of his and the second time to ask me to become a member of the PPF. I politely refused.

A man named Douillet, honorary university professor and award-winner of the Académie Française, provided a grand-sounding defense. He writes an emphatic private letter addressed to Prefect Charvet, whose past credentials as inspector of the Académie he does not forget to underscore; in the name of culture and ethics, he asks to spare *"this World War I veteran, Knight of the Legion of Honor… who did not mean any harm, if he made some mistakes and if they are real."*

But it is the letter from Sylvain Grumbacher to Dr. Badier which goes to the heart of the matter. Grumbacher was a 35-year-old Jewish refugee from Mulhouse, listed in the Apt census from 1941 to 1944. He was registered as an accountant when he was discharged from the military in 1941. On September 10, 1944, he wrote:

Dear Doctor,

It is with great sadness that I learned the predicament in which you have been during the last few days. I want to express my testimony by taking part in your tragic situation. I would be happy to reciprocate as a mark of gratitude for the kind help you gave me, during the perilous days spent in Apt, in May, when you offered asylum in your home to a hunted Jewish refugee.

I will not fail to mention the conscientious thoughtfulness you have demonstrated while caring for my ailing mother, and for other refugees.

I will be entirely at your disposal, should you need me to demonstrate my gratitude in any way I possibly can.

Dear Doctor, please accept the expression of my deepest devotion.

Welcoming a Jew in his own house was not a simple thing to do. And yet, this former member of "Croix de Feu," an informer of de Camaret's network, did do so. Let us however notice that Grumbacher was not really hidden, since he had been listed in the census.

3.
Louis Boyer

Louis Boyer's case brings us closer into the eye of the storm, even if the charges against him were to be dismissed.[5] The owner of a grocery store on place du Cloître St. Pierre in Avignon was a regular of bar Carnot. In the food business since August 1943, he had practiced several trades: construction worker, driver, bar manager, and notably of the Brasserie du Sporting in rue Bancasse.

He was engaged in trafficking. According the exposition of the facts, "*he is suspected of having had questionable relations with agents of the Gestapo; however, he did not seem to belong to that organization, although he benefited once—he claims against his will—from the influence of Georges Parietas, aka Boyer, when he was caught red-handed on the black market. He cannot be charged with any specific activity susceptible to damage the external security of the state.*"

Costa, a Gestapo agent, very active in the persecution of the Jews and talkative about his own misdeeds, provided more concrete facts:

> I met Louis Boyer at the bar Carnot, where he was a regular until mid-March 1944. I presume that he was involved in the resale of merchandise stolen from Jewish merchants during the break-ins, with the participation of Victor Bruni and Raphael Duble. I saw them several times at the bar Carnot. They were having a drink in company of Gestapo agents, like Roger Boyer [Boyer from Mondragon] and Alfred André. Louis Boyer took part in the theft of cigarettes at the Avignon railway station. He was arrested afterwards, but I do not know the disposition of that case. I cannot tell you whether Louis Boyer had his case dismissed through the protection of the Gestapo.

During his audition of February 3, 1945, while he was detained at the Avignon railway station, Louis Boyer limited his role to the sale of butter on the black market.

> In June 1944, I received a summons for the seizure of 8.850 kg of butter that I was about to liquidate on the black market. On that day, the gendarmes had just done a search in my apartment in my presence. As I was returning to rue Bancasse where I live, I was hailed by Georges Boyer [*aka* Parietas] in front of the bar Carnot. Boyer asked "What's happening to you?" I answered "It's because of a small amount of butter; leave it alone!" Boyer insisted and told the gendarmes "I belong to the German police, and this butter belongs to me." Following this intervention, the gendarmes took me to the gendarmerie where I was released almost immediately. On the same evening, I met Georges Boyer again at the bar Carnot. He did not speak to me, and I did not speak to him. Later, I saw him several times at the same bar without ever starting a conversation with him, because I knew him only by sight...

Georges Boyer is heard on the same day as Louis Boyer, but it is only in his statement given at the prisons of Les Baumettes on March 17, 1945, that he mentions he knew Louis Boyer and that they went together for a drink at the bar Carnot after his intervention.

> [Louis] Boyer did not seem to approve my intervention. He even told me "Will this not harm me after the war?" I told him that, since he had never worked for the Germans or the French members of the Gestapo, he should have nothing to fear and that it would be easy to prove his good faith in any case.

Did Louis Boyer limit himself to the profit he derived from the black market of the cigarette thefts? Did he dump the merchandise stolen from the Jews on the black market, as Costa had claimed? He could have made far more money, had he entered the active service of the rue Bancasse gangsters, instead of just having occasional drinks with them. Apparently, he was not seduced by the appeal of the hunt for the Jews. Did he prefer sitting on the fence?

The Idzkowski couple (the managers of the bar Carnot) spared him and reduced his role to that of a bistro clown. Marcel Idzkowski went even further in his statement of October 5, 1944:

> I, undersigned Marcel Idzkowski, certify that M. Louis Boyer came to know my whereabouts when I was hiding a few kilometers away from Avignon. If he had belonged to an anti-French organization, he could have denounced me since he suspected me of being an Israelite. I have already stated that I had mostly met Mr. Louis Boyer at the bar Carnot where his conduct did not raise any suspicion.

In her written statement of October 6, 1944, Marie Riz, the owner of the restaurant Le Coq Hardi in rue Bancasse, mentions that Louis Boyer could have easily caused harm to her.

> I, undersigned Marie Riz, state that I know Mr. Louis Boyer as a regular in my restaurant. He knew where I was hiding to elude the Gestapo and he never did anything against me.

We find the same spirit and even more on the part of Isaac Pinto, domiciled 3, rue Grande Fusterie in Avignon, who appears in the census of 1941.

> I, undersigned Isaac Pinto, am keen to add to my previous declaration that:
> 1- Mr. Louis Boyer who knew I was hiding in Livron to elude the Gestapo transferred food for me every week through a member of my

family. This food supply was transiting through Mme. Passalacqua, domiciled at 4, rue Grande Fusterie, who is also testifying.

2- One day, I called Mr. Louis Boyer on the phone at the bar Carnot. According to Mr. Boyer, a member of the Gestapo enjoined him, at the end of the phone call, to provide the location of my hiding place. He refused to do so.

This is bordering on an act of bravery. Was he then a friend of the Jews or did he simply have ties with some of them?

4.
Augustin Brémond

The Cavaillon purge committee, more precisely its political section, called him a collaborator in its note of January 29, 1945. He was accused of being on friendly terms with Kesleim, an interpreter at the Cavaillon Kommandantur. He was said to have stated at a barbershop that "*all those who helped young people join the Maquis were bandits.*"

Augustin Brémond, 51 years old, a fabric merchant in Cavaillon, must have been in deep trouble before the report of the inspector of the Sureté Nationale of February 3, 1945, softened the infamy hovering over his head.

Augustin Brémond is jailed because of his talk against the Maquis and his collaborationist opinions…

He has never lived anywhere else but Cavaillon. In 1943, he resigned from the Cavaillon municipality where he had been appointed by the government. Brémond denies having expressed himself against the Maquis. He claims having only said: "If the young people do not leave for Germany, the Germans are capable of sending the older ones." As for the collaborationist opinions attributed to him, he denies them again, claiming that he opposed the Germans by refusing the requisition of his apartment building, and instead making it available to bombing victims; he also provided a safe haven to four Israelite families.

Sought by the Legion, Brémond refused to take over the presidency he was offered at the head of the movement. There is no doubt that the accusations against Brémond are of such a little weight, and if the accusations are in any way justified, they are largely dominated by the importance of the help he provided to the four Jewish families. His resignation from the municipality in May 1943 and his refusal to accept the presidency of the Legion make him a very poor collaborator.[6]

Indeed, those Jews would not forget the help they were given. On September 8, 1944, Maurice Szczercowski wrote to the public prosecutor at the Avignon court.

> I, undersigned Maurice Szczercowski, Faubourg Tour Neuve, am honored to inform you that, after learning about the arrest of Mr. Augustin Brémond,... for reasons unknown to him, I feel compelled to bring to your attention the following facts in his favor.
>
> While the undersigned was being urgently sought (as an Israelite) by the Gestapo and had also imperatively been summoned to work on fortifications in Germany, he was able to avoid this trouble thanks to the voluntary intervention of Mr. A. Brémond, who did not hesitate to take the heavy responsibility to hide the undersigned in one of his buildings in Faubourg Terre Neuve. In addition, he did provide other help, food supplies, visits, etc.
>
> Thanks to this efficient and unselfish help, he was able to elude, during eight months until Liberation, the searches he was subjected to.
>
> It is in gratitude for this tremendous help that the undersigned wishes to testify on his behalf and seeks all your indulgence.

Henri Goldstein testified on September 27, 1944. He is probably related to Perla Goldstein, on the 1944 Cavaillon census of foreign Jews.

> I, undersigned Henri Goldstein, domiciled 27, rue Lamartine in Cavaillon, declare that Mr. A Brémond lent me a gas stove when I arrived in Cavaillon as a refugee. I kept this stove for one and a half year, and he refused to accept any payment. He told me that I should come and see him if I needed anything.

A man named Benveniste (not registered in the census), domiciled 46, rue de la Cannebière in Marseille provide an affidavit on September 28, 1944.

> Monsieur,
>
> About to leave Cavaillon, I want to reiterate my thanks and I will never forget your kindness and welcome to my very large family. Moreover, your help during their settling in and above all the fact that you did not declare them (this could have cut their stay short) contributed enormously to easing their shelter.
>
> I must add that I felt more confident when I learned that one of your sons was an [STO] dodger. We thus stood behind each other before the German.
>
> I do hope that the coincidences of life will soon provide an opportunity for us to return to Cavaillon and enjoy the pleasure of meeting you.

Finally, Mme. Adlerstein provides an affidavit on October 4, 1944. Four members of her family were registered in the 1944 foreign Jews census, as domiciled in Cavaillon.

> I, undersigned Mme. Adlerstein, state that Mr. A. Brémond volunteered to hide my son at his own brother's home when I was being hunted as an Israelite.

In the end, was Augustin Brémond a victim of the fiery zeal of last-minute members of the Resistance or a real collaborator? In any case, he was more than a good man with the Jews.

5.
Lucien Carrel

This is sheer misfortune. If the milicien Albert Marin, an occasional persecutor of Jews and a lieutenant of Thesmar, had not been a customer of Lucien Carrel, a barber in Avignon, domiciled at Place Jérusalem, Carrel would probably not have rejoined the ranks of the Milice. He justified himself during his interrogation of March 10, 1945.

> I had been summoned several times for the STO in Germany. Since I was really troubled by it, I opened up to one of my customers, named Marin who answered "Do not worry, I will fix it." He took my summons, and later he made me sign a paper. Since I do not know how to read and write, I did not understand immediately; later on, however, I understood that I had signed my enrollment in the Milice.[7]

Of course, rather than blindly trusting a bastard like Marin, he could have become a dodger and even joined the Maquis. But what did he know about it? Was he aware of the dodger networks, but was he ready to go the distance? Moreover, not everyone is cut out to become a member of the Resistance.

The fact remains, that he finds himself in uniform at the Lycée Mistral where miliciens are stationed. The exposition of the facts tells us that:

> … at the end of June 1944, he left with an expedition of the Milice to Clermont-Ferrand, still as a barber, then disgusted, he deserted. Carrel seems to have joined the Milice not out of an ideal, but to avoid being sent to Germany. While he was a milicien, he did hide in his home a family of Jews, the Leimans [it

should read Lehman] and had the archives and the relics of the synagogue for safekeeping.

Because of his time at the Milice, he was sentenced to a jail sentence of 10 months for intelligence with the enemy. In 1953, the state prosecutor deemed Carrel eligible for the benefit of Article 4 of the amnesty law of August 6. He reiterated that his membership in the Milice was susceptible to spare him the STO; he also stressed that Carrel did not participate in any operation and even deserted.

At his audition of January 23, 1945, Carrel gives more details.

> During the persecution of the Jews, I hid in my home a family of Israelites named Lehman during a month and a half from May to June [1944]. I have also hidden in my home the archives and the synagogue relics which had been entrusted to me by the caretaker, Miss Blanche.

Who was "Miss Blanche"? The "Miss Blanche" in question was really Blanche Amoyel, née Lisbonne, and listed in the census of the Jews. The Amoyels are an old Jewish family of Avignon. Blanche Amoyel would return to her post as synagogue caretaker at the Liberation.

Carrel's barbershop is situated a few yards away from the synagogue. They surely met frequently and had known each other for a long time. So Blanche Amoyel entrusted him with the religious objects. We realize that her choice was very effective when we read the declaration of David Fresco on April 5, 1945:

> During the occupation, I left Avignon for a hiding place and when I came back, the caretaker told me that the religious books and silver objects had been hidden by the man named Lucien Carrel, barber at Place Jérusalem. All these objects were returned to the synagogue as soon as the Germans left.

In his audition, David Fresco is introduced as the rabbi of the synagogue, whereas he is in fact the officiating minister. Fresco does not know about the Lehman family. But the Lehmans were registered in the census at 54, rue Thiers in Avignon. Moïse Lehman's name is etched as a "deportee and member of the Resistance who died for France" on the commemoration plate at city hall. Moïse was arrested in Buis les Baronnies and deported on convoy 76 from Drancy to Auschwitz.

One can imagine that if Lucien Carrel had not been illiterate, only his remarkable conduct would have remained, without the stain of his Milice adhesion that even the 1953 amnesty could not wash away. But it is also in the realm of possibilities that he walked a delicate path in his defense and that his argument was not sincere.

6.
Fernand Chamond

His file suggests that this man had switched camps. Born in Grenoble in 1905, Fernand Chamond became an electrical engineer. In 1928, he landed a job at "Sud Electrique" in Avignon. With the war he was mobilized as a second lieutenant in the 22nd Colonial Artillery Regiment. After the armistice, he joined the Legion and belonged to the SOL since its creation. Rapidly, he climbed the ladder: chief of "thirty," then chief of a "hundred." He paraded in uniform during Pétain's visit to Avignon.

During his interrogation on April 7, 1945, Chamond declared:

> ... I left Avignon on March 14, 1943. From that date, I indeed worked as an engineer at the electrical public service of Marseille (38 bis, avenue de Toulon). I left Marseille on November 1, 1943, and was assigned to Grenoble where I have been residing since then.[8]

In his interrogation on May 15, 1945, Chamond denies having belonged to the Milice: "I was chief of a *"hundred"* at the *SOL, but I returned my stripes* [resigned] *in February 1943. I have never been a milicien and I did not receive any summons from that group in 1943 and 1944.*" The presentation of the facts is less categorical: "*He was automatically transferred into the Milice and demoted to the rank of a simple milicien because of his lack of enthusiasm. He claims to have resigned twice in 1943.*" The public prosecutor noted that when he left Avignon "*his political activity was insignificant.*"

His departure which coincides with the creation of the Milice, suggests that he had likely taken advantage of it to distance himself politically. Anyway, the court of justice mentioned that he had rehabilitated himself after the actions he was charged with. Through a friend of his, he was able to provide members of the Resistance with public servant badges.

During his interrogation, Chamond underscored:

> I am currently drafted by the military government in Lyon after being assigned to the commander of the Anti-aircraft Ground Forces of the 27th alpine division. I am providing the transfer document dated May 7, 1945, ordering me to immediately return to my unit.

At the end of the war, he was on the right side.

But, his Avignon period is particularly interesting, since he mentions his relations with some Avignon Jews in the declaration he wrote in Grenoble on February 27, 1945.

> Mr. Zarade, an Israelite merchant, the owner of two stores in Avignon ("Lydie" and "Jean Claude") where an administrator is substituted to the owner by Vichy. I used to meet him on a daily basis and kept him informed about the anti-Jewish machinations. I have been able to provide him with useful information, since he was already gone 48 hours before his planned arrest. I do not know his whereabouts at the moment.

Information about the Zarades is available: they were registered in the census with several relatives from Dunkerque who joined them during the occupation. Chamond continues:

> Mr. Moïse—his family name is too difficult to pronounce and remember, he was known and usually called by his first name, a stallholder, domiciled rue Four de la Terre; I was personally giving him information about the anti-Semitic activities taking place in the streets of Avignon. In April 1944, he was not bothered.

This statement raises a few questions. Although Moïse is the first name of several Avignon stallholders, it is probably Moïse Asmanoff who lived near rue Four de la Terre. When Chamond mentions "anti-Semitic activities," is he referring to the dispossession of the Jews or to the threats of arrest? Moreover, he does not say how he knows that Moïse was not bothered in April 1944 since he had already moved to Marseille by that time. Did he keep a connection and had he advised him to flee? He then cites another Jew:

> Mr. Charles Kestenberg came to see me at my home and shared his worries. I gave him my support. I held him in high regard since he had participated in the 1939–1940 war in the foreign legion. He took refuge in my brother's home where his brother-in-law and sister in-law were already hidden (Villa "Mon Repos," in Uriage) in the company of other hunted Jews...

In the 1944 census of foreign Jews, we found the presence of Izyk Kestenberg. This is possibly the same person, if one takes into account that many foreign Jews did use French first names.

The absence of testimony by those who benefited from Chamond's help does not allow positive confirmation of his statement, but it is quite apparent that this chief of a "hundred" of the SOL was not an anti-Semite.

7.
Victor Chanoux

D escribed as the president of the Cavaillon SOL, chief of "thirty" in the Milice and a member of the PPF, Victor Chanoux was convicted of collaboration with the Germans and received a six year prison sentence on November 23, 1944. His name was proposed to de Camaret by d'Oléon as a possible administrator of Jewish assets.[9]

At first glance, this 33-year-old manufacturer was clearly a collaborator. But did he hold firm political beliefs? He claimed having resigned from the SOL on December 20, 1942, and never having been a member of the Milice. This is plausible since members of the Legion and the SOL were automatically moved to the Milice when it was created in 1943. He admits having paid dues to the PPF but denies having been a member. He paid the dues at the request of one of his employees as "he paid a lot of dues for various associations." Indeed, his file does not show any marked serious commitment to Doriot's views.

It is difficult to figure out this busy man who gets rid of intruders by putting his hand in his pocket. The same may be said for his presence at the founding meeting of the Milice. He attended "only out of curiosity."

Chanoux has a gift for slipping through our fingers, but he is not necessarily lying. He recognizes having paraded wearing a khaki shirt and a Legion armband during Pétain's visit, and his employees praised his consideration for his employees, even those belonging to the Communist party. They add that Chanoux was welcoming STO dodgers and hired them even if he did not need them, just to prevent them from being taken to Germany. This statement follows an article in "Cavaillon Libre" of September 13, 1944, claiming that the personnel of the Chanoux enterprise was in complete support of the PPF.

But, the statement by Guy Cupfer (at times written Kupfer) on October 14, 1944, is most provoking. A former attorney at the Paris court of appeals and an expert in Cavaillon, listed in the 1944 census of the Jews, Cupfer provides a flattering portrait of Chanoux.

During 1942, Mr. Victor Chanoux who had sought my advice about legal questions warned me that a list of suspects had been established during a meeting of the Legion. Mr. Chanoux stated that he did not pay attention to the list until he heard that I was considered as the head of Gaullist propaganda in Cavaillon.

Since he knew I was Jewish, he advised me to be on guard. In November 1943, Mr. Chanoux who was a member of the special delegation of Cavaillon came one evening at about 7 p.m. to warn me that he had heard accidentally that a roundup of Jews was about to take place in Cavaillon during the night and he suggested that I leave my home immediately. He specified that three people were in the know: himself, Mr. Roche, the Cavaillon police Superintendent, and Mr. Dame, president of the Cavaillon special delegation. I used this information to warn other people in my situation who were able to elude the Gestapo…

Since I was hiding close to Cavaillon, I was able to meet Mr. Chanoux who spontaneously proposed to take advantage of his interim Superintendant function to get an ID card without the stamp "Jew."

Cupfer who was called to testify on November 23, 1944, was present at the hearing. He reiterated that the roundup in question actually took place a few days later and that 13 people were arrested.

Clearly Cupfer was not the only one who benefited from the kindness of the accused. Chanoux added "*Among other Israelites, I hired and hid Judith Siliava who being was sought.*" A Jewish refugee bearing this name was indeed listed in the Cavaillon census.

8.
Emile Estachy

Emile Estachy, a 65-year-old surgeon at the Cavaillon hospital, seemed to display a good sense of timing when he published his travel impressions of Germany in 1940 in *Le Petit Vauclusien*, a newspaper he labels as being "national socialist" because of a marked sympathy for Jacques Doriot. On September 4, 1944, he stated:

I went to Germany in 1899 when I was 19, since I had a pen pal from school, and in 1937, I spent the month of August in Fribourg… Concerning the national socialist newspaper *Le Petit Vauclusien*, I recognize having published in 1940 two articles about my trip in Germany. Those articles were reprints of articles previously published in medical journals. I am the one who signed the articles. I also wrote a third article, exclusively philosophical about the doctrines of Fichte and Nietzsche. I firmly state that I have never been remunerated for the aforementioned articles, and that I never wrote a word in favor of collaboration in those articles.

His defense becomes more specific when he states:

> I should mention that I have always demonstrated a good attitude toward people detained or sought by the Gestapo. For instance, I provided a false certificate which was used to liberate Mr. Margulius from Nexon;* he will be able to confirm it. I also took in Mr. Marton, an Israelite at the moment of a roundup by the Gestapo.[10]

In his October 5, 1944, interrogation, he added another name, Mr. Lemmel. All were registered as foreign Jews, and Herman Margulius, who should have suffered the same fate as the Jews arrested by the prefecture in August 1942, was able to survive. As to Alfred Marton, he was deported to Auschwitz on convoy 64 on July 12, 1943. Estachy claims he has the copies of 19 medical certificates he delivered. Two of them concern two Jews, Mr. Cukier and Mr. Pulvermacher – two names we recognize.

It is difficult to understand how this case was thrown out of court, while in the eyes of public opinion of that period the interest for Germany and its philosophers was undoubtedly connected to the fascination for its daemons. Emile Eustachy does not seem to take into account that the Nazis had taken the reins of power, and that when he writes his articles, France is under their heel.

9.
Henri Guillerault

The man named Guillerault was a milicien. His rank was equivalent to that of a captain. Miliciens, Gestapo agents and Germans used to visit his home. On May 18, 1944, he does not hesitate to open fire on young members of the Resistance until the magazine of his submachine gun was empty. Guillerault, who attended the school for officers of the Milice, was also a member of the PPF.[11]

Sentenced to death on July 6, 1945, Guillerault owes his life to the decree enacted by the Provisional Government President, Charles de Gaulle, on August 1, 1945, commuting some death sentences to forced labor for life.

His active participation in operations against the Maquis was clearly established. He personally provided the names of miliciens, who attacked the

---

* French concentration camp in the *département* of Haute-Vienne.

Maquis Suzette, in collaboration with the GMR Comtat.* According to the witness Casimir Biscarat interrogated by the Vaison brigade on March 13, 1945, while Guillerault was on the run, *"He was chief of thirty, and after an internship in Savoie,† he was promoted to chief of hundred... The Heads of the Gestapo and of the Kommandantur were visiting his home."*

"His home" meant his "family home in Séguret," an inn belonging to his wife. He had met his future wife, a young war widow, in that boarding house where he had come to convalesce after a serious illness.

Guillerault's probably had a troubled childhood. Born in Marseille, he was the child of an unknown father. He was 6 years old when his mother died in 1919 and he was put up for adoption, and became a boarder in several schools before being taken in by his maternal grandparents. At a young age, he developed a strong liking for literature and with two friends, he launches "l'Académie de l'Art des Jeunes" (Academia of Arts for Youth). His file does not go beyond that and his political ideology remained unknown.

Later, he became an advocacy journalist in the collaborationist press; he worked as a reporter for *Le Ventoux*, and was sought as a freelancer at *Le Petit Marseillais, Marseille Libre. Sud Magazine, Alpes et Midi*, and finally at *L'Emancipation Nationale*, the mouthpiece of the PPF.

He knew Doriot personally, since his "family home" has been honored by his visit on April 9, 1939—a sign that Guillerault is not a newcomer to the PPF. The purge committee of Seguret kept an updated list of the VIPs who made a point of stopping at his inn:

Joseph Delest	Manager of the newspaper *l'Action Française*
Henri Lèbre (an alias for F. D. Auture)	Translator of excerpts of Adolf Hitler's *Mein Kampf* under the title *Ma Doctrine*
François Robin	Columnist at Gringoire
Henri Barbe	General secretary of the PPF, reporter
General Gaston	General Aviation Secretary in the Pétain-Laval government—1943
A. Brunet	General Governor of the Colonies, collaborator of Prime Minister Léon Bourgeois

But things didn't last, and at Liberation, Guillerault joined the ranks of fugitives. On August 19, 1944, he left for Lyon in the trucks of the Milice. Guillerault and a few others decided to stay in that city. In the hearing notes

---

* The GMR Comtat (a name reminiscent of the old Comtat Venaissin) is a unit of the GMR stationed in Avignon.
† This is "l'Ecole des Cadres d'Uriage" closed in December 1942 and replaced by "l'Ecole des Cadres de la Milice Française" in the same location

of July 6, 1945, he says: "*I was put on a truck like the other miliciens for the departure to Germany, but I was able to slip away from my group in Lyon. I went to a comrade belonging to the Resistance; I participated with him in the liberation of Lyon and took part in the fighting. I stayed for a while in Lyon, and then I left for Marseille where I enlisted in the* [foreign] *legion. That is when I was arrested.*"

This sudden but real U-turn is insufficient to impress the court of justice. However, if we want to assess the "Jewish dimension" of the file, it is necessary to slightly go back in time. While Guillerault is on the run, his wife is also targeted. A letter from the prefecture to the government commissioner accuses her on October 7, 1944, of being an active collaborator of her husband and proposes a penalty of one year in prison and national degradation. It is now appropriate to read the request of Maurice Weil "*to M. Captain Grangeon about the arrest of Mme. Gullerault from Séguret.*"

> It is upon the recommendation of Captain Rique from Orange that I am writing to you to explain the following facts which I described in detail this morning at your office in the Gendarmerie in Vaison.
>
> First, let me mention that I am a 1914–1918 war veteran, Military Cross and Verdun medal, a refugee in Orange since June 1940 and incapable, as an Israelite, of returning to my home in Paris.
>
> In Orange, I can provide references confirming that my action has been among those that you approve of.
>
> I was a friend of Mr. Benaroya of "Paris—Lainage," of Mr. Colion, etc… whom you can question. I am mentioning them to assure you that if I intercede today on behalf of Mme. Guillerault, it is not out of sympathy for miliciens' actions, but to fulfill what I believe to be my duty as a human being.
>
> On about April 15 I was told that the Gestapo was seeking my family and me. I immediately took an obvious measure, namely I left my home at 15, avenue de l'Arc in Orange.
>
> I looked for a refuge in St. Cécile, in Uchaux, etc., to no avail, and finally, someone suggested Séguret. I arrived at the "Auberge en Montagne" in Séguret, I gave the pretext of the poor health of my eldest daughter. But two or three days later, I learned that Guillerault belonged to the Milice.
>
> My wife and I, discussed what our behavior should be because we were afraid. And we decided to speak about it with Mme. Guillerault who was alone, since her husband was away from home. Without hesitation, Mme. Guillerault, to whom we confessed we were Jewish, replied that we could stay without fear and that our hotel registration would not be transmitted.
>
> On the next day, Mr. Guillerault returned and confirmed that he indeed was a milicien, but that he was taking us under his protection and that nothing would happen to us as long as we were in his home!
>
> In the mean time, the Gestapo came three times to Orange to arrest us.

On June 6, as soon as the allies landing became known, the hotel had to be closed since Mr. Guillerault was called to Avignon and would no longer be able to provide food.

On that day, my wife and I, as well as others, did whatever we could to convince Mme. Guillerault not to leave for Avignon; his wife had begged him to leave the Milice and flee with her, but alas, without success!

My wife, my two daughters and I, were again on the street and exposed to the reach of the Gestapo. At that moment, Mme. Guillerault told us to stay, and to keep our rooms; she made the dining room available to us, she had a stove installed so we were able to cook safely.

In one word, she saved our lives and what she did must be told; this must be brought to full light in order to counterbalance the accusation hanging over her head.

I am therefore asking you to return a mother to her 10 year old son and to her pregnant daughter; above all, I am asking you to take my deposition into consideration so that justice can be rendered truly "à la française"

Maurice Weil
September 3, 1944
L'Auberge en Montagne
Séguret (Vaucluse)

The Weil family, originally from Paris, is listed in the Orange census of the Jews.

Maurice Weil is grateful to Mme. Guillerault, but her husband did better than agreeing to his wife's proposal: he offered his protection. Was he debating a problem of conscience, or was he thinking about the near future when he was making his offer? In any case, he brought it up in his statement on June 21, 1945.

And what if this man—who had also been a member of the informers' network of de Camaret—had just obeyed a code of honor of his own? Although it is often difficult to separate personal interest from more honorable motivations, do the actions of Guillerault, seemingly in contradiction with each other, not make him all the more human?

10.
Antoine Guisset

His actions did not match his ideas. Although Antoine Guisset, 34 years old from Avignon, belonged to the SOL and the Milice, he did not do much, and if he acted, it was not as expected. An excerpt of the CDL deliberation of September 24, 1944, discusses his case:

A milicien—did resign more than one year ago—did help the Resistance considerably—hired an accountant aide arrested for Gaullist propaganda—has taken in the wife and child of an Israelite and safeguarded a stock of merchandise belonging to them.[12]

At the hearing of October 13, 1944, Pierre Godefroy, the accountant in question, confirms:

> Hired by M. Guisset, I knew he was a milicien and I fought his opinions. He helped me when I was hunted down because I was on the side of the Resistance. He destroyed documents which could have harmed me, if the Germans had found them.

As to Berthe Cécile Freiberg, née Szafrajzen, registered in the census of the Jews, her testimony strengthens the CDL's opinion.

> My husband and I, are Jews. Mr. Guisset was helpful to us. He used to warn us so that we can hide when there was a roundup. When we left, he took us in and kept our merchandise in his home. He moved us at night together with Mr. Godefroy. On my return, I found the merchandise which would certainly have disappeared if they had remained at my home which was looted.

Guisset received a two year suspended sentence, rather as a matter of form. But something else stands out in this file. In her deposition, Cécile Freiberg does not mention the arrest of her husband, Jacques Freiberg, who was deported on convoy 73. Probably, she still hoped to see him alive, but he would not return from Auschwitz. The help of the milicien was not sufficient to spare him.

11.
Alfred Hentzen

The war brought this student in literature from the University of Nancy to the Vaucluse. Enlisted in 1939, Alfred Hentzen was appointed, at the armistice, as the chief of a group of discharged soldiers in Piolenc.[13]

Having become a member of the Legion, in 1942, Hentzen joined the SOL and in 1943, the Milice, becoming département secretary in June of the same year. At the time, he was therefore the direct subordinate of Bonnefoy, the doctor in Sorgues and boss of the Milice, who would later enroll in the Waffen-SS.

What were the inner thoughts of Hentzen about the horrors of the time? His file provides some ambiguous indications. In 1943, he resigned from the Milice. In his defense, he explained this decision in a report dated September 10, 1944:

> I had not joined the Milice to denounce, arrest and assassinate French people. That is the reason why I resigned.

But in his resignation letter uncovered in a moving box, his decision seemed to be driven by his desire to bring harmony to his family; a reason which is picked up by the government commissioner. Hentzen wrote to his boss:

> … Nevertheless, since I had been pressured to promise my wife that I had given a complete resignation, I would ask you to call me at a phone number which I will provide, in case you need to summon me.

Was it a ruse designed to avoid problems with his former boss? One could think so, if we take at face value his statement during his interrogation on October 14, 1944.

> I belonged to the Milice from February 1943 to November 1943. In June 1943, I accepted the position of département secretary, since I had lost my job; I was making 3,500 francs per month. Since my resignation, I did not have any relations with that organization. At some point, I even had to hide because the Milice was seeking me to incorporate me into the Franc Garde*.

But this was not a key issue. Hentzen was an important officer in the Milice, even if he did not participate in operations against the Resistance. For that, he was sentenced on March 8, 1945, to 10 years in prison and 20 year ban from residing in the Vaucluse. His sentence was reduced to 5 years in prison by a decree of September 17, 1945.

His role in the Arokas case is particularly interesting. On November 21, 1944, Marthe Angel, née Arokas, domiciled in Avignon and registered in the census, gave a statement:

> My father, my mother, my sister and my husband were arrested as Israelites in July 1943. I took steps to try and free them, and through a connection with a Marseille friend, I obtained a letter of introduction for Mr. Bonnefoy, chief of

---

* Free Guard, the armed branch of the Milice.

the Vaucluse Milice. I arrived at the headquarters of the Milice where I was greeted by Mr. Bonnefoy who promised to do his best to try and free my relatives. The next day, or perhaps two days later, I returned to the Milice headquarters where I saw Mr. Hentzen. He was alone in his office. He shared his surprise with me about Mr. Bonnefoy's promise, and added that nothing could be done, given who my relatives where. I returned a third time to see Dr. Bonnefoy who simply kicked me out. It is probably during that third visit that he said: "For the Jews, no mercy!"

The testimony of Edmond Gabet (the last name is probably Gabay or Gabai) modifies somewhat the memory of his cousin Marthe, but most of all, he gives a different picture of Hentzen:

I have met Mr. Hentzen when we were both working at the Anglès Company, and I have always maintained excellent friendly relations with him. At some point, my relative, Mme. Angel, née Arokas, who knew my relationship with Hentzen and his position in the Milice, asked me to intervene in order to free her father, mother, brother and sister, arrested a few days earlier by the Gestapo and incarcerated at St. Anne. Indeed, my cousin went to the Milice headquarters, where Hentzen welcomed her kindly. He asked her to return a few days later... During the second meeting, Hentzen was not alone in the office; Mr. Bonnefoy was also there. This is when my cousin was kicked out. I am convinced that the change of attitude is exclusively due to the presence of his boss in Hentzen's office. I need to add that Hentzen knew my personal situation well and that he did nothing to cause me any trouble or to get me arrested. I am also aware that Hentzen left his position of administrative secretary at the Milice in November 1943 and that since then I never saw him in uniform or in contact with the miliciens.

This version seems to be the most credible if one puts it side by side with Hentzen's interrogation.

As to Mme. Arokas, it is true that I tried to get her father, brother and mother freed. She had been referred to me by her cousin Gabet... I met her the first time at the Milice headquarters where I promised to do my best to get her relatives freed. She had indicated that they had been arrested by the Milice, but since the Milice had not yet become involved in arrests, I thought that the relatives of Mme. Angel had been arrested by the Gestapo and I told her that I could not intervene.

The Arokas were indeed deported and did not survive, and it is possible that Hentzen tried to help. However, his testimony is useful in another context. According to Hentzen, the Milice had not started to take part in the arrest of Jews in July 1943. This reinforces the possibility that, at that time, the Germans were dependent on auxiliaries, like the members of the Avignon gang of Alfred André and Lucien Blanc, before the arrival of help from the Marseille gangsters.

Although the existence of a political disagreement between Hentzen and his organization cannot be established with certainty, a concrete fact concerning another Jew was recorded in his declaration:

> Summoned for the STO in January 1944, I was first assigned to the Somatras Company, and then transferred to the Guillet Company upon my request. In both companies, I did everything in my power to prevent the departure to Germany of workers required for the STO. I even arranged to provide a French ID card for an Israelite.

Hentzen names the Jewish individual in his deposition of September 10, 1944:

> I had a French ID card established for M. Janover, an Israelite from Avignon, and I listed him fictitiously in our site workforce.

Samuel Janover was registered in the 1944 census of foreign Jews; he was residing at 16, rue Deveria in Avignon.

12.
Denise Layet

She was the manager of the "Central Bar," a bistro on the place de l'Horloge and a favorite hangout of the Avignon who's who of collaboration. Denise Layet[14] was arrested with her husband in August 1944. She survived the wild justice which ended her husband's life, when he was executed on September 9, 1944, before the court of justice started its proceedings.

The presentation of the facts exonerates her.

> The wife of a milicien, Denise Layet was arrested at the same time as her husband. She was presumed to be a milicienne, but the investigation proves that this was unfounded, although she was once in June 1944 forced to wear the armband by her husband whose activity she was aware of. Since there are no specific charges against her, nothing justifies referring her case to the court of justice or the civic chamber.

Raymond Layet was not small fry in the Milice. He had been implicated in a number of important cases. There was some logic in the initial suspicion against her, as she recognized that Milice chiefs and Gestapo agents were regulars in her bar. But she was very clear during her interrogation of March 10, 1945:

> I have never been joined the Milice or any antinational group. I recognize having been forced by my husband to accompany him on June 1, 1944, while I was wearing the armband with the insignias of the Milice. If I displayed this armband, it was only after a long discussion with my husband. The woman named Simone Cabassole witnessed this discussion. I only walked 50 yards with these insignias and I got rid of them as soon as my husband lost sight of me.[*]
>
> My husband had asked Simone Cabassole and me to come with the miliciens to rue Joseph Vernet[†] on our return from the cemetery. Instead of listening to him, we went… to the Bar Clémenceau as soon as we left the cemetery.

Simone Cabassole was a waitress at the Central Bar. But Denise Layet did not mention that she was also the girlfriend of Robert Conrad, Müller's ledger clerk, who was far more involved in the roundups than in translations.

From Ste Marthe hospital, where she was scheduled for surgery, Denise Layet wrote a very interesting letter to the government Commissioner on March 25, 1945.

> I am taking the liberty of asking you to examine my case to the light of the information I am providing below.
>
> Arrested on August 23, 1944, I was interrogated on March 10, 1945, by Mr. Perrier, the investigating judge. As I was convinced, no charges were filed against me. After investigation, it appears that if my husband was a milicien (executed for that reason on September 9, 1944), I have not joined a party nor done anything that could be held against me. Quite the opposite, married for only one year and a half, I succeeded in obtaining from my husband to resign from the Milice. Moreover, two Jews known in Avignon, Mr. Bruisky, wine trader, and Mme. Mossé, midwife, are ready to testify that they were able to elude the Germans because I hid them. I am asking you, Mr. Commissioner, to hasten the decision that needs to be made on my case and that can only be freedom, since nothing can be held against me.

---

[*] Denise Layet evokes the procession organized by the Milice in memory of the bombardment victims at the end of May 1944.
[†] This is the address of the Milice headquarters in Avignon.

Bruisky, the wine trader, was not registered on the census of the Jews. Noémie Mossé, listed at 40, rue Guillaume Puy, was the wife of Gabriel Mossé, a founding member of the Oeuvres Laïques (Non-Religious Charities) of the Vaucluse, arrested on April 16, 1943, in Avignon and deported on convoy 58. Denise Layet would not actually need those two witnesses.

13.
Gaston Lefebvre

Gaston Lefebvre bought a vineyard in Vaison la Romaine in 1938 after trying his hand at several trades.[15]

Born in Liévin (Nord) in 1904, he first attended an agriculture school. Then, he worked as a miner, before becoming a clerk for a stockbroker. We learn from his interrogation of July 4, 1945, that he had also lived in Paris, in rue St. Paul in the Marais, with his wife who worked as a seamstress in the clothing industry.

After serving in the 1939–1940 war, he belonged to neither the Legion nor the SOL. It is only very late, in May 1944 that he joined the Milice. The presentation of the facts expands on that:

> In June 1944 he answered the mobilization call of Darnand and went to the Lycée Mistral in Avignon. He wore the uniform and was armed with a carbine, he stood guard and in one word he fulfilled all the duties of a milicien. On July 8, 1944, he left for Clermont Ferrand with a Milice detachment; he made a few sorties in that town, in particular to the Aulnat airfield. Then he left for Germany where he served as a worker.
>
> While he was in Vaison in the summer of 1943, he had denounced a Resistance group in the area of Vaison to the gendarmerie.

Lefebvre did not dispute the facts, but he tries to exonerate himself.

> If I joined the Milice, it is on the advice of Mr. Barra who was not yet a milicien. The denunciation of the dodgers to the gendarmerie of Vaison was done by Barra and I admit I was present. In my mind, the idea was not to get the young people arrested but only to have the gendarmerie watch them.

As for his departure for Germany, his version does not rest on his loyalty to the occupier, who was triumphant in not such a distant past.

On July 23 [1944], I left the Milice and tried to return to Vaison. On July 25 or 26, I was arrested between Pierrelatte and Montélimar by the Germans who took me to Germany.

He was jailed, and then he worked in clearing the railroads before his repatriation on May 24, 1945, as a STO draftee.

Clearly, the court of justice which sentenced him to forced labor for life was not moved by his story, and the document he provided in his defense did not weigh much. Yet it is still worthwhile to examine it.

In a letter with "Dresses Silk and Wool" letterhead, Léon Czerikowsky, domiciled 22, rue de Turbigo in Paris, wrote on July 26, 1945, to Mme. Lefebvre, then living at Mme. Guerin's home, 26, rue Petite Fusterie in Avignon:

Madame,
I eagerly wish to oblige you and fulfill your request. Moreover, I found the postcard of Mr. Lefebvre indicating to me a refuge where I could hide during the period of persecution which dealt ruthlessly with the Jews at the time.

I hope that this letter and the attached postcard will be able to rightfully serve him. Anyway, I have kept warm memories of you and Mr. Lefebvre when you were working in our enterprise.

While the Lefebvres were living in the Marais in Paris, Augustine Lefebvre worked as a seamstress in Czerikowsky's enterprise and their relationship was strong, since this Parisian Jew seeks out the Lefebvres in the Vaucluse to find shelter from persecution.

The file does not specify when this silk and wool trader came to the Vaucluse, and he is not registered in the census of the Jews. We understand however why Czerikowsky, who was known in Paris because of his business, deemed it prudent not to notify the local authorities of his presence.

14.
Louis Manca

It is difficult to believe that Louis Manca simply became the accounting supervisor of the Milice—not a low level job—exclusively because of his friendship with Max Knipping, at the time the head of the SOL in the Vaucluse.[16]

Born in Vedène in 1902, Manca studied in Aix en Provence at the preparation school for the Arts et Métiers.* At 18, he volunteered for the 34th Air Force regiment at Le Bourget, and spent a few years in the military before joining the Crédit Commercial de France. Following a brilliant banking career and the creation of his own company, the "Société de Gérance et de Participation" in Avignon, he was drafted in the air force in 1939, and joined the Legion after the armistice, and later the SOL. Finally, the Milice episode takes place and is described in his interrogation of October 23, 1944:

> In February 1943 people insisted that I join the Milice by singling out the help I could provide as an accountant. In fact, I never signed anything. I served Knipping whom I knew because he was an officer in my regiment and I was aware of his brave record during the two wars.

He quickly resigned from the Milice, a few days after joining, but he still attended a meeting later on. In his interrogation of September 9, 1944, he gave the deeper reasons that led him down that path as well as those that would turn him away.

> I have joined these antinational groups because I thought that they were French movements aimed at maintaining order. I became aware that a certain number of items in their programs did not satisfy me, in particular the paragraph related to the Jews and the freedom of religion. I resigned when I became aware of the tight coupling between the Milice and the Germans. I was already no longer a member when the collaboration I was afraid of became a reality. In summary, I made a platonic mistake, but on a practical level, I did nothing wrong. On the contrary, I helped young people in trouble with respect to the STO.

He did not save lives—and maybe the opportunity did not arise—but one of his actions must be noted. In another part of his interrogation, he states:

> I was not at all a sectarian and I sold a building to Mr. Rozenblit, in spite of the fact that he was denied the authorization by the prefecture because he is a Jew. To work around the difficulty, I executed the operation with a front man, while I well knew that Rozenblit was the real buyer.

This is confirmed by a letter from Israel Rozenblit on October 11, 1944:

---

* Elite engineering school in Paris.

I, undersigned Israel Rozenblit, domiciled at Chemin de Monclar in Avignon, certifies that Mr. Manca, domiciled at 20, rue Buffon in Avignon, representing Mme. Baldevin, domiciled in Bedarrides (Vaucluse) sold to Mr. Armand Renard, police secretary in Avignon a building situated at Chemin de Monclar in Avignon in which I live with my family and run a small business. I had not been able to personally acquire this building at that time, since I had been denied the authorization due to my Israelite religion.

On that occasion, Mr. Manca who was well aware of my personal situation allowed me to safeguard my future economic interests without any remuneration for it.

Louis Manca was sentenced to a one year suspended sentence. The procedural file does not say whether the significant and risky help granted to Israel Rozenblit had anything to do with the lightness of the sentence.

15.
Albert Pilat

The president of the Carpentras purge committee asked the court of justice on October 23, 1944, to find a proportionate sentence in the case against Albert Pilat.[17]

> Considering that Mr. Pilat belonged to the Milice as a chief, that as such, he has taken voluntary or involuntary anti-national action, considering on the other hand that he has on several occasions helped the Resistance by his moderation,
> Regrets that no article of the law leaves enough latitude for a sentence proportionate to the mistakes made,
> Estimates that the dismissal would not be just, but that the death sentence would be excessive, and asks the Tribunal to find a middle of the road solution allowing a proper sentence, even light, including national indignity.

It is not that easy to be fair to this 30-year-old insurance agent, who becomes the chief of the Carpentras Milice, in spite of his objection to transforming the SOL into the Milice. During his interrogation of March 7, 1945, he claimed having raised the issue with Darnand, who received him for two or three minutes, and irritated by such trivial ethical problems, shot back at him: "*Are you a milicien, yes or no? If you are, then you have no choice but obey!*"

However, in its presentation of the facts, the government Commissioner observed an association that was something more than undesirable:

The man named Albert Pilat has belonged to the SOL from the day of its creation in Carpentras in January 1942. He becomes the local chief of this organization. He participated in various meetings in that capacity. It must be noted that he was associated with the local chief of the PPF Barbarant with the obvious goal of coordinating the action of these two political formations. Pilat pretends he has resigned from the Milice at the end of June [1944].

To put this in context, the engineer Barbarant, the local chief of Doriot's party "*received the death sentence, commuted to forced labor for life, for having among others established lists of communists, Jews, and freemasons, destined for the German authorities, thus provoking or attempting to provoke the arrest of numerous French people.*"[18]

Finally, the court of justice sentenced Pilat to national degradation for 10 years on June 30, 1945. There are two Jews who possibly thought that this sentence was still too heavy. They made every possible effort for Pilat to be spared. First, Jules Kahn, registered in the census of the Jews, an administrator of the company Lorraine et Provence, wrote on October 4, 1944, to the president of the purge committee:

I wish to report the attitude of Mr. Albert Pilat following the police operation by the Gestapo against my person and my assets on November 24, 1943. At the time, I was the tenant of Mr. Pilat. On the very evening of the failed arrest by the German police, Mr. Pilat immediately proposed his help to save as many of my assets as possible.

Mr. Pilat then proposed to change the rental contract for the empty house to a contract for a furnished house, suggesting that the house and the furniture belonged to him. Together, we established a detailed inventory of every room included in the rental, and with this document in hand, Mr. Pilat was able to defend our interests before the Germans and the Gestapo; of course, this caused him difficulties with the Germans who became suspicious of him.

I state that I was able to recover all my furniture and appliances and others thanks to Mr. Pilat's initiative. I have particularly appreciated the Mr. Pilat's gesture at a time when it was difficult for people hunted down by the Gestapo to find any support.

This is why I consider it my duty, today when we are free again, to testify on behalf of Mr. Pilat, whom we have always considered to be an honest and loyal man; he has never denounced anyone or acted brutally against anyone, which constitutes an exception among the members of the Milice.

But this testimony pales in comparison to a true speech for the defense delivered by Jean Kahn, registered in the census, arrested and interned in Drancy. He wrote on October 5, 1944:

I was arrested as a Jew in Carpentras on March 17, 1944, by the German authorities, successively transferred to Les Baumettes prison in Marseille, to the Drancy internment camp, to the Deutsche Dienststelle* at 43, quai de la Gare in Paris, and then back to Drancy; I was finally released recently on August 19 following the Nordling agreement.†

I could return home on September 24.

I particularly suffered and witnessed suffering, but I cannot charge Albert Pilat with a responsibility that weighs on the group he was affiliated with.

I have known Albert Pilat since his childhood, we studied together, then we served together and we cemented 40 years of relationship interrupted by the war. If we have been able to maintain our friendship, it is because the private man has always had precedence over the Public Man and because his political functions have never affected his honesty and his integrity, as far as I know.

From our conversations, it emerges that his momentary position of Milice chief was first and foremost the result of circumstances (he was first appointed in the context of the SOL because of his youth and his military record, before the SOL was transformed into the Milice).

He has always assured me that he has curbed and generally prevented any action decided or planned by the Milice, when it was clear to him that it was stained by any kind of injustice and he often told me that he had decide to resign "on the day he would be ordered to do a dirty trick" (I am reporting his exact words).

He did inform me that he had resigned shortly after my arrest.

Here are a few "dirty tricks" he did not commit:

While rumors of arrests of patriots and Jews, attributed the Milice and its chief, were periodically circulating in Carpentras, I did frankly ask Albert Pilat about them. He calmed me down man to man and guaranteed to warn me and my family, if such an eventuality were to occur; and I remain convinced that if arrests were done under the initiative of the Milice—officially or not—they were done without his knowledge.

Without naming anybody, Albert Pilat informed me several times that he had given favorable recommendations during investigations of some of my co-religionists. I will mention for the record—this case was probably presented to you—his role during the arrest attempt of the Kahn family (from Lunéville) and the way he safeguarded the furniture of Jules Kahn. At the time, he immediately informed me of his action.

As for my own arrest during a roundup by the SS on March 17, Albert Pilat was out of town; Mme. Pilat who was aware of her husband's opinions and

---

* "German Service Station," where truckloads with the entire content of looted Jewish homes were un-loaded, often by Jewish Drancy internees.
† Raoul Nordling, the Swedish representative in Paris, conducted multiple dialogues with the Germans ahead of the Allies' invasion, and a large number of releases of Jews and non Jews were attributed to him. Note that Aloïs Bruner, the Drancy commander, left on August 17, 1944, with 51 Jewish hostages, among them 25 survivors.

feelings toward me, immediately made herself available to my wife and connected her with the local Milice leaders for attempting eventual proceedings on my behalf, unfortunately to no avail.

As soon as he arrived on March 18, Albert Pilat volunteered to go to Marseille in order to submit our case to the regional chief of the Milice; we did not take the offer because my wife had already started her own efforts. This shows—and Albert Pilat always affirmed it—that he never had any relations with the German authorities; he even avoided contact with the Germans whose contact would have become necessary for his position as a city council member.

One immediately notices the power of loyalty to a childhood friendship that continued far beyond youth. But isn't that too simplistic? Perhaps, other Carpentras Jews also took advantage of Pilat's advice. Moreover, the note from the purge committee praising his moderation that benefited the Resistance cannot be forgotten.

On the other hand, what were his real relations with Barbarant? Did Pilat play with fire? Indeed, Barbarant is an open door to the world of Gaston Mouillade who operated hand in hand with the Germans during the arrests of Jews and members of the Resistance.

Part Four

Summing Up the Effectiveness of Anti-Semitic Violence

> Whoever destroys a single life is deemed by Scripture as if he had destroyed a whole world;
> And whoever saves a single life is deemed by Scripture as if he had saved a whole world[1]

As early as the summer of 1940, the Vichy institutions—prefecture, CGQJ, Legion and later SOL and Milice—constituted the main threat the Jews had to face.

The round ups of foreign Jews of August 1942 ended in one hundred or so arrests and deportations; almost half of the victims were not targeted by the "list of 111"* of Aimé Autrand.

The targeted Jews who had eluded arrest and those who had been forgotten came out with the feeling that it was possible to reach an arrangement with the French institutions, even if the Statut des Juifs mandated a significant reduction of their individual "lebensraum." All the more so since by the end of 1942 the prefecture did not seem eager to arrest the Jews who had been spared by the recent deportations. This sentiment was reinforced by the attitude of the French authorities that tolerated a limited practice of religion.

> On July 28, 1942, the office of the chief Rabbi sent a letter to Blanche Mossé… to inform her that the chief Rabbi of France wants to come for the re-opening of the Carpentras synagogue.
>
> On August 31, 1942, the ministry of the interior informs the prefect of the Vaucluse… that the Cavaillon synagogue is exempt from the shutdown rule…[2]

Those Who Said "No!"

Even before the occupation of the southern zone, a small fraction of the Jewish population rose up against the anti-Semitic measures of Vichy and saw in them as unacceptable collaboration with the Germans. For the most part, these were French Jews or foreign Jews who had lived in France for a long time.

---

* In the "list of 111," one person was listed twice.

In 1941, de Camaret informs Xavier Vallat that Mr. Achille Naquet, staff captain, and Mr. Lévy, infantry lieutenant, were still members of the board of the Avignon Reserve Officers Association, in violation of the Statute of the Jews. The General Commissioner for Jewish Questions did not take long to answer, and the prefecture—specifically Autrand—is requested to get them to resign. Mr. Lévy gives up, but Achille Naquet "who had objected" is struck off administratively on February 23, 1942.

In an inquiry of August 21, 1943, Lebon writes that the Gak-Gorny family *"has been stripped of the French nationality in March 1941. This nationality was restored on July 28, 1943, by the judgment of the Orange tribunal..."* Without naming the judge who was known to be Judge Pierre Burgède, Lebon adds:

> However, an issue remains obscure. What right did the Orange tribunal have to restore a French citizenship that had been stripped by the Ministry of the Interior? ...[3]

The members of the Gak-Gorny family had "dared" sue the government for having illegally stripped them of French citizenship, in violation of the law of August 10, 1927, that broadened access to citizenship by naturalization. This law still being on the books made Burgède side with the plaintiff against an illegal act by Vichy. This kind of independence explains why Judge Burgède will be chosen to preside over the Avignon court of justice at the Liberation, despite his service as a Vichy magistrate during the war.

Once again, this brings to light a typical characteristic of that period when traditional institutions were upside down, without necessarily appearing abnormal. Jean Lebon, a raging subaltern of the SEC, expected justice to rule according to his own wishes, while ignoring the law when it did not suit him. The investigation about Burgède will take an unexpected turn when a loaded question is asked by the isn't the Gak-Gorny family enjoying "secret support from people in high places"?[*]

This kind of civil disobedience was more frequent before the invasion of the southern zone, but some went even further.

Georges Manberger, a Jew from Strasbourg, the manager of the Duparcq factory in Carpentras, was involved in the demonstrations against Vichy on July 14, 1942. Jointly with Dr. Uhry, Humbert, a tradesman, and Desbrun, an industrialist, he wrote a letter to the American embassy in Vichy. This letter, probably written before November 1942, was seized and copied by the censors. Here are a few paragraphs.

---

[*] Judge Pierre Burgède distinguished himself more than once by his independence from Vichy.

… Our press and our radio proclaim that president Roosevelt and the American People show a total lack of understanding toward the French People.

If you believed them, you would think that all of France is entirely won over to totalitarian doctrines; it accepted with delight the replacement of republican institutions by dictatorship and the burial of its now defunct parliamentary regime.

These voices speak French but they are not French voices. Mr. Ambassador, you are not without knowing who leads them and which impure inspiration is driving them. You must be aware. But we think it useful for some citizens, suffering to see their most precious sentiments and ideals trampled upon, to rise and bring you, the most distinguished representative of America, the testimony of their love for your free and generous country; and to tell you that we have faith in your country, that ravaged France is under the victor's yoke, and that, being gagged, it cannot think and speak its mind freely…[4]

On January 8, 1943, this letter, probably intercepted by the RG, is provided by Jean Lebon, the SEC delegate, to his boss in Marseille. Jean Lebon, who already had an eye on Georges Manberger, had invited him on December 18, to appear in his office—at the home of de Camaret at 13, rue de la Banasterie in Avignon—"*to discuss a matter which concerns you.*" On January 25, 1943, Jean Lebon sent to his boss his report about the Duparcq enterprise, belonging to Valentine Garcin, the "catholic" widow of René Duparcq. This "Aryan" business is managed by "the Jew" Manberger. The conclusions of Jean Lebon's boss are not late in coming:

1. Manberger is a French Jew
2. The Duparcq enterprise is entirely under his influence
3. His income declaration is notoriously false and hides more significant profits
4. It is common knowledge that Manberger is engaged in an anti-national activity, and consequently, he is dangerous.

    Therefore, I am asking

1. The director of the Economic Aryanization in Marseille to put the Duparcq enterprise under a provisional administrator so as to eliminate any Jewish influence.
2. The Prefect of the Vaucluse, with copy to the Regional Prefect, to take a measure of administrative internment against Manberger.

On February 25, 1943, Aimé Autrand informed the prefect of the Bouches du Rhône, in the name of the prefect of the Vaucluse, that Manberger has been committed to a residence in Sault, a softer measure than the internment recommended by Lebon's boss. Unfortunately, before the end of this bureaucratic maneuvering, Georges Manberger was already arrested in Marseille, sent to Drancy on January 24, 1943, and from there, deported to Sobibor on convoy 53.

Did Jean Lebon's report play any role in the arrest and deportation of Manberger or was he randomly picked up in the great roundups of January 22, 1943? We will never know, but Georges Manberger left behind a legacy of honor and courage.

He was not alone.

Maxime Fischer, a friend of Manberger, pays no heed in 1941 to the CGQJ ordering him to cease his activity as a lawyer. He was summoned by the sub-prefect in Carpentras: "Come on, resign at once, and stop making trouble for me!" Maxime Fischer replies: "Who is making trouble for whom?" Together with reserve Lieutenant Colonel Philippe Beyne, Fischer set up the Maquis Ventoux. He fought and fortunately survived. He was joined by numerous Jews.[5]

The Prefecture Takes the Pulse of the Jews

On January 4, 1941, prefect Valin underscored for the benefit of the minister of the interior that *"numerous people… hope for England's victory, but this does not mean they all are followers of Mr. de Gaulle, whose most loyal supporters are recruited among the sizeable Israelite community of our region."*[6]

In September 1942, shortly after the deportation of the foreign Jews by Vichy, Prefect Piton went a little further in pointing the finger at Jewish opposition. He focused on the cost of living: *"All this dissatisfaction is exploited by the communist, Gaullist, and Jewish propagandas which secretly work on public opinion—and one must agree—successfully so."*[7] In his reports of October and November 1942, Piton detected the desire of some to increase the measures against the Jews:

> Finally, those in complete support of the Maréchal and the government do not understand why measures—be it only as reprisals—were not taken to intern all Anglo-Saxons and numerous Jews who are still free among us, while the loyal supporters of the Maréchal are being executed or imprisoned in North Africa.

Then, the tone changed. The prefecture and its allies perceive a growing worry among the Jews. Commander Tainturier, head of the Vaucluse gendarmerie shared his observations on December 23, 1942:

The foreign population is calm. The Italians regularly visit their compatriots from the armies in operation… The British make every possible effort to go unnoticed out of fear that the German or Italian authorities require that measures be taken against them. Moreover, it is the same for the Israelites who in large parts have fled from the sea shore toward remote Vaucluse cities, where their only concern is to look for better living conditions, while spending lavishly and buying everything they can at any price.

"Going unnoticed" does clearly not mean getting out of sight of informers of the gendarmerie and prefecture.

Avignon Under German Rule

The weekly RG bulletin of November 30, 1942, reported a recent demonstration of open hostility against the Jews by the PPF. *"Numerous graffiti against the Jews were painted in various Avignon streets during the night from the 25 to the 26 of this month. These inscriptions seem to come from the PPF."*[8] It looks like the arrival of the Germans galvanized the PPF into a show of loyalty toward the occupiers.

From then on, the weekly bulletins indicate both a growing worry and a wait-and-see attitude among the Jews. During the week of December 19, 1942, *"the recent measures against the Jews did not cause any major reaction in Jewish circles that are nevertheless worried about their future."* For the week of February 20, 1943:

> As far as the Jews are concerned, a substantial worry emerges among them following rumors in the département about the creation of a "forbidden zone" which would include the city of Avignon.
>
> During the night of February 6 to 7, the windows of two Jewish stores, situated in rue de la République in our town, were smashed by unknown individuals using cobblestones. This action was disapproved of by most of the Avignon population and seemed instead to elicit a strong reaction in favor of the Israelites…

The open hostility toward the Jews seemed to be limited to fanatics—PPF or other collaborationists.

The report of the week of March 1 to 6, 1943, indicated that the Jews with resources were still residing in the Avignon hotels and *"do not work while families of workers have been expelled from Avignon."* These "expulsions" from Avignon were in fact the product of the commission headed by Aimé Autrand and in charge of assigning foreign workers to GTEs and their families to mandatory residences; the transfers generally took place within the boundaries of the Vaucluse, and of course, the new addresses of the expelled individuals were tracked by the prefecture.

During the following months, *"the Israelites do not seem very reassured, they particularly dread new measures susceptible to curtail their activity more efficiently ..."* (Week of March 14 to 20, 1943), *"the Israelites continue to worry about their future..."* (Week of March 21 to 26, 1943), *"the Israelite elements are taking an increasingly self-effacing stand..."* (Week of April 10 to 16, 1943), *"... seek rather to not be seen. They are concerned by the arrests conducted by the German authorities and move into the zone controlled by the Italians..."* (Week of April 17 to 24, 1943), *"... Departures are noted among the richer Jews following arrests in their social circles and they live in expectation and fear of new measures..."* (Week of May 16 to 22, 1943), *"... The vast majority of Israelites make every effort to go unnoticed. Those who can afford it have left the big centers and retreated to small villages where they are less known..."* (Week of June 20 to 26, 1943), *"... Moreover, many leave their residences clandestinely ..."* (Week of June 27 to July 3, 1943).

Most Jews used to live in the open, and few had truly gone underground, although this would have provided them better protection. But even this proved to be at times unrealistic. For instance, the Cohen family was living in Bedoin under an assumed name, Audibert. So a visiting relative who did not know their exact address asked a local for the whereabouts of the Audiberts. The man replied: "Ah, do you mean the Cohens?" The arrival of a stranger could not possibly go unnoticed.

Of course, we must take into account that the geography of those days seemed much larger than that of today. It will suffice to consider the transportation difficulties of Jean Lebon, before his boss agreed to provide him a motorcycle.

> Because of fuel shortages, public transportation had to cancel several lines, so much so that some villages are totally devoid of means of transport.
>
> Example: When I had to conduct an investigation in Ménerbes, here are the details of my trip
>
> Train from Avignon to Cavaillon at 5:15 a.m.; arrival in Cavaillon 6:25 a.m.; I have to wait until 9:00 a.m., namely the time when offices open, to borrow a bike at the police station. Ménerbes is 15 km away from Cavaillon and the location of my investigation is 4 km further away.
>
> The result is that the day is completely wasted for a one-hour investigation since I am coming back to Avignon at 9:25 p.m.[9]

Ménerbes was in the middle of nowhere.

Except for the lucky few, people were not moving around that much, as if there were tall mountains between Carpentras and Marseille or even

Entraigues and Avignon. That is why moving away was tantamount to hiding. The benevolent or even neutral attitude of some municipalities strengthened that feeling of safety.

One must also remember that the hunted Jews were not professionals of covert activity, and that for most Jews, hiding often came down to being out of sight of the Avignon SiPo-SD by settling in a remote village. However, everyone needed food ration cards and other documents, and they did not necessarily realize that a request made at the municipality or the gendarmerie was often transmitted for approval to the sub-prefecture and the prefecture. The list of foreign Jews was also provided to the Germans by the prefecture itself... not to mention the legion of local informers already discussed.

Moreover, the gangsters had a significant number of loyal antennas in the towns and villages. They only needed to make contact and ask. Also, the information provided by the CGQJ to the Germans found its way to the gangsters in their services.

Around July 1943 the atmosphere was changing and those who could left secretly (but not unbeknown to the RG); this exodus would steadily continue during the following months. The departure of the Italians left a clean sweep for the Germans signaling a significant worsening of the Jews' anxiety. "*The announcement of the arrival of a German commission in charge of arresting young Jews to force them into the STO is badly received in Israelite circles, who believe that the internment and deportation measures are continuing...*" (Week of September 5 to 11, 1943). Worry was mixed with the hope of an allied landing suggested by the Italian capitulation. Jews huddled down. "The Jews try more and more to be forgotten..." (Week of October 31 to November 6, 1943).

The report of the week of November 14 to 20, 1943, is particularly revealing. No place was safe anymore.

> The Israelite circles of the département still seem in the grip of the arrests conducted in Carpentras and Cavaillon where a certain number of Jews were included. At the present time, most Jews in that sector expect to be arrested at any minute. Moreover, they think that a general measure is about to be taken in France by the German authorities to secure the arrest of all the Israelites who are still free on French territory.

The anxiety kept on growing, but the tone changed with the first big roundups. The report of the week from March 26 to April 1, 1944, observed the departure of the registered Jewish stallholders and their families who had been in the open all along.

For the week of April 2 to 8, 1944, a worried wait-and-see is nevertheless still detected:

> The Jews appear very worried by the police operations executed by the German authorities and aimed at seeking a large number of Israelites. They wonder whether they too will not meet the same fate as their co-religionists.

Then, for the week of April 9 to 16, 1944:

> … Many think that in the near future similar measures will be taken in the entire département in the context of general reprisals against the Jewish population, in expectation of the landing of the Anglo-Saxon forces on French soil.

The effect of the great roundup of the end of March continued to be felt, and the report of April 30 to May 6, 1944, goes even further:

> Following an operation conducted by the German police in Avignon at the end of March (during which a number of foreign nationals of the Israelite race were arrested), most of Avignon Israelites have adopted a more unassuming attitude. Most of the place Pie stallholders have ceased they commercial activity, and a number of Jews have left town for a residence where they would be safer.

Buis-les-Baronnies, the Hub

The proceedings against Palmieri confirmed that the great roundup in Avignon at the end of March 1944 was based on the census of the foreign Jews. This must have shaken up the others, who felt more particularly targeted and fled.

Some of them were to be caught up in Buis-les-Baronnies, in the Drôme, during the following weeks. Their hiding places were not as watertight as they thought. We know through numerous testimonies that the French auxiliaries of the Germans were aware of the presence of Jews and members of the Resistance from the Vaucluse in Buis-les-Baronnies and the surrounding area. In fact, in 1944 that village had become a hub for the clandestine resistance, the hidden Jews, the informers of the German police and the gangsters at their service—a little Switzerland without neutrality. As in part of Mme. Marthe Angel's testimony of March 24, 1945:

> After discussion, my husband gave Merle the amount he was asking and on his advice, he left for Buis-les-Baronnies where I joined him.

One month after we left Avignon, my husband was arrested by three German soldiers and three French civilians.

Marthe Angel refers to the great roundup of Buis-les-Baronnies which seemed unavoidable. Palmieri knew how to catch up with his victims, because he had steered some of them toward that safe haven.

Furthermore, Bergeron had been sent to Buis-les-Baronnies to protect the Achard family whose father had been wounded during an assassination attempt by the Resistance. During the same period, Esther Felzner, the wife of Abraham Felzner, a member of the Maquis Ventoux—both registered in the 1944 census in Entraigues—found shelter at the Hotel du Lion d'Or, where she gets a job and serves as a mailbox for the Resistance, with the full knowledge of the hotel owner who also belongs to the Resistance. She had obtained forged identity documents in the name of Madeleine Lefèvre.

The Census and the Lists of Jews

In spite of the "departures," the total number of Jews in the census does not seem to change. This was because of a simultaneous exodus and an influx. The prefecture report of December 12 to 18, 1943, explained those "departures."

> The number of Jews living in the département is approximately 1500; one-third of them are foreigners. 40% came after the armistice mostly from Paris and Alsace-Lorraine.
>
> Most of the refugees settled in the villages where they feel safer and they find better food… Most of them have normally submitted to the obligation of the law of December 11, 1942…

When comparing the census of 1941 with that of 1944, one finds that 871 individuals (642 French Jews and 229 foreign Jews) appear in both. Therefore, a significant number of newcomers replaced the people who left and mingled with the rest of the population; at the same time, a drift of the Jews toward the remote villages took place, but most of them regularized their situation with the prefecture and the local authorities. This is another indication that they did not really hide. Moreover, the census lists of September 1943 and May 1944 still show a significant number of people still living in Avignon, completely in the open. In spite of this Jewish population drift, the prefecture was still able to keep the census up to date. This should be attributed to the municipalities which served as gate keepers for various essential requests, like work permits, ID cards and food cards.

Jews registered in the census had little difficulty in finding a place to live even in the most remote cities and villages of the Vaucluse. This brings up an important distinction between a person who was taking the risk of secretly hiding non registered Jews and a villager who was opening his door to a registered Jew in exchange for rent or for participation in the work of the farm. The first one was acting heroically while the second was providing a welcome hospitality that was not negligible in times of hardship. We found a large number of cases in the second category and a small number in the first one—and this rather late.

But how many Jews remained at their usual address and in particular in Avignon where the danger was greater? We have seen the double blackmailing of Marie Riz at the same address—that of her restaurant "Le Coq Hardi"—first by the Parietas gang, and then by the Palmieri gang. And Jacques Senator who was arrested on May 30, 1944, in a café on the place de l'Horloge, the meeting place of the gangsters; he was carrying money in the lining of his coat. And Estréa Asseo in the middle of the street on June 6, 1944, and Sarah Levendel, in her store on the same day; both of them had momentarily returned to their homes…

In short, a large part of the Jews in the Vaucluse, whether hidden or not, in their original homes or far away, were easy prey for those seeking their elimination. Palmieri was holding many victims within his reach. He kept a reserve list of 200 names, which he probably continued to feed while verifying new addresses. He was not running out of Jews to arrest.

The Genocidal Intent

The appointment of Aloïs Brunner in July 1943 to handle operations against the Jews in France testifies to the impatience of the German leaders to finish the job. In that sense, it was also a slap in the face of Helmut Knochen,* head of the security police in Paris, and his subordinate Heinz Röthke,† who had replaced Théo Dannecker at Jewish affairs (Judenreferat) in August 1942. Brunner who pulled rank on Knochen was receiving his orders directly from Adolf Eichmann in Berlin. This was to be a source of tension, and probably of competition between the two men.

---

* Knochen, sentenced to death in France in 1954, had his sentence commuted in 1956 and was released in 1962 after being pardoned by President Charles de Gaulle.
† Röthke died in the sixties without ever being indicted.

In May 1943, General Karl Oberg,[*] supreme chief of the German police forces, and Röthke had tried in vain to obtain from Vichy the denaturalization of a new slice of the Jewish population. However, the Germans had not waited for the end of these fruitless "negotiations" before they arrested a number of French and foreign Jews in the Vaucluse. The Germans were to progressively have a growing tendency to ignore Vichy.

In March-April 1944 Knochen issued secret directives aimed at accelerating the process of arrests and deportation of Jews,[10] and Brunner approved. There would be no distinction any more between French and foreign Jews, and since the Germans could not rely on the French government, they would use all the means at their disposal. To discover hidden Jews, relatively small bonuses, between 500 and 1.000 francs, would be granted to informers at the discretion of the local chiefs of the German police.

How did the genocidal intentions of Berlin's Section IV B 4 turn out in practical terms in the Vaucluse?

Successful Operations and the Capabilities of the System

During the trial of Reynoir, a gangster who helped Quinson in the hunt for the Jews in the Var, Jean Gibelin, a member of the Palmieri gang, declares during his deposition on September 18, 1944:

> … Around the end of March [1944], the Avignon agent Lucien Blanc arrived at the office with a list of about 60 Israelites to be arrested in the region; this when Charles [Palmieri] decided to launch an operation in cooperation with the Avignon SD. The participants in this operation were Charles, Alfred [Palmieri], Simon, Heiter and the Avignon agents. The operation yielded about 40 people all delivered to the Avignon SD.[11]

This operation started on March 28, 1944, after sundown and ended two days later in the morning.

Ten weeks later, on the evening of June 6, 1944, Palmieri phoned Carteron (Jean Gibelin) at the office of 8, rue Paradis in Marseille, and left a message for Rodolphe Bride.[12] Bride was ordered to join Palmieri and his gang, who had left the previous evening to arrest Jews in Avignon; he must bring his typewriter because the boss wanted to prepare a report about his

---

[*] Oberg was sentenced to death in France in 1954, had his sentence commuted in 1958 and was released in 1965 after being pardoned by President Charles de Gaulle.

activity during the day. On June 7, 1944, in the morning, Bride arrived at the Avignon train station where Lucien Blanc picked him up and drove him to the Grand Nouvel Hotel, at 4, rue Molière, requisitioned by the Germans to host their auxiliaries when they came to town. According to Bride's statement:

> The owner [of the hotel] seemed to know Palmieri very well and behaved with him in a servile way... the people accompanying Palmieri were: Bergeron, *aka* Toto, Fasciola, *aka* Olivier, Albert Simon, Lucien Blanc, Mouillade,... a Gestapo officer who had his own car and whose name was Billartz... I understood that the gang had wreaked havoc in the region, since Charles Palmieri had me type at the hotel a pretty long list of Jews whom he had arrested. This list was typed in several copies and I saw Charles Palmieri hand them over to the German Billarz* and keep a copy for himself...

The presence of Bilharz is corroborated by Charles Palmieri during his confrontation with Moïse Benyacar, an Auschwitz survivor arrested on June 6, 1944: "*I do not contest this arrest with Billartz who was the boss. He belonged to the Marseille Gestapo under the orders of Bauer...*"[13]

Rolf Bilharz was the subordinate of Aloïs Brunner (and not Bauer). Today we know that Bilharz had eluded detection until 1983.[14] Stationed in Nice at the time, his presence demonstrated Brunner's determination to accelerate the rate of arrests in the southeast. The harnessing of Palmieri and his men, French members of the "anti-Semitic" service of the Marseille SiPo-SD, indicated the collaboration between the networks of Brunner and Rolf Mühler. Palmieri's confusion about the hierarchy above Bilharz originates from the fact that the reporting structure tends to become blurred within tight collaboration.

After having established a "delivery slip" which would allow him to cash the promised bonuses, Palmieri left his victims in the hands of the Germans at the Hautpoul barracks in Avignon and returned with his gang to Marseille on June 7, 1944. Bilharz and his small entourage (the Frenchmen "Jean" and "Pierre") took their own car. As we have already seen, we know the next steps from Estréa Asseo,[15] who was among those arrested. We also know independently that Palmieri and his gang had arrested at least 38 people in the Vaucluse on that day.

In each case, on March 28–29 and on June 5–6, about 40 Jews were arrested during two days of work. The gangsters knew how to do the job.

---

* This name has been spelled in several ways: Billartz, Billarz, and even Bilarts. His real name was Rolf Bilharz.

A Lack of Vigor

The 300 arrests during German occupation of the southern zone took place from November 11, 1942, to August 15, 1944, over a 644 day time span. September 7, 1943, coincides with the departure of the Italians and March 1, 1944, with the arrival of Palmieri.

Period	Days	% of arrests	% of interval	Average rate
11/11/42–9/7/43	301	24%	47%	1 Jew/4.18 days
9/8/43–2/28/44	174	11%	27%	1 Jew/5.27 days
3/1/44–8/15/44	169	65%	26%	1.15/days

We observe a slight decrease of the arrest activity after the departure of the Italian occupation troops at the beginning of September 1943. However, there is a perception that, in September 1943, the Jews lost the protection of the Italian occupation troops. Is that perception real? Between November 11, 1942, and September 8, 1943, there were 72 arrests of Jews in the Vaucluse. During the same period, 17 Jews (22%) were arrested in Carpentras, Pernes, Mormoiron, Pertuis and le Thor (see Appendix C) through German incursions in the Italian zone, as we have seen in the case of Henri Dreyfus, the former mayor of Carpentras. On one hand, obviously, the Italian "sovereignty" over most of the Vaucluse did not prevent the Germans from conducting arrests there. On the other hand, given that about half of the Jews were living under Italian occupation, one is tempted to attribute the smaller percentage of arrests in that area to the Italian protection of Jews. However, two other factors must be taken into consideration. First, the towns in the Italian zone were distant from Avignon, thus making arrests less cost effective. Secondly, the larger concentration of Jews in Avignon, close to the German police headquarters, made them easier targets. Therefore, the lower percentage of arrests in the Italian occupation zone of the Vaucluse does not imply that the Jews benefited from a significant protection.

The arrival of Parietas in November 1943 to head up Alfred André's gang and help the GFP did not yield any significant change in the pace of arrests of Jews. On the other hand, Palmieri's "reign" shows a very large increase in anti-Jewish activity, and comparatively, attests to a new sense of urgency. It is however certain that Palmieri is not the sole factor of this quickening pace, since we are aware that his Marseille associates and the other Avignon gangs also joined the hunt for the Jews. It is probable that this increase was due to the impetus of the Germans and their hierarchy.

At a rate of 40 Jews per operation, people like Palmieri and his gang would have needed 8 operations to arrest the 300 Jews of our list. Based on two-day operations, 16 days would have been sufficient out of 644 available days. This would have left 628 "idle days." We know that the Avignon and Marseille gangsters took advantage of these "idle days" to line their pockets by setting up bogus police raids. On more than one occasion, it is clear that the gangsters did not want to kill "the goose that lay golden eggs." In fact, witnesses—mainly those released after payment—testified about their deals with their hunters between official roundups. Although Palmieri demonstrated his organizational skills during the various raids he coordinated in the spring and early summer of 1944, the "limited" bogus cop operations and targeted arrests fit in better with the style common to gangsters than large scale operations. They also provided additional sources of income behind the backs of their German bosses.

We must take into account that the "Vaucluse men"—the Parietas gang, the "favorites of the Germans" and Lucien Blanc's men—were also serving their masters in other capacities, in addition to their own personal "idle time." The activity of the Palmieri gang, based in Marseille, also spanned the Basses Alpes, the Alpes Maritimes, the Var and the Bouches du Rhône départements. In some cases, he was accompanied by Vaucluse men; Bergeron was also seen in the Var. All this implies that the availability of the gangsters in the hunt of the Jews was at best limited.

Their German bosses in Avignon did not project a greater sense of urgency than their French "employees." They were aware of the "secondary" sources of revenue of their "favorites," albeit not in the details. But, had they applied more pressure, would they have had better results, and above all, would they have continued to benefit from the generosity of the auxiliaries? Who else would have organized their Sunday outings to the racetrack in Le Pontet, as Rodolphe Bride mentioned in his deposition?

The Germans and their French cronies acted in fits and starts, as if they were responding once in a while to prodding from above. The pace of the big roundups fits this pattern. Moreover, we know that Aloïs Brunner, who had been sent to France by his boss Adolf Eichmann to accelerate the deportation of Jews, was concerned by the small number of Jews coming from the southeast. This was why he took a number of trips to the Mediterranean coast, in particular to the Nice area, but also to Marseille. Fanny Deyns, arrested in Pertuis on January 5, 1944, was interrogated in Marseille by Aloïs Brunner. On April 29, 1946, she testified before the gendarmes Louis Mouret and Marcel Richaud.

I was taken with my sister [Suzanne Tibi*] directly to Gestapo headquarters, 425, rue Paradis in Marseille, where we were interrogated by other Gestapo agents, in particular by a man named Brunner. This interrogation was aimed at finding out my opinions as well as other members of my family. I was threatened with guns to get me to talk... At the camp of Drancy, I was interrogated again by Brunner and brutalized by a man named Brückler†...

In her testimony of June 7, 1946, Fanny Deyns added: "*Every time* [anti-] *Jewish operations were taking place in various French cities, Brunner was going there to rule on the prisoners and to direct them to Drancy.*"

Brunner had also set up a procedure to "recover" the close relatives of the arrested Jews that were still at large, and he did not hesitate to get personally involved, as indicated by Fanny Deyns' testimony. He also used, on the southeast coast and later in the Paris region and in Brittany, the services of Oscar Reich, an Austrian Jew, as a tout to get at other Jews. Around the end of May 1943, Oscar Reich, a former soccer player in Vienna,‡ had been chased by Jean Lebon, the SEC delegate for the Vaucluse, out of the Avignon Sports Association, where he had been hired as a coach in violation of the Vichy laws.[16] After the Liberation, Reich was executed by firing squad in Montrouge.

Much has been said about Aloïs Brunner, a sadistic and fanatical anti-Semite, and we will add only one remark. The arrival of Palmieri and his Marseille helpers in Avignon, and the sudden burst of energy that we noticed in the arrests from that moment on, were clearly the result of Brunner's orders and of the coordinated action between him and the Marseille SiPo-SD. Although it was considerable, this spurt will nevertheless come up against a corrupt system. One thing is certain: under the pressure of his chain of command, the boss of the Marseille SiPo-SD was not satisfied at all with Palmieri's results, in spite of a slight improvement in the pace of arrests. He even reprimanded him. His excessive interest in the money of the Jews and lack of interest in their arrest resulted in his incarceration by his German bosses at the beginning of August 1944.

That's how the SiPo-SD, overwhelmed by all their duties and unable to count on Vichy, was led to hire subcontractors from the underworld. It must be noted that the local gangsters were already operational when the Germans

---

* Suzanne Tibi domiciled in Pertuis, deported on convoy 69.
† This is likely to be Ernst Brückler, the loyal torturer at the service of Aloïs Brunner.
‡ Austrian born Léo Bretholz, a soccer fan in Vienna before 1939, told Isaac Levendel that Oskar Reich, then in his twenties, had played before the war in the ranks of the Brigittenau Athletic Club of Vienne (BAC), then for Hakoah (Vienna Jewish club). Léo who jumped off the train en route for Auschwitz says that Drancy echoed the name of Oskar Reich.

arrived long before the big chiefs were sent to keep them in line. The Germans found a few recruits in the collaboration organizations. But, with the exception of a few "favorites of the German," they were unable to mobilize organizations like the PPF and the Milice, in their entirety. The loose attribution of the word "milicien" to describe a French collaborator may have induced some to conclude too quickly that the Milice, as an organization, was dedicated to the hunt for the Jews. Our investigation does not support this claim in the Vaucluse.

Were German military reversals a factor in the "lack of energy" evidenced in the deportation of the Vaucluse Jews? Probably not to a significant degree, because the gangsters, like many of their compatriots, were convinced that the inferior position of the Jews had become a French asset that would outlast the war, and that their extortions and thefts would be pardoned once the gangsters switched to serving new masters. This thinking surfaces in the purge trials; the gangsters easily admit their actions against the Jews, while focusing the attention away from their crimes against the Resistance. Others were deeply aware of the approaching allies, but were too implicated against the Resistance to change course; Mouillade had put it very clearly to an employee at the Vaucluse prefecture named Reau:

> "We are cleaning up to shut the mouth of the Gaullists. As for myself, I have decided to act, because I would be dead meat if the Americans were to land."[17]

1942 and 1943–1944

Whatever the reasons, the "yield" of the Germans and their French auxiliaries in 1943-1944 pales in comparison with the arrests of August 1942 made by Aimé Autrand. Within a few days he had organized and carried out the arrests of one hundred of foreign Jews, while it took almost two years for the gangsters to arrest 300 Jews out of a total population of about 2,000. It also took months to gather some speed. The Germans would have needed many more gangs, to be able to organize surprise operations at once—like the prefecture did in 1942. But they had to make do with whatever was available: a small number of auxiliaries that were drawn in by lucrative "private enterprise." Even with the German "spurts" of March 1944, it was too little and too late.

The persecution of the Jews in the Vaucluse did not end up in the catastrophe it could have been. But this is often not because the local population was hiding the Jews. The French gangsters did not put their hearts in this work, and they were holding the employers in check. The sole means of pressure the Germans had was not to renew the temporary SiPo-SD permits of their "employees." But did they really have a choice and could they have managed without their auxiliaries? In this case, would they have given up on the final solution or would they have moved to brutal action, as in eastern Europe, at the risk of rapidly alienating the local population?

In any case, one can hardly imagine the resulting slaughter, if the German police and their helpers had been able to hunt the Jews with steady consistency instead of working in bursts, and if they had more auxiliaries at their service as well as the active collaboration of the prefecture.

On the other hand, no hindrance of the aryanization process mitigated the fate of the Jews of the Vaucluse. Even if the prefecture did not participate in arrests during the occupation, some threads of the information spider network weaved by the Germans and their helpers are connected to Vichy institutions. A society that had first marginalized the Jews also enabled what appears to be a sinister lottery.

The history of the deportation of the Vaucluse Jews must be based on an examination, where the genocidal intent is seen in the context of local variations. It should also be viewed at the confluence of the deportation routes, from the villages and towns of the Vaucluse to Marseille, from Marseille to Drancy and from Drancy to Auschwitz. The closer we get to the end of the voyage, the higher the likelihood of achieving the extermination goal. Conversely, at the bottom of this hierarchy, far from Auschwitz, the genocidal intent must take into account the reality on the ground where its success is far from absolute.

In the end, the reality in the Vaucluse may resemble that of other parts of France, and certainly in the neighboring départements which we have come to know better. The extent and the depth of the damage will certainly vary according to the geography. It is however probable that a certain number of elements that emerge from our study—greed, villainy, absence of moral compass, the decomposition of the institutions—played a significant role in Nazi Europe in general. In any case, it is evident that neither Europe nor France in particular can be considered as homogeneous blocs. More local studies would provide significant contributions to the development of regional, national and European syntheses. Without the differentiation of operational realities, it is impossible to understand what happened through the sole study of Nazi strategy.

Part Five

SS Commander Rolf Mühler

The Epicenter of German Police Repression in the
Marseille Region

In the struggle against all forms of liberal ideology, one fact must be underscored: these ideological groups which are today too weak to actively intervene in the political process, are hiding behind Moscow. However, one decisive factor remains: the Jews are at the helm in soviet Russia as well as in the most important democracies.

Rolf Mühler's final examination
at the school of SD Cadres in Bernau (c. 1936)[1]

All the loose ends of the German police web may now be brought together, starting with the southern occupation that swept the Vaucluse. The KdS of Marseille served as the nerve center, with Rolf Mühler at the top from January 1943 to June 1944. A complex network of relationships grew around him—as a boss to his subordinates in the SiPo-SD, as a customer to his subcontractors, the French auxiliaries, as supplier of intelligence to the regional German military units, as collaborator and competitor with other police services, in particular, but far from exclusively, the hunters of Jews and the other intelligence networks.

In 1941-1942, Rolf Mühler had been the head of the SiPo-SD for the Rouen region; he was then briefly transferred in November 1942 to head the Lyon region, before he was sent to Marseille. Surprisingly, no document concerning his service in Rouen was ever presented at his trial, although significant proof of his repressive anti-Semitic activity are available at the Centre de Documentation Juive Contemporaine.

Since he was the hub of police activity in all the départements of the Marseille region, he was responsible for its successes as well as its shortcomings. At his trial, he stated in impeccable French:

In general, it must be said that—given the enormous load of the service—the staff was scant. It included—and I can only give approximate numbers—100 men and 25 to 30 German women employees.* This number includes the officers and men and women employees of all the subordinated services which were very small, except that of Nice. In general, such a service counted 5 or 6 men. Approximately 50% were professional police officers; the remainder was composed of former members of the Geheime Feldpolizei (German military

---

* The KdS of Marseille started with about 30 employees, and grew with the Italian defection and the increase in sabotage actions.

police). All professions were represented: businessmen, merchants, waiters, reporters, teachers, drivers, peasants, etc. A small minority were able to speak French. This made it necessary to use several interpreters. With the exception of a few rare cases, these were not individuals of considerable value; strictly speaking, most of them did not have a motherland. For want of better ones, they had to be kept...[2]

The numbers put forward by Mühler are in line with what we have learned from other sources—the testimonies of Ernst Dunker, the London files and the investigation files of military justice. In particular, Avignon counted about 10 people, including a secretary and drivers. Mühler's numbers follow the general pattern in France, although the KdS of Marseille seems to have been somewhat understaffed by comparison to the average. This must be kept in mind for a better understanding of the strategy of the German police in France.

In his deposition, Mühler clarifies that some ambiguity remained between the GFP and his own organization:

> The GFP (Secret Military Police) was a very important service. I have already mentioned that the members of my service had been recruited in a large extent among former members of the GFP. Indeed, this service had played a key role in France until May 1942. From that moment, most of its units had been incorporated into our service. Until 1942, our service was not allowed to execute searches, arrests, etc. It was rather the GFP that did such police actions... Until May 1942, the GFP was the police proper in France. Later, there were nevertheless GFP units in the headquarters of the large military units... In principle, the GFP dealt with all the matters related to the members of the Wehrmacht. I was not allowed to get Germans soldiers or officers arrested, that was the business of the GFP. But the GFP had the right to arrest French people or foreigners...

We have indeed observed that the Avignon GFP was connected to Major Von Bock of Aix-en-Provence, and that some members were working with and for Wilhelm Müller during operations against the Jews and the Resistance. The boundary between the GFP members at the service of the SD and those serving the army was blurred.

However that may be, these events, that were not presented at Rolf Mühler's trial, clearly show his involvement and his initiatives in the deportation of the Jews.

On March 6, 1943, Rolf Mühler announced the arrest of 20 Jews in Marseille, and he signed two telexes, dated March 30 and April 5, 1943, each one informing Section IV-B ("Jewish" section) of the Paris SiPo-SD of the arrival of 10 Jews coming from Marseille.[3]

The account of Raymond Raoul Lambert has already shown that Rolf Mühler had played an active role in the arrest of Jewish hostages following the assassination of two SS on May 1, 1943, in Marseille.[4]

Another event a few months after Muhler's arrival in Marseille adds to our skepticism about his defense. According to a report to his bosses, Guido Lospinoso, the Italian police superintendent in Menton, received two envoys from Rolf Mühler who were bringing a request seemingly in contradiction with the orders from Rome. Indeed, they were coming to arrange for the exchange of Austrian and German Jews under Italian control with Italian Jews under German control. A few days later, Lospinoso received a telegram from Rome ordering him to "*satisfy the request of the German police that German Jews be delivered to them.*"[5] Mühler informs Knochen, who does not seem aware of this issue, clearly indicating that this was a local initiative by Mühler.[6] Shortly thereafter, this agreement was nevertheless canceled by Rome "*due to the recent reorganization of the Italian government.*"[7] (the overthrow of the Mussolini regime on July 25, 1943). Following this change, Rolf Mühler informed his boss of a meeting he had, this time in Marseille, with Lospinoso before the latter's departure to Rome for new instructions. On that occasion, Mühler told his boss that he had returned to Lospinoso the list of Austrian and German Jews the Italian superintendant had lent him, but that these lists "*had not been copied... because Guido Lospinoso had promised to return them after he comes back from Rome.*" Of course, we can be sure that the head of the Marseille SiPo-SD was very careful not to copy the lists of Jews that he had been entrusted with!

He was therefore linked to the affairs of Section IV-B. But who were his associates?

"These Gentlemen," the French Auxiliaries of the SiPo-SD

Mühler confirms in his deposition a series of relationships we already know for the Vaucluse.

> Needless to say that I and several of my officers and employees, we had contacts of differing closeness with the collaborationist parties and groups. This state of affairs followed orders we had received from Paris. As for me, I have above all been acquainted with the regional heads of the PPF and the Milice,

Messers. Sabiani, Knipping, de Vaugelas and Dr. Durandy*... In Marseille, the PPF was very important because Mr. Sabiani was a personality full of energy. I know that, before the occupation of the southern zone, he had tight contacts with our service in Paris... I was obliged to call him in very often because his men were less or more shocking the population. I even had to arrest a good number of PPF members who were working for the services of Dr. Baumel (work force for Germany).

The PPF was providing a lot of intelligence, some of its members were employed in Section VI of my service; others worked for Section IV (executive). They often were denouncing compatriots and receiving varying amounts... Since the PPF was mostly composed of Mr. Sabiani's gangsters, it had in its ranks many individuals for sale...

My service heads in the other cities of the region all had contacts with the collaborationist parties. The contacts were very tight, in Avignon for instance. I personally met the head of the PPF in Toulon, a doctor named Jamin. I know that he was well acquainted with my officers in Toulon...

I know very well that the true gangster bosses in Marseille, Messers. Carbone, Spirito, Palmieri, etc. have worked in Section VI in Paris. Once—at the very beginning of 1943—the French police had tried to arrest these Gentlemen. Our service in Paris intervened to prevent their arrest...

"These Gentlemen" were too valuable at the time in the eyes of their SiPo-SD customers to rot in a French cell. Mühler confirms it. Thus he provides weighty information. The utilization of underworld auxiliaries, similarly observed in Avignon, was clearly in line with the SiPo-SD strategy from top to bottom. Mühler added that this state of affairs was not limited to his services.

A certain Monsieur Ottavi who preferred to be called Norbert came several times to see me. He too was one of the great black market aces. He was in close cooperation with several German economic services... Especially with several officers whose offices were at the "Splendid" hotel. These officers were making very big purchases. It is certain that he made a lot of money through his collaboration with the Germans. One day, he was arrested by the French police. Before arresting him, Mr. Andrieu came to ask for my approval...

There was hardly a German service with which Mr. Sabiani had no contact...

---

* Max Knipping, Jean de Vaugelas, and Dr. Paul Durandy, followed one another at the head of the Milice of the Marseille region. Knipping would become the assistant to Darnand and the head of the Milice for the northern region; he was executed on June 18, 1947. Jean de Vaugelas, enrolled as an officer in the Charlemagne division, and eluded justice in Argentina, but he would die in an accident in 1957. Paul Durandy, enrolled as an officer in the Waffen-SS, and was killed in Pomerania.

One Monsieur Carbone was very closely connected with a certain Monsieur Mayer who was working for the AST in Cologne. This Monsieur Mayer who was playing a big role in Marseille had very good relations with all the big gangsters. One could even say that he was himself one of the biggest gangsters in Marseille. The role he was playing on the black market was considerable. That was the reason why many German soldiers and officers were going and seeing him for purchases… He was in contact with all the German economic services, therefore also with Section V of my service…

Here, we are faced with what looks like a true paradox. Mühler had direct contacts with the "aces of black market" who supplied the German units with all kinds of products in exchange for good cash payments while Section V of his own services was in charge of the repression of this kind of trafficking.

The head of the KdS continues:

There were other members of the PPF providing us with such intelligence [about the Resistance], for instance in the département of the Vaucluse… I do not know whether Monsieur Sabiani was receiving money personally; there were however many PPF who were paid by our service and by other German services. It was not a secret that the PPF in Paris had been officially subsidized by Germany.

Of course, Müller was not relying solely on the PPF. *"The Milice had also established a contact with us… actually, I do not know whether the information given to us by the Milice was very valuable or not."*

Mühler kept going into the description of his networks and disclosed name after name, and organization after organization, on the German military side as well as on the French side. He was well informed about the personalities of the French auxiliaries that the German units, including his own services, were dealing with. The gangsters were not working only for the German police and not only in hunting the Jews. This situation was probably not limited to the southeast of France.

This symbiosis between the SiPo-SD and the underworld led to some obvious contradictions on the national scale, like the destruction of the Vieux Port, shortly after Mühler's arrival in Marseille. One wonders why the Germans decided early on to launch a war against the people of the underworld whom they were about to utilize so profusely. However, this stops being surprising if we consider that the Germans alternated between the carrot and the stick in their relations with the mob. So they started with a big stick. As Rolf Mühler explained:

Mr. Himmler gave Colonel [Bernhard] Griese the order to go to Marseille with his regiment to maintain order in that town... A terrorist attack had taken place in a brothel. Several German soldiers and several women had been wounded... It was there [the high command of the Wehrmacht] that a plan to set an example was hatched in line with the order of Mr. Himmler to Colonel Griese. The intention was to deal a blow to the criminals and the gangsters of Marseille.

This was a measure to get the Marseille underworld to toe the line and become more malleable in the future.

The Organization Chart of Political Repression and the Hunt for the Jews

Based on the body of depositions, interrogations and testimony during Rolf Mühler's trial, it is possible to reconstruct the organization chart of the SiPo-SD, while focusing on the chain of command from Berlin, down to Paris, Marseille, and Avignon in particular (see Appendix D). This chart reflects the unification of most of the German police forces under the authority of Heinrich Müller, head of Berlin's Section IV, starting in April 1942. With the departure of the Italians, the SiPo-SD completed the deployment of its antennas all over the Marseille prefectoral region and beyond.

Overall, General Karl Oberg* relied on a force of about 5000 people. Approximately one half, the Ordnungspolizei—the police used to maintain law and order—was an auxiliary force, whose divisions and units were scattered on French territory. This police, composed of six battalions, was stationed next to the most important KdS headquarters, and played a relatively small role in France. The second half was under the command of Helmut Knochen, head of the SiPo-SD in France.[8] Needless to say, that was small in size compared with the magnitude of the task under its authority.

The second striking feature of the organization chart is the multiplicity of links and chains of command between Knochen and his subordinates down to the lowest level. For instance, Knochen controlled Section IV in Marseille through his direct subordinates in Paris and through Rolf Mühler in Marseille. Beyond the specialization of those links at the national and regional level, this had both advantages and disadvantages. On one hand, Knochen could place loyal individuals along those chains who would become his eyes and ears, while keeping an eye on one another. Berlin used the same pattern

---

* Sentenced to death in France in 1954; sentence commuted in 1958, released in 1965 after a pardon by Charles de Gaulle.

at the highest level. Authoritarian regimes often use this subterfuge, but this also has negative side effects: the mutual distrust and above all an opportunity to offload one's own responsibility onto others, when things don't go as planned. Such an organization is seldom efficient.

The structure of the SiPo-SD anti-Jewish operation is represented on the second chart in Appendix D. Section IV, an executive section which included elements of the Gestapo, had to rely heavily on Section VI for its intelligence. It is important to notice that the segmentation into 6 sections disappeared in the small antennas where the small staff was unable to maintain a complete structure. This is why we have seen members of the GFP participate in the arrests of Jews, while their main function was to collect intelligence about the Resistance. Wilhelm Müller used his subordinates according to his boss's pressure and the needs of the day.

Finally, Aloïs Brunner, vested with Adolf Eichmann's mandate,[*] grafted himself onto the anti-Jewish activity of Knochen's SiPo-SD as soon as he arrived in France. With Berlin's support, he was able to acquire the cooperation of the national, regional and local chiefs and harness parts of their resources in the pursuit of his mission. As we have seen, he was not always exceptionally effective.

In his written deposition, Mühler lists a few police forces, operating in Marseille that had been left out of the unification of the police units:

1. The AST (Abwehrstelle), the counter-espionage service of the Wehrmacht, was in charge of military affairs, while the SiPo-SD was dealing with political questions. But, over time, issues took both military and political aspects, at the same time, thus eliminating much of the distinction between the tasks of the two police forces.
2. A few GFP services remained under the control of the large military units, which lobbied for the need of an emergency contingent under their direct orders while promising to coordinate their action with the SiPo-SD.
3. The Feldgendarmerie was attached to the military administration, but its responsibilities overlapped those of the SiPo-SD
4. Service for the control of bars and vehicle circulation
5. Port and coast police
6. Customs service

---

[*] Adolf Eichmann, Section IV-B-4 of the Reichssicherheitshauptamt—RSHA (Reich Security Main Office).

Some units were intentionally redundant with the SiPo-SD. Mühler also mentions two organizations belonging to the unified police and constituting services parallel to the SiPo-SD in France:

1. The intelligence unit led by Hans Senner was attached to the German consulate in Marseille, but it was directly controlled by Section VI in Berlin. This service competed more that once with the Mühler's sections IV and VI, especially in recruiting French auxiliaries.
2. The Ordnungpolizei was in charge of the relations with the French police, the Gendarmerie and the GMRs. Mühler had tighter relations with the units stationed in Marseille because their chains of command both went up to Oberg.

How It Worked on the Ground

Jean Isidore Kahn testified on July 10, 1946:

On March 17, 1944, at about 10 a.m., I was in Carpentras, when all the German SS started a roundup. I was able to reach the boulevard des Platanes, but I was stopped by a German soldier in front of the Kommandantur; he hit me in the lower back with the butt of his rifle, because I had tried to flee.

In the afternoon, at about 3 p.m., we leave Carpentras by truck toward Avignon. We spent the duration of the trip lying down; as soon as we lifted our head we were hit with the butts of the rifles. We were guarded by SS soldiers and by a civilian who was speaking both German and French very well; his hair was graying, he was medium-sized and looked about 45 years old. This man, whose name I do not know was armed with a pistol held in a discreet shoulder belt.*

As soon as we arrived at the Gestapo, in Avignon, boulevard St. Ruff,† the villa of Doctor Pons, I was booked by a young blond woman‡ speaking a perfect French; I do not remember her first name which I heard from the German officers; very politely, she asked me for my identity, the address of my wife and my civil status.

When we came out of the Gestapo, we were driven by the same crew to Ste Anne prison. On the way, the civilian who accompanied us went off at the Auberge de France.

Upon our arrival at St. Anne, we were received at the gate by a man, armed with a colt, young looking, about 35 year old, wearing a light colored suit; I assume he was Palmieri, *aka* Merle, since I had already seen him in the

---

* This description seems to fit Gaston Mouillade..
† Jean Kahn is mistaken. It should be Monclar.
‡ The woman is probably Frida Magey, Müller's secretary; she received German citizenship

Carpentras area. Furthermore, I recognized his face on photographs that appeared in newspapers during his trial.

I was registered, upon my arrival by the head of the Avignon Gestapo, tall and lean, speaking French very well, 50-60 years old, wearing a dark suit; it could be Müller, but I cannot be in the affirmative.

After my interrogation, I was beaten on my face with a blackjack by two men, the professional boxer type, wearing only pants; this was because I was a Jew and did not want to disclose the whereabouts of my mother.

Then, I was put in a cell with 17 other poor souls, with whom I spent the night, and on the next day, Saturday, I was transferred to les Baumettes by truck with 8 other comrades: the two Mitrani cousins, one from Avignon and the other from Lyon, and a man named Horn, a stallholder in Avignon; I never heard about them again. There was also a British family which was later interned in the St. Denis camp, especially reserved for them.

On our way, between St. Cannat and Lambesc, they stopped so that we could urinate; we were put in one line and photographed. We were escorted by 8 soldiers and 2 civilians; a civilian took our picture.

At les Baumettes, I was jailed together with Horn and the young British man; on Sunday night, we got food for the first time since my arrest. From March 18 to April 6, 1944, I tasted the regimen of blows and humiliations of les Baumettes, without omitting food deprivation.

On April 8, 1944, I arrived at Drancy after a two day journey in a passenger car; my head was shaved and my hands and feet were shackled; I got food but no drink.

At this camp from which 1400 were able to escape out of 80,000, I had to deal with Brunner, Bruckner* and Weisel.†

On May 6, 1944, I was transferred to the Deutsche Dienstelle W, near the Gare d'Austerlitz, in Paris, as a worker; there we were guarded by Cossacks and Mongolians.

On August 12, I was taken back to Drancy, until August 18, the day of Liberation. This is when we suffered the most, because this was the last breath of the Reich...[9]

A Killer with Clean Hands

In his confrontation with the head of the Marseille KdS, on July 29, 1947, Dr. Beltrami mentions the arrival of Mühler during a torture session he endured at 425, rue Paradis. Mühler objected: "*I persist to say that I heard these noises* [screams and howls of the victims!!!] *only twice, and I did not know where they were coming from; in those cases I intervened.*" The witness added that after the conver-

---

* This is Ernst Brückler, mentioned earlier.
† Joseph Weisel, who lived in Austria until 1983.

sation in German between Mühler and his torturer, the blows redoubled after his departure.

One can easily imagine one of the reasons for Mühler's "deafness": eventually, it will provide an opportunity to pass the buck to his subordinates. Out of frustration, Commissioner Léon Castellan wrote a few lines on a service note of July 22, 1947: "*It is difficult to establish the direct responsibility of Rolf Mühler who takes cover behind the initiative of his subordinates and the excess of zeal of his French auxiliaries.*" He adds: "*To hear him, Rolf Mühler was a simple mail box!*"

Mühler continuously contradicted himself all along the procedure.

On the occasion of Fanny Deyns' testimony about her arrest in Pertuis and the death of her husband, Georges Deyns, in the offices of 425, rue Paradis, Mühler insists on explaining the death of M. Deyns. He affirmed that "this Monsieur" volunteered to help the Brunner Kommando. Because of his informer's role, Mühler would grant him a weapon; he explained that he was the only one able to do it and that a severe weapons control was carried out by Section I. This weapon was given to Deyns by interpreter Hecht. It is during the weapon transfer that an accident caused the death of Mr. Deyns.

In the CGQJ files, we found a testimony that gives a contradictory version of the events. The SEC director, Guilledoux, wrote a report to his boss on March 16, 1944:

> Deyns has always stated he was catholic although there was a strong presumption that he was Jewish, and serious information let it be known that his real name was Guikovaty...
>
> On Wednesday, March 8, 1944, I got the visit of a police inspector who informed me that since the Deyns case had been reopened by Public prosecutor's office, he had been sent to the interested party, who had provided a letter in German accrediting him to the Gestapo as a member of the police of this organization...
>
> After contacting the Jewish Affairs of the Gestapo, I was informed that it was nothing of the sort and that the document in the hands of Deyns had no significance...
>
> 1. On the same day, Deyns was summoned to the Jewish section of the Gestapo; he arrives at noon.
> 2. After a discussion about his identity and his racial situation, Deyns was brought to German doctor and asked to submit to the check that would prove his non belonging [to the Jewish race]; since Deyns was recognized Jewish because of his circumcision, he is said to have shot himself in the head.
> 3. His death was said to be instantaneous

4. Seals were said to be put on the store owned by Deyns in Marseille, and the German section for Jewish affairs asked for the immediate designation of a Provisional Administrator.[10]

Was it a real suicide or an assassination? We come close to the center of this episode with the independent testimony of Juliette Fellous, the daughter of Fanny Deyns. Georges Deyns had taken the identification documents from a Belgian who had died during the German invasion, and sold the Deyns name to Fanny Pouchkoff through a fictitious wedding. Juliette continues:

His was a Hungarian Jew whose real name was Guicovaty (I am not sure about the spelling). He did not die executed, but tortured at 425, rue Paradis. I am the one who caused his arrest, and I would do it again because one of the men who came to arrest my mother and my aunt told me that Georges Deyns was the denouncer. He gave me his name and even his address... I immediately went to Marseille where I knew a police detective who worked for Vichy; he was a friend of my aunt and my uncle [Suzanne and René Tibi]. I told him everything. I was a fearless teenager or rather completely unconscious about the danger... He told me "Go back home, don't move from there, don't tell anybody, I am going to take care of this!" And this is what he did...

Juliette Fellous adds: *"Georges Deyns was tortured to death. This is what I was told at the time..."* One can only speculate about the reason why Mühler gave to the Court of Justice a "sterilized" version of the event.

Then, there is the testimony of Robert Andrieu, former Police Superintendent in Marseille, who was arrested by Vichy in February 1944. Andrieu had among others participated in the negotiations with Müller for the liberation of the Jewish hostages in May 1943. In his September 17, 1947, deposition, Andrieu who was in charge of the relations of the French police with Mühler added:

... However, I intervened once to apprise him that public rumors accused the SD services of torturing arrested people to get them to confess; his approximate response was that "he did not go down to his services and that he needed only to read the reports"...

The SD services were nevertheless using French people, miliciens, PPF and the francists. Mühler was barely hiding his disdain for the informers in his service...

Mühler wanted apparently to look like a soldier, but we know that his subordinates behaved like criminals...

To which extent is Mühler responsible for his services?

To which extent can a chief ignore the methods and the missions of his services?

A complete ignorance would appear highly implausible.

Passing the Buck

In any case, in his deposition, Mühler sheds tears over the "departure" of Robert Andrieu whose removal had been demanded in 1944 by the SiPo-SD itself, because he opposed the measures against the Jews.

> … I knew that Mr. Andrieu was a good Frenchman and an excellent officer. I thus made every possible effort to keep him in the region, in spite of many attacks directed at him, on the part of both our Paris services and the collaborationist groups. I have always preferred to work with true French patriots, as long as they do not actively sabotage the measures of the occupying authorities.[11]

Of course, it was "our Paris services" that got Andrieu arrested. In most cases, Mühler unloads his responsibility on his direct boss, Helmut Knochen, who in turn deflects them towards his own hierarchy. In his audition of October 25, 1948, Knochen specified that he was taking care of all the sections reporting to him, but that he personally belonged to Section IV. He too was removed from those under his orders.[12] *"When someone was arrested by a KdS, his interrogation report was transmitted to us with proposals related to this individual. After studying the file, we did transmit it with our own proposals to Berlin which decided in all cases… It is true that the Jewish questions have been more particularly handled by specialists, notably by Dannecker who reported directly to Berlin."*

According to Knochen, Dannecker, his subordinate, was under direct Berlin orders. Mühler and Knochen are trying to lead us to believe an absurd scenario: that they had no control over their subordinates and that every detail was decided in Berlin; this went for both particular cases and political issues. They would want us to accept as a fact that nothing was done without a specific order from the German capital!

As for the "Merle Bureau," that of Charles Palmieri, Mühler stated that he had not been aware of its existence. He added that the name of Kompe had been mentioned as a founder of the bureau, but he affirmed having known nothing… He indicated that other services were using the SD building, and this explains his ignorance.

In the trial notes of March 16, 1949, Mühler picks up once more on the classic theme of his defense, but he nevertheless recognizes his limited and passive collaboration in the arrest of Jews.

> The arrests of Jews, refugees in the Mediterranean zone, these were done by a special organization "The Brunner Kommando," installed in Nice, reporting to

a certain Eckmann*. He [Mühler] admits that the men of the SD have been brought to arrest Israelites, but he added that this was either to help the Brunner Kommando who had the power to require it from him, or the arrest of Israelites from the Resistance arrested as such by the SD. There were a few men detached by Brunner to Marseille. He had a strict order to collaborate with them. The arrested Jews were assembled in Drancy.

Mühler added that Section IV-J (or IV-B) had only an administrative link to his service and was not reporting to him. He knew nothing either about the passage through Marseille of 54 arrested Jews mentioned in one of the testimonies at his trial. He reaffirmed that *"the Brunner Kommando was taking care of the racial arrests; the SD was only summoned to help in some cases."*

Concerning the hunt for the Jews, Mühler points his finger in the direction of Brunner, while his boss, Knochen, had pointed it toward Dannecker, one of his Section IV subordinates in Paris. But Knochen assures us that the orders were reaching Dannecker directly from Berlin.

"It's not Me; it's Meyer!"

Mühler's defense was significantly damaged by a series of witnesses who always come back to the same point: some saw him during actions and others had informed him.

And Mühler attempted once more to diminish his role, when he writes at the end of his deposition:

> To summarize, it can be said that our service was relatively small in comparison with its assignment. Section IV was the largest… I mostly took care of Sections I, II, and VI. Meyer [Mühler's assistant] took care of Section IV in particular, and to some degree, of Section V. Section III was collaborating tightly with Section VI…

This makes everything crystal clear. Mühler took the responsibility for intelligence, since he had to take some. But it was his subordinate, Commandant Gustav Meyer, who committed the crimes, since he was more particularly in charge of Section IV, the executive section.

After his death sentence, Ernst Dunker, *aka* Delage of Section IV in Marseille, shattered this scaffold. He insisted on testifying at the trial of Rolf Mühler, his boss's boss. On May 13, 1947, Dunker, a former GFP member attached to the SD in August 1942, stated about the French auxiliaries: *"The*

---

* Is Mühler referring to Otto Eckmann, the alias which Adolf Eichmann used to disappear after the war?

weapon permits and the SD cards were exclusively signed by Mühler after a report was written about the quality of these collaborators... One rule of the Paris Section IV was to obtain confessions by all possible means when the security of the German troops was concerned. These telegrams were passing through Mühler...”

The boss, who probably realized the skepticism of the military judges, reiterated once more that the Jewish section did not report to him, but he recognized that *"the arrests were done under his responsibility, but not under his orders.”*

During Dunker's trial, Charles Palmieri had testified on the same issue. His testimony is cited in the report of June 30, 1945:

> He [Palmieri] pretends he was a double agent, while dealing only with the Jews on the German side. Palmieri receives a protection letter signed by Commandant Mühler...[13]

We know that, after Palmieri's move under Bauer, the salaries and the expenses of Palmieri and his gang were paid by Mühler. The head of the Marseille SiPo-SD inadvertently revealed the depth of his knowledge of the functioning of his organization, which he pretended otherwise to be ignorant of. At his trial, a witness from Avignon, Raoul Gros, arrested and transferred to Marseille where he was brutalized, testified that *"Boyer and André did hesitate between La Cigale and Monclar”* to deliver him to the Germans. Mühler denied having seen and hit the witness, and he attributed the arrest to the GFP, since *"the witness mentioned the Hotel de la Cigale in Avignon and Commissaire Boyer.”* Mühler was therefore aware of the existence of Parietas, *aka* Commissaire Boyer, one of the French auxiliaries of his Avignon subordinate, Wilhelm Müller; he also knew the nature of the staff in the Avignon antenna. He didn't hesitate to unload his responsibility on the members of the GFP, hoping that the Court would not associate them with his services. Moreover, the witness, Raoul Gros, did provide information already known, namely that the GFP of rue Bancasse collaborated with the service of Monclar, since Boyer and André had hesitated between the two.

Heard Nothing, Saw Nothing

In his handwritten deposition of January 25, 1947, Rolf Mühler summarized the situation. He stressed that he was an honest man, and that if there were any blunders, it was really not his fault. The true culprits were: his superiors who were giving the orders, the German military units who often lost their cool and retaliated thoughtlessly, and his subordinates, who used excessive violence behind his back.[14]

These were excesses he hastened to prohibit when third parties tipped him off. Why did he not hear the screams of the victims at 425, rue Paradis? This was because he was in his office reading his subordinates' reports and bosses telegrams all the time. And there were so many of them—thousands he assures us: "*At the beginning of our activity in the region, I tried to sign every report, later it became impossible.*" He did not hear anything from his apartment next to his offices either. In fact, he heard them one evening only:

> Twice in the evening, I heard noises in the Section IV offices. I intervened to see what it was all about. I noticed that detained people had been beaten; this was strictly prohibited. I announced to the people who were present—these were the members of the Dunker team together with Dunker himself—that I would arrest everybody if they continued the beating. Since I was living in the same house, I would be able to observe whether my orders were followed or not. Later, I heard nothing …

One observation is however timely: Mühler places all the blame on his subordinate Dunker. This explains the eagerness of Dunker to testify.

What about the Jewish affairs? He thought he remembered that Section IV-B was under his responsibility, but it came under the orders of Aloïs Brunner and his Sonderkommando (special unit). He knew that Brunner had sent Jews to Paris where their fate was decided, but he never saw any of them at 425, rue Paradis. As for the prison of les Baumettes, it was under army control. He had even demanded that the detention conditions be improved.

The Pencil Pusher

According to Mühler, he was a simple pencil pusher; he was just relaying orders from above and reports from below. He even tells us that, before the war, in Berlin he had been a member of the service "*that took care of literary, philosophical and scientific questions, in the press, etc. In its ranks, this service counted many gentlemen who had studied at German or foreign universities. The boss himself was a professor at Berlin University.*" Effectively, there are two telegrams sent from Berlin by Rolf Mühler, the first one on December 14, 1938, concerning the elimination of Jews from the German economy, and the second one on January 27, 1939, concerning the securities seized from Jewish communities. Literary, philosophical and scientific issues, obviously?[15]

He added about his job in Marseille: "*I am taking the liberty to point at the fact that I was one of the rare service heads who did not come from the executive section. There were several attempts to replace me with a gentleman of the executive... But in May 1944, the Central Office in Berlin—strictly speaking the head of Office IV who belonged to the executive succeeded in naming a successor, who did belong to the executive. This was Mr. Nolle, to whom I transferred my functions as a Kommandeur on June 1, 1944.*"

Commander Rolf Mühler wanted us to believe that he moved up the SS ladder exclusively on the base of his cultural knowledge, and that his bosses were not happy with him because he did not come from the Gestapo. This being said, it is quite plausible that he had started to hobble along in view of the ominous allied victory; hence his dismissal on June 1, 1944.

In reality, we have every indication that he was more active than he claimed. It is however plausible that he personally took a more active part in the hunt for members of the Resistance than in that for the Jews.

One question was not asked during his trial: what happened to Mühler after his departure from Marseille? Everything indicates that he returned to Berlin's Section VII. Indeed, toward the end of 1944, he became the commander of Schlesiersee, a retreat centre in Poland for the RSHA archives, where he heads a force of 65 subordinates. In this centre, situated 100 km southeast of Poznan, the RSHA had concentrated archives stolen in occupied countries as well as archives from the Berlin command. In his diary, Mühler describes the destruction of sensitive RSHA archives before his hasty departure westward ahead of the Russians toward the end of January or the beginning of February 1945. The remainder of the archives will be picked up by the Russians during close to 50 years.[16]

A Justice in Serious "Default"[17]

On November 7, 1947, three indicted members of the SiPo-SD of the Marseille region were in the hands of the military justice: Ernst Dunker, August Moritz,[*] head of Section VI, and Rolf Mühler. Arrest warrants had been issued against 142 other members of the SiPo-SD of the Marseille region.

As of today, there are 169 files in default[†] for individuals who had been attached to the SD of Marseille at one moment or another.[18] Among them, we find names that we have met previously in the Vaucluse.

Rolf Bilharz, the man who accompanied Palmieri in his actions against the Jews (Avignon, Cannes, etc.): on April 14, 1950, the warrant for his arrest

[*] August Moritz was sentenced to death in absentia, and unmasked by the Klarsfelds in 1973 in Hambourg.
[†] A file in default is a file that cannot be brought to trial for any number of reasons

issued on March 7, 1947, was *"cancelled, since the aforementioned man has benefited of a dismissal of the charges because of non-identification… However, the search for this individual needs to continue until April 14, 1960."* Bilharz will be uncovered in 1983 by a reporter of *Der Spiegel.*[19]

The file of Willy Bauer, head of the anti-Jewish section IV-B in Marseille, will also remain in default.

Wilhelm Müller: on April 14, 1950, the warrant for his arrest issued on March 7, 1947, was *"cancelled, since the aforementioned man has benefited of a dismissal of the charges because of non-identification… However, the search for this individual needs to continue until April 14, 1960."* He will not be found.

The charges against Wilhelm Müller were, however, not negligible: criminal conspiracy, assassinations, thefts, false imprisonment of individuals, looting, illegal arrests, voluntary homicide and homicide attempts, barbaric acts, daylight robbery, malicious wounding, and acts of violence. Moreover, these charges were similar to those against his Marseille boss, Rolf Mühler: criminal conspiracy, illegal arrests, malicious wounding, complicity with illegal arrests, complicity to malicious wounding, complicity to looting, complicity to arson, and complicity to assassinations.

Mühler—who was rumored to have gotten himself transferred just before Liberation—was arrested by the Americans, transferred to France, and sentenced to death on January 26, 1954, by the Permanent Tribunal of the Armed Forces in Marseille. He appealed before the Permanent Tribunal of the Armed Forces in Lyon in 1955, and just before the verdict he added that *"the events submitted to the tribunal date back to 10 or 11 years earlier; he underscores the difficult situation of the German army in 1944; his men and he had not asked to serve in France; he asks the tribunal to reflect on it."* And the tribunal reflected on it alright, since his death sentence is commuted to 20 years forced labor and 20 years of ban from the area. His sentence will be reduced twice more on the occasion of partial amnesties, and he is finally pardoned and freed in 1962. He would die of natural causes in 1967 in Wuppertal.

At first glance, Mühler had chosen a defense strategy paradoxically opposite to that of Charles Palmieri. Rolf Mühler admitted his action against the Resistance, on the condition that he had executed orders coming from superiors and that he was not aware of his subordinates' abuses; in addition, he insulated himself from Jewish affairs. In contrast, Palmieri took responsibility for his actions against the Jews, while keeping his distance from the hunt for the members of the Resistance. Palmieri knew well that actions against the Resistance would have led to a sentence of treason; however, he deemed the hunt for the Jews less serious in the context of the period. On his side, Rolf Mühler understood that the struggle against the resistance had pitted soldier against soldier, while hunting the Jews was a war crime against civilians. Judging by the outcome, the strategy worked.

As to his subordinate, Ernst Dunker, he had been sentenced to death on January 24, 1947, and executed on June 6, 1950. In the eyes of justice, there was a clear border line between the responsibility of Dunker and that of the big boss of Marseille. Rolf Mühler seemed not to have been included in the "handful of scoundrels" who incurred the harshness of the new French republican justice.

The case of Jakob Trumpfehler of the Avignon SiPo-SD deserves some attention. He participated as a driver to a multitude of actions against the Resistance and the Jews. He belonged to Section I. And yet, the Military Court of justice of Marseille takes note that "*the Nuremberg Tribunal did not include Sections I, II, and V of the Gestapo units as targeted by its declaration of criminality.*" The dismissal of charges is pronounced on December 18, 1948. While the argument can be understood, it is still a little, from the point of view of the victims, as if one had exonerated the driver of a gang during an armed robbery.

In a similar way, Heinrich Krabbe, a professional policeman and a member of the Avignon SiPo-SD, also benefited from a dismissal of the charges thanks to the testimonies of his German vicar and of a man from Avignon to whom he had confided that his work at the SD disgusted him. Moreover, the court took into consideration that "*being a professional policeman, he had not volunteered.*"

In these two latter cases, "*the mere affiliation with the Gestapo was not recognized as a crime.*"

Some individuals with a heavy police record attempted to elude justice by offering their services to the masters of the new republican regime. The recovery of some, like Palmieri, was not a success. One case however stands out.

Hans Sommer, *aka* Senner, was tried on July 9, 1948.[20] He denied being a member of the SD, and a dismissal of charges was issued on March 2, 1949, by the military Tribunal of Marseille. At that time, he lived at Mr. Perroux's home, 22, rue de la Paix in Paris. It must be noted that a high ranking intervention had shifted the wind in his favor. The Squadron Head of the Central Intelligence Bureau of the southeast wrote to the government Commissioner at the Tribunal of the 9th Military Region in Marseille:

> Hans Senner presents a genuine interest for our services and I have been charged by my direction with approaching you about his case.

He has already been used for several missions, and it appears that he could be very useful, because of his knowledge and the relationships he has preserved.

If there is no absolute objection to our request, I would be obliged to you to take into account the Senner case with the goal of considering his provisional liberation or a dismissal of the charges.

A report from the American Intelligence services, dated April 27, 1947, by the detachment in Dachau of the group against war crimes confirmed the importance of Senner during the war and the value of using him after the war:

> He had his office in Marseille from April 1940 until August 1944, and in San Remo from August 1944 to May 1945. His organization had branches in Spain, Portugal, England and North Africa, and hundreds of millions were put at his disposal.
>
> He was working for the RSHA in Berlin (Amt VI)

Senner is one more name in the list of German intelligence agents who had been planted in the free zone, long before November 11, 1942. The text confirms that he was indeed affiliated with Section VI of the RSHA, in particular the foreign intelligence agency headed by Walter Schellenberg.

In the new order after Liberation, all available means were used.

The Resistance Tops the List

On one hand, the prefectural apparatus had progressively reduced its collaboration activity: few actions against the Resistance and the STO dodgers, and no more roundups of Jews. Vichy was however pursuing its plan to eliminate Jews from the economy and society without directly collaborating toward their deportation. Only a reduced nucleus of reliable collaborators remained: the hard core of the Milice, the French volunteers to the Waffen SS, the CGQJ fanatics and "those Gentlemen" the auxiliaries.

On the other hand, with time, there was a steady increase in Resistance actions against German troops. With rudimentary means, the Resistance mounted guerilla operations against German strategic targets, soldiers and war material transport. Railroad tracks and main roads became less and less secure. The STO dodgers did not only escape from the German military effort, but they had become a pool of new recruits for the Resistance. Mühler was deeply aware of the situation.

I have underscored several times that, from the point of view of public security, police, etc., the Marseille region remained relatively quiet, much longer than other regions, those of Lyon, Limoges, Toulouse and Clermont-Ferrand, for instance. Enemy activity ended seldom in acts of sabotage and terrorism. The resistance was passive rather than active...

Toward the end of 1943 and at the beginning of 1944, information about the Resistance was growing. There were camps above all in the mountain districts. At that time, it was the beginning of 1944 if my memory is correct—the Wehrmacht took the initiative of a systematic fight against the Resistance. In Avignon, the site of the XIXth Army headquarters, we formed a central organization which coordinated all the intelligence about the maquis. It goes without saying that this central organization also disposed of all the staff needed to combat the maquis efficiently. The army often provided the "Brandebourg" unit, I have already mentioned... All the services susceptible to provide intelligence about the Resistance were assembled one day to organize this central group. I went to Draguignan twice where the Army corps headed by General [Baptist] Kniess was headquartered. Similarly, I took a part in negotiations in Aubagne, the site of the staff headquarters of a division headed by General [Hans] Schäfer... In Digne, there was a special battalion whose exclusive task was to combat the maquis, which started increasing dramatically in this region in March 1944. The head of this unit, a Commandant, came to see me several times. I know that, in May or at the beginning of June 1944, a few members of this unit and the head of our service in Digne were shot by the Resistance...

By the way, "the head of our service" in question was probably Wilhelm Wolfram, *aka* Gauthier, executed by the Resistance on June 6, 1944, during an ambush near Digne. In addition, this confirms that Gauthier, a member of the GFP who had been operating from the Hotel de la Cigale until his transfer to Digne, was also a member of the SiPo-SD of Avignon.

According to the circumstances described in his deposition, Mühler would have had a hard time not obeying the orders of his military associates, who had a higher rank. Therefore, he focused increasingly his attention on the repression of the "terrorists," all the more so since the hunt for the Jews was in good hands and he could not find a "Brunner" to take the lead on the Resistance business. Because they had no scruples, Dunker, Komp and their associates needed to be taken in hand and watched. His military associates would not have forgiven him anyway, had he discharged his responsibility on others. Moreover, Mühler had inherited a large contingent of GFP men whose job it was to protect the rear of the army.

It is therefore not surprising that, in the middle of the conflict between military needs and the racial policies of the Third Reich, it is the military pressure that won, thus leaving the execution of the racial policies in the hands of Mühler's subordinates, the members of the Brunner Kommando, and "those Gentlemen" the French auxiliaries; a truly dreadful team, but one with limited resources and conflicts of interest that have been amply described.

Paradoxically, the harassment by the Resistance, which did not place the rescue of the Jews at the top of its priorities, had contributed to monopolize the attention of the German police, and as such, slowed down its mission of extermination. Rolf Mühler did not pull out all the stops in carrying out his mission.

Epilogue:

In Front of the Barracks...

Vor der Kaserne
Vor dem großen Tor
Stand eine Laterne
Und steht sie noch davor
So woll'n wir uns da wieder seh'n
Bei der Laterne wollen wir steh'n
Wie einst Lili Marleen – Wie einst Lili Marleen.[*]

"Lili Marleen"
Lyrics of Hans Leip (1915) and music of Norbert Schultze (1938)

However dreadful it had seemed to be, the German repression machine collapsed in the face of the liberating forces, and the Vaucluse witnessed its crumbling under the pounding of the western allied armies. First, bombs landed on strategic spots: train tracks and roundhouses, bridges and main roads, material and ammunition depots, airfields. The retreating German army rushed into the Rhône valley where it became a prime target for the allied air force. British Spitfires hedgehopped just above the cypresses. From the roof tops, in the darkness of the sky, the air base of Orange was set ablaze. Gruesome rumors spread across the Vaucluse: national highway 7 was strewn with German bodies amid scattered heaps of military vehicles, weapons and supplies.

---

[*] In front of the barracks,
At the dawn of day,
The old street light suddenly flares up and shines.
It's in that corner that at night
We wait for each other, filled with hope
The two of us, Lily Marlène. (First verse of the French version by Henry Lemarchand in 1940)

No sooner was the last German soldier out of sight, that the towns and villages resounded with a parody of "Lili Marleen"—the old time favorite of the Afrika-Korps, made famous in English, on the allied side, by Marlene Dietrich in 1943. During recess, children broke into this song of revenge.

> In front of the barracks,
> A German soldier,
> Is mounting guard,
> While sniveling.
> I ask him: why are you crying?
> He answers me: we've had it!
> The Russians are right on our tail - The Russians are right on our tail.

In the school children's song, the demons of the German occupation were still present, the fear that they inspired had not yet vanished. One makes a mockery of what had been a source of terror, and we are almost convinced that the Germans were just clowns. But not just yet, because, for many, the wounds had not yet healed.

At the conclusion of this study about the Vaucluse, in looking at our return to the past, may be in itself a lingering exorcism of those early daemons, we are overwhelmed by the power of the Nazi police machinery, even if it broke down in the face of the massive attacks of the allied forces. The German police tracked down and turned Resistance fighters to discover the hideouts of the Maquis-Ventoux, at the edge of the Vaucluse. We have seen how that police unleashed the massive fire power of the German army—a detachment composed of a ground crew of the Luftwaffe, SS, members of the "Brandebourg Division," and Militia men. We have witnessed the massacre without hesitation of 35 Résistance fighters, who were surprised in their sleep. The disparity between that war machine and its victims was overpowering.

This was the same police apparatus the Jews of the Vaucluse had to face. They could all have been discovered and reduced to dust—every single one of them, since they carried so little weight. The machine had the means to do it, and furthermore, its bosses in Berlin had devoted all their energies to the elimination of the Jews. If in the Vaucluse the German police did not fulfill the desires of its leaders, it is because, under the pressure of events, it did not put the extermination of the Jews at the top of the list of its objectives.

One still trembles at the thought that it could have done so, that it makes us feel the urge to start singing the parody of "Lili Marleen" all over again.

Appendix A

The value of 100 French Francs in dollars of 2010

Year	2010 Value
1945	$ 16.4
1944	$ 24.3
1943	$ 29.7
1942	$ 36.9
1941	$ 44.4
1940	$ 52.2

Appendix B

Organization of the Milice

Main (Hand)	5 miliciens
Dizaine (Ten) = 2 Mains	10 miliciens
Trentaine (Thirty) = 3 Dizaines	30 miliciens
Centaine (Hundred) = 3 Trentaines + one group de command staff	100 miliciens
Cohorte (Cohort) = 3 ou 4 Centaines + one Trentaine of command staff	About 400 miliciens
Centre = several Cohortes	-

Appendix C

Arrest of Jews in the Italian zone

Last Name	First name	Place of Birth	Arrest location
Dreyfus	Claire	La Ferte s/Jouarre	Carpentras
Dreyfus	Francine	Paris	Carpentras
Dreyfus	Henri	Mulhouse	Pernes
Dreyfus	Jacques	Paris	Mormoiron
Dreyfus	Jean-Pierre	Paris	Carpentras
Dreyfus	René	Mulhouse	Pernes
Frank	Friedel	Somborn*	Carpentras
Frank	Henriette	Frankfurt*	Carpentras
Hochster	Emile	Bonn*	Pertuis
Karpiol	Bernard	Cologne*	Cadenet
Lyon	Leopold	Frankfurt*	Carpentras
Lyon	Rosa	Ruckerhausen*	Carpentras
Naquet	Adrien	Carpentras	Carpentras
Naquet	Gaston	Carpentras	Carpentras
Naquet	Marcelle	Nimes	Carpentras
Naquet	René	Carpentras	Carpentras
Weil	Joseph	Piltz*	Le Thor

The list includes 7 foreign Jews (*) and 10 French Jews.

Appendix D

Organization Chart of the Unified German Police and of Jewish Persecution 1943–1944

Legend

⟶ Direct Hierarchy

- - - ➤ Knochen has a line around his subordinates, the KdS heads

━ ➡ The Jewish Affairs in Berlin go around Oberg and Knochen

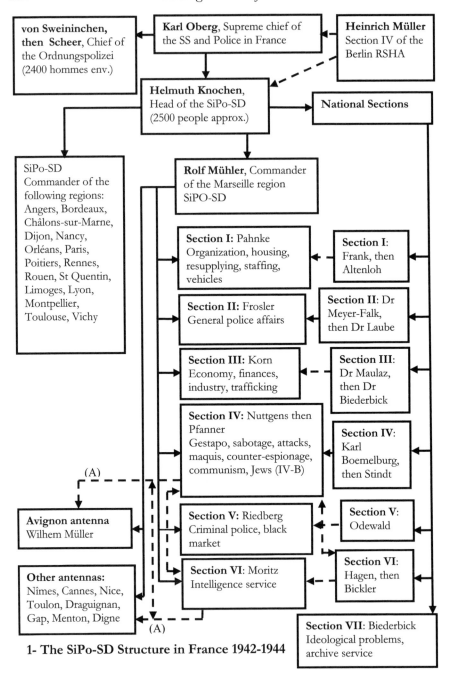

1- The SiPo-SD Structure in France 1942-1944

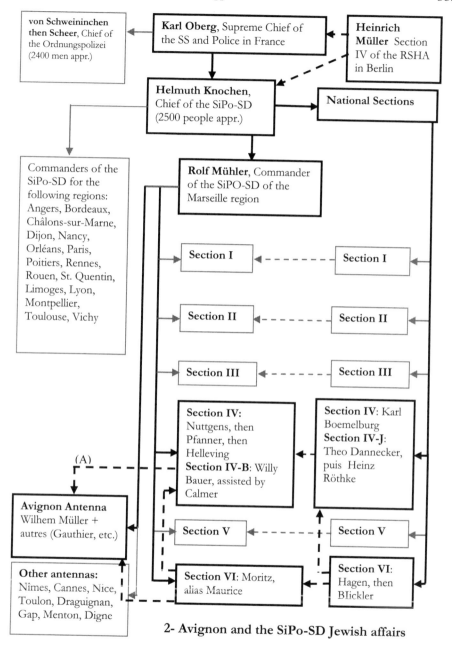

2- Avignon and the SiPo-SD Jewish affairs

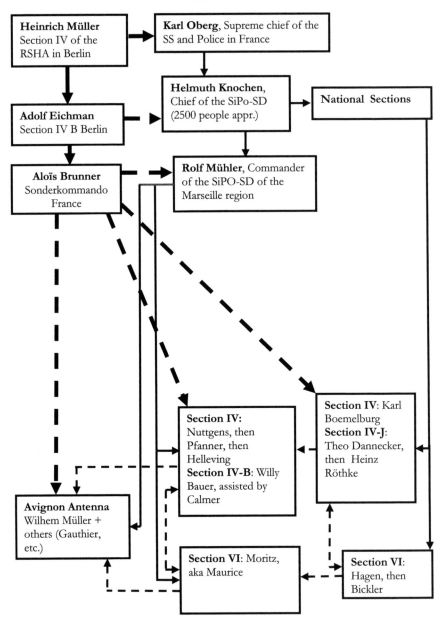

3- Aloïs Brunner injects himself into the Jewish affairs of the SiPo-SD

Notes

Preface

1. Isaac Levendel, *Not the Germans Alone*, Northwestern University Press, 1999 and 2000.

Foreword

1. François Bedarida, *La Shoah dans l'Histoire*, Esprit, juin 1997.
2. Isaac Levendel, *Un Hiver en Provence*, Editions de l'Aube, 1996.
3. Isaac Levendel, *Not the Germans Alone*, Northwestern University Press, 1999 and 2000.

Introduction: From State Anti-Semitism to Mob Rule

1. Saül Friedlander, *Les années de l'extermination*, Editions du Seuil, Paris 2008.
2. AJ 38 3807, Direction Régionale de Marseille, Archives Nationales.
3. http://www.not-the-germans-alone.org.
4. Isaac Levendel, *Un Hiver en Provence*, Editions de l'Aube, 1996.
5. Testimony of a person from Le Pontet, Gaston Vernet, in 1992.
6. Pascal Convert, Raymond Aubrac, *Résister, reconstruire, transmettre*, pp. 264-265, Editions du Seuil, 2011.
7. Philippe Bourdrel, *L'épuration sauvage*, 1944-1945, Perrin, 2002.
8. Pierre Bouisson, *Le Vaucluse à l'heure du provisoire, Mémoire de maitrise*, Avignon, 1997.
9. 3 W 21, Rapports du préfet de Vaucluse au Commissaire régional de la République des 10 et 23 novembre 1944, Archives Départementales de Vaucluse.
10. Philippe Bourdrel, *L'épuration sauvage*, 1944-1945, Perrin, 2002.
11. Lucie Favier, *La Mémoire de l'Etat: Histoire des Archives Nationales*, Editions Fayard, Paris, 2004.
12. 55 W 148, Dossier Palmieri, Rapport du Capitaine CRUCIANI, Archives Départementales des Bouches du Rhône.

Part One: The "French Solution" to the Jewish Question in Vaucluse

Chapter 1 : The Forgotten Jews of 1942

1. Aimé Autrand, *Le Département du Vaucluse: de la Défaite à la Libération*, Editions Aubanel-Avignon, 1965.
2. Ibid., p. 52.
3. http://www.yadvashem.org/wps/portal/IY_HON_Entrance.
4. Ibid.
5. Michèle Bitton, *Des noms pour mémoire—Les victimes de la Deuxième guerre mondiale à Pertuis (Vaucluse)*, Marseille, 2008 (édité sous l'égide de la Mairie de Pertuis).
6. Michèle Bitton et Jean Priol, *La guerre 1939-1945 et ses inscriptions à Villelaure (Vaucluse)*, Association Mémoire et Histoire, Marseille, 2010.
7. http://www.not-the-germans-alone.org/AMEJDVF/index.
8. Isaac Levendel, *Un Hiver en Provence*, Editions de l'Aube, 1996.
9. In the "111" list, one person was mentioned twice.
10. Robert Bailly, *Avignon 39/44—Histoire d' Avignon et des Avignonnais pendant la dernière Guerre (Septembre 1939–Septembre 1944)*, Editions A. Barthélémy, Avignon, 1986.
11. AJ 38 3817, Archives du CGQJ, Archives Nationales.
12. Aimé Autrand, *Le Département du Vaucluse: de la Défaite à la Libération*, Editions Aubanel, Avignon, 1965, pp. 231-232.

13. 3U7/459 Jacques Petit, Procédures de la Cour de Justice de Vaucluse, Archives Départementales du Gard.
14. Joseph Cucumel, personal communication to Isaac Levendel in January 1995.
15. 27 W 16, Mesures contre les Juifs, Archives départementales de Vaucluse.
16. Stéphane Courtois et Adam Rayski, *Qui Savait Quoi ?*, La Découverte, Paris, 1987.
17. Joseph Cucumel, personal communication to Isaac Levendel in January 1995.
18. Maxime Fischer, personal communication to Isaac Levendel, Paris, June 1995.
19. 6 W 37, Arrestations 43-44, Archives départementales de Vaucluse.
20. Robert O. Paxton, communication personnelle à Isaac Levendel en 1993.
21. Document LXXII-7 & 8 - Centre de Documentation Juive Contemporaine.
22. Robert Zaretzky, *Nîmes at War* (Nimes pendant la Guerre), Pennsylvania State University Press, 1995.
23. Haute Cour de Justice, Compte rendu in extensor des audiences, Imprimerie des Journeaux Officiels, Paris, 1945.
24. *Laval Parle* - Notes et mémoires rédigés par Pierre Laval dans sa cellule, Constant Bourquin, Genève, 1947.
25. Aimé Autrand, *Le Département du Vaucluse: de la Défaite à la Libération*, op. cit., page 29.
26. Maxime Fischer – personal communication.
27. Ibid.
28. Martyn Cornick, "The BBC and the Propaganda War Against Occupied France: the Work of Emile Delavenay and the European Intelligence Department," *Oxford Journal, French History*, Vol. 8, No. 3, pp. 316–354.
29. *Secret Intelligence and the Holocaust*, edited by David Bankier, pp. 171-186, Enigma Books, New York.
30. Bernard Wasserstein, *Britain and the Jews of Europe, 1939-1944*, p. 297, Clarendon Press, Oxford, 1979.
31. Estéra et Rose Margolis, personal communication.
32. 22 W 3, Archives Départementales du Vaucluse.
33. Michel Hayez, En Parcourant nos Quartiers et nos Rues, Gazette de la Paroisse St Joseph – Avignon, No 213, Hiver 2000.
34. Conversation between M. Hayez and Isaac Levendel, December 1992.

Chapter 2 - The CGQJ: Legalized Looting

1. AJ 38 3803, Rapports de la PQJ, Archives du CGQJ, Archives Nationales.
2. AJ 38 6332, Antoine d'Ornano, interception téléphonique concernant d'ORNANO, Archives du CGQJ, Archives Nationales.
3. Laurent Joly, *Vichy Dans la Solution Finale, Histoire du Commissariat Général aux Questions Juives 1941-1944,* Grasset, 2006.
4. 3U7/223, Antoine D'Ornano, Dossier de Procédure de la Cour de Justice du Gard, Archives Départementales du Gard.
5. Renée Dray-Bensoussan, *Les Juifs à Marseille (1940-1944),* Les Belles Lettres, 2004.

Chapter 3 - Henri de Camaret and His Network:
The CGQJ Delegate for the Vaucluse

1. 3U7/460, Dossiers de Procédure de la Cour de Justice de Vaucluse, Archives Départementales du Gard.
2. Ibid.
3. 3U7/410, Henri de Camaret, Dossiers de Procédure de la Cour de Justice de Vaucluse, Archives Départementales du Gard.
4. AJ 38 988, Dossier de de Camaret, Archives du CGQJ, Archives Nationales.
5. AJ 38 3806, Rapports de Jean Lebon, Archives du CGQJ, Archives Nationales.
6. The original documents are parts of various files covering the activity of the Jewish Affairs section at the Prefecture of Vaucluse (1st Division, 2nd Bureau) and are kept at the Archives Départementales.
7. Aimé Autrand, *Le Département de Vaucluse de la Défaite à la Libération : mai 1940–25 août 1944,* p.232, Aubanel, Avignon, 1965.
8. 7 W 15, Archives Départementales de Vaucluse.
9. 3U7/417, Régis Dubout, Dossier de Procédure de la Cour de Justice de Vaucluse, Archives Départementales du Gard.

10. Ibid.

11. 3U7/443, Maurice Rambaud, Dossier de Procédure de la Cour de Justice de Vaucluse, Archives Départementales du Gard.

12. 3U7/461, Henri de Camaret, Dossier de Procédure de la Cour de Justice de Vaucluse, Archives Départementales du Gard.

13. Aimé Autrand, *Le Département de Vaucluse de la Défaite à la Libération : mai 1940–25 août 1944*. p. 17. Aubanel, Avignon, 1965.

14. Laurent Joly, *Vichy dans la « Solution Finale » : Histoire du Commissariat Général aux Questions Juives, 1941-1944*, p. 775, Grasset, 2006.

15. Archives départementales de Vaucluse – Service éducatif.

16. Ordonnance n 45-770 du 21 avril 1945.

17. 3U7/ 417, Victor Dupeyre, Dossier de Procédure de la Cour de Justice de Vaucluse, Archives Départementales du Gard.

18. Comité International de la Croix Rouge, Genève, http://www.icrc.org/dih.nsf/FULL/350?OpenDocument.

19. 3U7/473 Henri de Camaret, Dossier de Procédure de la Cour de Justice de Vaucluse, Archives Départementales du Gard.

20. Ibid.

21. 3U7/410, Henri de Camaret, Dossier de Procédure de la Cour de Justice de Vaucluse, Archives Départementales du Gard.

22. 22 W 4, Comité Départemental de Libération, Archives Départementales de Vaucluse.

23. AJ 38 3801, SEC de Marseille, Archives Nationales.

24. 3U7/460, Henri de Camaret, Dossier de Procédure de la Cour de Justice du Vaucluse, Archives Départementales du Gard.

25. 3U7/410 et 461, Henri de Camaret, Dossier de Procédure de la Cour de Justice de Vaucluse, Archives Départementales du Gard.

26. 3U7/473, Henri de Camaret, Dossier de procédure de la Cour de Justice de Vaucluse, Archives Départementales du Gard.

27. 3U7/461, Henri de Camaret, Dossier de procédure de la Cour de Justice de Vaucluse, Archives Départementales du Gard

28. AJ 38 3803, Archives du CGQJ, Archives Nationales.

29. Renée Dray-Bensoussan, *Les Juifs à Marseille (1940-1944)*, Les Belles Lettres, Paris, 2004.

30. 8 W 4, Groupements de Collaboration, Renseignements Individuels, Archives Départementales du Vaucluse.

31. 3U7/461, Henri de Camaret, Dossier de Procédure de la Cour de Justice de Vaucluse, Archives Départementales du Gard.

Chapter 4 – The Trial of Jean Lebon

1. AJ 38 3803, Dossier Lebon, Archives Nationales.

2. AJ 38, Archives Nationales, Paris.

3. Max Fischer, personal communication 1995.

4. AJ 38 3801, SEC de Marseille, Archives Nationales.

5. AJ 38 3802, Dossier personnel de Jean Lebon, Archives Nationales.

6. Aimé Autrand, *Le Département de Vaucluse de la Défaite à la Libération*, Aubanel, 1965.

7. 7 W 16, Mesures contre les juifs, Archives Départementales de Vaucluse.

8. In his last function, Lebon was in fact an Inspector of the SEC, and not of the Jewish Affairs. He was an Inspector for Jewish Affairs police between February 13, 1942, and his appointment to the SEC (AJ 38 3801).

9. Jean-Pierre Aazema, *Les Libérations de la France: Prologue*, French Cultural Studies, 1994, 5:223-226.

10. Laurent Joly, *Vichy dans la Solution Finale—Histoire du Commissariat aux Questions Juives, 1941-1944*, Grasset, 2006.

11. Ibid.

12. AJ 38 3801, Dossier de Lebon, Archives Nationales.

13. AJ 38 3801, SEC de Marseille, Archives Nationales.

14. Laurent Joly, *Vichy*.

15. AJ 38 5837, Archives du CGQJ, Archives Nationales.

16. AJ 38 3806, Rapports de Jean Lebon, Archives du CGQJ, Archives Nationales.

17. 3 W 18, Rapport mensuels du préfet, Archives Départementales du Vaucluse.

18. AJ 38 5837, Cas divers, Archives Nationales.
19. AJ 38 3806, Rapports mensuels, Archives Nationales.
20. Léo Taxil, *Les Frères Trois Points,* Letouzey et Ané, Paris, ca. 1885.
21. 3U7/410, De Camaret Henri, Procédure de la Cour de Justice de Vaucluse, Archives Départementales du Gard.
22. Aimé Autrand, *Le Département de Vaucluse de la Défaite à la Libération,* Aubanel, 1965.
23. AJ 38 3802, Dossier Jean Lebon, Archives Nationales.
24. Aimé Autrand, *Le Département de Vaucluse de la Défaite à la Libération,* Aubanel, 1965.
25. AJ 38 3803, Dossier Jean Lebon, Archives Nationales.
26. AJ 38 3802, SEC de Marseille, Archives Nationales.
27. AJ 38 3803, Dossier Jean Lebon, Archives Nationales.
28. 27 W 16, Mesures contre les Juifs, Archives départementales de Vaucluse.
29. Ibid.
30. Papiers de René de Chambrun, Coffret No 1, Document No. 76, Hoover Institution Archives, Stanford, Californie.
31. AJ 38 3807, Rapports mensuels du Directeur régional de la SEC de Marseille, Archives Nationales.
32. Voir audition Henri Dreyfus, 28 février 1945.
33. AJ 38 3803, Dossier Lebon, Archives Nationales.
34. Ibid.
35. Laurent Joly, *Vichy.*
36. 3 W 29, Bulletins hebdomadaires des Renseignements Généraux 1942-1944, Archives Départementales de Vaucluse.
37. 55 W 80, Albert Simon, dossier de procédure, Archives Départementales des Bouches du Rhône.
38. Laurent Joly, *Vichy.*
39. 3U7/428, Jean Lebon, Procédure de la Cour de Justice de Vaucluse, Archives Départementales du Gard.
40. AJ 38 3803, Dossier Lebon, Archives Nationales.

Chapter 5 - A State-Sponsored Network of Profiteers of Jewish Assets

1. Matthew 21:33—The Parable of the Tenants.
2. Gaston Bunel, *Guide des Vignerons et Caves des Côtes du Rhône,* p. 148, Paris, Lattès, 1980.
3. Conservation des Hypothèques, Archives Départementales du Vaucluse.
4. Document CXCV-1, Centre de Documentation Juive Contemporaine.
5. AJ 38 – 3806, Jean Lebon, Rapports d'enquêtes, Archives du CGQJ, Archives Nationales.
6. Gaston Brunel, *Guide des Vignerons et Caves des Côtes du Rhône,* pp. 148-149, Paris, Lattès, 1980.
7. Jean Laloum, La restitution des biens spoliés, Les Cahiers de la Shoah, Les belles lettres, 2002/1 – No. 6.
8. Mission d'étude sur la spoliation des Juifs de France, sous la direction du président MATTEOLI, Rapport Général, La Documentation Française, Paris, 2000.
9. Données de l'Institut National de la Statistique et des Etudes Economiques: http://www.insee.fr/en/indicateur/achatfranc.htm.
10. Matthew 21:33–46—end of the Parable of the Tenants.
11. AJ 38 3813, Direction Régionale du CGQJ de Marseille, Archives Nationales.
12. AJ 38 988, Direction Régionale du CGQJ de Marseille, Archives Nationales.
13. 3U7/460, Henri de Camaret, Dossier de procédure, Cour de Justice du Vaucluse, Archives départementales du Gard.
14. Ibid.
15. Table des propriétaires (Table of owners), Archives Départementales du Vaucluse.
16. Félix Terrier, grandson of Stanislas Terrier, personal communication, Châteauneuf du Pape, July 25, 2008.
17. Jean-Marc Dreyfus, personal communication, August 13, 2008.
18. AJ 38 3800, Direction Régionale du CGQJ de Marseille, Archives Nationales.
19. AJ 38 3803, Direction Régionale du CGQJ de Marseille, Archives Nationales.
20. 22 W 11, Séances du CDL, Archives Départementales du Vaucluse.
21. Dossiers du CGQJ de de Camaret et de Lebon.
22. AJ 38 3803, Direction Régionale du CGQJ de Marseille, Archives Nationales.
23. 3U7/461, Henri de Camaret, Dossier de procédure de la Cour de Justice du Vaucluse, Archives Départementales du Gard.

24. AJ 39 3819, Dossiers de restitutions, Archives du CGQJ, Archives Nationales.
25. AJ 38 5837, Archives du CGQJ, Archives Nationales.
26. AJ 38 3806, Archives du CGQJ, Archives Nationales.
27. 7 W 16, Mesures contre les Juifs, Archives Départementales du Vaucluse.
28. AJ 38 3803, Direction Régionale du CGQJ de Marseille, Archives Nationales.
29. 3U7/460, Henri de Camaret, Dossier de procédure de la Cour de Justice de Vaucluse, Archives Départementales du Gard.
30. AJ 38 5837, Archives du CGQJ, Archives Nationales.
31. Série 1200 W, Actes originaux sous seings privés, Archives du Tribunal de Commerce, Archives Départementales du Vaucluse.
32. AJ 38 3807, Rapports mensuels de la SEC, Archives du CGQJ, Archives Nationales.

Chapter 6 - Régis d'Oléon, President of the *Légion Française des Combattants* of Vaucluse

1. 3 W 17, Bulletins des Renseignements Généraux, Archives Départementales de Vaucluse.
2. 3U7/426, Jules Joly, Dossiers de Procédure de la Cour de Justice de Vaucluse, Archives Départementales du Gard.
3. Henri du Moulin de Labarthete, *Le Temps des Illusions*, Editions du Cheval Ailé, Genève, 1946.
4. 3U7/464, Régis d'Oléon, Chambre Civique, Archives Départementales du Gard.
5. AJ 38 3801, Rapports de de Camaret, Archives du CGQJ, Archives Nationales.
6. 47 W 5, La Légion, Archives Départementales du Vaucluse.
7. 3U7/403, Gaston Barbarant, Dossiers de Procédure de la Cour de Justice de Vaucluse, Archives Départementales du Gard.
8. 3U7/464, Chambre Civique de Vaucluse, Rapport de Police du 10 février 1945.
9. 22 W 4, Délibérations du CDL, Archives Départementales de Vaucluse.
10. 1035 W 1, 2 et 3, Tribunal d'état de Lyon, Archives départementales du Rhône.
11. Catherine Fillon, personal communication (AN BB30 1707, Papiers Gabolde).
12. 3U7/419, Bernard Faucon, Dossiers de Procédure de la Cour de Justice de Vaucluse, Archives Départementales du Gard.
13. AJ40/541, Archives Nationales, Paris.

Part Two - The Germans and Their Associates: The "German Solution" to the Jewish Question in Vaucluse

1. Raymond Raoul Lambert, *Carnet d'un Témoin 1940-1943*, Editions Fayard, Paris, 1985.

Chapter 7 - The Purest Riffraff Around

1. Document Numéro 014-PS, http://www.yale.edu/lawweb/avalon/imt/document/014-ps.htm, The Avalon Project, Yale University.
2. 55 W 148, Dossier Palmieri, Cour de Justice de Marseille, Archives Départementales des Bouches du Rhône.
3. 3U7/423, dossier Marie-Claire Jean, Archives départementales du Gard.
4. 55 W 148, Dossier Palmieri, Archives Départementales des Bouches du Rhône.
5. 3U7/283, dossier Blanc Lucien, Archives départementales du Gard.
6. 3U7/431, dossier Auguste Manzon, Archives départementales du Gard.
7. 3U7/420, dossier Tiziano Feroldi, Archives départementales du Gard.
8. 3U7/420, dossier Tiziano Feroldi, Archives départementales du Gard.
9. Marceline Loridan-Ivens, *Ma vie Balagan*, Rober Lafont, 2008.
10. 3U7/473, Henri de Camaret, Cour de justice de Vaucluse, Archives départementales du Gard.
11. AJ 38 3803, Archives de la SEC, Archives Nationales, Paris.
12. 6 W 37, Rapport de Police, Archives Départementales de Vaucluse.
13. 3U7/413, dossier Jean Costa, Archives départementales du Gard.
14. Jacques Delarue, *Histoire de la Gestapo*, Fayard, 1962.
15. Brown, Paul B., *The Senior Leadership Cadre of the Geheime Feldpolizei, 1939-1945* Holocaust and Genocide Studies - Volume 17, Number 2, Fall 2003, pp. 278-304.
16. Ibid.

17. The indictment list of the military tribunal counts about 10 members in the Avignon SiPo-SD ; this number somewhat underestimates the size of the Avignon German police.
18. 58 W 20, Ernst Dunker, Déposition, Cour de Justice de Marseille, Archives Départementales des Bouches du Rhône.
19. Dossier de Londres No 1068 ; summaries can be found in many procedural files of the civilian and military courts.
20. 6 W 37 Archives Départementales de Vaucluse.
21. 3U7/429, dossier Roger Leonetti, Cour de justice de Vaucluse, Archives départementales du Gard.
22. 3U7/447, dossier Pierre Terrier, Cour de justice de Vaucluse, Archives départementales du Gard.
23. 3U7/409, dossier Victor Bruni, Cour de justice de Vaucluse. Archives départementales du Gard.
24. Conversation between Ginette Kolinka and Isaac Levendel, on July 23, 2008.
25. 3U7/447, dossier Denis Teyssier, Cour de justice de Vaucluse. Archives départementales du Gard.
26. Harry de Quetteville, I said no to art lessons from Henri Matisse, The Telegraph, February 7, 2001.
27. Nelcya Delanoë, personal communication.
28. 3U7/437, dossier Maurice Pardini, Cour de justice de Vaucluse. Archives départementales du Gard
29. 3U7/413, dossier Jean Costa, Cour de justice de Vaucluse. Archives départementales du Gard.
30. 55 W 100, Boyer « de Mondragon », Dossier de Procédure de la Cour de Justice de Marseille, Archives Départementales des Bouches du Rhône.
31. 55 W 102, Jean-Baptiste Cabagno Dossier de Procédure de la Cour de Justice de Marseille, Archives Départementales des Bouches du Rhône.
32. 55 W 104, Antoine Cappe, Dossier de Procédure de la Cour de Justice de Marseille, Archives Départementales des Bouches du Rhône.
33. 55 W 100, Boyer « de Mondragon », Dossier de Procédure de la Cour de Justice de Marseille, Archives Départementales des Bouches du Rhône.
34. 3U7/413, dossier Jean Costa, Cour de justice de Vaucluse. Archives départementales du Gard
35. Conversation on February 8, 2008.
36. 55 W 104, Antoine Cappe, Dossier de Procédure de la Cour de Justice de Marseille, Archives Départementales des Bouches du Rhône.
37. 55 W 100, Roger Boyer (de Mondragon), Dossier de Procédure de la Cour de Justice de Marseille, Archives Départementales des Bouches du Rhône.
38. Ibid.
39. 55 W 104, Antoine Cappe, Dossier de Procédure de la Cour de Justice de Marseille, Archives Départementales des Bouches du Rhône.
40. 55 W 148, doc. 448, dossier Palmieri, Archives départementales des Bouches du Rhône.
41. 3U7/445, dossier Pierre Terrier, Cour de justice de Vaucluse. Archives départementales du Gard.
42. AJ38 3807, Archives du Commissariat Général aux Questions Juives, Archives Nationales.
43. 55 W 100, Roger Boyer (de Mondragon), Dossier de Procédure de la Cour de Justice de Marseille, Archives Départementales des Bouches du Rhône.
44. 55 W 102, Jean-Baptiste Cabagno, Dossier de Procédure de la Cour de Justice de Marseille, Archives Départementales des Bouches du Rhône.
45. 55 W 100, Roger Boyer (de Mondragon), Dossier de Procédure de la Cour de Justice de Marseille, Archives Départementales des Bouches du Rhône.
46. Grégory Auda, *Les Belles années du Milieu 1940-1944*, Editions Michalon, Paris, 2002, p. 187-189.
47. Ibid., p. 132.
48. 55 W 100, Roger Boyer (de Mondragon), Dossier de Procédure de la Cour de Justice de Marseille, Archives Départementales des Bouches du Rhône.
49. 3U7/283, Lucien Blanc, Dossiers de Procédure de la Cour de Justice du Gard, Archives Départementales du Gard.
50. 3U7/449, dossier Marcelle Veran, Cour de justice de Vaucluse. Archives départementales du Gard.
51. 3U7/283, dossier Lucien Blanc, Archives départementales du Gard (deposition of Palmieri).
52. 3U7/201, dossier Joseph Allemand, Archives départementales du Gard.
53. Gregory Aauda, *Les Belles Années du "Milieu" 1940–1944*, Editions Michalon, 2002.

Chapter 8 - Wilhelm Müller's Favorites

1. AJ 38 3815, Archives du CGQJ, Archives Nationales.
2. 58 W 20, Ernst Dunker, Déposition, Cour de Justice de Marseille, Archives Départementales des Bouches du Rhône.

3. La Résistance en Vaucluse, Documents et témoignages, Service Educatif des Archives Départementales de Vaucluse et Collection Begou, Archives Départementales de Vaucluse.

4. 3U7/447 Pierre Terrier, dossier de procédure de la Cour de Justice de Vaucluse, Archives Départementales du Gard.

5. 3U7/433 Jean-Daniel Michon, dossier de procédure de la Cour de Justice de Vaucluse, Archives Départementales du Gard.

6. 3U7/410 Robert Conrad, dossier de procédure de la Cour de Justice de Vaucluse, Archives Départementales du Gard.

7. « Vaucluse 44, l'année de la liberté retrouvée, » publication réalisée par le service départemental de l'office national des Anciens Combattants et Victimes de Guerre (Mission du 60ème anniversaire des débarquements et de libération de la France).

8. 3U7/447 Jean Terrier, dossier de procédure de la Cour de Justice de Vaucluse, Archives Départementales du Gard.

9. 3U7/426 Marie-Claire Jean, dossier de procédure de la Cour de Justice de Vaucluse, Archives Départementales du Gard.

10. 3U7/424 Gisèle Guyon, dossier de procédure de la Cour de Justice de Vaucluse, Archives Départementales du Gard.

11. 3U7/423 Antoine Guidoni, dossier de procédure de la Cour de Justice de Vaucluse, Archives Départementales du Gard.

12. 3U7/230 Walter Garattoni, dossier de procédure de la Cour de Justice du Gard, Archives Départementales du Gard.

13. 3U7/450 Michel Versin, dossier de procédure de la Cour de Justice de Vaucluse, Archives Départementales du Gard.

14. "Vaucluse 44, l'année de la liberté retrouvée," publication réalisée par le service départemental de l'office national des Anciens Combattants et Victimes de Guerre (Mission du 60ème anniversaire des débarquements et de libération de la France).

15. 3U7/447 Pierre Terrier, dossier de procédure de la Cour de Justice de Vaucluse, Archives Départementales du Gard.

16. 3 U 7/410, Robert Conrad, Dossier de procédure, Cour de Justice de Vaucluse, Archives Départementales du Gard.

17. 3 U 7/448, Yves Thesmar, Dossier de procédure, Cour de Justice de Vaucluse, Archives Départementales du Gard.

18. Ibid.

19. AJ 38 3801, Dossier de Lebon, Archives Nationales.

20. 3 W 19, Rapport du préfet, Archives Départementales du Vaucluse.

21. 3 U 7/405, Albert Bathelier, Dossier de procédure, Cour de Justice de Vaucluse, Archives Départementales du Gard.

22. 3 W 19, Rapports du préfet, Archives Départementales du Vaucluse.

23. 3 W 28 Bulletins hebdomadaires des Renseignements Généraux 1942-1944, Archives Départementales de Vaucluse.

24. Christelle Fageot, Milice et milicien(ne)s en Vaucluse, Université d'Avignon, 2007.

25. 3 W 19, Rapport du préfet, Archives Départementales du Vaucluse.

26. 3 W 28 Bulletins hebdomadaires des Renseignements Généraux 1942-1944, Archives Départementales de Vaucluse.

27. 3 W 28 Bulletins hebdomadaires des Renseignements Généraux 1942-1944, Archives Départementales de Vaucluse.

28. 3 U 7/442, Giqueaux du Crouzet, Note des RG d'Avignon aux RG de Vichy, Dossier de procédure, Cour de Justice de Vaucluse, Archives Départementales du Gard.

29. 3 W 19, Rapport du préfet, Archives Départementales du Vaucluse.

30. 8 W 4, Documents de la Milice, Archives Départementales de Vaucluse.

31. Personal communication, 1995.

32. 3 W 20, Rapport du préfet, Archives Départementales du Vaucluse.

33. 3 U 7/425, Alfred Hentzen, Dossier de procédure, Cour de Justice de Vaucluse, Archives Départementales du Gard.

34. 3U7/410 René Caprio, Procédures de la Cour de Justice du Vaucluse, Archives Départementales du Gard.

35. 3U7/426 Pierre Kuhling, Procédures de la Cour de Justice du Vaucluse, Archives Départementales du Gard.

36. 3U7/416 Paul Desjardin, Procédures de la Cour de Justice du Vaucluse, Archives Départementales du Gard.

37. 3 U 7/421, Auguste Gandon, Dossier de procédure, Cour de Justice de Vaucluse, Archives Départementales du Gard.

38. 3U7/421 Auguste Gandon, Procédures de la Cour de Justice du Vaucluse, Archives Départementales du Gard.

39. 3 U 7/423, Jules Gondoin, Dossier de procédure, Cour de Justice de Vaucluse, Archives Départementales du Gard.

40. SAP-R2-BCRA Londres-Alger, réseau l'Archiduc.

41. Pierre Bonvallet, *Histoire du Maquis Ventoux 43-44*.

42. 6 W 37, Arrestations 1943-1944, Archives Départementales de Vaucluse.

43. Jean-Louis Medveowski, *Mémoire d'Automne*, Editions SAMSARA, 2001.

44. 3U7/420 Tiziano Feroldi, Procédures de la Cour de Justice du Vaucluse, Archives Départementales du Gard.

45. 55 W 148 Dossier Palmieri, Archives Départementales des Bouches du Rhône.

46. Today, Sathonay has been split into two villages, Sathonay Camp and Sathonay Village, both attached to the Rhône département (69).

47. 3U7/473 Henri de Camaret, Procédures de la Cour de Justice du Vaucluse, Archives Départementales du Gard.

48. 3U7/431, Albert Marin, Procédures de la Cour de Justice du Vaucluse, Archives Départementales du Gard.

49. Dossier Cruon, Archives de la Justice Militaire, Le Blanc.

50. 3U7/432 Gilbert Mercier, Procédures de la Cour de Justice du Vaucluse, Archives Départementales du Gard.

51. 3U7/432 Marie-Louise Mesley, épouse Rousset, Procédures de la Cour de Justice du Vaucluse, Archives Départementales du Gard.

52. 3U7/407 Raymond Bonabel, Procédures de la Cour de Justice du Vaucluse, Archives Départementales du Gard.

53. 3U7/424 Henri Guillerault, Procédures de la Cour de Justice du Vaucluse, Archives Départementales du Gard.

54. The significant participation of Jews in the Résistance has been confirmed multiple times. Among the 35 executed members of the maquis of Izon la Bruisse, 6 were Jewish : Alfred Epstein, Samuel Franck, Pinchus Hoffmann, Nathan Hoffmann, André Picard, José Polak.

55. 8 W 4 Groupements de collaboration, PPF, Milice, etc. Archives Départementales de Vaucluse.

56. 3U7/420 Tiziano Feroldi, Procédures de la Cour de Justice du Vaucluse, Archives Départementales du Gard.

57. 3U7/430 Denise Layet, Procédures de la Cour de Justice du Vaucluse, Archives Départementales du Gard.

58. 3U7/448, Yves Thesmar, Dossier de procédure, Cour de Justice du Vaucluse, Archives Départementales du Gard.

59. 3U7/423 Antoine Guidoni, Procédures de la Cour de Justice du Vaucluse, Archives Départementales du Gard.

60. 3U7/447 Pierre Terrier, Procédures de la Cour de Justice du Vaucluse, Archives Départementales du Gard.

61. Renzo De Felice, *The Jews in Fascist Italy. A History*. New York: Enigma Books, 2001.

62. 3U7/437 Jeanne Nesme, Procédures de la Cour de Justice du Vaucluse, Archives Départementales du Gard.

63. 47 W 33, Arrestations opérées à la libération, Archives Départementales de Vaucluse.

64. Serge Issantier (Correspondant de l'Histoire de la Seconde Guerre Mondiale), Contribution à l'Etude de l'Esprit Public du Vaucluse, mai/juin 1940 – août 1944.

65. 3U7/255 Jean Poutet, Procédures de la Cour de Justice du Gard, Archives Départementales du Gard

66. 3U7/438 Suzy Pommier, Procédures de la Cour de Justice du Vaucluse, Archives Départementales du Gard.

67. Le Bulletin Annuel d'Informations de l'Association 1901 « Les Amis de la Galicière », January 2003.

68. This information was partially provided by Vincent Feroldi (Lyon, France).

69. 3U7/449 et 474, Charles Uhl, Dossiers de Procédure de la Cour de Justice de Vaucluse, Archives Départementales du Gard.

70. La Résistance en Vaucluse – Documents et Témoignages, Service Educatif des Archives Départementales de Vaucluse.

71. 3U7/425, Laurent Idlas, Dossiers de Procédure de la Cour de Justice de Vaucluse, Archives Départementales du Gard.
72. 3U7/449 et 474, Charles Uhl, Dossiers de Procédure de la Cour de Justice de Vaucluse, Archives Départementales du Gard.
73. 3U7/420, René Le Flem, Dossiers de Procédure de la Cour de Justice de Vaucluse, Archives Départementales du Gard.
74. 3U7/421, Joachim Gatto, Dossiers de Procédure de la Cour de Justice de Vaucluse, Archives Départementales du Gard.
75. 3U7/442, Maurice Riety, Dossiers de Procédure de la Cour de Justice de Vaucluse, Archives Départementales du Gard.
76. 47 W 33, Arrestations opérées à la Libération, Archives Départementales de Vaucluse.
77. 3U7/407, Raymond Bonabel, Dossiers de Procédure de la Cour de Justice de Vaucluse, Archives Départementales du Gard.
78. 3U7/468, Georges Passelegue, Dossiers de Procédure de la Cour de Justice de Vaucluse, Archives Départementales du Gard.
79. 3U7/459, Jacques Petit, Dossiers de Procédure de la Cour de Justice de Vaucluse, Archives Départementales du Gard.
80. 3U7/473, Henri de Camaret, Dossiers de Procédure de la Cour de Justice de Vaucluse, Archives Départementales du Gard.
81. Pierre Giolitto, *Histoire de la Milice*, Perrin, 1997.
82. 22 W 3, Comité départemental de Libération, Archives Départementales de Vaucluse.
83. AJ 38 3800, Archives du CGQJ, Archives Nationales.
84. 8 W 4, Groupements de collaboration 43-45, Archives Départementales de Vaucluse.
85. 3U7/470, Registre des arrêts—Procès verbaux d'audiences, septembre 44–juillet 45, Archives Départementales du Gard.
86. 3 U 7/420, René Le Flem, Dossier de procédure, Cour de Justice de Vaucluse, Archives Départementales du Gard.
87. 3 W 24, Note des Renseignements Généraux du 30 août 1945, Archives Départementales de Vaucluse.
88. 58 W 20, Ernst Dunker, Déposition, Cour de Justice de Marseille, Archives Départementales des Bouches du Rhône.
89. 3 W 24, Note des Renseignements Généraux du 30 août 1945, Archives Départementales de Vaucluse.
90. 3 U 7/255, Jean Poutet, Dossier de procédure, Cour de Justice de Gard, Archives Départementales du Gard.
91. 3 U 7/444, Vahan Sarkissoff, Dossier de procédure, Cour de Justice de Vaucluse, Archives Départementales du Gard.
92. 3 W 28 Bulletins hebdomadaires des Renseignements Généraux 1942-1944, Archives Départementales de Vaucluse.
93. Renée Dray-Bensoussan, *Les Juifs à Marseille 1940-1944*, Les Belles Lettres, 2004.
94. 3 U 7/410, René Caprio, Dossier de procédure, Cour de Justice de Vaucluse, Archives Départementales du Gard.
95. 3 U 7/404, Gaston Barbarant, Dossier de procédure, Cour de Justice de Vaucluse, Archives Départementales du Gard.
96. 3 U 7/421, Victor Gaillard, Dossier de procédure, Cour de Justice de Vaucluse, Archives Départementales du Gard.
97. 47 W 18 Notes sur l'épuration, Archives Départementales de Vaucluse.
98. 3 W 28 Bulletins hebdomadaires des Renseignements Généraux 1942-1944, Archives Départementales de Vaucluse.
99. 8 W 4 Groupements de Collaboration, Archives Départementales de Vaucluse.
100. 22 W 14 Comité de Libération, Archives Départementales de Vaucluse.
101. 55 W 148 Dossier Palmieri, Archives Départementales des Bouches du Rhône.
102. 3 U 7/410, René Caprio, Dossier de procédure, Cour de Justice de Vaucluse, Archives Départementales du Gard.
103. Paul Jankowski, *Communism and Collaboration—Simon Sabiani and Politics in Marseille 1919–1944*, Yale University Press, 1989.
104. 3 U 7/425, Laurent Idlas, Dossier de procédure, Cour de Justice de Vaucluse, Archives Départementales du Gard.

105. Henri du Moulin de Labarthete, *Le Temps des Illusions—Souvenirs (Juillet 1940–Avril 1942)*, Les Editions du Cheval Ailé, 1946.
106. 8 W 4, Groupements de collaboration, PPF. Milice, etc. Archives Départementales de Vaucluse.
107. 3 U 7/404, Gaston Barbarant, Dossier de procédure, Cour de Justice de Vaucluse, Archives Départementales du Gard.
108. 3 U 7/425, Laurent Idlas, Dossier de procédure, Cour de Justice de Vaucluse, Archives Départementales du Gard.
109. 3 W 28 Bulletins hebdomadaires des Renseignements Généraux 1942-1944, Archives Départementales de Vaucluse.
110. Ibid.
111. Ibid.
112. 3 U 7/425, Laurent Idlas, Dossier de procédure, Cour de Justice de Vaucluse, Archives Départementales du Gard.
113. Dossier Jacques Tricon, Archives de la Justice Militaire, Le Blanc.

Chapter 9 - The Palmieri Gang: Serving the SiPo-SD

1. 3U7/283 Lucien Blanc, Procédures de la Cour de Justice du Gard, Archives Départementales du Gard.
2. Isaac Levendel, *Un Hiver en Provence*, Editions de l'Aube, 1996.
3. 3U7/425 Laurent Idlas, Procédures de la Cour de Justice du Vaucluse, Archives Départementales du Gard.
4. 3U7/434 Gaston Mouillade, Procédures de la Cour de Justice du Vaucluse, Archives Départementales du Gard.
5. 3U7/404, Gaston Barbarant, Procédures de la Cour de Justice du Vaucluse, Archives Départementales du Gard.
6. 8 W 4, Groupements de collaboration, PPF. Milice, etc. Archives Départementales de Vaucluse.
7. 3U7/412, Rose Chauveau, Procédures de la Cour de Justice du Vaucluse, Archives Départementales du Gard.
8. 8 W 4, Groupements de collaboration, PPF. Milice, etc. Archives Départementales de Vaucluse.
9. 3 W 28, Bulletins hebdomadaires des Renseignements Généraux, 1942-1944, Archives Départementales de Vaucluse.
10. Ibid.
11. 55 W 148, Dossier Palmieri, Archives Départementales des Bouches du Rhône.
12. 3U7/283, Lucien Blanc, Procédures de la Cour de Justice du Gard, Archives Départementales du Gard.
13. 55 W 148, Dossier Palmieri, Archives Départementales des Bouches du Rhône (Déposition de Rodolphe Bride).
14. 8 W 4, Groupements de collaboration, PPF. Milice, etc. Archives Départementales de Vaucluse.
15. 55 W 148 Dossier Palmieri, Archives Départementales des Bouches du Rhône.
16. Ibid.
17. 822-823, Tribunal Permanent des Forces Armées à Lyon, Archives de la Justice Militaire, Le Blanc.
18. Philippe Aziz, Au Service de l'Ennemi, Fayard, 1972. Note: Aziz chose for some indivuiduals fictitious names, which need to be decoded by cross-checks.
19. 58 W 20, Ernst Dunker, Déposition, Cour de Justice de Marseille, Archives Départementales des Bouches du Rhône.
20. Paul Jankowski, *Communism and Collaboration—Simon SABIANI and Politics in Marseille 1919-1944*, Yale University Press, 1989.
21. 3U7/283, Lucien Blanc, Procédures de la Cour de Justice du Gard, Archives Départementales du Gard.
22. 55 W 148, Dossier Palmieri, Archives Départementales des Bouches du Rhône.
23. 876, Dossiers de Paris, Archives de la Justice Militaire, Le Blanc.
24. 8 W 4, Groupements de collaboration, PPF. Milice, etc. Archives Départementales de Vaucluse.
25. 55 W 80, Albert Simon, Dossier de procédure de la Cour de Justice des Bouches du Rhône, Archives Départementales des Bouches du Rhône.
26. Grégory Auda, *Les Bandits Corses*, Editions Michalon, 2005.
27. 3U7/283, Lucien Blanc, Deposition of Palmieri on March 10, 1945, before Judge Larat, Procédures de la Cour de Justice du Gard, Archives Départementales du Gard.
28. Gregory Auda, *Les Belles Années du "Milieu" 1940-1944*, Editions Michalon, 2002.

29. 3U7/283, Lucien Blanc, Procédures de la Cour de Justice du Gard, Archives Départementales du Gard.
30. 55 W 148, Palmieri Charles, Dossier de Procédure de la Cour de Justice de Marseille, Archives Départementales des Bouches du Rhône.
31. 55 W 148, dossier Palmieri, Archives départementales des Bouches du Rhône.
32. 3U7/283, Lucien Blanc, Procédures de la Cour de Justice du Gard, Archives Départementales du Gard.
33. 8W4 Groupements de collaboration, PPF. Milice, etc. Archives Départementales de Vaucluse.
34. 3U7/201, Allemand Joseph, Cour de Justice du Gard, Archives Départementales du Gard.
35. 56 W 21, Rodolphe Bride, Dossier de non lieux, Archives de la Cour de Justice des Bouches du Rhône, Archives Départementales des Bouches du Rhône.
36. Personal communication of Gaston Vernet, a neighbor of the Levendels.
37. Gregory Auda, *Les Belles Années du "Milieu" 1940-1944*, Editions Michalon, 2002.
38. 58 W 20, Ernst Dunker, déposition, Cour de Justice de Marseille, Archives Départementales des Bouches du Rhône.
39. 55 W 148, Confrontation du 7 août 1945, dossier Palmieri, Archives Départementales des Bouches du Rhône.
40. 55 W 148, dossier Palmieri, Archives Départementales des Bouches du Rhône.
41. 56 W 21, Rodolphe Bride, Dossier de non lieux, Archives de la Cour de Justice des Bouches du Rhône, Archives Départementales des Bouches du Rhône.
42. 3U7/434 Gaston Mouillade, Procédures de la Cour de Justice du Vaucluse, Archives Départementales du Gard—Rapport du Commissaire de Police Rotton Victor sur l'affaire Mouillade—2 mai 1945.
43. 47 W 15, Archives Départementales du Vaucluse.
44. Estrea Asseo, conversation with Isaac Levendel in 1992.
45. Marc Olivier Barouch (sous la direction de), *Une Poignée de Misérables*, Fayard, Paris, 2003.
46. 55 W 130, François Heiter, Dossier de procédure de la Cour de Justice des Bouches du Rhône, Archives Départementales des Bouches du Rhône.
47. Ibid.
48. Gregory Auda, *Les Belles Années du "Milieu" 1940-1944*, Editions Michalon, 2002.

Part Three - Shades of Grey

1. Adam Rayski et Jean Courtois, *Qui Savait Quoi?*
2. 3U7/403, Edmond Autran, Cour de Justice de Vaucluse, Archives Départementales du Gard.
3. 3U7/447, Pierre Terrier, Dossier de procédure, Cour de Justice de Vaucluse, Archives Départementales du Gard.
4. 3U7/404, Edouard Badier, Dossier de procédure, Cour de Justice de Vaucluse, Archives Départementales du Gard.
5. 3U7/408, Louis Boyer, Dossier de procédure, Cour de Justice de Vaucluse, Archives Départementales du Gard.
6. 3U7/409, Augustin Bremond, Dossier de procédure, Cour de Justice de Vaucluse, Archives Départementales du Gard.
7. 3U7/411, Lucien Carrel, Dossier de procédure, Cour de Justice de Vaucluse, Archives Départementales du Gard.
8. 3U7/411, Fernand Chamond, Dossier de procédure, Cour de Justice de Vaucluse, Archives Départementales du Gard.
9. 3U7/411, Victor Chanoux, Dossier de procédure, Cour de Justice de Vaucluse, Archives Départementales du Gard.
10. 3U7/418, Emile Estachy, Dossier de procédure, Cour de Justice de Vaucluse, Archives Départementales du Gard.
11. 3U7/424, Henri Guillerault, Dossier de procédure, Cour de Justice de Vaucluse, Archives Départementales du Gard.
12. 3U7/424, Antoine Guisset, Dossier de procédure, Cour de Justice de Vaucluse, Archives Départementales du Gard.
13. 3U7/425, Alfred Hentzen, Dossier de procédure, Cour de Justice de Vaucluse, Archives Départementales du Gard.

14. 3U7/428, Denise Layet, Dossier de procédure, Cour de Justice de Vaucluse, Archives Départementales du Gard.
15. 3U7/428, Gaston Lefebvre, Dossier de procédure, Cour de Justice de Vaucluse, Archives Départementales du Gard.
16. 3U7/430, Louis Manca, Dossier de procédure, Cour de Justice de Vaucluse, Archives Départementales du Gard.
17. 3U7/438, Albert Pilat, Dossier de procédure, Cour de Justice de Vaucluse, Archives Départementales du Gard.
18. 3U7/404, Gaston Barbarant, Dossier de procédure, Cour de Justice de Vaucluse, Archives Départementales du Gard.

Part Four - Summing Up the Effectiveness of Anti-Semitic Violence

1. The Talmud of Jerusalem, Sanhédrin 4:8.
2. 4 W 3309, Situation religieuse dans le département—rapports, correspondance (42-44), Archives Départementales de Vaucluse.
3. AJ 38 3803, Enquêtes de Jean Lebon, Archives du CGQJ, Archives Nationales.
4. AJ 38 3637, Archives du CGQJ, Archives Nationales.
5. http://www.not-the-germans-alone.org.
6. 3 W 17, Rapports mensuels du préfet, Archives Départementales de Vaucluse.
7. 3 W 18, Rapports mensuels du préfet, Archives Départementales de Vaucluse.
8. 3 W 28, Rapports hebdomadaires des Renseignements Généraux 1942-1944, Archives Départementales de Vaucluse.
9. AJ 38 3806, Rapports mensuels de Jean Lebon, Archives du CGQJ, Archives Nationales.
10. Adam Rutkowski, «Directives Allemandes concernant les arrestations et déportations de Juifs de France en avril-août 1944,» *Le Monde Juif*, No 82, avril-juin 1976, pp. 53-65.
11. 56 W 161, Reynoir, Dossier de procédure de la Cour de Justice des Bouches du Rhône, Archives Départementales des Bouches du Rhône.
12. 56 W 21, Rodolphe Bride, Dossier de non lieux, Archives Départementales des Bouches du Rhône.
13. 55 W 148 Dossier Palmieri, Archives Départementales des Bouches du Rhône.
14. *Der Spiegel*, 13/1983, 28 mars 1983, p. 61.
15. 3U7/283 Lucien Blanc, Procédures de la Cour de Justice du Gard, Archives Départementales du Gard.
16. AJ 38 3806, Archives du CGQJ, Archives Nationales.
17. 55 W 148, Palmieri Charles, Dossier de Procédure de la Cour de Justice de Marseille, Archives Départementales des Bouches du Rhône.

Part Five - SS Commander Rolf Mühler

1. Joachim Wolf, Schulungsort für den Massenmord (Centre de Formation pour Massacre), http://www.bpb.de.
2. 822-823, Tribunal Permanent des Forces Armées à Lyon, Archives de la Justice Militaire, Le Blanc.
3. XXVc-216 et XXVc-236, Centre de Documentation Juive Contemporaine, Paris.
4. Raymond Raoul Lambert, *Carnet d'un Témoin 1940-1943*, Editions Fayard, Paris, 1985.
5. Michele Sarfatti, "Fascist Italy and German Jews in South-Eastern France in July 1943," *Journal of Modern Italian Studies* (L'Italie fasciste et les Juifs allemands dans le sud-est de la France en juillet 1943, Journal d'Etudes Italiennes Modernes), 3 (3) 1998, pp. 318–328.
6. XLVIIIa-29, deux télégrammes (26-8-1943 et 1-9-1943) de KNOCHEN à Rolf MÜHLER, archives du CDJC.
7. XLVIIIa-28, trois télégrammes (du 19-8-1943 au 2-9-1943) de Rolf MÜHLER à KNOCHEN, archives du CDJC.
8. Adam Rutkowski, Directives Allemandes concernant les arrestations et déportations de Juifs de France en avril-août 1944, Le Monde Juif, No 82, avril-juin 1976, pp. 53–65.
9. No 76/487, Dossier du SD d'Avignon, Tribunal Permanent de Marseille, Archives de la Justice Militaire, Le Blanc.
10. AJ 38 3806, Archives du CGQJ, Archives Nationales.
11. Raymond Raoul Lambert, *Carnet d'un Témoin 1940-1943,* Editions Fayard, Paris, 1985.

12. 822-823, Audition de Helmut Knochen, Dossier de la SD de Marseille, TPFA de Lyon, Archives de la Justice Militaire, Le Blanc.

13. 80, Dossier Delage, Tribunal Militaire Permanent de Marseille, Archives de la Justice Militaire, Le Blanc.

14. 822-823, Tribunal Permanent des Forces Armées à Lyon, Archives de la Justice Militaire, Le Blanc.

15. I-5 et I-7, Centre de Documentation Juive Contemporaine.

16. Patricia Kennedy Grimstead, "Twice Plundered or 'Twice Saved'? Identifying Russia's 'Trophy' Archives and the Loot of the Reichssicherhetshauptamt," Oxford Journals, *Holocaust and Genocide Studies*, Volume 15, Issue 2, pp. 191–244.

17. 821, SD d'Avignon et 822-823, SD de Marseille, Tribunal Permanent des Forces Armées à Lyon, Archives de la Justice Militaire, Le Blanc.

18. 817 et 822-823, SD de Marseille, Tribunal Permanent des Forces Armées à Lyon, Archives de la Justice Militaire, Le Blanc.

19. *Der Spiegel*, 13/1983, 28 mars 1983, p. 61.

20. 822-823, SD de Marseille, Tribunal Permanent des Forces Armées à Lyon, Archives de la Justice Militaire, Le Blanc.

Index